Web Performance Tuning

Web Performance Tuning

Patrick Killelea

O'REILLY™

Beijing · Cambridge · Köln · Paris · Sebastopol · Taipei · Tokyo

Web Performance Tuning

by Patrick Killelea

Copyright © 1998 O'Reilly & Associates, Inc. All rights reserved.
Printed in the United States of America.

Published by O'Reilly & Associates, Inc., 101 Morris Street, Sebastopol, CA 95472.

Editor: Linda Mui

Production Editor: Madeleine Newell

Printing History:

      October 1998:   First Edition.

ISBN: 1-56592-379-0

Table of Contents

Preface

When I told people I was writing a book called *Web Performance Tuning*, the usual response I got was that the title should be "Web Server Performance Tuning." Most people believe that the server is the only part of the Web that you can tune. When you're desperate to improve performance, however, you become much more creative about finding other parts of the Web that you can tune. You may not be able to do much about the public network or about remote clients, but you can tune entire intranet systems, including clients, networks, servers, and databases, and you can improve your access to the public network through better connections and strategic locations for clients and servers. Yes, you can tune the web server itself, but the server is only one piece.

Thinking in terms of individual machines is rapidly becoming obsolete. An isolated machine, whether PC or mainframe, is increasingly rare. There is a very good reason for this: a collection of machines is far more powerful, flexible, and reliable than any individual machine. The network takes on the characteristics of a bus connecting the components of a larger and better computer. To have a network connection to another machine is to have more power available from your own machine. To be connected to the Internet is to have access to millions of machines. The biggest disk in the world is simply all disks wired together.

What Is This Book Good For?

This book is good for improving web site performance, estimating web site hardware and software requirements, and clarifying scaling issues. It covers client and network issues as well as server-side issues, because many web sites are on intranets, where a system administrator has control over the client and network. While most web performance discussion centers on the HTTP server, the HTTP server itself is not usually the performance bottleneck. To improve performance, we must also look at other issues.

The performance I care about is from the end user's point of view: how quickly the Web satisfies the user's request. There are other kinds of performance, such as total server throughput or availability, but this book focuses on the user's perception of speed.

Although it presents some general principles of performance tuning, this book concentrates on practical advice much more than on theory. The principles are presented only to show patterns that unify typical web performance problems and solutions. While any book on performance tuning is to some degree a collection of tips and tricks, I hope the principles help to bring some order to this collection.

Another goal of this book is to present a clear picture of the chain of events involved in viewing a web page. Having a clear mental model of exactly what happens and why is critical to reasoning through new performance problems and finding solutions.

In the end, performance tuning is about spending money and time wisely to get the most out of your resources. A lot of life is like that.

Audience for This Book

Web Performance Tuning will be of interest to anyone responsible for a web site, from the person running a personal site off a Linux PC at home up to large corporate sites with multiple enterprise-class servers and redundant Internet connections. The book assumes you are familiar with the fundamentals of setting up a web site and getting connected to the Internet. If you need advice on setting up a web site, see *Apache: The Definitive Guide*, by Ben Laurie and Peter Laurie (O'Reilly & Associates). If you need advice on how to get connected to the Internet, see *Getting Connected*, by Kevin Dowd (O'Reilly & Associates).

This is a book of practical advice on the configuration and application-level programming of commodity components, not a book for operating system programmers, compiler writers, or chip designers. In other words, the book goes over what you can change right now from the system administration and application level.

To some degree, you are at the mercy of the market to supply you with good building blocks. Since the performance of a web site is a function not only of the tuning parameters and options but also of the raw hardware and software products involved, this book also includes information on how to select the appropriate products. The issues of scalability and conformance with open standards will also be covered.

Here are some representative titles of people who might have an interest in this book:

- System Administrator

- System Architect

- System Integrator

- Web Applications Programmer

- Web Content Developer

- Webmaster

Assumptions of This Book

This book assumes a basic familiarity with the technical components of the Web. Throughout the book, there are descriptions of the events that occur in a typical HTTP operation. There are also references in the text and the appendixes to other books and web sites for those who need more background or want to explore a subject in more depth.

The server examples are drawn from the Unix world because a majority of web servers use the Unix operating system, and because Unix has proven suited to running a scalable high-performance web site. To be completely honest, it's also because my experience has been mostly with Solaris and Linux, and I like them. If you use a non-Unix web server, you'll find that most of the advice in this book is still applicable to your server, but the specific details will vary.

It is assumed that the reader has some programming experience with C, Java™, or Perl, but that is not a requirement for using this book.

How This Book Is Organized

The first part of this book goes over topics of general interest to anyone running a web site, including quick and simple performance boosts, estimating what hardware and software you need for a given load and level of performance, common measures of web site performance, case studies of some web sites, and principles of performance tuning.

The structure of the second part of book is modeled on what actually happens when the user of a web browser requests an HTML page from a web server. We'll follow an HTML request from client to network to server to CGI to database (see Figure P-1). We'll also cover what happens when a Java applet is downloaded from the server and started in the browser. From the browser's point of view, after the request is sent, the answer magically appears on the network. From the net-

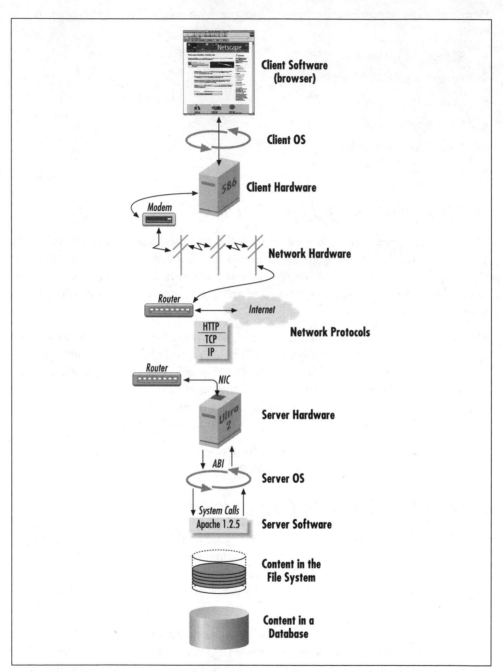

Figure P-1. The chain of events

work's point of view, the answer magically appears at the connection to the server, and so on. We'll trace the process back one stage at a time to point out performance issues along the way and to eliminate the unknown. We'll also give tips for finding out which side of each interface is slower so that you can figure out where the bottleneck is and how to bring the performance of that section into line with the rest of your web site.

Part I, Preliminary Considerations

Chapter 1, *The Blunt Instruments*, describes crude but often effective measures to increase your site's performance when you just don't have time to analyze your system and tune it the "right" way.

Chapter 2, *Capacity Planning*, helps you make decisions about what kind of hardware and software you'll need to allow your site to perform well and scale for the future.

Chapter 3, *Web Performance Measurement*, describes web performance benchmarks and why they may be unreliable indicators of real-world performance.

Chapter 4, *Case Studies*, gives some examples of performance problems and solutions, and describes major commercial web sites, including what hardware and software they use.

Chapter 5, *Principles and Patterns*, describes some general principles to keep in mind when thinking about the performance of your web site.

Part II, Tuning in Depth

Chapter 6, *Client Software*, tells you what's going on in your browser and how to help it along, especially when it seems to be hanging.

Chapter 7, *Client Operating System*, gives tips on the differences between the various OSs and how these affect browser performance.

Chapter 8, *Client Hardware*, describes what the bottlenecks are on the client hardware and what you can do about them.

Chapter 9, *Network Hardware*, describes the hardware of the Internet. There's not a lot you can do about hardware that belongs to someone else, but you can at least influence the parts of the Internet you use. If you're running your own intranet, you can modify many parameters to tune performance.

Chapter 10, *Network Protocols*, describes the protocols at the core of the Web and gives you tips on how the protocols interact and how to get them to play nicely together.

Chapter 11, *Server Hardware*, describes issues constraining the server, such as disk bottlenecks.

Chapter 12, *Server Operating System*, gives tuning hints for the typical Unix web server.

Chapter 13, *Server Software*, discusses the free and commercial HTTP server software available.

Chapter 14, *Content*, goes over the various kinds of data you return to the user and the performance implications of each.

Chapter 15, *CGI Programs*, gives you tips and tricks for reducing the amount of time spent in CGI processes.

Chapter 16, *Java*, goes over some issues in optimizing your Java applications.

Chapter 17, *Databases*, describes the performance and cost of various database systems.

Part III, Appendixes

Appendix A, *Netscape Enterprise Server 3.0 Tuning*, contains Netscape's own advice for tuning their web server.

Appendix B, *Apache Performance Notes*, written by one of the authors of Apache, discusses performance issues for the Apache web server.

Appendix C, *Solaris 2.x—Tuning Your TCP/IP Stack and More*, gives detailed Solaris TCP advice from Jens-S. Vöckler.

Font Conventions

Italic

is used for URLs, filenames, program names, and hostnames, and for emphasizing words.

`Constant width`

is used for HTTP headers, text to be typed literally, and function and system call names.

 This symbol indicates a tip.

 This symbol indicates a warning.

How to Contact Us

We have tested and verified all the information in this book to the best of our ability, but you may find that features have changed (or even that we have made mistakes!). Please let us know about any errors you find, as well as your suggestions for future editions, by writing to:

> O'Reilly & Associates
> 101 Morris Street
> Sebastopol, CA 95472
> 1-800-998-9938 (in the U.S. or Canada)
> 1-707-829-0515 (international/local)
> 1-707-829-0104 (FAX)

You can also send messages electronically. To be put on our mailing list or to request a catalog, send email to:

> *nuts@oreilly.com*

To ask technical questions or to comment on the book, send email to:

> *bookquestions@oreilly.com*

The author can be reached at:

> *webperf@patrick.net*

Web Site Updates and Code Examples

Be warned that web pages frequently change without regard to references to them. For the latest corrections and collection of my links, and also for the book's code examples, see *http://patrick.net/*. You can also find the code examples at *http://www.oreilly.com/catalog/webpl/*.

Other Books and Resources

Books

In reading this book, you'll find that I frequently refer to other books that explain concepts more completely than I can (at least, not without making this book twice its size). The following is a brief listing of the books that I recommend:

Albitz, Paul and Cricket Liu, *DNS and Bind* (O'Reilly & Associates, 1997).

Ballew, Scott, *Managing IP Networks with Cisco Routers* (O'Reilly & Associates, 1997).

Blake, Russ, *Optimizing Windows NT* (Microsoft Press, out of print).

Brooks, Fredrick P., Jr., *The Mythical Man-Month* (Addison Wesley, 1995).

Chapman, Brent and Elizabeth Zwicky, *Building Internet Firewalls* (O'Reilly & Associates, 1995).

Cockcroft, Adrian and Richard Pettit, *Sun Performance and Tuning* (Prentice Hall, 1998). Everything about tuning Solaris and Sun hardware. The new edition includes Java and web tuning.

Dowd, Kevin, *Getting Connected* (O'Reilly & Associates, 1996).

Frisch, Æleen, *Essential System Administration* (O'Reilly & Associates, 1996).

Gancarz, Mike, *The Unix Philosophy* (Digital Press, 1996). Wonderful explanation of what makes Unix Unix.

Garfinkel, Simon, *PGP: Pretty Good Privacy* (O'Reilly & Associates, 1995).

Gray, Jim, *The Benchmark Handbook for Database and Transaction Processing Systems* (Morgan Kauffman Publishers, 1993).

Gundavaram, Shishir, *CGI Programming on the World Wide Web* (O'Reilly & Associates, 1996).

Gurry, Mark and Peter Corrigan, *Oracle Performance Tuning* (O'Reilly & Associates, 1996).

Harold, Elliotte Rusty, *Java Network Programming* (O'Reilly & Associates, 1997).

Laurie, Ben and Peter Laurie, *Apache: The Definitive Guide* (O'Reilly & Associates, 1997).

Libes, Don, *Exploring Expect* (O'Reilly & Associates, 1994).

Loukides, Mike, *System Performance Tuning* (O'Reilly & Associates, 1991). The standard text on Unix system performance.

Nassar, Daniel J., *Ethernet and Token Ring Optimization* (M&T Books, out of print). The accumulated experience of a network tuner. Includes TCP/IP tips.

Orfali, Robert and Dan Harkey, *Client Server Programming with Java and CORBA* (John Wiley & Sons, 1998).

Partridge, Craig, *Gigabit Networking* (Addison Wesley, 1994).

Stern, Hal, *Managing NFS and NIS* (O'Reilly & Associates, 1991).

Stevens, Richard, *Advanced Programming in the Unix Environment* (Addison Wesley, 1993); and *TCP/IP Illustrated*, Volumes 1 and 2 (Addison Wesley, 1994).

Tannenbaum, Andrew S., *Computer Networks* (Prentice Hall, 1996). The canonical networking book.

Ware, Scott, Michael Tracy, Louis Slothouber, and Robert Barker, *Professional Web Site Optimization* (Wrox Press, Inc., 1997).

Wall, Larry, Tom Christiansen, and Randal L. Schwartz, *Programming Perl* (O'Reilly & Associates, 1996).

Wong, Brian L., *Configuration and Capacity Planning for Solaris Servers* (Prentice Hall, 1997). See especially Chapter 4, on configuring web services.

Wong, Clinton, *Web Client Programming with Perl* (O'Reilly & Associates, 1997).

Web Sites with Performance Information

http://help.netscape.com/kb/server/971211-7.html
   The Netscape tuning page included in this book.

http://www.apache.org
   The Apache home page. See especially *www.apache.org/docs/misc/perf.html*.

http://www.apacheweek.com/tips/
   Tips for running Apache.

http://louvx.biap.com/webperformance/
   Lou Slothuber's web performance page.

http://www.cam.org/~agena/computer.html
   Extensive PC hardware performance site.

http://www.cmg.org/
   The Computer Measurement Group's home page.

http://www.cs.cmu.edu/~jch/java/optimization.html
   Jonathan Hardwick's Java optimization page.

http://www.sysopt.com/
   Very popular page packed with information on optimizing PCs.

http://www.1computers.com/f/ftomhardware.html
   Tom's Hardware Guide. Rightly famous for PC hardware information.

http://www.nlanr.net/Papers/data-inet97.html
   Excellent review of the state of performance measurement of the Internet.

http://www.rational.com/
   Includes some papers on application performance tuning.

http://www.sun.com/workshop/java/wp-javaio/
http://www.sun.com/solaris/java/wp-java/
   Information about running Java quickly on Solaris 2.6.

http://www.sun.com/sunworldonline/swol-03-1996/swol-03-perf.html
   Good web server performance article.

http://www.sgi.com/Technology/web/
> SGI's Web Performance Tuning Guide.

http://www.techweb.com/speed/
> Lots of tuning tips, but only for Windows platforms.

http://www.cerberus-sys.com/~belleisl/mtu_mss_rwin.html
> The definitive site for Winsock tuning.

http://www.w3.org/
> Has the RFCs on which the web is based.

http://www.sun.com/javastation/whitepapers/serversizingguide/
> How big should your JavaStation™ server be?

http://www.yahoo.com/Computers_and_Internet/Hardware/Benchmarks
> A set of links to other benchmark and tuning sites.

Newsgroups with Web Performance Content

> *comp.benchmarks*
> *comp.infosystems.www.authoring.html*
> *comp.infosystems.www.misc*
> *comp.unix.solaris*

Disclaimer

I hate to yell in all caps, but here it is:

1. THE INFORMATION IS PROVIDED "AS-IS" AND WITHOUT WARRANTY OF ANY KIND, EXPRESS, IMPLIED OR OTHERWISE, INCLUDING WITHOUT LIMITATION, ANY WARRANTY OF MERCHANTABILITY OR FITNESS FOR A PARTICULAR PURPOSE.

2. IN NO EVENT SHALL THE AUTHOR, CONTRIBUTORS, OR THEIR EMPLOYERS BE LIABLE FOR ANY SPECIAL, INCIDENTAL, INDIRECT, OR CONSEQUENTIAL DAMAGES OF ANY KIND, OR ANY DAMAGES WHATSOEVER RESULTING FROM LOSS OF USE, DATA, OR PROFITS, WHETHER OR NOT ADVISED OF THE POSSIBILITY OF DAMAGE, AND ON ANY THEORY OF LIABILITY, ARISING OUT OF OR IN CONNECTION WITH THE USE OR PERFORMANCE OF THIS INFORMATION.

Not a single suggestion in this book is guaranteed to help any particular situation. In fact, if you simply change configurations and parameters without analyzing the situation and understanding what you are changing and why, you may experience hardware damage, data loss, hair loss, dizziness, and nausea. Back up everything, don't work directly on production servers, and be careful.

Also note that the opinions expressed in this book are those of the author and have nothing to do with the author's employer, Sun Microsystems Professional Services, or with the book's publisher, O'Reilly & Associates, Inc.

Acknowledgments

Thank you to Linda Mui, my editor at O'Reilly, for her patience and good questions. Thanks to my father, Thomas, for instilling ambition, and to my mother, Diane, for saying I ought to write a book. My wife Leah and son Jacob deserve enormous credit for letting me sit and work in the evenings. Thanks to John Leavitt for the initial review, and to Adrian Cockcroft, Richard Gates, Dan Klein, and Scott Mattoon for reviewing the full draft. Thanks to Mike Connor for the hummingbird cover inspiration, and to Edie Freedman for the great cover art. Michael Wight deserves credit for putting up with silly questions. I told Robert Hellwig I'd mention him here. Jens-S. Vöckler, Dean Gaudet, and Netscape's Suzanne Anthony were all kind enough to let me include their web pages or portions thereof in the appendixes. Thanks to Sun Microsystems Professional Services for their encouragement. And thanks to everyone on the Internet who is willing to share what they know just because it's a nice thing to do.

I

Preliminary Considerations

1

The Blunt Instruments

Let's say you have a web performance problem and you hate it. You should probably take time to consider what you're about to do, but you pick up the nearest blunt instrument, and . . . . What are those blunt instruments that kill performance problems, at least some of the time? Here are a few you can try right off without investing much brainpower or patience, though you may have to invest money. Some are not very elegant and might not help. But then again, they might.

Improving Performance from the Browser Side

Turn off automatic loading of images.

Turning off autoloading of images will help performance dramatically if the problem is simply that your bandwidth is limited to that of a modem on a regular dial-up telephone line (also known as a POTS line, for Plain Old Telephone Service). Of course, without graphics you won't enjoy a lot of what the Web is about, which is, well, graphics. In Netscape 4.0, you turn off automatic loading by choosing Edit → Preferences... → Advanced and then unchecking the "Automatically Load Images..." box.

Even if you turn off automatic loading of images, you can load and view an interesting image by clicking on the associated image icon. Your next question should be how to tell whether an image looks interesting before you've seen it. This is exactly what the HTML <ALT> tag is for: the HTML author is supposed to add a text description of the associated image, which the browser will display if image loading is off. ALT stands for "alternate text." Here is an example:

```
<img src="images/foo.gif" alt="Picture of a Foo" width=190 height=24>
```

Most browsers also have a button which forces all unloaded images to load at once.

Many sites offer a light-graphics or text-only link for the bandwidth-impaired user. Another option is to use a text-only browser such as Lynx, which also has the advantage that it can be run remotely over a VT100 or other terminal-mode connection rather than requiring a TCP/IP connection all the way to the client. That is, your ISP may let you dial up and run Lynx on the ISP's computer rather than on your computer at home.

It is frequently helpful to set the browser to start on a blank page, so that the user does not have to wait for a default page to load when starting up. The Netscape page can be particularly heavy with graphics and features, so it's a poor choice to leave as the default. To change the startup page to blank in Netscape, choose Edit → Preferences... → Navigator and then click the radio button for "Navigator starts with blank page".

When loading a web page, sometimes you first see an image loading at the top of the screen, followed by a long delay before the text of the page appears. More often than not, this image is an animated GIF advertising something you don't want. This usually happens because the page designer didn't include the image size in the HTML. The browser doesn't know how much space to set aside for the image until the image is completely loaded, so it delays laying out the page until it has the entire image.

If you notice this happening, you have a couple of options to stop it. First, try hitting Netscape's Stop button. This forces Netscape to stop loading, to show the rest of the page, and to stop any animated GIFs. Remember that the HTML text of a page is necessarily downloaded before any images. If you think about it, this must be so, because the HTML contains the link to the image, not the other way around. You might think that the text should therefore be visible before any images, but it doesn't always work that way. The browser needs to know the size of the images before it can lay out the HTML text correctly, but when you hit Stop, Netscape will go ahead and do the best it can to display the HTML because it's not getting any more image data.

Another way you can avoid the ugly-ad-image syndrome is to turn off automatic loading of images, as described above. Remember that you can always hit the Show Images option to get the images if you want them.

Finally, you can switch to another browser. It seems that Internet Explorer does not delay HTML rendering until images are loaded, unlike Netscape 4.*x*. The text-based browser Lynx, of course, never waits for images, because it can't display them.

On the other hand, if you're a content designer and you want to inflict this suffering on your viewers because it pleases your sponsors, there are a couple of ways you can make viewers watch the commercial before starting the show. First, you can simply leave the image size out of the HTML <IMG> tag, as described earlier. This doesn't work for Internet Explorer users, so it's not a general solution. A second way to force the user to look at the image before viewing the HTML is to send an image with an HTTP `Content-length` header that deliberately lies about the size of the image, claiming that it is bigger than it really is, so that the browser hangs waiting for more until the user hits the Stop button. A third way to achieve the same effect is to put the GIF in its own HTML frame and to put the content in another frame—but delayed by the server until a good while after the GIF loads. The delay can be generated several ways. One way is to load a blank page in the bottom frame and include a <META> tag in its HTML, like this:

```
<meta http-equiv="refresh" content="5;url=Show.html">
```

The *Show.html* page will be loaded after the user waits for 5 seconds.

Turn off Java.

Java is not yet as popular in web advertising as animated GIFs are. Still, there are enough sites using gratuitous Java that it may be worthwhile for you to turn off Java if you can't spare any bandwidth for the applet download. Another performance problem with Java is that it can take 15 or 20 seconds to start up the Java virtual machine the first time you hit a page with Java in it. This Java initialization freezes the browser and cannot be interrupted, which can be very annoying.

Like the ALT text, the text within the <APPLET ...></APPLET> tags will be displayed when Java is off, so you will have an idea of whether you want to turn Java back on and reload the page. This text can include any valid HTML, and it is possible that the content designer has created a useful alternative to the applet and put it within the applet tag, so you may not even know that Java is disabled. In some cases, you really need Java: if you must use a Java applet as the client in a client/server application, it won't work with Java disabled.

Preinstall applets.

Another crude trick that gives the appearance of better bandwidth is to install most of your applet's class files on the client with the browser's own Java class libraries. You can put them in the same directory or even in the same *.zip* or *.jar* file that comes with Netscape (unzip it, add them, and zip it up again). You can also put them in some arbitrary directory and ask the user to add that directory to his or her CLASSPATH. You then download a stub applet from the web server and use that applet to refer to the bulk of the locally installed code. This requires installation work and isn't practical for publicly available applets, but it's a big help for intranet applets you'll need for long periods of time.

Buy a faster machine.

A faster client machine will parse HTML faster and retrieve pages from the cache faster, as well as run Java applets faster. This may be an obvious tip, but it won't help much if the bottleneck is your network connection or the speed of the web server at the other end of that connection.

Buy a better graphics card.

Your video performance is limited by your graphics card and CPU, not by your monitor. If you buy a faster video card, your display and scrolling performance should improve. Another option is to include more video RAM (VRAM) on the video card. This will help only up to the point where you have enough VRAM to store the entire display buffer.

Buy a worse graphics card.

Ironically, 8-bit color video cards, or even black-and-white cards, are often faster than 24-bit color video cards, because they have much less work to do and put less of a load on the CPU.

Find a mirror site if the one you're interested in is slow or down.

If you're trying to read a popular site, consider that there may be mirror sites that are less heavily loaded. Mirror sites are usually mentioned on the home page of a site. AltaVista (*altavista.digital.com*), for example, has mirror sites around the world, as does the Apache site (*www.apache.org*).

Don't verify document freshness.

Browsers cache the documents you view and then retrieve an item from the browser's cache if you request it again. Because the document may have changed in the meantime, the browser will by default contact the original server to validate the freshness of every cached page. If the document has changed on the server, the new version will be downloaded. If the locally cached copy is up to date, then it is displayed. The validation request may require only a little network traffic if the document has not been modified, but you'll still get better performance from using what's in the cache without verification, and you won't have to download any pages with trivial changes. You may get stale pages, but at least you'll get them quickly.

To get the performance gain from not verifying cached documents in Netscape, set Options → Network Preferences... → Verify Document: to "Never". If you suspect you've got a stale page, it's an easy matter to force Netscape to get the current version. Simply hold down the Shift key and hit Reload. Setting Verify Document: to "Once per Session" is second-best; this will verify the timeliness of the document just once for that Netscape session. Setting Verify Document: to "Every Time" is worst from a performance point of view. This instructs Netscape to check with the original server for a fresher version every time you view that page.

Tell your computer to read ahead while you're browsing.

There are a number of "read ahead" products that immediately retrieve all of the pages linked to by the page you've just loaded, whether you intend to look at them or not. While this definitely speeds up perceived performance if you spend a bit of time reading the current page and then jump to a link from of the current page, it's really not a neighborly thing to do. You probably won't read most of the content that is downloaded to your machine, so this makes someone else's server and network do a lot of work for nothing. Take a look at your modem's read light to get an idea of how much more it is working when you're using one of these products. Normally, you see the read light when loading a page, and then the light goes off, showing that you're not reading anything more off the network. With one of these read ahead products, the read light will probably never turn off. Two read ahead products for Windows 95 and NT are Blaze (*http://www.xspeed.com*) and PeakJet (*http://www.peak.com*).

Browse late at night or very early in the morning.

If you are on the West Coast of the U.S., be aware that there is a lot of traffic in the morning because the East Coast has been up and surfing for three hours already. So the East Coast gets better speed early in the morning because the Californians are asleep, and the West Coast is faster late at night because the New Yorkers are asleep.

Listen to the hardware.

You can tell if your disk is working hard by listening to the machine. Hard disks are noisy things, so if you hear a lot of crunching going on when your hit the Back button, for example, you know that the machine is getting the previous page from disk and not from memory. This may be because the browser has used up the RAM you allocated to the memory cache or because the operating system is paging. If you hear silence but the machine still takes several seconds to show the previous page, it's a good bet that your machine is just slow to parse and display HTML, so you'd probably be better off with more RAM for the browser's cache, or a better CPU, video card, or bus. To get a better bus, you have to get a new machine.

Buy a faster modem.

It has always been well worth the money for dial-up users to buy the fastest modem available. If you are dialing in over a POTS phone line, that's currently 56kbps. 56K modems have incompatibilities between brands due to the use of chip sets that follow different standards. You should check what sort of modem is going to be on the other end, say at your ISP or company dial-in port, and purchase the same brand or one known to be 56K-compatible with it. If the modems include the same chipset, they're probably compatible.

Many higher-bandwidth access services are available, but all have a higher cost. You can get 128kbps from ISDN by "bonding" the two 64kbps channels together. ISDN, unlike 56K, has limited availability and steep startup and per-minute costs because the service is available only through local phone monopolies. Some local monopolies also offer Asymmetric Digital Subscriber Line (ADSL) at rates up to 1.5Mbps, but both ADSL and ISDN require that you pay two bills: one to the phone company to rent the physical wire, and another to your ISP for Internet connectivity. In some areas of the country, you can get cable modem service for $50–100/month, approximating ADSL bandwidth. Cable modem providers also act as ISPs. I have had both ISDN and cable modems, and I prefer the cable modem, because it has higher band-width, it's always on, and it's been more reliable than ISDN. Your local cable monopoly can tell you whether they offer this service in your area.

Dial direct, bypass the Internet.

A PPP connection over a modem, dialing direct to another modem attached to a web server, has reasonable latency and sometimes better throughput than the Internet even at only 28.8kbps. This is a very rare solution, but the moral is that the Internet is not the only way to get to a web server. If you need good access to a web server at work, find out if you can dial into a modem attached to your LAN at work.

Get a dedicated line.

Whether you're browsing or serving, a dedicated digital line is almost always better than using a modem over a POTS line. The first step up is ISDN, cable modem, or a 56kbps dedicated line. These connections are more expensive than an analog line, but they have much better throughput.

Get an account with the server's ISP.

If you are spending most of your time getting data from one server, it may be worthwhile to get an account with the ISP that connects that server to the Internet. You'll probably see better throughput and latency working from an account on the same ISP than from somewhere else. Telecommuters probably want an account with their company's ISP.

Use a proxy server for caching.

A proxy server between your organization and the Internet will cache fre-quently requested pages, reducing the load on your connection to the Inter-net while providing faster response time to the users for cached pages. The benefit you see depends on the number of times the requested page is in the cache. If all web requests were for unique URLs, then a proxy would actually reduce performance, but in practice, a few web pages are very popular and the cache is well used. The proxy server has a particular need for speed, since it must act as both client and server. Proxies are write-intensive, so they can benefit a lot from a caching disk controller.

Also, keep in mind that proxies are likely to make some Java applets unusable, since applets can currently connect back only to the server they came from. The server they came from will be the proxy, which is not where the applet probably thinks it came from.

Check DNS response times.

DNS servers can become overloaded like anything else on the Internet. Since DNS lookups block the calling process, a slow DNS server can have a big impact on perceived performance. Consider setting up additional servers or simply pointing your DNS resolver to another DNS server.

Improving Performance from the Server Side

Make sure the web server is not doing reverse DNS lookups.

Web servers are often set by default to take the IP address of the client and do a reverse DNS lookup on it (finding the name associated with the IP address) in order to pass the name to the logging facility or to fill in the REMOTE_ HOST CGI environment variable. This is time consuming and not necessary, since a log parsing program can do all the lookups when parsing your log file later. You might be tempted to turn off logging altogether, but that would not be wise. You really need those logs to show how much bandwidth you're using, whether it's increasing, and lots of other valuable performance information. CGIs can also do the reverse lookup themselves if they need it.

Increase the TCP retransmit timeout.

TCP will assume a segment has been lost if it has not been acknowledged within a certain amount of time, typically 200 milliseconds. For some slow Internet connections, this is not long enough. TCP segments may be arriving safely at the browser, only to be counted as lost by the server, which then retransmits them. Turning up the TCP retransmit timeout will fix this problem, but it will reduce performance for fast but lossy connections, where the reliability is poor even if the speed is good.

Locate near your users.

Internet Protocol data packets must go through a number of forks in the road on the way from the server to the client. Dedicated computers called routers make the decision about which fork to take for every packet. That decision, called a router "hop," takes some small but measurable amount of time. Servers should be located as few router hops away from the audience as possible;

this is what I mean by "near." ISPs usually have their own high-speed network connecting all of their dial-in points of presence (POPs). A web surfer on a particular ISP will probably see better network performance from web servers on that same ISP than from web servers located elsewhere, partly because there are fewer routers between the surfer and the server.

National ISPs are near a lot of people. If you know most of your users are on AOL, for example, get one of your servers located inside AOL. The worst situation is to try to serve a population far away, forcing packets to travel long distances and through many routers. A single HTTP transfer from New York to Sydney can be painfully slow to start and simply creep along once it does start, or just stall. The same is true for transfers that cross small distances but too many routers.

Buy a bigger pipe.

The most effective blunt instrument for servers and users alike is a better network connection, with the caveat that it's rather dangerous to spend money on it without doing any analysis. For example, a better network connection won't help an overloaded server in need of a faster disk or more RAM. In fact, it may crash the server because of the additional load from the network.

Buy a better server.

While server hardware is rarely the bottleneck for serving static HTML, a powerful server is a big help if you are generating a lot of dynamic content or making a lot of database queries. Upgrade from PC hardware to workstation hardware from DEC, HP, Sun, or SGI. They have much better I/O subsystems and scalability.

Buy more RAM and increase cache sizes.

RAM accesses data thousands of times faster than any disk. Really. So getting more data from RAM rather than from disk can have a huge positive impact on performance. All free memory will automatically be used as filesystem cache in most versions of Unix and in NT, so your machine will perform repetitive file serving faster if you have more RAM. Web servers themselves can make use of available memory for caches. More RAM also gives you more room for network buffers and more room for concurrent CGIs to execute.

But memory doesn't solve all problems. If the network is the bottleneck, then more RAM may not help at all. More RAM also won't help if all of your content is already in memory, because you've already eliminated the disk as a potential bottleneck. Another way to boost performance is with level 2 cache RAM, also known as SRAM, which is several times as fast as ordinary DRAM but also several times more expensive. More cache RAM will help performance by keeping frequently used code close to the CPU.

Buy better disks.

Get the disks with the lowest seek time, because disks spend most of their time seeking (moving the arm to the correct track) in the kind of random access typical of web serving. A collection of small disks is often better than a single large disk. 10000 rpm is better than 7200 rpm. Bigger disk controller caches are better. SCSI is better than IDE or EIDE.

Set up mirror servers.

Use multiple mirrored servers of the same capacity and balance the load between them. See Chapter 2, *Capacity Planning*, for information on load balancing. Your load will naturally be balanced to some degree if you are running a web site with an audience scattered across time zones or around the world such, as a web site for a multinational corporation.

Get the latest software.

Software generally gets faster and better with each revision. At least that's how things are supposed to work. Use the latest version of the operating system and web server and apply all of the non-beta patches, especially the networking- and performance-related patches.

Dedicate your web server.

Don't run anything unnecessary for web service on your web server. In particular, your web server should not be an NFS server, an NNTP server, a mail server, or a DNS server. Find those things other homes. Kill all unnecessary daemons, such as *lpd*. Don't even run a windowing system on your web server. You don't really need it, and it takes up a lot of RAM. Terminal mode is sufficient for you to administer your web server.

Use server APIs rather than CGIs or SSIs.

While CGI is easy to program and universally understood by servers, it relies on forking additional processes for every CGI-generated page view. This is a big performance penalty. Server-side includes, also known as server-parsed HTML, often fork new processes as well and suffer the additional penalty of the parsing, which is compute-intensive. If you need to insert dynamic content such as the current date or hit count in the HTML you return, your performance will be much better if you use your server's API rather than CGI or SSI, even though the API code won't be portable across web servers. Other options that have better performance than CGIs are FastCGI, Java servlets, and Apache's Perl module, but these are not quite as fast as server API programs. If you do use CGI, compile the CGI rather than using an interpreted language. See Chapter 15, *CGI Programs*, for additional tips.

By the way, SSI and CGI also have associated security hazards. For example, if FTP upload space is shared with the web server, then it may be possible for a user to upload a page including an SSI directive and to execute whatever he or she likes. With CGI, users may write naive scripts which inadvertently accept commands from anyone viewing the web page.

Examine custom applications closely.

Any custom applications used by the web server should be profiled and carefully examined for performance. It is easy to write an application with correct functionality but poor performance.

Preprocess all of your dynamic content.

Unless you are generating content that depends on a huge number of possible inputs from the user, you can trade storage for performance by using all possible inputs to create static HTML. Serving static HTML is much faster than creating any kind of dynamic content.

Let a professional host your server.

Use one of the web hosting services like Genuity, Globalcenter, or Exodus to host your web site at multiple locations close to the Network Access Point (NAP). It's expensive, but they do all the hosting work for you, leaving you free to work on your content.

Key Recommendations

- Turn off images on the client.

- Turn off Java on the client.

- Turn off cache validation on the client.

- Put more RAM on the server.

- Put more RAM on the client.

- Don't use CGIs.

- Buy a better connection to the Internet.

- Let a professional host your server.

- On a LAN, if you can cache static content in RAM, you can probably serve it at full network speed. If you can't cache content, then your disk is probably the bottleneck.

- On the Internet, the Internet is usually the bottleneck; the next bottlenecks are CGI startup and database queries.

2

Capacity Planning

Capacity Planning Is Preemptive Performance Tuning

Since this is a book on web performance tuning, you might think a chapter on capacity planning is out of place. Not so. Capacity planning and performance tuning are in a sense the same thing: choosing system components, placement, and parameters based on performance criteria. The difference is in when they are carried out. Capacity planning is part of planning; it is generally done before any of the system has been assembled. Tuning, on the other hand, is done after the initial architecture is a fact, when you have some feedback on the performance of the architecture. Perfect capacity planning would eliminate the need for performance tuning. However, since it is impossible to predict exactly how your system will be used, you'll find that planning can reduce the need to tune but cannot eliminate it.

Methodology

How should you go about planning the performance of your web system? To limit the scope of the problem, it helps to think of capacity planning for web services as an algorithm, with two kinds of input and one kind of output. The inputs are your constantly changing requirements and the constantly changing characteristics of the available components. The output is an architecture that meets those requirements. By considering the problem this way, you've reduced it to collecting information and using that information to decide on a suitable architecture.

Unfortunately, the algorithm that gets you from here to there is still more art than science, particularly because you undoubtedly have additional requirements beyond performance, such as cost, security, and freedom from platform lock-in, and because requirements and components are moving targets (almost always in the direction of more performance). There are probably many configurations that would satisfy your performance requirements alone, but you may find that it is not possible to satisfy them simultaneously with all your other requirements, especially if those requirements include a small budget or a certain throughput and latency from the Internet. Read the rest of this book for details on how the pieces behave and interact. Then expect to go through several iterations of modifying your requirements and evaluating potential architectures before you find an architecture that meets all of your requirements. It is, like life, an ongoing process of adaptation.

Do the Math . . .

When you evaluate a potential architecture, the most critical part of the job is to compare your required latency and bandwidth to the rated capacity of every link in your proposed configuration. Each component should meet those requirements with an additional margin for component interaction inefficiencies and increasing load over the life of the architecture. You could skip the calculations and forecasting, buy something that satisfies your immediate requirements, and forge ahead, planning to upgrade when necessary—but there are a few reasons why you're well advised to do the math and think about where you want the system to go in the future.

First of all, management likes to have a good idea of what they're going to get for the money you're spending. If you spend money on a system that cannot deliver because you didn't do a few calculations, you then have the embarrassing task of explaining why you need to spend more. You may not even be able to use what you have already bought if it's not compatible with the higher-performance equipment you need.

Second, unplanned growth has penalties associated with it, for example, barriers to scalability, upgrades, or platform changes. You'll need more capacity next year than you do this year. If you cannot easily migrate your content and applications to higher-performance equipment, you will suffer.

Third, unplanned systems are more difficult to manage well because they are more difficult to comprehend. Management is inevitably a larger cost than the equipment itself, so whatever you can do to make management easier is worthwhile.

. . . But Trust Your Eyes More Than the Math

It is possible, however, to plan too much. Requirements change and new technologies are making older ones obsolete, so you can't know for sure what you'll need in a year or two. It is a good idea to choose a few pieces of flexible, scalable equipment of adequate rated capacity and try them out together, knowing you can add capacity or alter the architecture as you collect real-world data and as new options become available. Choose components that "play nice" with products from other manufacturers. Starting this way has the substantial advantage of giving you continuous feedback on the performance and reliability of live, interacting equipment.

Don't bet the farm on vendor specifications and advertising. They are less reliable sources of information than firsthand experience or the experience of trusted friends. It is shocking, but true, that some vendors have fudged benchmark and scalability tests in their quest for sales. A real system to build on also gives you a gut-level feel for the kind of performance you can expect. You can use this feel to check your analytical model against reality.

Remember that component ratings are the maximum the vendor can plausibly claim, not necessarily what you'll see. 10Mbps Ethernet will give you a maximum of about 8Mbps of data throughput in practice. Cause a few problems yourself, just to see what's going to happen next year. Better that your server crashes right in front of you, for known reasons, than at 4 a.m. when you're in bed, for unknown reasons. Try the load generation tools mentioned in Chapter 3, *Web Performance Measurement*, but be sure that the load and network match your production environment: test over 28.8kbps modems if your customers will be using them. Generating relevant and complete tests is tricky. Watch to be sure that latency remains bounded when you test at very high throughput. Also watch to see what happens when latency does go up. Many applications are sensitive to latency and simply give up if they have to wait too long for a response. You can buy or build hardware delay boxes for testing at different latencies.

Given that the hardware of your server defines its maximum capabilities, you might be tempted to buy and assemble the highest performance components, thinking that this will result in the highest performance server. It ain't necessarily so. For example, small commodity disk drives are less reliable and have lower capacity than more expensive, larger drives. Nonetheless, you will get better availability and performance for the money from a set of small drives working together in a Redundant Array of Inexpensive Disks (RAID) configuration than from a single large drive. Smaller disks often have lower seek times precisely because they are physically smaller. Server vendors add value to components by working out these interactions and encapsulating them for you, giving you the ability to plan at a higher level.

The output from your capacity planning will be a specification that includes the following:

- Network type and speed
- Internet connection provider
- Server hardware:
  — Number and kind of CPUs

  — Size of CPU cache

  — Amount of RAM and number and kind of disks

  — Whether you need disk striping or RAID
- Web server software
- Load balancing and scaling strategy
- Client hardware/software (if you have control over that)

Questions to Ask

The first step in capacity planning is to clarify your requirements and get them down on paper. Here are some questions that will help you pin down what you need:

How many HTTP operations per unit time do you expect?

Unlike the client/server paradigm where the most important sizing parameter is the number of concurrent users, the relevant parameter for web servers is HTTP operations per second, also referred to as *hits* per second. Few websites receive more than 25 hits per second. Web servers do not maintain a dedicated connection to the browser because HTTP 1.0 is a connectionless protocol. The user connects, requests a document, receives it, and disconnects. HTTP was implemented in this way to keep the protocol simple, to conserve bandwidth, and to allow a web page to consist of components from multiple servers. Even though the user has the impression that he or she has been connected during an entire session of reading pages from a web site, from the server's point of view, the user disappears after each request and reappears only when requesting a new page and associated content, like images. This loading characteristic of web servers is changing because HTTP 1.1 does allow the user to remain connected for more than one request. Also, Java applets sometimes open a connection back to the web server they came from and can keep this connection open.

Because of the simple nature of HTTP, it is easy to make overly simplified assumptions about what "connections per second" actually means. For example, we usually assume that HTTP requests are fulfilled serially and that the connection time is very short. These assumptions are valid if we are serving relatively few users on a fast LAN connection, but not if we have many users on slow modem connections. In the case of many users with slow access, connections are likely to last more than a second. Each connection will require buffer space and processor time, so the server load calculations should measure the load in concurrent users, which is the typical form of client-server load.

So we see that network speed has an important effect on server sizing. Even though HTTP loads are expressed in hits per second rather than number of concurrent users, you have a qualitatively different load if your users are all on Ethernet than if they are on 28.8kbps modems. The differences are that the Ethernet users will expect lower latency and that the server will have fewer concurrent connections for Ethernet. So in one sense, high-speed users place a larger load on the server, since their latency expectations are more demanding. In another sense, they require less of it, because fewer concurrent connections require less memory.

At any speed, HTTP requests tend to cluster because of the need to get embedded images and other such content. The arrival of one connection is a good indication that several others are very likely to arrive soon. If servers were more clever and more powerful, they'd parse HTML as it was served to find embedded images or applets that belong with each HTML page. They could then begin the retrieval of an HTML page's embedded content *before* the browser even asks for it.

Load on a server is statistically a function of the time of day. Figure 2-1 shows a typical graph of the load on a web server throughout the day. For content with a global audience, the load rises to a gradual peak about noon in California (which is 3 p.m. in New York and 9 p.m. in London). Depending on the market for the content, the shape of this curve will vary somewhat over the day and over the week. Stock quote servers will be busiest during working days. Servers advertising specific events can expect a flood of users during the event and relatively few thereafter. Peaks of three to five times the average load are typical during special events. As a general rule, permanent web sites see a continuous rise in load as more people get connected to the Internet, so you must build for this expected growth. The web is not only expanding, but may even be accelerating its growth as it moves to encompass non-computer devices.

Keep in mind that even a million hits per day, which until recently would put your site into the top rank of web sites, is not a particularly heavy load per second when averaged smoothly over the day: $1000000 / (60 \times 60 \times 24) = 11.6$ hits/second. Given a 10K average transfer size, this load is within the capabili-

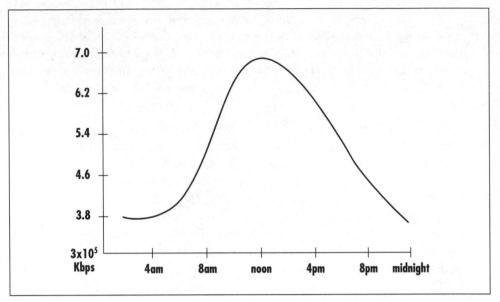

Figure 2-1. Typical Sprint NY NAP usage data from http://www.nlanr.net/

ties of even modest machines, but requires a network capable of handling 10240 bytes × 11.6/second × 8 bits/byte × 1.3 for network overhead = 1.2Mbit/ second, which is theoretically within range of a T1 connection. It is unlikely that a million hits will be so evenly distributed in time, but the point is that it is within reach of most organizations to run a very substantial web site.

See *Getting Connected,* by Kevin Dowd (O'Reilly & Associates), for a worksheet on estimating your Internet bandwidth requirements.

What is the purpose of the web site?

The purpose of the site will affect the distribution of the load over time. For example, a site used to support a classroom lecture will see a large jump in hits during the class and possibly synchronized hits during the class hour. Sizing for the average number of hits over the day will result in a system that is wholly inadequate for this class. You may need to size with the assumption that all users will need near-simultaneous access to the same pages. So if there are 30 class members, you may need to provide a server that can handle 30 hits per second, even though this could also be expressed as several million hits per day.

Have you analyzed your log files?

How can you know the number and distribution of connections to expect? If your web server is already live, then you have an excellent source of information about the sort of load you should tune for, because your web server logs can tell you how much bandwidth you are currently using, whether it's increasing or decreasing, and how quickly. Of course, the log may merely reflect a bottleneck in your system and not the system's potential capacity or the potential demand from users. Web server log files are almost universally in Common Log Format (CLF) as one line per HTTP operation, giving the domain name or IP address of the requesting machine, user and password if supplied for access-controlled files, parsed date, request issued by client, the HTTP response code, and number of bytes transferred. See *mod_log_config.html* in the Apache distribution for more information on the format and on custom modifications you can make. Neither Netscape, Apache, or NCSA servers include the headers in the count of bytes transferred, so your throughput calculation result will be slightly low if you just use the log file to calculate bytes transferred.

For example, here is a log file line from the NCSA server:

```
client8.isp.com - - [21/Aug/1997:16:56:57 -0500] "GET /recipe.html HTTP/1.0"
200 217
```

You can calculate the number of completed HTTP operations per second by looking at the number of lines in any time interval and dividing by that interval. Similarly, you can figure out your throughput in bytes per second by adding up the bytes transferred over some interval and dividing it by that interval. Again, most servers do not include the header data in the recorded number of bytes transferred. In the example log file line above, *recipe.html* is exactly 217 bytes long, yet the server also transmitted HTTP headers back to the client but didn't record them in the log file. Those headers look like this:

```
HTTP/1.0 200 Document follows
Date: Sat, 30 Aug 1997 04:31:18 GMT
Server: NCSA/1.4.2
Content-type: text/html
Last-modified: Mon, 16 Dec 1996 04:51:12 GMT
Content-length: 217
```

This header itself is 174 bytes, which is 45% of your server's output in this case. Header size has been creeping up as more capabilities are added to web servers.

Your log file can give you a feel for how hard your server is being hit right now via the Unix *tail -f* command. Find your server access log file (e.g., *access_log*) and try this:

```
% tail -f access_log
```

The *tail* command shows the last few lines of a file, and the *-f* option tells the *tail* command that the file isn't yet complete and that it should continue to print new lines as they are added to the file. You'll see new lines in the log file as they are added when users hit the site.

While useful for giving you a picture of the current state of affairs, log files are limited as a performance diagnosis tool. For example, your log file will not tell you if the user tried to contact your server but was unable to, nor if the reply took so long that the user gave up, although transfer errors are logged. A lightly loaded server could be an indication of performance problems rather than an indication of unused capacity. Maybe your site is unpopular because the performance is poor.

The one-line-per-transfer format is difficult to analyze by directly reading it. The need to extract as much useful information as possible from log files has given rise to a small industry of log parsing and graphing packages like Interse and Analog. These products are useful, but it is also not difficult to write a simple Perl script to parse your log file into a format readable by spreadsheet programs. A good spreadsheet program will have graphing ability similar to dedicated log graphing packages, and the added advantage is that you may already own one. To provide additional information, some web servers use extended log formats, including details such as how long the transfer actually took to complete.

Your log file can also tell you where your users are. Are they across the whole Internet? In a 50-location extranet? All in one building? Analyze any log files you may have, and try to locate your servers close to the largest concentrations of users.

How tolerant are your users?

Put another way, what are your throughput and latency goals? It is essential to attach numbers and distributions to these goals if you are serious about improving performance. For example, you might establish a goal of satisfying 90% of HTTP requests for files under 10K at a rate of 5 seconds or less for each file. Given such a specific goal, you not only have a concrete starting point for planning, but also a clear indication of whether your planning was successful. User happiness can also be a numerical goal if you decide to measure it. While happiness will vary with the patience of the user and is a "soft" psychology question, surveys give hard numbers which at least tell you whether satisfaction is rising or falling.

This does not mean that you need only one set of goals. Most sites give all users the same priority, but it is certainly feasible to segment the market. That is, you can provide restricted access to a high-performance server for some users and broader access to a lower-performance server for others. You can even provide differing grades of access to the exact same content if you serve the content from a high-speed NFS server and refer to the same NFS-mounted files from the two web servers of varying capacity. Or, you can dual-serve content from a database. In either case, simply restricting the number of users on one web server may define that machine as higher-performance, since it will have a lighter load.

You can also differentiate service on the basis of network speed, server capacity, and many other factors. This differentiation may seem elitist, but there are often practical reasons for it. For example, doctors need immediate access to patient records, while insurance companies can tolerate a longer wait, though both may need access to the same information. So providing a restricted higher performance service to one group may be a viable solution to complex goals.

Your throughput and latency goals should be checked against the hard limits of your users' network access potential as well as user expectations. A goal of 50kbps throughput per user is simply unreachable for end users accessing the data through 28.8kbps modems. Similarly, a latency goal of 10 milliseconds just can't be met for access from Europe to California because that's faster than the speed of light. Expectations vary with network access quality as well. A user with a 28.8kbps modem might be happy waiting 10 seconds for a static 5K page of HTML text, and may be even more forgiving for images or CGI-calculated output. Ethernet LAN users accessing an intranet site will have higher expectations, but they may actually see worse throughput during peak loads, because Ethernet performance degrades nonlinearly with throughput. As an Ethernet network approaches its maximum throughput, its latency increases dramatically, to the point where it is no longer usable. In grim Darwinian fashion, when some users give up in frustration, performance gets significantly better for those who remain.

What is the average transfer size going to be?

The typical size for an HTTP transfer is about 10K. Text tends to be smaller: figure 2K per page. Images tend to be larger, say 15K. If you have a document tree of static HTML text and GIF images, it's quite simple to calculate the average size of a file. Here's a little script I wrote that will do it for you (you may need to change the path to *perl* and make sure the *find* command is in your PATH environment variable):

```perl
#!/usr/local/bin/perl
# Finds the average size in bytes of all .html and .gif files below
# the given directory, or the current directory if none given.

@ARGV[0] = "." unless @ARGV[0];

@files = `find @ARGV[0]`;
chop @files;

foreach (@files) {
    if (/\.html$/ || /\.gif$/) {
        $count++;
```

```
        $sum += -s;
        # print -s, "\n"; # Uncomment to see all file sizes.
    }
}

$avg = int($sum/$count);
print "Average size is $avg bytes.\n";
```

You run this script by giving it the name of your public_html directory:

```
% avgsize.pl /home/patrick/public_html
Average size is 12038 bytes.
```

Although this script is an easy way to get an idea of the average size of your static content, it is just a starting point because it tells you only the size of the average file available to the user, not the average size of files actually sent, which is the total bytes transferred during some time interval divided by the number of files. Your log file will give you a better picture of your true average transfer size because it will have a record of the actual content transfer sizes, including CGI-generated content.

Here's a modified version of the previous script that looks at the transfer size, which is the last number of each line in a common log format log file, and prints the average size transferred, excluding headers. Lines ending in a dash (-) indicate something other than a successful transfer and will be added in as a 0-byte transfer by this script:

```
#!/usr/local/bin/perl
# Finds the average size in bytes of all file transfers recorded by a CLF
# log file.

while (<>) {
        / (\d*)$/;
        $count++;
        $sum += $1;
}

$avg = int($sum/$count);
print "Average size is $avg bytes.\n";
```

You run this script by giving it the name of your log file:

```
% avgsize.pl /opt/apache_1.2.4/logs/access_log
Average size is 5515 bytes.
```

The average size actually transferred in a web transaction was less than half the average size of my content, because most transfers were my home page, which is very small and only text.

Log files themselves are not completely accurate because, as we've seen, they do not include the size of header information and have no mechanism for recording the load created by other non-HTTP activity, such as socket connections created by Java applets or non-parsed-header files.

The distribution of transfer sizes can be more important than the average size. Implicit in most discussions of web planning is the assumption that the distribution of transfer sizes falls into a classic bell curve. It may not be that way. You may find that 95% of your transfers are around 10K, but that your average is skewed upwards to 50K because 5% of your transfers are downloads of large files like executable software and high-resolution images. This is more a bimodal distribution than a bell curve and is quite common. A more useful script than the one already shown would give you the distribution of file sizes as well as the average size.

The distribution in time of these large transfers can also be irregular. For example, if you happen to be distributing software from your site, you can expect a surge in downloads of large software files when you post new versions. If your web site supports operators in a call center by providing them applets for database access, you can expect many large transfers when work starts in the morning and users need to load the applets. A good architecture for these kinds of problems is to have two web servers: one sized for the average of many small transfers and one that serves the few large files. HTTP is perfectly suited for transparently distributing hits among servers. There is nothing to say that a JPEG embedded in a page must be served from the same server that provides the surrounding HTML. There may be a slight penalty to this in the form of an additional DNS lookup for the JPEG, or not, if you use the IP address in the embedded JPEG link.

Will you provide any streaming media?

Streaming media such as continuous audio or video need to be sized separately from the web server, because they are different in nature and may be of indeterminate size. They use up a lot of network bandwidth and have strict latency requirements. A stream can also last minutes, which is far different from the connect time of a standard HTTP transfer, which should last only milliseconds. Streaming media servers should be sized by the number of simultaneous connections desired, not by connections per second.

Will the web server spawn additional processes?

While serving static HTML and images is rarely enough load to make the server the bottleneck, using CGIs or server APIs to dynamically generate HTML or other content can slow your server to a crawl, especially if the content generation requires database access. The load generated by CGIs and databases varies enormously with the application, so it is impossible to make sizing calculations without detailed analysis or experience with the application. When planning a web application, size the server around the application, because that will be more resource-intensive than serving the results. Also consider that it is often possible to push some of the processing work onto the client by using Java or JavaScript. See Chapter 16, *Java*, for more

details. Database tuning is a huge field in its own right. See *Oracle Perfor-
mance Tuning*, by Mark Gurry and Peter Corrigan (O'Reilly & Associates).
Also, see Chapter 15, *CGI Programs*, for hints on how to reduce the impact of
CGI.

What other processes need to run on the web server or over the network?

Don't forget to size for other services that may be running on your web server
at the same time. Small companies may be forced by economics to use their
web server for additional purposes, such as DNS or NFS services. The load
imposed by these other services will reduce the performance of your web
server. A particularly bad additional use for a web server is as a programmer's
workstation. I've been the programmer assigned to use a test web server as
my work machine, and I found it unacceptable for the usual programming
work of coding, compiling, and testing because of large drops in compilation
and network performance when the test web server was being hit, even
though keyboard response remained good due to the very high priority of
keyboard interrupts. Conversely, web server performance suffers from the
presence of a programmer on the web server machine.

Also take into account the possible need to share your web server's connection to the Internet with users inside your company who browse the Internet.
On a more local scale, if your web server must share a LAN with an NFS
server, for example, you need to take into account the bandwidth required by
that NFS server in sizing the LAN.

What sort of scalability do you need?

A tentative web architecture is like a theory in physics. It's an idea about how
things might work, but it has not yet been thoroughly tested. I've been told
that physicists like to shoot down each other's theories for sport, and that
when other avenues of attack are exhausted, they resort to this trump question: "Your theory sounds reasonable, but how does it hold up in the gigaelectronvolt range?" The odds are that your opponent has not considered whether
a theory works in the gigaelectronvolt range because it is on an entirely different scale than most current research and is impractical to investigate. Even better, you don't have to actually understand the theory to ask the question.

For web servers, the gigaelectronvolt question is this: When you have reached
the limits of the current configuration, can you gracefully add more hardware
to increase capacity, or will you have to rework everything? Can you upgrade
the operating system to handle the new hardware? The ability to gracefully
increase the capacity, of an architecture is known as *scalability*. Scalability
even has a number associated with it: the ratio of performance increase relative to the hardware you've added, such as RAM, CPU cards, network interface cards, etc. If you get x performance with one CPU and $1.6x$ performance

with 2 CPUs, then your CPU scalability is 1.6. Scalability can also be less than one, meaning that you get worse performance with more hardware! Scalability of less than one happens because of the overhead in coordinating the activity of all of the components.

Note the word "gracefully" in the scalability question. It should not require blood, sweat, or tears to add additional capacity, meaning no major system or database overhauls. It is simple to add more servers next to the first one. The hard part is to add them without turning access to your data into the bottleneck. You might think you can simply replicate or partition your data among machines to provide better access, but replication and partitioning require synchronization and coordination, which are complicated. If you haven't planned for it, you don't have scalability. Scalability is the reason why adding CPUs to a single machine is preferred over adding entire mirror machines: it is very quick and simple. Mirror machines may work fine for serving static HTML, but you still have to keep them synchronized. Web servers for database input or transaction processing always require real planning for scalability.

It is depressingly easy to build a system that satisfies your immediate needs, only to find that you have to rework it entirely when your needs increase or otherwise change. Given that the Internet is still expanding rapidly and new uses are still being found for it, it is certainly advisable to build as much as possible for growth. The downside is that scalable components almost always cost more. Here are a few examples:

— IDE disks and controllers are cheaper, but SCSI scales to much higher throughput.

— A 56K leased line is usually cheaper than the same bandwidth of fractional T1, but the fractional T1 can be upgraded via a computer in the central phone office, while the 56K line cannot be upgraded at all.

— An ordinary PC is limited in the amount of RAM it can take. You may absolutely need more RAM, but find that your machine simply has no extra place to put it, meaning you have to buy not only the RAM, but an entirely new machine.

— It is easier to get started with Windows NT than with Unix, but Unix scales all the way from very cheap 386 hardware (that cannot run NT) up to supercomputers (which also cannot run NT) and also scales sideways across various CPUs.

The scalability of various components is considered in their respective chapters in Part II of this book. The scalability of entire architectures is considered later in this chapter.

What is your budget?

Money is an important capacity planning parameter, too. Although how much you can spend defines a hard upper limit on the possible performance of your web site, the range of attainable performance at any given level of spending is huge. You can waste all of your money on equipment that doesn't work together, essentially throwing it away. Alternatively, careful planning can help you surpass the performance of far more expensive but ill-conceived sites.

It is critical to budget for ongoing maintenance and upgrades when planning your web site. In the long run, these costs will be larger than your initial outlay for equipment. Network connection fees, costs for system administration tasks (such as pruning and interpreting log files), and performance monitoring and adjustment costs should all be included in your budget.

How available does your site have to be?

Availability refers to the percentage of time your system is up. Some web sites require very high availability, especially transaction processing sites, such as banking and brokerage sites. The Internet itself is reasonably reliable because of its built-in ability to route around problems, although it is common for servers providing only static content to be mirrored at several places around the Internet for availability and performance reasons. Transaction sites are still generally not mirrored because of the difficulty in coordinating data access across multiple servers. So we must look to individual servers for high availability transaction sites.

The disk drive is by far the component most likely to fail, since it has moving parts. Disk drive unreliability can be overcome, however, by using RAID. See Chapter 11, *Server Hardware*, for a discussion of RAID and disk availability.

Other parts of the server hardware and operating system also have an impact on availability. Commodity PCs are not built for extremely high reliability and occasionally have problems such as thermal shutdown when connectors disengage due to expansion caused by heat. Workstations are more expensive but have higher quality components and manufacturing. Mainframes are extraordinarily stable but extraordinarily expensive, so most web sites are run from PC or workstation hardware.

As for operating systems, Windows and Macintosh, though simple, are not stable enough for very important sites. Unix is the most stable operating system for workstations and PCs, sometimes running for *years* without needing to be rebooted. There are also special high-availability operating systems, such as Solaris HA, and hardware failover solutions at additional cost. Web servers and your web applications themselves have a large impact on your availability. Those that leak memory will slow down your system. Tools that find memory leaks, such as Purify (*http://www.pureatria.com/*), can help you fix leaks in your applications, but not leaks in commercial applications like web servers.

All commercial web sites should run on uninterruptable power supplies (UPS), both to have a reserve of power in the event of a blackout and to be protected from power surges which can damage equipment. Large commercial web hosting companies often have emergency diesel generators that can be run as long as needed for the power to return. Finally, consider automatically paging your system administrator when performance drops below a certain level. Performance can be monitored from a failover machine or even from somewhere else on the Internet.

Clustering machines, that is, setting up several machines that act as one, can give you better reliability and scalability than is possible with one machine. In a cluster, each machine is equivalent and is monitoring the health of the others. If one machine fails, the others just pick up its load. The machines may share a RAID disk so that they all have access to the same data, yet there is no single point of failure. Note that this is different than a server farm, which is simply a group of distinct machines. Unix machine clustering has been well worked out over the last several years. NT clustering is also starting to arrive.

Can you force suppliers to compete?

There is a temptation to buy whatever solution is the cheapest or requires the least work to get started. This may work just fine for small installations that you know won't grow, but there is a well-known hazard to single-vendor solutions. Once your content or application is tied to some proprietary format, then your vendor has you over a barrel.* The cost of reworking your content and architecture for some other platform is usually large enough that the vendor can charge exorbitant fees for upgrades or maintenance and you will find it cheaper to simply pay up than to consider switching. It may in fact cost you more to switch vendors than it cost to implement the solution in the first place. You can't just throw everything out and start over; you may have to spend time and money to undo what you've done, for example to extract your data from some proprietary format or to retrain programmers. Worse, you may find that even though you've paid for repeated upgrades, you still cannot get the scalability, performance, or functionality you need.

One solution to this problem is to use only open standards, by which I mean free, published specifications that have been implemented in fact, not just potentially, by multiple vendors. Open standards include TCP/IP, SVR4 Unix, Java, CORBA, and the standards that have made the web as valuable as it is: HTTP and HTML.

---

* The expression comes from the last century, when it was a common punishment to be tied over a barrel and whipped.

Hey kid, want to try a browser?

So why does anyone use proprietary platforms? One reason is that proprietary platforms are sometimes given away for free. This is because vendors can make back an initial loss many times over once users are dependent on a platform. In the web space, Internet Information Server and Internet Explorer are good examples. They are bundled with Windows, so commodity PC hardware includes them. Naive web developers may consider them a good deal regardless of performance because they have not explicitly had to pay for and/or install them, unlike Netscape's products. Unfortunately, once they write content for any of their proprietary features such as ISAPI or ActiveX, they no longer have the option of using Netscape servers for that content. Not that Netscape doesn't play a lot of the same games: they have their own web content hooks, such as extensions to JavaScript and HTML. At the risk of repeating myself, the lesson is that the free market will fail you in matching proportion to the difficulty of switching to a competing vendor's products.

The rational motive for using proprietary platforms is that they often actually do provide better performance than any implementation of open standards. For example, CGI is an open standard, yet its performance is intrinsically poor. NSAPI and ISAPI easily beat CGI in performance, but they tie your work to one server platform. So you have a tradeoff to make. Just be aware of what you're getting yourself into. Before you start, ask yourself: "If I don't like this, can I get out easily?"

Other questions.

There are many other requirements to establish before you can complete a web architecture, and these go beyond the performance issues of this book. Among them are the degree of security your web site needs, what programming environment your programmers are used to, and whether you can integrate new and existing equipment.

How Much Bandwidth Do You Need?

Server bandwidth is the single most important factor in the performance of your web site. The math to determine what bandwidth you need is, in essence, very simple:

```
hits/second * average size of a hit in bits = bits/second
```

That is, you need some estimate of the number of hits per second you want to be able to serve. Then you need to know the average size of one of these hits. From this, you know what sort of network bandwidth you need.

Thinking About Bandwidth

You can get some perspective when thinking about bandwidth from the following chart. Note that Table 2-1 uses the decimal million (1000000) and not "mega" which is $2^{20} = 1048576$.

Table 2-1. Bandwidth Comparison

Mode of data transfer	Million bits/ second	Comments
Fast typist	0.000035	70 words/min $\times$ 5 chars/word $\times$ 6 bits/char $\times$ M/10^6 $\times$ min/60 seconds.
4800bps modem	0.004800	4800 bits/sec $\times$ M/10^6 This is also about maximum human reading speed.
POTS sampling rate	0.064000	Voice over plain old telephone service is sampled at 64kbps.
ISDN, two channels bonded	0.128000	
One million 10000-byte web hits in one day, evenly distributed	0.925925	10^6 hits/day $\times$ 80Kbits/hit $\times$ day/ 86400 seconds $\times$ M/10^6.
Audio CD	1.280000	40000 samples/second $\times$ 16 bits/ sample $\times$ 2 (stereo) $\times$ M/10^6.
T-1 (DS-1 or primary ISDN)	1.544000	Carries 24 POTS channels with 8kbps overhead.
Ethernet	10.00000	
Token Ring	16.00000	
IDE Hard disk	16.00000	Sustained throughput.
T-3 (DS-3)	44.60000	672 DS-0's, 28 DS-1's, or 7 DS-2's.
FDDI and Fast Ethernet	100.0000	
ISA Bus	128.0000	16 bits @ 8MHz.
Broadband ISDN	135.0000	
ATM	154.0000	
250 million 10000-byte web hits in one day, evenly distributed	231.4812	About one hit for every U.S. citizen.
EISA bus	264.0000	
Wide Ultra SCSI disk controller	320.0000	
100-nanosecond RAM	320.0000	32 bits / (100 $\times$ 10^{-9}) seconds $\times$ M/ 10^6.
Gigabit Ethernet	1000.000	
PCI Bus	2112.000	64 bits @ 33 MHz.
AT&T Sonet	2400.000	Long-distance fiber trunk.
CPU	3200.000	Hypothetical CPU processing 32-bit instructions at 100Mhz, one per clock cycle.

Table 2-1. Bandwidth Comparison (continued)

Mode of data transfer	Million bits/ second	Comments
Human eye-to-brain rate	5600.000	Estimated.
Highest achieved fiber optics	16000.00	Bell Labs.
Theoretical fiber capacity	64000.00	

This chart ignores latency, which varies even from bit to bit, and can be huge, especially on startup of any component. If you're a bit romantic, you can imagine a blurry picture of virtual reality coming into focus over the years in this chart, from short symbol transmissions twenty years ago, to the limit of human audio perception today, to the limit of visual perception in the coming years.

Estimating Web Server Network Bandwidth

Table 2-2 displays an estimate of the number of hits per second of a given size (*y*-axis) a given amount of bandwidth (*x*-axis) can handle with a 30% deduction for TCP/IP and other network overhead. Numbers are truncated to integers, so 0 means "less than one per second" rather than truly zero.

Table 2-2. Web Server Bandwidth Requirements

Hit size	28.8K	56K	ISDN(2)	T1	10bT	T3	100bT Ethernet
1KB	2	4	10	132	854	3845	8544
2KB	1	2	5	66	427	1922	4272
4KB	0	1	2	33	213	961	2136
8KB	0	0	1	16	106	480	1068
16KB	0	0	0	8	53	240	534
32KB	0	0	0	4	26	120	267
64KB	0	0	0	2	13	60	133
132KB	0	0	0	1	6	30	66
264KB	0	0	0	0	3	15	33
512KB	0	0	0	0	1	7	16
1MB	0	0	0	0	0	3	8
2MB	0	0	0	0	0	1	4

You can use Table 2-2 to estimate, for example, how many 4K files per second your T1 line can handle. The answer is 33. Keep in mind that the table refers just to the network capacity and does not say whether the load was generated by static HTML or CGIs. That is, network capacity says nothing about the capacity of your disk or server CPU, or of a database behind the web server.

In fact, the capacity of a server to fill a network connection is distinctly nonlinear. Smaller transmissions require a larger overhead in terms of interrupts and packet header processing. This means that sending two packets will require more of the server than combining them into one larger packet.

Table 2-2 is also a bit deceptive in that you will rarely see a smooth distribution of hits filling your network capacity. Rather, there will be peaks of three to four times the average rate per second and long troughs of no load at all.

To scale any of these connection types, you can add more network cards or modems until you reach the maximum number of cards or modems the server has room for. Then you can move up to the next connection type or to a bigger server. This is the easy way to do things, throwing more hardware into a single server. Scaling across multiple servers is typically more complicated, requiring load balancing strategies.

How Fast a Server Do You Need?

Given a certain network bandwidth, how fast a server do you need? More server disk speed, bus speed, and CPU speed all cost money. From the network bandwidth, you have an upper limit on the HTTP server hardware you need for serving static content such as HTML and images. Remember that there's no point in buying server hardware that has vastly more throughput capacity than the network it's connected to if you can't use that server's throughput. The web server software and operating system determine how efficiently you can use your server hardware. In practice, HTTP server software is not a bottleneck. For example, Apache running on Linux on a low-end Pentium machine can fill a 10Mbps line with static HTML content. If a significant load is put on your server, it will be from dynamic content generation, such as CGIs, Java servlets, and database queries. If you have any dynamic content, you should size your server around that.

The whole connection time for an Internet HTTP transfer is typically 2 to 20 seconds, most of which is usually caused by modem and Internet bandwidth and latency limitations. While this may be frustrating, it does leave quite a bit of breathing room for the server. It makes little sense to insure that a lightly loaded server can generate a response to an HTTP request in one millisecond if the network is going to consume thousands of milliseconds.

This is not to say that web server performance on the Internet is not important; without planning and tuning, a site that performs very well at low volume can degrade dramatically at high volume, overwhelming network considerations, especially if dynamically generated content is involved. But you can easily set up a server and get reasonable performance at light loads without any tuning, giving you some time to figure out what you want to do in the long term for the inevitable increase in load as the web expands.

Symmetric Multi-Processing (SMP) machines have multiple equivalent CPUs. SMP servers scale well because you simply add more CPUs, I/O boards, and storage to get more capacity. SMP machines also have load balancing and redundancy built in. Since most of HTTP's work is done by TCP and since TCP implementations formerly were single-threaded, there was no way to allocate different threads to different CPUs. So, there was no way to take advantage of the multiple CPUs. This has changed with Solaris 2.6 as well as operating systems from other vendors; they now have multithreaded TCP. You may also use SMP to scale multithreaded FastCGI programs or Java programs which use native threads.

Benchmark tests are not useful for forecasting absolute performance because test conditions are very artificial, involving extremely high-speed networks not normally used for surfing the web. The use of benchmarks in capacity planning is rather to get some idea of the *relative* performance of different components.

How Much Memory Do You Need?

The worst thing short of total failure that can happen to your server is a memory shortage serious enough to start the swapping of entire processes out to disk. When that happens, performance will quickly drop, and users will wonder if it's worth their time to wait for your content. It is better to refuse the excess connections you cannot handle well than for all of your users to get unacceptable performance. Servers that run as multiple processes, such as Apache, have a configurable limit to the number of processes and simultaneous connections per process. Multithreaded servers provide limits to the number of active threads. See Chapter 12, *Server Operating System*, for details. You can also limit incoming connections by setting the TCP listen queue small enough that you are assured of being able to service the users who have connected.

A system that is short of memory may show high CPU utilization because it constantly needs to scan for pages of memory to move out to disk. In such a case, adding CPU power won't help. You have to add more memory or reduce memory usage. Look at the rate of page scanning with *vmstat* under Solaris or with the Performance Monitor under NT. Under Solaris, the *sr* column of *vmstat* will tell you the scan rate. Sustained scanning is an indication of a memory shortage. Under NT, the clue is that your processor time will be high and almost identical to privileged time, meaning that the CPU is doing almost no work on behalf of the web server, but only on behalf of the OS itself.

There is a limit to the amount of memory any particular machine physically has room for. Be aware that this is a hard limit on scalability for that machine. When you hit that limit, you will have to replace the machine or offload some of the processing, for example, by using FastCGI (described in Chapter 15).

Memory for the Operating System

First, let's consider the operating system. Linux 2.0 can run well in less than 8MB, while you should budget 32MB for Solaris 2.6 or NT 4.0 unless you know your configuration requires less. And that's just for the operating system, not the web server or applications. Also, it is ironic but true that your OS itself will require slightly more memory when you have more memory. This is because the kernel uses memory to keep tables which track memory usage.

One reason more RAM helps very busy web servers is that impolite clients that disconnect abruptly leave open TCP connections, which consume RAM in the kernel until they eventually time out. The number of such connections can rapidly accumulate on busy web servers. The Unix *netstat* command is an easy way to see how many connections exist at the moment. See the "Keepalive interval" item under TCP in Chapter 10, *Network Protocols*, for more about the TCP "keepalive" timeout, which clears out the unused connections. Another reason more RAM helps very busy web servers is that many actively used connections can accumulate due to the bandwidth limitations of the Internet. Each of these connections requires on the order of 50KB TCP/IP socket buffer memory.

Memory for httpd

Now, you should budget for the number of server daemons you have running on top of the memory you have for the OS. Allocate 1 or 2 megabytes per server daemon running as a separate process; you can see memory usage of *httpd* processes with *top* or *ps*. For threaded servers, Adrian Cockcroft, a Sun performance expert, made a rough recommendation of 1M per server process plus 100K per thread, because he measured Netscape 2.0 processes—which can spawn up to 32 threads—and found that they used about 1M when idle and grew to be 3M to 4M when busy, probably due to caching of content. From this it can be assumed that the 32 threads took up 3M, so that's about 100K each. You should also allocate about 50K for each network connection, the number of which will be the same as the number of threads running.

Memory for Content

Another rule of thumb is to provide enough RAM to hold all the content that you expect will be accessed within a five-minute interval. This should prevent the web server from having to access the content disk more than once in any five-minute interval. Many servers cache recently accessed pages in memory, even though the pages may already be in the filesystem cache. This caching by the server may improve performance slightly over the user of the filesystem cache alone, but it could also double your memory usage. Try turning off the web server's cache and compare performance and memory usage. You may save memory and not lose any performance.

Memory for CGIs

To budget memory for CGIs, you need to know how many CGIs will be running concurrently. To really know the number of concurrent CGIs you'll be running, you need to know the number of requests to run the CGI per second and the time each CGI takes to complete. But that completion time depends on how many CGIs are running! The recursive math quickly gets daunting.

The safe thing is to budget enough memory to run as many CGI processes as you have server threads or daemons, on the assumption that each thread or daemon may run a CGI concurrently with all the others. CGI processes can easily require more memory than the *httpd* process itself, especially if the CGI is written in an interpreted language, which requires loading the interpreter, or if the CGI accesses a database, which often has large connection libraries that must be loaded before a connection can be made. The use of Transaction Processing (TP) monitors can help performance by managing a pool of open database connections rather than opening a new connection for each CGI. See Chapter 15 for additional hints on how to reduce CGI executable sizes.

The number of different CGI executables that you run has an impact on the amount of memory you need, since the text segment can be shared between concurrent instances of the same program, although the heap and stack can not. Use the Unix *size* program to determine the size of the text, data, and bss (uninitialized data) segments of your CGI. The data and bss give you a lower limit for how much additional RAM each instance of the CGI will use. The CGI can and probably will use more memory as it runs. Use *ps* and *top* to see how much unshared memory is really being used for a typical copy of the CGI. Budget RAM for one copy of the text segment of the CGI, plus RAM for stack, heap, and both initialized and uninitialized data for each concurrent user you expect. Then consider that you need more RAM if users are connecting over 28.8kbps than over a LAN because the connections are around longer (since the user can't get data out as fast). This means more concurrently running connections and CGIs. A slow CPU will have a similar effect, requiring more RAM.

Architecture Scaling Options

HTTP Is Scalable

Although HTTP is inefficient in the sense that it goes to the trouble of setting up and tearing down a TCP connection for a stateless and generally short transfer of data, HTTP happens to be quite scalable exactly because the connections are stateless and so short-lived. Connections are unlikely to be concurrent with each other because each is so brief, and each connection is likely to have good access to the server's resources. For example, you probably won't run out of socket connections, because they're constantly being closed after use. Since the protocol is stateless, it is entirely transparent to users if some of their requests are fulfilled by one server and some by another. This makes it easy to add more identical servers on the fly to accommodate larger loads in serving static content and is a fundamental advantage of the Web over, say, client-server systems.

CGI scripts, which have been notoriously difficult to scale, can be accommodated reasonably well with the FastCGI protocol, which keeps CGI processes continuously running on multiple machines. See Chapter 15 for details.

Replication and Consistency

Adding identical web servers, however, brings up the question of whether you should replicate your content, that is, whether you should keep multiple copies of the same data or simply partition data across different servers. If you choose to replicate content, then you have the additional burden of keeping that content synchronized across the different servers. With relational database content, if you do not replicate, you will find a bottleneck at the point of data access, particularly write access, because database transactions must satisfy the so-called ACID criteria of Atomicity, Consistency, Isolation, and Durability. These criteria are more important than performance in most organizations. To be sure of the self-consistency and durability of the transaction, you must lock the data you are going to operate on before beginning the transaction (isolation), so that no other process can modify and potentially corrupt the data during the transaction, which either runs to completion or is entirely aborted (atomicity). Because you have a single data set with strict serial access, you will find your transaction rate limited to how fast you can lock, modify, and unlock the data in the database, with no opportunity for parallel processing. This reduces performance.

It is often forgotten that you do not really need complete consistency of a database all the time. You can let the database be inconsistent, i.e., have contradictions, for some period of time without too much risk. Even in the case of a bank which has a central database of account information, say that each ATM machine has a local data cache and a rule that each account is allowed to withdraw $200 per hour per ATM machine without any immediate database access to the current balance figure. This makes the transaction much quicker for the user. The database can be synchronized within an hour after the transaction takes place, making use of cheap low-priority packet communication. The bank takes some small risk that the user will go around to many ATM machines and withdraw $200 from all of them in that hour before the database is guaranteed to be consistent, but the risk is rather small relative to the benefits to the user and the bank, particularly if the bank has some minimum balance requirement. The bank officials know exactly how much money was in each account an hour ago, but they can't be exactly sure how much is in each account right this instant. It's a tradeoff between wait time for the user, risk for the bank, communication costs, and complexity of programming.

It makes sense to partition data across multiple regional servers when you have regional rather than global content. If you have content of global interest, there are a number of tools to help you replicate it. Inktomi's Traffic Server caches pages at the ISP level. Bright Tiger Technologies (*http://www.brighttiger.com/*) has a software package called ClusterCATS which also does replication. Unix has a built-in facility for replication called *rdist*. See the Unix manual page on *rdist* for more information. Sun's Netra includes proxy caching. See also the end of Chapter 13, *Server Software*, for more information on proxy servers.

NFS for Replication

If you have read-only content, a good step up from a single web server without introducing the complexity of replication is to keep HTML and images in an NFS filesystem and to set up multiple web servers on the same LAN to refer to that filesystem for their content. Properly tuned for a high-speed LAN, NFS has much higher performance than HTTP, so you can supply content to multiple web servers from one NFS server without needing to replicate that content. Using NFS insures that the content provided from each server will be exactly the same. If you need geographically dispersed web sites to overcome the latency and throughput problems of the Internet, the NFS method probably will not work because it is very difficult to get high NFS performance over a wide area network. See Brian Wong's book, *Configuration and Capacity Planning for Solaris Servers* (Prentice Hall), for examples of NFS configurations.

Directing Server Traffic

Whenever you have mirrored web servers, whether they are on a LAN or a WAN, you have to come up with a mechanism for deciding where to direct each request. The most primitive mechanism is to present the user with a web page of alternate servers and require the user to manually select a server by clicking on a link. (Well, forcing the user to type in the selected URL might be yet more primitive.) Though primitive, this method is actually the standard for selecting FTP download sites. Its advantages are that the user has control over which server is used and that it requires no effort on the part of the download site administrator. The user can select the geographically nearest server, perhaps by clicking on an imagemap, under the assumption that the closest server will also be the quickest. Of course this method gives no guarantee that the server selected will be running or have sufficient capacity to handle the request. If the selected site is unusable, the user has to hit the Back button and try a link to another site. This is not efficient or user-friendly, and it does not attempt to balance the load across servers.

The situation can be improved with a variety of simple scripts that automatically run when the user needs to be redirected to an appropriate server. For example, the user's domain name can be detected and then used by some algorithm on a master server to decide which slave server would be best. The master can then send the user's browser an HTTP redirect header, like `Location: http://someserver.com/`, which redirects the browser to the given server. This occurs without the user even knowing that he or she has been redirected. One difficulty with this approach is that domain names do not reliably map to geography. Another is that there is still no attempt to verify availability or balance the load.

An improvement would be to automatically run a script that follows links to anonymous FTP servers until it discovers one that is clearly available. The Expect scripting language is very useful for tasks like this, involving remote logins and time-outs. An Expect script as a CGI could easily ping several servers and pick one that is running, but it would take a significant time to run the script. Another improvement would be to formalize a method for FTP servers to report their loading status.

There is nothing to stop you from setting up two servers on opposite sides of the country and assigning them both the exact same IP address. The nature of the BGP routing protocol ensures that TCP packets don't get confused; the load is automatically balanced across them.

Round Robin DNS

The above solutions, while functional, are mostly slow and inelegant. A more sophisticated solution works at the DNS level, where server names are resolved to IP addresses. This solution is called *round robin DNS*. The idea is that you set your local DNS server to return a different IP address each time it is queried for the IP associated with your web server's hostname, cycling through a set of addresses. This distributes DNS replies evenly across a set of servers. While round robin DNS does achieve this distribution easily, it may not be exactly what you expect or need for three reasons:

- First, even though the replies are distributed evenly among web servers, round robin DNS makes no attempt to find the closest or otherwise most appropriate server for a particular client; it simply points the user to the server next in line, or rather, next in circle. There could be a wide variation in response time if those servers are geographically dispersed.

- Second, round robin DNS makes keeping state for a user more difficult. Say a user is trying to use a "shopping cart" CGI application which records multiple transactions in a session for a single user. If the servers use round robin DNS, then the user may not get the same server for each HTTP operation. DNS results are cached by the user for a time called the *time to live* (TTL). If the whole user session is within the TTL, then the user will be talking to the same machine for the whole session. Once the user goes over the TTL, another DNS query will happen and the user will start talking to another randomly assigned server—perhaps the same one, perhaps not. To be sure of a coherent session, there must be a timeout to the user's session, or the servers themselves must communicate to share the user's state. This timeout or synchronization of data in real time adds complexity. The most appropriate use of round robin DNS is when the content is read-only.

- Third, round robin DNS is lacking in load balancing. Round robin DNS is not true load balancing, but it does balance the load in simple cases. True load balancing would be measuring the utilization of servers and assigning connections based on that utilization, so that connections are always assigned to servers with enough spare capacity to handle them. This is very important for, say, a CGI accessing a database. You don't want two complex queries going to the same server when another server is lightly loaded with a simple query. True load balancing can also improve the availability of your site, since one server can go down and the others will automatically take over its load.

There are a few catches with the implementation of round robin DNS. Round robin DNS is a recent feature of DNS and is not supported by all DNS servers on the Internet. Older DNS servers will use just one of the IPs provided by the authoritative name servers. This defeats products like Cisco's DistributedDirector, described later. In addition, if you want to remove an IP address, you have to contend with the fact that DNS changes propagate slowly and that many users' DNS servers will have the IP cached for that DNS name for a certain length of time, the TTL. This means that users will attempt to access the wrong IP address if you have changed it before the cache has expired or before the change has propagated to them. DNS has the capacity to assign a 0 TTL to addresses so that they don't get cached locally. Round robin DNS records also have a limit of 32 entries per record, so you can't scale past 32 IP addresses per DNS name. For more information on round robin DNS, see *http://www.cisco.com/warp/public/787/49.html*.

Multicasting

Another clever method of using native Internet protocols for load balancing is to apply multicasting to the problem. Multicast is a publish-and-subscribe mechanism for data at the IP level. Some IP addresses are designated as multicast addresses. The data sent to a multicast IP address is copied to everyone who has expressed an interest in it, but is not copied to anyone else, saving considerable bandwidth over other broadcasting models. The way multicasting can be used for web load balancing is to subscribe several web servers to the same multicast address, while instructing each server to respond *only* to requests for a particular class of URL, say a URL from a certain IP address range, or a URL requesting a certain kind of data. Each server should ignore all other requests. One problem with multicasting is that all of the routers in between the source and destination have to understand the multicast protocol for the transmission to proceed, but currently many routers do not. For more information on multicasting for web load balancing, see *http://gizmo.lut.ac.uk/~martin/wwwcac/wwwcac.html*.

Load Balancing Products

Load balancing is simpler to implement and more efficient if you are balancing across servers of similar capacity. Round robin DNS works best in this case. Although a good load balancing product will measure the available capacity of all servers and allocate load based on capacity so that you can balance across very different servers if you want to, there is still the hazard that the stronger server will fail for some reason, leaving the weaker server overwhelmed. It is better from an availability standpoint to balance across similar servers.

LocalDirector and DistributedDirector

Cisco (*http://www.cisco.com/*) sells load balancing products named LocalDirector and DistributedDirector. LocalDirector rewrites IP headers to redirect a connection to the local server with the most available capacity. It apparently judges capacity by network usage rather than server machine statistics because it runs no processes on the actual web server. Because of this, it is not a true load balancing tool and may not be appropriate for use with servers of differing capacity. The end user, application, and DNS server have no idea that this sort of balancing is happening; it's transparent to them. This lets many servers share one externally visible IP address.

DistributedDirector is intended for geographically dispersed servers. You can either set up a DistributedDirector DNS service that will return the IP of the closest server or you can have it send the HTTP reply status code "302 Temporarily Moved" containing the name of the most appropriate server, which the browser will then use to get the page. DistributedDirector figures out the distance in router-hops and directs the user to the closest server. It does not, however, analyze the performance of the servers and make judgments based on that information, so you may indeed be using the topologically closest server, but that may not give the best performance.

You can use DistributedDirector to maintain one URL that redirects users to your other web servers around the world. One downside of these products is that they are based on proprietary hardware which has a single point of failure, namely the hardware itself. Another problem is that since they map one IP address to many, you have the same problem maintaining state that you do with round robin DNS. DistributedDirector provides a "sticky" option to keep a user hitting the same server for this reason.

HydraWeb

HydraWeb (*http://www.hydraweb.com/*) is the name of both a company and their load-balancing product. Hydraweb is a hardware product, so it has a single point of failure. There is an option to buy a second identical unit and set the two units to fail over to each other, but this is obviously more expensive. Hydraweb does maintain state so that you can use it to load balance a transaction processing site.

Dispatch

Dispatch from Resonate, Inc. (*http://www.ResonateInc.com/*) is a software-only load balancing tool with no single point of failure. It does not require redundant hardware for failover. Dispatch sets up a single IP address as the address of multiple web servers, rather like Cisco's products. It uses resource-based scheduling to allocate load, so it is a true load balancing tool. Dispatch does maintain state and can be used for transaction processing sites.

lbnamed

lbnamed is a load balancing name daemon which allows one DNS name to map to a dynamically changing group of machines. The actual machine chosen depends on the loading of the various machines. A machine may be in multiple groups and so have more than one DNS name under *lbnamed*.

lbnamed was written in Perl by Roland J. Schemers III, and it is freely available from *http://www-leland.stanford.edu/~schemers/docs/lbnamed/lbnamed.html*.

Network Dispatcher

IBM's Network Dispatcher is another load balancing solution which maps a single IP address to a set of servers connected by a LAN. Network Dispatcher chooses a machine according to a set of weights you specify and rewrites IP headers to direct a request to one of the servers, so it is independent of DNS. Network Dispatcher is available from IBM at *http://www.ics.raleigh.ibm.com/netdispatch/netspec.htm*.

Web Server Director from RND

Web Server Director (WSD) is an intelligent load-balancer for identical-content machines. It is a hardware product supporting two or four Ethernet or two fast Ethernet ports. A single virtual IP address can represent and load balance a "farm" of servers. WSD can handle 512 virtual IP addresses and up to 50,000 servers. The load is balanced according to one of three load balancing algorithms which allow some servers to operate at higher loads than others. Servers can be configured to backup other servers. Server failure detection is supported physically and/or in the application.

More information is available from *http://www.rndnetworks.com/*.

Load Balancing Services

There are companies willing to mirror your web content at geographically scattered sites: LocalEyes (*http://www.localeyes.com/*), which buys distributed colocation from Genuity; ANS (*http://www.ans.net/*), owned by AOL; Exodus Communications; GlobalCenter (*http://www.isi.net/*), which bought ISI; GTE/BBN; InterNex; and MCI.

Mirroring services and products can save you telecommunications costs because users are closer to content, especially if you are currently running an extranet with dedicated long-distance links. Note that mirroring is also a good way of getting fault tolerance if the system is set up to reroute requests when a server is down. Software to manage the mirroring (that is, to choose the best server for a given request and to ensure that data is replicated quickly and correctly across the servers) is still immature. Currently, the options for directing requests are Cisco's DistributedDirector, described above, or Genuity's Hopscotch, which takes server and link availability measurements rather than simply choosing the topologically closest server. Hopscotch is currently available only as a Genuity service, not as a separate product. See *http://www.bbn.com/products/hopscotch.htm*. Note that Genuity has been bought by BBN.

Content replication across mirror sites is possible with products from F5 Labs (*http://www.f5labs.com/*), Inktomi (*http://www.inktomi.com/*), StarNine (*http://www.starnine.com/*), Studebaker (*http://www.tigereye.com/*), and Versant (*http://www.versant.com/*).

The DRP Replication Protocol

Rather than using a proprietary content distribution protocol or relying on the Unix-specific *rdist* functionality, you also have the option to use the Distribution and Replication Protocol (DRP) created by Marimba, Netscape, Novell, Sun, and @Home. DRP is intended to replicate content over the Internet, which can simplify the task of maintaining synchronized servers at multiple locations. DRP has been proposed as a standard to the World Wide Web Consortium (W3C), but has not as of this writing been accepted as a standard.

DRP makes no assumption about the content of the files, so any kind of content can be replicated. It is assumed that the files are in a hierarchy, and this hierarchy is replicated to the clients. After the initial download of files to clients, updates of the content are done through differential transfers to conserve bandwidth, that is, only the parts of files that have changed are sent to the clients, along with instructions on how to update those files. This is rather like an automated use of the Unix *diff* and *patch* commands.

Not only does DRP allow replication of content between servers and between a server and a set of clients, it also includes a provision to tell a client which alternate servers are available for the same information.

More information on DRP is available from *http://www.marimba.com/drp/*. Also see Chapter 13 for information about caching proxy servers, which have similar functionality.

Key Recommendations

- Write down your requirements.

- Remember that the network constrains the server output.

- Size your server first for the back-end applications, because these are almost always heavier than simple web serving.

- For every architecture, ask yourself "If I decide I don't like this, can I migrate away from it easily after having implemented it?"

- Plan for future scalability, not just for your immediate needs.

- Keep performance records so you know whether your site is meeting expectations.

3

Web Performance Measurement

Parameters of Performance

There are four classic parameters describing the performance of any computer system: latency, throughput, utilization, and efficiency. Tuning a system for performance can be defined as minimizing latency and maximizing the other three parameters. Though the definition is straightforward, the task of tuning itself is not, because the parameters can be traded off against one another and will vary with the time of day, the sort of content served, and many other circumstances. In addition, some performance parameters are more important to an organization's goals than others.

Latency and Throughput

Latency is the time between making a request and beginning to see a result. Some define latency as the time between making a request and the completion of the request, but this definition does not cleanly distinguish the psychologically significant time spent waiting, not knowing whether your request has been accepted or understood. You will also see latency defined as the inverse of throughput, but this is not useful because latency would then give you the same information as throughput. Latency is measured in units of time, such as seconds.

Throughput is the number of items processed per unit time, such as bits transmitted per second, HTTP operations per day, or millions of instructions per second (MIPS). It is conventional to use the term *bandwidth* when referring to throughput in bits per second. Throughput is found simply by adding up the number of items and dividing by the sample interval. This calculation may produce correct but misleading results because it ignores variations in processing speed within the sample interval.

The following three traditional examples help clarify the difference between latency and throughput:

1. An overnight (24-hour) shipment of 1000 different CDs holding 500 megabytes each has terrific throughput but lousy latency. The throughput is $(500 \times 2^{20} \times 8 \times 1000)$ bits/$(24 \times 60 \times 60)$ seconds = about 49 million bits/second, which is better than a T3's 45 million bits/second. The difference is that the overnight shipment bits are delayed for a day and then arrive all at once, but T3 bits begin to arrive immediately, so the T3 has much better latency, even though both methods have approximately the same throughput when considered over the interval of a day. We say that the overnight shipment is *bursty* traffic.

2. Supermarkets would like to achieve maximum throughput per checkout clerk because they can then get by with fewer of them. One way for them to do this is to increase your latency, that is, to make you wait in line, at least up to the limit of your tolerance. In his book *Configuration and Capacity Planning for Solaris Servers* (Prentice Hall), Brian Wong phrased this dilemma well by saying that throughput is a measure of organizational productivity while latency is a measure of individual productivity. The supermarket may not want to waste your individual time, but it is even more interested in maximizing its own organizational productivity.

3. One woman has a throughput of one baby per 9 months, barring twins or triplets, etc. Nine women may be able to bear 9 babies in 9 months, giving the group a throughput of 1 baby per month, even though the latency cannot be decreased (i.e., even 9 women cannot produce 1 baby in 1 month). This mildly offensive but unforgettable example is from *The Mythical Man-Month*, by Frederick P. Brooks (Addison Wesley).

Although high throughput systems often have low latency, there is no causal link. You've just seen how an overnight shipment can have high throughput with high latency. Large disks tend to have better throughput but worse latency: the disk is physically bigger, so the arm has to seek longer to get to any particular place. The latency of packet network connections also tends to increase with throughput. As you approach your maximum throughput, there are simply more packets to put on the wire, so a packet will have to wait longer for an opening, increasing latency. This is especially true for Ethernet, which allows packets to collide and simply retransmits them if there is a collision, hoping that it retransmitted them into an open slot. It seems obvious that increasing throughput capacity will decrease latency for packet switched networks. While this is true for latency imposed by traffic congestion, it is not true for cases where the latency is imposed by routers or sheer physical distance.

Finally, you can also have low throughput with low latency: a 14.4kbps modem may get the first of your bits back to you reasonably quickly, but its relatively low throughput means it will still take a tediously long time to get a large graphic to you.

With respect to the Internet, the point to remember is that latency can be more significant than throughput. For small HTML files, say under 2K, more of a 28.8kbps modem user's time is spent between the request and the beginning of a response (probably over one second) than waiting for the file to complete its arrival (one second or under).

Measuring network latency

Each step on the network from client to server and back contributes to the latency of an HTTP operation. It is difficult to figure out where in the network most of the latency originates, but there are two commonly available Unix tools that can help. Note that we're considering network latency here, not application latency, which is the time the applications running on the server itself take to begin to put a result back out on the network.

If your web server is accessed over the Internet, then much of your latency is probably due to the store and forward nature of routers. Each router must accept an incoming packet into a buffer, look at the header information, and make a decision about where to send the packet next. Even once the decision is made, the router will usually have to wait for an open slot to send the packet. The latency of your packets will therefore depend strongly on the number of router hops between the web server and the user. Routers themselves will have connections to each other that vary in latency and throughput. The odd, yet essential thing about the Internet is that the path between two endpoints can change automatically to accommodate network trouble, so your latency may vary from packet to packet. Packets can even arrive out of order. You can see the current path your packets are taking and the time between router hops by using the *traceroute* utility that comes with most versions of Unix. (See the *traceroute* manpage for more information.) A number of kind souls have made *traceroute* available from their web servers back to the requesting IP address, so you can look at path and performance *to* you from another point on the Internet, rather than *from* you to that point. One page of links to traceroute servers is at *http://www.slac.stanford.edu/comp/net/wan-mon/traceroute-srv.html*. Also see *http://www.internetweather.com/* for continuous measurements of ISP latency as measured from one point on the Internet.

Note that *traceroute* does a reverse DNS lookup on all intermediate IPs so you can see their names, but this delays the display of results. You can skip the DNS lookup with the *-n* option and you can do fewer measurements per router (the default is three) with the *-q* option. Here's an example of *traceroute* usage:

```
% traceroute -q 2 www.umich.edu
traceroute to www.umich.edu (141.211.144.53), 30 hops max, 40 byte packets
 1  router.cableco-op.com (206.24.110.65)  22.779 ms  139.675 ms
 2  mv103.mediacity.com (206.24.105.8)  18.714 ms  145.161 ms
 3  grfge000.mediacity.com (206.24.105.55)  23.789 ms  141.473 ms
 4  bordercore2-hssi0-0.SanFrancisco.mci.net (166.48.15.249)  29.091 ms
39.856 ms
 5  bordercore2.WillowSprings.mci.net (166.48.22.1)  63.16 ms  62.75 ms
 6  merit.WillowSprings.mci.net (166.48.23.254)  82.212 ms  76.774 ms
 7  f-umbin.c-ccb2.umnet.umich.edu (198.108.3.5)  80.474 ms  76.875 ms
 8  www.umich.edu (141.211.144.53)  81.611 ms *
```

If you are not concerned with intermediate times and only want to know the current time it takes to get a packet from the machine you're on to another machine on the Internet (or on an intranet) and back to you, you can use the Unix *ping* utility. *ping* sends Internet Control Message Protocol (ICMP) packets to the named host and returns the latency between you and the named host as milliseconds. A latency of 25 milliseconds is pretty good, while 250 milliseconds is not good. See the *ping* manpage for more information. Here's an example of *ping* usage:

```
% ping www.umich.edu
PING www.umich.edu (141.211.144.53): 56 data bytes
64 bytes from 141.211.144.53: icmp_seq=0 ttl=248 time=112.2 ms
64 bytes from 141.211.144.53: icmp_seq=1 ttl=248 time=83.9 ms
64 bytes from 141.211.144.53: icmp_seq=2 ttl=248 time=82.2 ms
64 bytes from 141.211.144.53: icmp_seq=3 ttl=248 time=80.6 ms
64 bytes from 141.211.144.53: icmp_seq=4 ttl=248 time=87.2 ms
64 bytes from 141.211.144.53: icmp_seq=5 ttl=248 time=81.0 ms

--- www.umich.edu ping statistics ---
6 packets transmitted, 6 packets received, 0% packet loss
round-trip min/avg/max = 80.6/87.8/112.2 ms
```

Measuring network latency and throughput

When *ping* measures the latency between you and some remote machine, it sends ICMP messages, which routers handle differently than the TCP segments used to carry HTTP. Routers are sometimes configured to ignore ICMP packets entirely. Furthermore, by default, *ping* sends only a very small amount of information, 56 data bytes, although some versions of *ping* let you send packets of arbitrary size. For these reasons, *ping* is not necessarily accurate in measuring HTTP latency to the remote machine, but it is a good first approximation. Using *telnet* and the Unix *talk* program will give you a manual feel for the latency of a connection.

The simplest ways to measure web latency and throughput are to clear your browser's cache and time how long it takes to get a particular page from your server, have a friend get a page from your server from another point on the Internet, or log in to a remote machine and run `time lynx -source http://myserver.com/ > /dev/null`. This last method is sometimes referred to as the *stopwatch* method of web performance monitoring.

Another way to get an idea of network throughput is to use FTP to transfer files to and from a remote system. FTP is like HTTP in that it is carried over TCP. There are some hazards to this approach, but if you are careful, your results should reflect your network conditions. First, do not put too much stock in the numbers the FTP program reports to you. While the first significant digit or two will probably be correct, the FTP program internally makes some approximations, so the number reported is only approximately accurate. More importantly, what you do with FTP will determine exactly which part of the system is the bottleneck. To put it another way, what you do with FTP will determine what you're measuring. To insure that you are measuring the throughput of the network and not of the disk of the local or remote system, you want to eliminate any requirements for disk access which could be caused by the FTP transfer. For this reason, you should not FTP a collection of small files in your test; each file creation requires a disk access. Similarly, you need to limit the size of the file you transfer because a huge file will not fit in the filesystem cache of either the transmitting or receiving machine, again resulting in disk access. To make sure the file is in the cache of the transmitting machine when you start the FTP, you should do the FTP at least twice, throwing away the results from the first iteration. Also, do not write the file on the disk of the receiving machine. You can do this with some versions of FTP by directing the result to */dev/null*. Altogether, we have something like this:

```
ftp> get bigfile /dev/null
```

Try using the FTP *hash* command to get an interactive feel for latency and throughput. The *hash* command prints hash marks (#) after the transfer of a block of data. The size of the block represented by the hash mark varies with the FTP implementation, but FTP will tell you the size when you turn on hashing:

```
ftp> hash
Hash mark printing on (1024 bytes/hash mark).
ftp> get ers.27may
200 PORT command successful.
150 Opening BINARY mode data connection for ers.27may (362805 bytes).
##########################################################################
##########################################################################
##########################################################################
##########################################################################
#############################################
226 Transfer complete.
362805 bytes received in 15 secs (24 Kbytes/sec)
ftp> bye
221 Goodbye.
```

You can use the Expect scripting language to run an FTP test automatically at regular intervals. Other scripting languages have a difficult time controlling the terminal of a spawned process; if you start FTP from within a shell script, for example, execution of the script halts until FTP returns, so you cannot continue the FTP session. Expect is designed to deal with this exact problem. Expect is well documented in *Exploring Expect*, by Don Libes (O'Reilly & Associates).

You can of course also retrieve content via HTTP from your server to test network performance, but this does not cleanly distinguish network performance from server performance.

Here are a few more network testing tools:

ttcp

> *ttcp* is an old C program, circa 1985, for testing TCP connection speed. It makes a connection on port 2000 and transfers zeroed buffers or data copied from STDIN. It is available from *ftp://ftp.arl.mil/pub/ttcp/* and distributed with some Unix systems. Try *which ttcp* and *man ttcp* on your system to see if the binary and documentation are already there.

nettest

> A more recent tool, circa 1992, is *Nettest*, available at *ftp://ftp.sgi.com/sgi/src/nettest/. Nettest* was used to generate some performance statistics for vBNS, the very-high-performance backbone network service, *http://www.vbns.net/.*

bing

> *bing* attempts to measure bandwidth between two points on the Internet. See *http://web.cnam.fr/reseau/bing.html.*

chargen

> The *chargen* service, defined in RFC 864 and implemented by most versions of Unix, simply sends back nonsense characters to the user at the maximum possible rate. This can be used along with some measuring mechanism to determine what that maximum rate is. The TCP form of the service sends a continuous stream, while the UDP form sends a packet of random size for each packet received. Both run on well-known port 19.

netspec

> NetSpec simplifies network testing by allowing users to control processes across multiple hosts using a set of daemons. It can be found at *http://www.tisl.ukans.edu/Projects/AAI/products/netspec/.*

Utilization

Utilization is simply the fraction of the capacity of a component that you are actually using. You might think that you want all your components at close to 100%

utilization in order to get the most bang for your buck, but this is not necessarily how things work. Remember that for disk drives and Ethernet, latency suffers greatly at high utilization. A rule of thumb is that many components can run at their best performance up to about 70% utilization. The *perfmeter* tool that comes with many versions of Unix is a good graphical way to monitor the utilization of your system.

Efficiency

Efficiency is usually defined as throughput divided by utilization. When comparing two components, if one has a higher throughput at the same level of utilization, it is regarded as more efficient. If both have the same throughput but one has a lower level of utilization that one is regarded as more efficient. While useful as a basis for comparing components, this definition is otherwise irrelevant, because it is only a division of two other parameters of performance.

A more useful measure of efficiency is performance per unit cost. This is usually called *cost efficiency*. Performance tuning is the art of increasing cost efficiency: getting more bang for your buck. In fact, the Internet itself owes its popularity to the fact that it is much more cost-efficient than previously existing alternatives for transferring small amounts of information. Email is vastly more cost-efficient than a letter. Both send about the same amount of information, but email has near-zero latency and near-zero incremental cost; it doesn't cost you any more to send two emails rather than one. Web sites providing product information are lower latency and cheaper than printed brochures. As the throughput of the Internet increases faster than its cost, entire portions of the economy will be replaced with more cost-efficient alternatives, especially in the business-to-business market, which has little sentimentality for old ways. First, relatively static information such as business paperwork, magazines, books, CDs, and videos will be virtualized. Second, the Internet will become a real-time communications medium.

The cost efficiency of the Internet for real-time communications threatens not only the obvious target of telephone carriers, but also the automobile industry. That is, telecommuting threatens physical commuting. Most of the workforce simply moves bits around, either with computers, on the phone, or in face-to-face conversations, which are, in essence, gigabit-per-second, low-latency video connections. It is only these face-to-face conversations that currently require workers to buy cars for the commute to work. Cars are breathtakingly inefficient, and telecommuting represents an opportunity to save money. Look at the number of cars on an urban highway during rush hour. It's a slow river of metal, fantastically expensive in terms of car purchase, gasoline, driver time, highway construction, insurance, and fatalities. Then consider that most of those cars spend most of the day sitting in a parking lot. Just think of the lost interest on that idle capital. And consider the cost of the parking lot itself, and the office. As data transmission costs continue to accelerate their fall, car costs cannot fall at the same pace. Gigabit connections between work and home will inevitably be far cheaper than the daily commute, for both the worker and employer. And at gigabit bandwidth, it will feel like you're really there.

Benchmark Specifications and Benchmark Tests

For clarity, we should distinguish between benchmark specifications and benchmark tests. There are several web benchmarks that may be implemented by more than one test, since there are implementation details that do not affect the results of the test. For example, a well-specified HTTP load is the same regardless of the hardware and software used to generate the load and regardless of the actual bits in the content. On the other hand, some benchmarks are themselves defined by a test program or suite, so that running the test is the only way to run the benchmark. We will be considering both specifications and tests in this section.

The point of a benchmark is to generate performance statistics that can legitimately be used to compare products. To do this, you must try to hold constant all of the conditions around the item under test and then measure performance. If the only thing different between runs of a test is a particular component, then any difference in results must be due to the difference between the components.

Exactly defining the component under test can be a bit tricky. Say you are trying to compare the performance of Solaris and Irix in running Netscape server software. The variable in the tests is not only the operating system, but also, by necessity, the hardware. It would be impossible to say from a benchmark alone which performance characteristics are due to the operating system and which are due to the hardware. You would need to undertake a detailed analysis of the OS and the hardware, which is far more difficult.

It may sound odd, but another valid way to think of a benchmark test is the creation of a deliberate bottleneck at the subject of the test. When the subject is definitely the weakest link in the chain, then the throughput and latency of the whole system will reflect those of the subject. The hard part is assuring that the subject is actually the weakest link, because subtle changes in the test can shift the bottleneck from one part of the system to another, as we saw earlier with the FTP test of network capacity. If you're testing server hardware throughput, for example, you want to have far more network throughput than the server could possibly need, otherwise you may get identical results for all hardware, namely the bandwidth of the network.

One downside of benchmark tests which measure the maximum throughput of particular components is that it is easy to extrapolate incorrectly, that is, to assume that the performance of a configuration is linear over a wider range of load than it really is. A good example, mentioned above, is the server on a very high speed connection. It so happens that high speed servers need less RAM for a given rate of HTTP connections, because memory usage for connections and CGI processes is far less likely to be an issue when connections are short-lived. To get, say, one-tenth the server performance over a network that runs at one-tenth of the benchmark speed, you will need more than one-tenth of the RAM in the benchmark server to be assured of sufficient storage for the overhead of concurrent connections and the simultaneously running CGI processes, while still meeting the overhead of the operating system itself.

Your network will make some benchmarks not exactly repeatable, because the number of collisions on an Ethernet network depend on very small differences in time. You may get the same statistical results over several runs of a trial, but you will not get exactly the same results twice.

The moral is that you should find a benchmark that reflects, as much as possible, what you will really be doing. If you will be serving 28.8kbps modem users, find a benchmark that calculates the maximum number of 28.8kbps users the server can handle rather than a benchmark that tests the server's ability to fill a T3 line. You should look carefully at the wording of the test before assuming that it has meaning for you. For instance, I regularly benchmark my server hardware for physical speed. It hasn't moved an inch in months, so the speed is zero. Nonetheless, it's pretty good as a web server. Since I don't really care whether my server can move, I'm using the wrong benchmark.

How do you determine what your server does in the real world so that you can find a good benchmark test? A good place to start is your log files. They reflect exactly what your server has been up to, at least in terms of HTTP operations and bytes transferred. You could replace your software, OS, or hardware with a trial version of something else, let it run for a while, and then compare the log files. But that may not be accurate, because loads vary over time, and you may be running well under peak capacity in both cases. Log files won't tell you your server's peak capacity; they only show what the server has attained so far. If, however, the log shows that the server was suddenly able to handle a much larger or smaller load when you changed some component, that is probably significant.

Be careful of the fine print in benchmark tests. Consider benchmarks in light of information theory: if you know exactly what's coming, then it isn't information. The point of a computer benchmark is to see how quickly you process information, that is, how quickly you can deal with the real-life uncertainty of what the user wants. If you tune the entire system specifically for the benchmark so that there is very little uncertainty left, you've effectively defeated the purpose of the test, and the results have no relevance to real users of the system. One of the benchmark programs used by the makers of the Zeus web server is rather like that. The test repeatedly requests the same file, so the file is cached in memory after the first request. The benchmark consequently tells you only the rate at which the server can accept connections and dump from a buffer to the connection, not the rate at which it locates the correct file.

This reminds me of a story a friend in a programming class once told me. He had to write a calculator program to work with Roman numerals. He was told exactly which calculations would be asked of the program as a test of its correctness, so rather than writing a useful Roman numeral calculator, which would take a lot of work, he just wrote a hashtable that looked up the question and spit out the right answer. You can imagine a naive web benchmark in which a tester, not realizing there is a file cached in the browser, repeatedly requests it and assumes that the server it originally came from is providing it at an incredible speed.

Similar to hypertuning for the details of a particular test is finding or creating a test that makes you look good, which is like shooting an arrow and then painting the bull's-eye around it. This is known as "benchmarketing," and is the rule rather than the exception for tests from vendors, who count on the fact that most buyers just don't have the time to verify the assumptions and methodology of a test. If you compare the contradictory claims of victory in advertisements from web hardware and software vendors, you'll start to see that exactly what is being measured varies quite a bit or is just so ill-defined that you're not sure what it means.

Following are brief reviews of the some standard benchmarks for web performance:

WebStone

> The first widely used benchmark of web servers was the WebStone benchmark created by Silicon Graphics. WebStone simulates the activity of many clients making requests of a web server via many client machines each requesting a standard set of files. Each client machine can run multiple instances of a test client. The latest version of WebStone can test CGI and server API performance as well as the serving of plain HTML.

> There are some problems with WebStone. The run rules of the test leave many decisions up to the tester, so there is a large opening for benchmarketing, as described previously. The client machines are usually connected to the web server over a 100Mbps network, but the network speed is not specified by the benchmark. The file set is also small enough that it can be cached, meaning that the test does not necessarily measure disk performance. WebStone tests only HTTP GETs, not HTTP POSTs. POST is used for sending form information to CGIs.

The WebStone specification is free to the public. A good overview of Web-Stone is available at *http://www.mindcraft.com/webstone/*. Mindcraft acquired WebStone from Silicon Graphics. Mindcraft runs WebStone benchmarks on popular hardware and software web server configurations and publishes the results on the Web.

SPECweb96

A more rigorous test of web server performance is available from the Standard Performance Evaluation Corporation (SPEC). The test specification is not free, but it has significant advantages over other web server benchmarks: there are more detailed run rules, including a required mix of HTTP GET content transfer sizes. The load is modeled on what a typical Internet service provider would experience. More significantly, it is the only web performance benchmark that did not originate with a vendor of web server hardware or software, so it is presumably free of deliberate bias toward one vendor.

Like Webstone and may other tests, SPECweb96 is usually run at 100Mbps, which has little to do with the reality of the Internet, where bandwidth is scarce and therefore connections and processes tend to be concurrent. This network connection speed is, however, a simple way to be assured that the server and not the network is the actual subject of the test.

A number of other features of the test make it more of a theoretical than a practical exercise. The file set is large to discourage caching, but vendors use even larger amounts of RAM to avoid accessing the hard disk, in a sort of benchmarking arms race. In practice, most web sites require disk access. The test is confined to static HTML access and does not attempt to test the performance of CGI, Java, dynamic HTML, database access, and other more interactive uses. Finally, the test does not allow the use of HTTP 1.1's performance-improving persistent connections.

In short, SPECweb96 measures a very limited subset of what a web server might encounter, so it should never be the sole basis for conclusions about the relative performance of more elaborate web service configurations. It is most relevant for a 100Mbps LAN intranet serving only static HTML. On such an intranet, the server is probably not going to be very busy anyway.

SPEC has recognized many of these shortcomings and is working on a new benchmark to be called SPECweb98, which will include HTTP GETs to CGIs in Perl, with allowances for server software APIs for those who do not wish to use CGI. Also included in the new test are HTTP POSTs to CGIs, HTTP 1.1, and a separate proxy server benchmark.

As an example result, Sun's Ultra Enterprise 2 claims 1488 SPECweb96 HTTP transactions per second running Solaris 2.6 and Sun WebServer. This machine has two 300MHz UltraSPARC II's with 2MB external cache each, and a 622 megabit-per-second ATM network. Some servers claim SPECweb96 results of up to 4000 transactions per second.

See *http://www.specbench.org/osg/web96/*. Also see *http://open.specbench.org/osg/web/results/* for some other benchmark results.

TPC-C, TPC-D

The same Internet infrastructure that lets a user request a particular HTML document can also be used to let the user request that the server perform transaction processing tasks, such as transferring money from one account to another. Transaction processing has stricter requirements than ordinary web services, such as insuring that a transaction either completes correctly or is rolled back, meaning that it is invalidated and discarded. There can be no ambiguity about whether you paid a bill or not, for example.

Transaction processing is fundamentally different from serving HTML in both protocols and complexity. There are benchmarks that existed long before the Web specifically for transaction processing. The standard transaction processing benchmarks are currently TPC-C and TPC-D, created by the Transaction Processing Council. The earliest widespread transaction processing benchmark was known as *debit-credit*, and simulated withdrawals and deposits into a bank account, but it was found to be fundamentally flawed because it was poorly specified, allowing a number of ways to get whatever results were desired—for example, by caching the entire data set in memory. Debit-credit was replaced by the well-specified benchmarks TPC-A and TPC-B, but these are now obsolete. TPC-C and TPC-D results are audited, and include not only raw performance, but also scalability and the total cost of ownership.

For a more detailed description of transaction benchmarking, see Jim Gray's *The Benchmark Handbook for Database and Transaction Processing Systems* (Morgan Kaufmann), or the TPC website at *http://www.tpc.org/*.

Vendor-standard benchmarks

For widespread but proprietary applications such as SAP and Oracle Financials, you may find that the only option is to use benchmark tests and results from the product vendors themselves.

CaffeineMark

The CaffeineMark benchmark for Java is identical to the testing tool: the score is simply how well it runs the tool. It has been called unreliable because it does not test method calls, allocation, synchronization, or runtime facilities. It is possible to customize Java applications to get arbitrary results on the CaffeineMark test.

The CaffeineMark was created by Pendragon. See *http://www.webfayre.com/cm.html*.

Web Performance Measuring Tools and Services

Now that we know about some web benchmarks, let's look at some tools and services that give us web performance information. Note that the IETF is working on standards for measuring performance of the Internet itself. See *http://io.advanced. org/IPPM/*. Merit has some analysis of Internet performance statistics at *http:// www.merit.edu/ipma/analysis/*.

Some web performance monitoring tools and services are included here as well. Web performance monitoring is automatic web performance measurement at regular intervals. This is very useful for site maintenance and can be linked to a pager so that the webmaster can get immediate notification when the site is down or unusually slow. Performance monitoring is important for planning capacity expansion:

AIM (http://www.aim.com/)
> AIM Technology provides performance measurement software and services for Unix and NT systems.

ARM (http://hpcc923.external.hp.com/openview/rpm/papers.armwp.htm)
> The Application Response Measurement API provides a standard way to characterize resource consumption by a particular application, even in a distributed environment. It was developed by Hewlett-Packard and Tivoli Systems. It is a good idea, but it requires that software developers instrument their code using this API. To date, few software vendors have released ARM-compliant code.

Baseline (http://www.teamquest.com/)
> Baseline is a product from TeamQuest that reports performance of CPU, disk, buffer cache, etc., for networks of Unix and NT machines, locating bottlenecks and providing detailed analysis and alarms. The reports are accessible via a web browser, and there is even a live demo at their web site.

Best/1 (http://www.bgs.com/)
> The Best/1 performance products from BGS run on most corporate computers including mainframes, Unix systems, and NT. They not only collect data, but they also feed the data into a capacity planning tool. You can set performance monitors, alerts, generate reports, and plan additional capacity.

BMC Patrol Knowledge Module for Internet Servers (http://www.bmc.com/products/ internet/)
> The suite of Patrol products from BMC monitor all kinds of corporate systems including web servers. You can set rules to automatically identify problems, then to try to correct the problems or notify you. The Patrol CGI Analyzer lets you monitor CGI performance in particular.

Cisco's NETSYS tools (http://www.cisco.com/warp/public/734/toolkit/index.shtml)

These tools are designed to monitor networks (routers in particular) rather than web servers, but, of course, the network is critical to your web performance.

Del Mar Solutions (http://www.delmarsol.com/)

DelMar's Service Watch monitoring tool monitors performance and availability for your network and web proxy servers, among other services, while Web-Eye monitors the performance of web servers. They both work with Sun's Netmanager and HP's Openview, or with SNMP.

Homegrown

You can easily measure web performance yourself by writing scripts that time the retrieval of HTML from a web server. Java and Perl are both well suited for this, but if you have the text browser Lynx from the University of Kansas, here's a simple way to get an idea of the time to get an answer from any server on the Internet:

```
% time lynx -source http://web.myserver.com/
0.05user 0.02system 0:00.74elapsed 9%CPU
```

On some systems the *time* command has been replaced with *timex*. Of course, the startup time for Lynx is included in this, but if you run it twice and throw away the first result, your second result will be fairly accurate because the Lynx executable won't have to be loaded from disk. Remember that network and server time is included as well; in fact, this includes all the time that is not system or user time: .67 seconds in the example above, which used a cable modem connection to a fast server. So even in the case of very good network connectivity, the Internet can still take most of the time. You can also use the free Perl tool *webget* in place of Lynx.

If you want to see how the performance or your site looks from elsewhere on the Internet, you can log in to a remote machine and run the *time lynx* command given above. The time given will be the time from the remote point of view.

If you'd like to monitor the performance of a web server rather than just measure it once, here is a trivial script that will do just that:

```
#!/bin/bash
while true
    do
        time lynx -source http://web.myserver.com/ > /dev/null
        sleep 600
    done
```

If you call the above script *mon* then you can capture the results to a file called *log* like this:

```
mon 2> log
```

You could also put in an automated email to notify you if performance drops below a certain level.

If you just want to hit your server hard with a specified number of hits, you can do it with the following script. Take the difference between the start and end times output by the script, and divide the number of hits in the script by that time to get the number of hits per second you delivered to the web server. This script forks a new Lynx browser process for each hit, so the script is not efficient and the total running time is not very accurate, but you can see how easy it is to write a simple load generation tool in a Unix shell language:

```
#!/bin/bash
CNT=0

date
while [ "100" -ne "$CNT" ]
    do
        lynx -source http://web.myserver.com/ > /dev/null &
        CNT=`expr $CNT + 1`
    done
date
```

As mentioned previously, you could also write these tools in Java or Perl and get a more accurate reading and heavier generated load by eliminating Lynx startup time.

Simple Network Management Protocol (SNMP) tools are another way to write your own scripts and discover patterns that are not otherwise obvious. SNMP is a large topic which is beyond the scope of this book.

HP Openview tools (*http://www.hp.com/openview/rpm/netmetds.htm, http://www.hp.com/openview/rpm/mwds.htm*)

Netmetrix is an RMON-based network monitoring tool that works with Cisco's IOS. It can extract data from routers for performance monitoring. The HP MeasureWare agent collects statistics on the performance of distributed systems in general, not just web systems. MeasureWare collects and analyzes application response times and system metrics such as disk, CPU, and network. It is well integrated with the other HP OpenView tools.

INS Enterprise Pro (*http://www.ins.com/*)

Enterprise Pro is a network monitoring service from International Network Services. They will monitor your web sites and provide web-based reports of latency, throughput, error conditions, and trends.

Keynote Perspective (*http://www.keynote.com/*)

Keynote Perspective is a monitoring service from Keynote Systems featuring real-time measurement and reporting of web site performance from almost 100 sites around the U.S. The reports can be viewed via the Web and include statistics on latency, so they provide a good overview of how users really perceive your site's performance from various locations.

RAPS (http://www.resolute.com/)

RAPS, or the Real-time Applications Performance System, is a product from Resolute Software that monitors applications, servers, and networks through lightweight agents that report back to a central server at regular intervals. Collected data can be analyzed to determine current capacity and predict when components will need to be upgraded to handle increasing load. A rules engine can look for certain correlations in real-time data and initiate corrective actions.

Resolve (http://www.crosskeys.com/cross/services/)

CrossKeys sells a product called Resolve that monitors WAN service-level agreements (SLAs) for frame relay, voice, and ATM. It generates reports that are valuable in determining whether you are actually getting the telecommunication services you are paying for.

SE toolkit (http://www.sun.com/sunworldonline/swol-01-1998/swol-01-perf.html)

The SE toolkit by Adrian Cockcroft and Rich Pettit is actually a Unix system performance monitoring and analysis kit, not a web performance monitoring tool per se. Since the operating system greatly affects web server performance, however, it is a good idea to keep this tool running to collect statistics for analysis. It monitors TCP throughput, TCP connections, TCP retransmits, NIC rates, collisions and overruns, CPU and disk utility levels, and memory residence time of applications.

The SE package also includes some log file data collection and analysis tools that work with the Common Log File format, but these are written in a custom interpreted dialect of C and run only on Solaris for SPARC or x86.

Visual UpTime (http://www.visualnetworks.com/)

Visual UpTime is another WAN service-level management system. It automates the collection, interpretation, and presentation of WAN service-level data for frame relay, ATM, leased lines, X.25, and the Internet.

WebBench (http://www1.zdnet.com/zdbop/webbench/webbench.html)

WebBench is a web server software test suite for both static and dynamic content, allowing not only CGI but also NSAPI and ISAPI.

WebSizr (http://www.technovations.com/)

WebSizr is a web loading client which can simulate up to 200 simultaneous HTTP users and record the results. The program runs on Windows only, but it can generate a load to test any HTTP server.

Log File Analysis Tools

In a sense, all web servers come with a performance monitoring tool, namely, the logging facility of the server. This, however, leaves the webmaster the problem of interpreting the logged data. A number of products have naturally arisen to fill this niche, for example, net.Analysis from net.Genesis (*http://www.netgen.com/*). You can also use Netscape's built-in *analyze* command, or simply import log files into a spreadsheet program and use the spreadsheet to plot the results in various ways. See Chapter 2, *Capacity Planning*, for more about analyzing log files.

Other Resources

A few more benchmarking resources on the web are the Linpack site, which compares Java to Fortran, at *http://www.netlib.org/benchmark/linpackjava/*; the Netperf site, which has a large database of network performance results found with the free Netperf tool, at *http://www.cup.hp.com/netperf/NetperfPage.html*; and a Java benchmark page at *http://www.cs.cmu.edu/~jch/java/benchmarks.html*.

Key Recommendations

- Don't put too much stock in benchmarks unless they're very closely related to what you actually intend to do.

- Do monitor your actual web performance, not just the server load, and keep records.

- Analyze your log files and be familiar with them so you have a feel for when things are good or bad.

4

Case Studies

In this chapter:
- *Example Performance Problems, Diagnoses, and Solutions*
- *Methodology for Performance Consulting*
- *Sample Configurations*
- *Key Recommendation*

Example Performance Problems, Diagnoses, and Solutions

Here are some hypothetical cases of web performance problems and their solutions. Any resemblance to situations you recognize is coincidental.

Not Enough Memory on Server

The Custom Pasta Corporation routinely gets most of its orders via its web site on Tuesday evenings. Unfortunately, the performance of its site also slows to a crawl at that same time every week. The webmaster is asked to check out the server configuration and fix the problem.

She figures, first of all, that the server is being overloaded somehow, because many clients have reported this problem, and there is no obvious reason for a surge in overall Internet traffic on Tuesday evenings. On Tuesday evening, she tries some tests. First, she connects from a client machine she knows to have good performance and places a test order for pasta. It does indeed take a very long time to get back to her with an acknowledgment page. So even a good client on a LAN connection to the web server has problems.

Perhaps the problem is that the LAN is overloaded. The webmaster logs in to the web server itself, a Sun Ultra, and runs the *snoop* utility. She stops the output and looks through it. There are a few HTTP requests and replies going back and forth, but they don't seem excessive, and there is not a particularly high number of TCP retransmits. There is no NFS traffic because all of the content is on this machine's local disk. The *netstat -i* command shows very few collisions, and *netstat* without any options shows that 20 or so concurrent connections are in the ESTABLISHED state. The network doesn't seem overloaded; rather, it seems that clients are waiting on the server.

Now the webmaster notices that she can hear the disk running continuously. This is odd, since she set up a separate disk for the log file and she knows that the HTML content is pretty lightweight: just a catalog of pasta types, simple HTML forms for ordering, and a few small graphics. The disk should easily be able to serve out this content for 20 users. She runs *top* and sees that *pageout* is taking 50% of the CPU time and that there are 20 or so instances of the pasta ordering CGI running along with numerous other processes spawned from the CGIs. The CGI is a rather large shell script. "Spaghetti code," she thinks, while trying to read it. Worse, shell scripts are very inefficient as CGIs because of the number of additional processes they usually start.

Using *top*, she sees that she's using more than 100% of physical memory. At least one problem is now clear: the server just doesn't have enough memory to run so many concurrent CGIs. The server is paging processes out to disk, that is, using virtual memory to try to give all of the processes a chance to run. But, since virtual memory is on disk, it is several thousand times slower than physical memory, and performance has degraded dramatically. The *vmstat* command confirms that paging is happening continuously: *vmstat*'s *pi* and *po* fields, for page in and page out rates, are both over 10 per second.

The webmaster exits the X Window System and checks the situation from terminal mode. It is slightly better because more memory is available, but there is still a great deal of paging going on. The CGIs were written by a contractor who has long since gone, so rather than try to decipher the code and rewrite it in a more efficient language, the webmaster simply buys more RAM to tide her over until she can plan how to get away from ordinary CGIs, perhaps by using NSAPI, FastCGI, or servlets. In any case, the server performance improves dramatically when the new memory is installed, and the webmaster has time to plan for the future.

Network Connection Too Slow

Telecommuter Tom lives in San Francisco, but he works as a marketer for Dev Null Drivers, Inc., in San Jose. It's an arduous commute, but Tom likes his job and he likes living in San Francisco. He suggests to his boss that he be allowed to telecommute a few days a week. Tom's boss likes the idea, because it frees up some expensive office space a few days a week, and because she wants to keep Tom happy.

Tom is responsible for a lot of content on the company's web site, and he is a fan of a Java chat applet that is very popular within the company. Most Dev Null employees leave it running so they can have private conversations in a crowded office. Tom also creates or edits many files every day. He goes out and buys a 56K modem, and signs up for service with Oversold ISP, which charges only $10 per month for unlimited access and a static IP address. When he logs in for the first time, his modem control program tells him that he's actually getting nearly 56kbps between his modem and the modem at his ISP in San Francisco, but the interactive response time between his home and work is awful. Tom has both a Mac and a PC, but the situation is the same with both of them. It's no better early in the morning or late at night. When he starts a telnet session to edit files at work, he finds he can type ahead for several words before they are echoed back to him. The chat applet is just as bad. This is very disappointing, because he is used to great response time from the LAN at work. The boss asks how it's going, and Tom has to tell her that he's actually having a hard time being productive because of the poor performance of the ISP.

Tom's boss describes the problem to Dev Null's system administrator and asks for advice. The sysadmin asks Tom for his IP address and runs a *traceroute* to it from Dev Null in San Jose. The *traceroute* shows huge latencies, on the order of five seconds, to intermediate routers with domain names ending in *.na* and one with the word *satellite* in the name. Not having seen the *.na* domain before, the sysadmin looks up the country assigned the *.na* ending. It's Namibia. Having no idea where Namibia is, he looks on a web search engine for some mention of the country. Ah, it's in southwest Africa. It seems that Oversold is routing all of Tom's traffic through Namibia via satellite because Oversold's only connection to the Internet is in Windhoek, its home town. The sysadmin silently thanks whatever Unix god wrote *traceroute* and suggests that Tom use the same ISP that Dev Null is using because Tom's traffic would then be on that ISP's private network between San Francisco and San Jose and would not have to traverse any other part of the Internet. Here's the *traceroute* output from *devnull* to Tom's computer in San Francisco:

```
% traceroute 196.27.12.12
traceroute to 196.27.12.12 (196.27.12.12), 30 hops max, 40 byte packets
1   router.devnull.com (206.24.110.65)   22.557 ms   24.554 ms   10.07 ms
2   sj103.mediatown.com (206.24.105.8)   37.033 ms   16.912 ms   79.436 ms
3   sf000.mediatown.com (206.24.105.55)   29.382 ms   66.754 ms   14.688 ms
4   bordercore2-hssi0-0.SanFrancisco.mci.net (166.48.15.249)   134.24 ms 38.762 ms
    18.445 ms
5   core4.SanFrancisco.mci.net (204.70.4.81)   165.704 ms   210.167 ms 125.343 ms
6   sl-stk-1-H9-0-T3.sprintlink.net (206.157.77.66)   30.076 ms   33.985 ms
    23.287 ms
7   gip-stock-1-fddi1-0.gip.net (204.60.128.193)   48.501 ms   30.192 ms 19.385 ms
8   gip-penn-stock.gip.net (204.60.137.85)   501.154 ms   244.529 ms 382.76 ms
9   204.60.137.90 (204.60.137.90)   503.631 ms   488.673 ms   498.388 ms
10  206.48.89.39 (206.48.89.39)   505.937 ms   680.696 ms   491.25 ms
11  196.27.64.202 (196.27.64.202)   1046.61 ms   1057.79 ms   1168.45 ms
12  oversold.com.na (196.27.12.3)   1074.49 ms   1086.45 ms 1257.85 ms
```

```
13   satellite.oversold.com.na (196.27.12.7)   1174.49 ms  1186.45 ms 1157.85 ms
14   usroutersf.oversold.com (196.27.12.9)   4074.49 ms   5086.45 ms 4257.85 ms
15   196.27.12.12 (196.27.12.12)   5293.84 ms 5230.90 ms 5148.39 ms
```

Tom switches accounts to Dev Null's ISP and finds that he can now get nearly 56kbps in download times from work, and that interactive response is nearly indistinguishable from that on the LAN at work. He has to pay an extra $10 per month, but it is money well spent. Here's the *traceroute* output from work to his new account:

```
devnull> traceroute tom.mediatown.com
traceroute to tom.mediatown.com (206.24.105.44), 30 hops max, 40 byte packets
1   router.devnull.com (206.24.110.65)   22.557 ms   24.554 ms   10.07 ms
2   sj103.mediatown.com (206.24.105.8)   37.033 ms   16.912 ms   79.436 ms
3   sf000.mediatown.com (206.24.105.55)   29.382 ms   66.754 ms   14.688 ms
4   tom.mediatown.com (206.24.105.44)   29.382 ms   66.754 ms   14.688 ms
```

Note that I have nothing against Namibia. I did a little research and found they happen to have an ISP at *http://www.iwwn.com.na/*, which has enough throughput that I can surf it quite comfortably in California. Latencies are just over one second, which isn't bad given the distance to the other side of the world. Running *traceroute www.iwwn.com.na* shows it really is over there and not just mirrored somewhere in the U.S.

Firewall Introducing Latency

The webmaster of the Antique Fruitcake website is experiencing a frustrating performance problem and having a hard time tracking it down. The website has a catalog of almost 10,000 fruitcakes searchable by year, model, serial number, and current owner in a database connected to a web server. This is not a large database by most standards, but customers are complaining that it can take 10 seconds to return the results of a simple query, while complex searches can take even longer.

The machines are overconfigured for their tasks, so the performance problem is that much more of a mystery. The web server machine is a dual-CPU Pentium 166 MHz Compaq with 256MB of RAM, a 4GB SCSI II disk used for both content and logging, and a 100Mbps Ethernet card. The database machine is a single-CPU Pentium 200Mhz Compaq with 164MB of RAM running SQL Server, a 5GB RAID 5 disk set, and again a 100Mbps Ethernet card. The two machines are not used for any other applications. The database machine is behind a firewall and is talking to the web server outside the firewall using just TCP/IP.

The configuration mostly uses the out of the box defaults, but a few optimizations have been performed. On the web server, all unnecessary services have been disabled, the memory available for Active Server Page (ASP) caching has been increased, and database connection pooling has been turned on so that the overhead of creating new ODBC connections to SQL Server is minimized. Pooling means connections are recycled rather than created new for each query. On the database machine, the data has been indexed by each of the search variables to reduce search time; *tempdb*, a temporary storage area in the database that gets heavy use, has been put in RAM rather than left on disk; and the cache size for SQL Server has been increased.

The NT performance monitor tool shows that the bandwidth between the database and the firewall and between the firewall and the web server is not highly utilized, and that memory utilization on both machines is also low. Simple tests from a web browser show that static pages are being delivered quite quickly, but pages that require database access are slow. When a query is submitted to the web server, its CPU utilization jumps for an instant as it interprets the query and passes it through the firewall to the database machine, which then shows a CPU jump for about a second. The ISQL utility on the database machine also shows that even complex queries are actually executing in less than two seconds. The mysterious part is that both machines are then mostly idle for about seven seconds before the data starts coming back to the browser, and this happens even for identical queries, which should be cached by the database and therefore returned extremely quickly on the second call.

Simply by process of elimination, the webmaster decides the problem must be with the firewall. A close examination of network traffic shows that the delay is indeed happening almost entirely within the firewall machine. The firewall is a 486 machine with an excessive default set of rules that includes blocking many kinds of application traffic in both directions, forcing the firewall to look far within each packet rather than just at the headers. An upgrade to a packet filtering router with a few simple rules for blocking inbound traffic from everywhere except the web server solves the performance problem. Unfortunately, this also makes the database less secure, because a break-in to the web server would mean that the database is exposed. Some security has been traded for better performance.

Slow Client

The doctors at Budget Surgeon would like to use the Web to research surgical journals. They subscribe to a commercial service offering access to a variety of surgical journals via the Web, but they are immediately disappointed by the performance when they try it out. The doctors see that Netscape indicates that it is downloading the articles at 2KB/s and assume that they need to upgrade their 28.8 modems. They ask the office computer expert for his recommendation, and he suggests a new cable modem service being offered in their area. The cable modem ads claim 500kbps downstream, which is 62.5KB/s (500kbps/8 bits per byte).

The doctors subscribe to the cable modem service but are astonished to try it out and find that they are still getting only about 4KB/s, rather than the 62.5KB/s advertised, and it still takes forever before any useful information shows up in their browser. They go back to the computer expert and complain that the cable modem is a fraud. The expert decides to try it for himself. He has an old Pentium 75Mhz laptop with a 512KB L2 cache and 24MB of RAM running Linux and Netscape. He hooks up the cable modem and views a few well-known sites. He sees that he is, in fact, getting better than 50KB/s viewing the surgical journals over the cable modem. The expert tries out one of their Macintosh PowerBook 5300cs laptops and finds that it does indeed get only 4KB/s. A little research reveals that this series of PowerBooks has no L2 cache at all, meaning that no executable code is cached; rather, every instruction must be fetched from RAM, which is about ten times slower than L2 cache. This accounts for some of the problem. The doctors seem to have enough RAM overall, and enough of it assigned to Netscape, because the disk is not particularly busy during downloads. The Macintosh has no place on its motherboard to put cache, so there's not much the doctors can do about that problem if they want to keep the same machines.

The expert also notices that the Macs are faster when not plugged into an outlet but running off the battery. This is really odd, because plugged-in laptops should have better performance because there is no special need to conserve power. Most laptop BIOS's or OS's are configured to turn off power conservation features (which slow down the machine) when wall power is available. It turns out that some of the first 5300s shipped ran slower when plugged in because of electromagnetic interference (EMI) within the machine. An EMI shroud is ordered from Apple to solve this problem.

The Macs are running MacOS 7. An upgrade to MacOS 8 provides another immediately noticeable improvement, partly because more of the MacOS 8 code is native to the PowerPC CPU than to the previous CPU, the Motorola 68K series. The 68K code requires a 68K emulator to run on the PowerPC, and this slows down the machine.

Finally, the expert tries Speed Doubler by Connectix. Speed Doubler improves performance in several ways, but the most important feature is a higher-performance replacement for the 68K emulator in the PowerMac. Not only do 68K applications run faster, but because parts of the MacOS 8 are still emulated, even native PowerMac applications see some benefit. In the end, the doctors get better than 25KB/s and are satisfied with the performance.

Methodology for Performance Consulting

Here is a methodology I use when beginning to look at a web site's performance problems. It reflects the point of view of an outside consultant brought in for a fresh look at the problems.

First, start a log and write down the date, who the customer is, and what the approximate problem is. Whatever you do or talk about, write it down. Not only will this help you when you need to remember passwords and what exactly you changed, but it is also useful for writing reports later.

Next, resist the urge to just start twiddling parameters. The webmaster you're working with may tell you what he or she thinks is wrong and ask you to change something right off. Just say no. That's a rathole you don't want to enter. You need to do some analysis first. Likewise, if the webmaster asks for your first impression, don't respond. If you do, he or she is quite likely to go into that rat-hole alone and drag you in behind. Point out that there are no magic bullets (or, at least, very few of them), and that slow and steady wins the race.

Write down, in as much detail as you can, what the perceived problem is and what the webmaster or users think caused the problem. Listen hard. Remember that performance problems always come down to unhappy people somewhere, and that success means making them happy rather than resolving all technical issues.

Ask what performance data has been collected so far. Has the customer run any benchmarks, or tried any solutions? Benchmark and duplicate the problem yourself. Get a good topology diagram with servers and connections clearly marked.

Consider changing the highest levels first, that is, the architecture of what the customer is doing, and identify steps that could possibly be eliminated. Low-level tuning should be saved for much later, because the gains are smaller, and any work you put into low-level tuning may be wiped out by architecture changes.

The most likely suspects for performance problems are home-grown CGI or server API applications, high-level architecture, the Internet, and hard disks. Try running a benchmark when no other users or processes are on the system, perhaps late at night, to find out what the best possible performance of the current configuration is. This helps clarify the difference between bad applications and excessive load on the system. If performance is bad for a single user with no network load, then the problem probably lies in the application. If performance is only intermittently bad, look for low-efficiency error handling by the application. Profile the application and really look at the results, because intuition about bottlenecks is often wrong. Look for memory leaks by monitoring process size.

Analyze the OS and hardware with the diagnostic tools at your disposal, again, from the highest levels first. Look at the server log files for errors. Run whatever sort of performance tools your server system has and look at CPU, disk, and memory usage. Look at router and switch configuration and throughput. Check physical cable connections and look for kinks or sources of interference. Get performance statistics from your ISP.

Once you have a hypothesis about where the problem is, back up everything, try a solution, and run your benchmarks again. Run whatever tests are needed to make sure you didn't break anything else. If your solution didn't help, you need to do some more analysis.

Sample Configurations

Here are a few tried-and-true configurations that have good performance relative to the cost of the setup. Beware that prices are volatile and these examples are only approximate.

Low Volume

A low-volume site gets one to ten thousand hits per day. Such a site can easily be run out of your home. A typical configuration for this level is good PC hardware ($2000) running Linux 2.0 (free), Apache 1.2.6 (free), with connectivity through a cable modem with 100kbps upstream ($100 per month). For database functionality, you may use flat files, or read all of the elements into a Perl hashtable or array in a CGI, and not see any performance problems for a moderate number of users if the database is smaller than, say, one thousand items. Once you start getting more than one hit per second, or when the database gets bigger than one thousand items or has multiple tables, you may want to move to the mSQL free relational database from *http://www.hughes.com.au/*. The database and connectivity are the weak links here. Apache and Linux, on the other hand, are capable of handling large sites.

Medium Volume

A medium volume site gets ten thousand to a million hits per day. A typical configuration for a medium volume site is a Sun Ultra or an Intel Pentium Pro machine with 64MB for the operating system and filesystem buffer overhead plus 2 to 4MB per server process. Of course, more memory is better if you can afford it. Such workstation-class machines cost anywhere between $3,000 and $30,000. You should have separate disks for serving content and for logging hits (and consider a separate disk for swap space), but the size of the content disk really depends on how much content you are serving. RAID disks or any other kind of disk array gets better random access performance because multiple seeks can happen in parallel. You can increase the number of network interfaces to handle the expected number of hits by simply adding more 10BaseT or 100BaseT cards, up to a limit of about 45 for some Solaris systems. Apache web server still works fine for medium volume web sites, but you may want to go to one of the Netscape or other commercial servers for heavier loads, or for formal support or particular security or publishing features.

One million hits per day sounds like a lot, but that's only about twelve hits per second if it's spread evenly throughout the day. Even twenty hits per second is within the capacity of most workstations if the site is serving only static HTML and images rather than creating dynamic content. On the other hand, twenty hits per second is a pretty large load from a network capacity point of view. If the average hit is about 10KB, that's 10KB × 8 bits/byte × 12 = 983040 bits/second, you might think that a single T1 line at 1544000 bits per second can handle one million hits per day, but remember that web traffic is bursty, because each HTML page results in an immediate request for all embedded images, applets, and so on, so you should expect frequent peaks of three to five times the average. This means you probably cannot effectively serve a million hits per day from a single T1 line, but you should be able to serve one hundred thousand hits per day.

If your site has a large database access component to it, you'll probably want to use one of the high-capacity commercial RDBMS systems like Oracle, Informix, or Sybase, which can have price tags in the $10,000 to $20,000 range. You'll get best performance by keeping database connections open with a connection manager package from the vendor, but you can also write a connection manager yourself or use a TP monitor to manage connections. You probably should not use CGIs at all, but rather servlets, FastCGI, or a server API such as the Apache API, NSAPI, or ISAPI.

High Volume

A high-volume site gets more than one million hits per day. There is no standard configuration for such high volume sites yet, so let's just consider a few examples.

AltaVista

AltaVista delivered about 20 million searches per day in late 1997, according to *http://altavista.digital.com/av/content/pr122997.htm*, which is very impressive given that each search required some sort of database access. AltaVista is one of the most popular sites on the Web, according to *http://www.hot100.com/*, and one of the best performing, according to *http://www.keynote.com/*.

The AltaVista query interface, which is the part you see when you go to *http://altavista.digital.com/*, is served from the site's web server, which is a set of 3 Digital AlphaStation 500/500s, each with 1GB of RAM and 6GB of disk running Digital Unix. The web server and database are both custom software written in C under Digital Unix, making heavy use of multithreading. But that's just the front end. The really big iron runs the search engine on the back end.

The AltaVista search engine runs on 16 AlphaServer 8400 5/440s, each with 12 64-bit CPUs, 8GB of RAM, and 300G of RAID disk. Each holds a portion of the web index and has a response time of under one second. Most queries are satisfied from RAM, minimizing disk access. Note that 8GB of RAM cannot be addressed with a 32-bit machine (2^{32} is 4G) so a 64-bit CPU is a necessity rather than a luxury.

AltaVista's Internet connection in Palo Alto is 100Mbps to UUNet plus two other connections of unspecified speed, to BBN and Genuity. The whole thing is mirrored at five sites distributed around the world.

See *http://altavista.digital.com/av/content/about_our_technology.htm* for more information on their site.

Netscape

As of the end of 1997, Netscape was getting over 135 million hits per day, which is over 1000 HTTP connections per second. There are probably peaks of three to five times the average, or 3000 to 5000 hits per second. If you were to direct a click to */dev/audio* for every hit on their servers, you'd hear a rather high-pitched whine. This is impressive.

Netscape's web site runs on more than 100 servers, representing every major server hardware manufacturer. A little test showed that hits on *home.netscape.com* or *www.netscape.com* are indeed redirected to one of 102 servers with names following the pattern *www#.netscape.com*. Here's a one-line Perl script that will show you the IP addresses for the 102 machines, with some help from the Linux *nsquery* program:

```
% perl -e 'for ($i=1; $i<103; $i++) { print `nsquery www$i.netscape.com`; }'
```

Telnetting to port 80 of one of the machines shows that it's running Netscape Enterprise 2.01. The web site itself contains a little more information about the setup, but not much detail. There are four T3 lines, one going to each gateway machine, and all of the gateways are connected by a 100Mbps FDDI ring. There are mirrors of the main site in Europe and Australia. Some machines are hosted at Globalcenter, *http://www.globalcenter.net/*, one of several large providers of space for web servers and high speed connectivity. See *http://home.netscape.com/site/*.

Sun

Sun Microsystems' web site at *http://www.sun.com/* gets more than 2 million hits per day, making it about the 30th-busiest site on the web. The web server is a pair of UltraServer 1/170 systems, each with a 167MHz UltraSPARC processor, 256 MB of memory, and a SPARCstorage Array. The two systems are in different physical locations for reliability and round robin DNS is used to split the load between them. The OS is Solaris 2.6 and server software is NS Enterprise/2.01. Internet connectivity is through a T3 from BBN to the local router, which is connected via 100Mbps Ethernet to the web server. See *http://www.sun.com/sun-on-net/ www.sun.com/.*

What Are the Busiest Sites on the Web?

There is a list of the 100 most trafficked web sites at *http://www.hot100.com/.* The data comes largely from analysis of proxy server logs. The site rankings vary over time, but the following sites are usually included:

> AltaVista
> AOL
> City.Net
> CNET
> CNN
> Excite
> Geocities
> Magellan
> Microsoft
> Netscape
> Pathfinder
> Starwave
> Warner Bros.
> Yahoo!

Connectivity and Server Software at Well-Known Web Sites

There is a list of Internet access providers and server software used for 40 big companies at *http://www.keynote.com/measures/business/business40.html.* You can figure out all of this information for yourself by using *traceroute* and telnetting to port 80 of well-known servers, but Keynote has been kind enough to publish the results of their own research. For the 40 sites they publish data on, the most popular Internet providers are UUNET, BBN, and MCI, and the most popular web servers are Netscape Enterprise and Apache.

Key Recommendation

*   Be aware of what others in the web industry are doing.

5

Principles and Patterns

If you ask any computer consultant for a concrete solution to a general problem, you will inevitably get the reply that each situation is different and that more information is needed before advice can be offered. While it is true that a specific solution can't be given without detailed knowledge of the problem, there are also some principles of performance tuning that apply in the general case and some patterns that unify the specific solutions.

Principles of Performance Tuning

Sometimes You Lose

You don't know whether or not you can improve the performance of a system until you study it, but you risk wasting your time just figuring out that there's nothing you can do, particularly when you are under tight budget or time constraints. You have to weigh the probable difficulty of the analysis against the potential gains. If the gains could be very large, it is a good bet to try to improve performance, but otherwise it's not worth your time.

To Measure Something Is to Change It

The physicist Werner Heisenberg pointed out that measuring anything changes it, if only slightly, so there is some uncertainty to all measurements caused by the act of measuring. This is called the *uncertainty principle*, and is certainly true when measuring computer performance. The classic example is running *ps -aux* to see what processes are running on your server, and noticing that the only thing you ever see in the run state is *ps* itself. This must be so because *ps* has to be the running process in order to check which process is currently running. Similarly, when you take performance measurements on a machine doing some work, you are necessarily measuring not only the load of the work, but also the load caused by measurement. Do not let this lead to disturbing recursive thoughts. The uncertainty is negligible if the measurement itself was small and quick. So keep your measurements small and quick.

Reading Is Fundamental

When you walk through a room in the dark, you tend to bruise your shins. When you turn on the lights, it gets much easier. The light gives you knowledge that lets you optimize your path. It's exactly the same for performance tuning. The better your mental model of the problem, the easier it is to solve. Your guiding lights are the manuals that come with your workstation, software, and routers, so do the right thing and RTFM. Manuals are not at all dull when they hold the keys to lessening your pain. It's OK to experiment with settings and measure performance, but it's better to know why settings make a difference and how they interact with other settings and subsystems. This knowledge is in the manuals. A performance increase in one place may come at the expense of a loss in another place. If you don't know what you paid, you don't know whether the change was worthwhile.

There Is No Free Lunch

While the point of performance tuning is to get more without necessarily spending more, you will have to pay something for every increase in performance, if only the effort you put into understanding the problem and the solution. In some cases, you will have to buy new hardware, re-architect your system, or perhaps lose on portability, maintainability, security, reliability, or developer time. You can overclock the system bus for better server performance, but then the system is more likely to crash. You can remove your firewall and any encryption for better performance, but then you are exposed to attack. You can write all of your web software in optimized assembly or build web-specific chips, but the maintenance difficulties or size of investment relative to the performance gain would almost certainly mean that you made a very bad business decision. It is also unfortunate, but true, that optimizations for known usage patterns will inevitably hurt under some different usage patterns. The trick is not to spend too much for what you get. A cheap lunch is possible.

Returns Diminish

Costs also tell you when you have finished tuning the hardware you've got. When you begin tuning a system, it is usually easy to find "low hanging fruit" problems and fix them. As the system is tuned, additional performance gains become harder to find and more dependent on the particular configuration and usage pattern.

When the investment is not worth the return, tuning is finished. Worth is subjective, but here are some clues that you're finished, at least for the moment:

- Your users no longer notice improvements.

- Your violations of good programming style in the quest for performance make the code unportable and unmaintainable.

- You are considering writing in assembly language.

- Your total cost per hit is greater than hiring someone to staff a telephone and fax the information on demand.

- You are getting very annoyed.

Perfect tuning is a moving target, because your configuration, usage patterns, and available components are also constantly moving, making it impossible to get and keep that last bit of optimal performance. You'll do better in the long run to tune to standard protocols and APIs rather than using proprietary solutions or inventing your own. Then your tuning efforts will pay you back in portability across multiple generations of systems, for a much greater long-term return on investment.

Performance Fights Portability

There is a conflict between performance and portability. The best performance is achieved by optimizing for one specific set of circumstances, but portability is defined as identical functionality under many different circumstances. You cannot optimize for all circumstances, so you have to choose just where to trade performance against portability. Completely optimized software is tied to a particular platform because it must take advantage of every available performance feature of that platform, such as the use of special CPU registers or system calls. Portable software, on the other hand, cannot take advantage of features which are specific to just one platform. If it did, it would not be portable. At another level, there can be dependence in optimizations which assume a particular usage pattern. These optimizations are likely to hurt rather than help performance in other situations. The tradeoffs are endless.

Loss of software portability to optimizations would not matter much were it not for the fact that portable software, in particular, is a very valuable commodity. Portability at the source code level means code does not have to be rewritten to run on another platform, just recompiled. This saves development costs and provides larger markets. Portability at the object code level, for example Java and Smalltalk, is a worthy goal for developers and users alike. Developers can concentrate on writing rather than porting, while users are free to choose whatever platform they like. There is never any benefit to the user in being tied to a platform.

A different kind of portability is achieved by following open networking standards, so that software which may not be portable itself can at least communicate
easily with other computers. The rise of the Web is directly due to the portability
of the HTTP protocol. HTTP may not give optimal performance on any particular
machine, but since it has been implemented on so many different machines, its
value for sharing content is more important. Any server on the Web can be
accessed by any browser, because they all speak the same language. The lesson
here is that you can trade portability for performance, but it's a Faustian bargain.
There will be a very high cost to pay eventually.

Memory Is Hierarchical

The Web can be thought of as simply the slowest and cheapest form of memory
on your computer. Even though the Web is not really on your computer and it's
mostly read-only, it fits in well with the rest of the memory hierarchy.

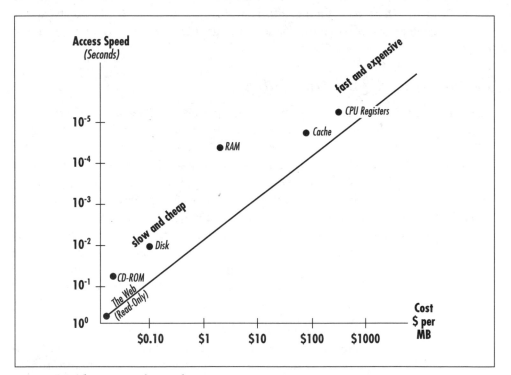

Figure 5-1. The memory hierarchy

Each level of the memory hierarchy makes a different tradeoff between cost and
performance, with cost always directly related to access speed (see Figure 5-1).
Recently used data from each level is usually cached by the next faster level. The
goal of caching is to maximize performance by using the fastest memory the most.

This can also be stated as minimizing the number of cache misses. Of course, cache reads must eventually miss, or you wouldn't need all the slower levels. A cache miss is expensive because of the relatively larger access time of the next slower level.

It is often said that the Web makes distance irrelevant, but that's not quite true. You pay just once for your local disk and you can use it for a long time, if not forever. You have to pay over and over to send and receive data over the Internet. So in the case of the Web, caching not only helps performance, but it also reduces cost. If you are going to use data many times, it is cheaper to store the data in a cache than to transmit it any significant distance.

Storing information is just transmitting it through time rather than space. To move a bit from now to later in some storage medium is analogous to moving a bit from here to there over some transmission medium. In both cases you are concerned with assuring that the bits are not changed along the way. The same error correction schemes work for both cases.

Caches Depend on Locality of Reference

If memory access were completely random, caching would not help performance much. Your cache would be constantly overwritten with new data from random parts of memory, so it would be unlikely that you would access the same data twice in an interval short enough to find it still in the cache. Fortunately, there is a pattern to memory access. Memory locations that were accessed recently are likely to be accessed again soon, as are nearby memory locations. This pattern is referred to as *locality of reference*. That is, memory accesses tend to cluster in address space and in time. This is why algorithms that cache the contents of recently accessed memory and nearby locations do in fact significantly help performance. This works quite well for the Unix filesystem buffer and for web browser caches, for example.

I/O Is Slow

I/O stands for Input and Output, the processes by which information enters or leaves your computer. I/O can also refer to input and output between components within the computer. I/O is not what computers do best. They are much better at calculating than at outputting the results of calculation. Unfortunately, I/O is what the Web is all about: network access, disk access, and screen rendering.

Mechanical devices are the worst I/O offenders. Anything with moving parts just can't keep up with the purely electronic speeds in the rest of the computer. This means the hard disk is the slowest part of your web server. How slow? Compare

50ns (10^{-9}) RAM to 10ms (10^{-3}) disk. That's on the order of 10^5 (or 100,000) times slower. You clearly want to minimize disk access if you can access RAM instead.

Network I/O has historically been much slower than bus speeds, but recent LAN I/O cards and networking equipment, such as gigabit Ethernet, are quite capable of saturating both the bus and the CPU of most computers. If this trend continues out to the WAN level and latency issues are resolved by clever use of caching, it will be possible to build a truly distributed computer, with processing power and storage scattered around the Internet. But for now, the Internet rivals your disk for last place in web component performance.

Information Is Relative

Information theory defines information as that which reduces uncertainty. When a computer is listening to a network connection, it is uncertain whether the next bit is going to be a one or a zero. When a bit of information arrives, that uncertainty is gone. Information tells us what we did not know. So whether or not bits are information depends on what we do know.

It follows that a server can reduce the number of bits transmitted simply by using what the client already knows. Caching mechanisms take advantage of this. When the client doesn't know whether its cached data is up to date, or fresh, it sends a request to the server describing the information it has. The server tells it whether that information is fresh. This is exactly how `If-modified-since` headers work in HTTP. It saves quite a bit of Internet bandwidth and improves performance.

Here are some rules of thumb for applying what your client already knows to web performance problems:

- First, send only the difference, or *delta*, when updating information. An example is the repeated use of a stock price query applet rather than a CGI. The CGI sends the entire HTML page and graphics with every result, wasting bandwidth and slowing performance. A stock query applet can receive and display just the stock price, a much smaller amount of information, avoiding retransmission of the graphics and HTML.

- Second, optimize using what you know about the pattern of requests that you'll get. You don't have to be ready for anything if only a limited number of things are likely to happen. For example, file access in HTTP servers is not random: the HTML text file contains links to other files, such as those containing the page's embedded graphics, which will definitely be requested immediately after the HTML file. To optimize for this, you could place the HTML file first on disk, followed immediately by the other files, reducing disk seek time. This might not help at all for heavily loaded servers with continuous requests for different pages, but you get the idea. As another example, if you knew the users were all going to ask for a certain page at a certain time, you could opti-mize for that, moving it from disk to filesystem cache or server cache in advance. Log files are a good source of information on usage patterns. In some ways, performance tuning for the Web is easier than general computer performance tuning, because you can learn a lot about the usage patterns of the HTTP server and client.

- Third, optimize using what you know about the data set. Bits are bits, but you can tune for a particular kind of data. For example, some data sets have a characteristic distribution of file sizes. A web site providing downloads of large files will get better filesystem performance by increasing the amount of data a single inode can refer to, and it will get better network performance by ensur-ing that the maximum transmission unit (MTU) is as large as the smallest MTU along the route.

- Fourth, optimize using what you know about the user. What sort of compres-sion does his or her browser understand? Does the browser understand the performance improvements of HTTP 1.1 or Java 1.2? What sort of latency and throughput does the user expect? Each of these things can help you to meet the user's expectations.

An interesting aside about compression and information: any compression scheme requires agreement between sender and receiver on an algorithm describing how to reconstitute the data. The agreement could be a simple mechanism for reduc-ing redundancy, but the agreement could also contain a data set itself. Code Excited Linear Prediction (CELP) speech compression works this way. Human beings produce a limited number of kinds of sounds. You can get good perfor-mance over low-bandwidth links by keeping a "codebook" of these basic sounds and simply transmitting an index pointing to the sound you want, along with some modification parameters to make it flow with the surrounding speech and sound more natural. There have been some proprietary attempts to make the Web work better through a similar scheme to send all users of a service a CD with images and sounds on it, so that surfing the proprietary site would be simply the retrieval of text along with pointers to images and sounds on the CD. It never caught on, because a single CD is so tiny and inflexible compared with the information on the Web.

Hardware Is Cheap, Software Is Expensive

I should qualify that: Custom software and support are expensive and hardware's not that cheap, but if you have to fix a performance problem quickly, throwing more or better hardware at it is often the most economical solution. Software, on the other hand, is expensive to write or debug, and you cannot amortize the cost of custom software over a large number of users. Software can take a long time to write, and good programmers charge a lot of money. And unlike hardware performance, programmer performance is not improving exponentially, because programmers are only human.

The Goal of Tuning Is Simultaneous Failure

A web system is considered to be in tune when there are no bottlenecks. This definition says nothing about the total throughput of the system—a very low throughput system can technically be in tune. The goal of tuning is to waste no capacity at all, in other words, for every component to reach its limits at the same time. This is not a new idea: Henry Ford supposedly commissioned someone to study cars in junkyards in order to find out which Ford parts wore out last. Then he reduced the quality of those parts in order to save money. It didn't make sense to have some parts of a system that lasted much longer than other parts.

I'm not recommending that you downgrade pieces of your system until all are equally bad. Ford was trying to cut costs on an assembly line; you are probably not churning out web systems for profit, but instead have a single system to improve. You'll want to do the opposite: find the weakest link and improve that.

Since web systems are usually dynamic, with new pieces constantly being introduced, finding the weakest link at any moment in time may be nearly impossible. Rather than spending all your time chasing the elusive bottleneck just to be in tune, it makes sense to specify a certain performance as good enough for the moment, even if a few components are underused. It is a problem, though, when most of the components are underused.

Better Is Relative

You should be monitoring performance and keeping performance records, which provide a baseline for evaluating changes as well as clues as to where bottlenecks might be lurking. Your log files contain valuable information that should be kept for years or forever, if you have the storage. The ultimate measure of performance is user satisfaction, so keep organized records of performance complaints. Think of complaints as free performance monitoring data.

Bits Are Cost

In the U.S. Postal Service, the size of the package doesn't affect its transit time much. On the Web, the smaller the package, the more quickly it arrives. No matter how tuned your system, excessively large content can crush your performance. Keep your content light and small. Don't throw everything into every page just because you can. It goes the other way, too. Don't accept arbitrarily large input from users; cut them off at some reasonable point.

Internet Performance Degrades Nonlinearly

Internet services tend to degrade ungracefully and quickly past a certain point, like hitting a wall, rather than just gradually getting slower with increasing load. This is mostly due to the fact that the Internet is a shared medium like a road and subject to similar traffic jams.

Tuning at the Highest Level Gives the Biggest Gains

You hardly ever get a performance tuning home run by tweaking some parameters. You get them by wiping out whole sections of your architecture or eliminating processing steps. To get the biggest gains, analyze your architecture at the highest level first. There is also less risk of wasting your work this way; if you tune some fine level of detail, you may waste your effort when you later realize that you can eliminate that entire step of processing.

It's Not What You Know, It's Whom You Know

In any case, *whom* you know is still more important than *what* you know. The details of web services and performance are changing so fast that it is impossible for any one person to keep up with it all. Your own trade secrets about how to improve your web site's performance are not going to help you nearly as much as a large set of friends in a similar situation who will share their experiences with you. To get their trust, you have to help them out. You can meet a lot of web people on *comp.infosystems.www.servers.** and *comp.infosystems.www.misc.*

As George Bernard Shaw once said, "If you have an apple and I have an apple and we exchange apples, then you and I will each have one apple. But if you have an idea and I have an idea and we exchange these ideas, then each of us will have two ideas."

Patterns of Performance Improvement

Performance improvements can be grouped into patterns which are generalizations of the way things tend to work rather than concrete advice. Here are some patterns which unify performance improvement techniques, each with three examples.

Amortization

Performance improvements often involve amortizing overhead among many transactions for an economy of scale:

- HTTP 1.1 allows a single TCP connection to be reused for multiple file downloads. This feature is known as *persistent connections*. The overhead of setting up and tearing down a TCP connection is spread among several files rather than reincurred for each file.

- Java *.jar* files work in a similar way, grouping Java *.class* files together into a package that can be downloaded in one TCP connection rather than setting up a separate TCP connection for each class. The downside here is that the *.jar* file may include classes you never use.

- A composite imagemap is another example. Rather than sending multiple small images to the user, send a single large image. If the original individual images were clickable, you can maintain the same functionality by making the large image a clickable imagemap.

Caching

Caching is the most important and widespread performance technique. The idea is simple: keep frequently accessed data close at hand. Caching helps only if some data is in fact more frequently accessed than other data, but this is usually the case:

- You can often trade storage space for more performance by running the most popular inputs to your CGI programs offline and caching all the results. Users can then rapidly access static HTML rather than forcing the generation of dynamic HTML.

- More memory will reduce the need for your servers to go to disk for content, increasing access time. Unix will cache frequently accessed files in physical memory rather than go to disk for them, if there is enough memory.

- Web proxy servers reduce the load on an organization's Internet access point as well as providing better access time for popular web pages by caching those popular pages.

Profiling

Profiling is looking at real-world usage patterns, either to find bottlenecks or to optimize for those usage patterns:

- Code profilers find the code that is most frequently accessed so that it can be most optimized, perhaps by rewriting it in assembly language. The HotSpot Java VM dynamically calculates which code is most heavily used and compiles it on the fly to native code.

- You can profile where your users are coming from and use that information to put your web site closer to them. For example, if most of your users happen to be coming from Japan, you'll probably give them better performance by putting your web server in Japan.

- It is possible to profile the download times of your customers and make assumptions about what sort of access throughput they have. Adjust your content to something reasonable for their access type.

Parallel Processing

Many problems in web serving benefit from letting more than one entity work on the problem at the same time:

- Netscape and some other browsers will open several simultaneous connections to the server and make multiple requests in parallel, hoping that the server can then figure out the most efficient order to serve the requests rather than letting the client make the requests in a random order.

- Java programs benefit from multithreading, which allows some threads to continue execution while others are blocked. For example, the user of a Java application may need to fill in a login screen. This is an opportunity to download additional class files in the background in a different thread.

- Symmetric multiprocessing (SMP) hardware is capable of mapping multiple threads to multiple CPUs and executing code in parallel.

Simplicity

Many gains come just from keeping things simple and minimal:

- Internal modems have no cable between the modem and the system bus, and are therefore not only faster but also cheaper. It is also impossible to buy the wrong cable for them simply because there isn't any cable.

- Making HTML content small and simple with no frames or tables and few images can have a dramatic improvement on download time. Yahoo!'s content is like this.

- Using only static content and no CGIs at all greatly improves service time at the expense of flexibility.

Key Recommendations

- RTFM.
- Be prepared to spend for performance.
- Minimize I/O.
- Send only deltas (where possible).
- Cache what you can.

- Match your components' latency and throughput to each other.
- Keep records.
- Keep content small.
- You're much better off sharing tips than hiding them.

II

Tuning in Depth

6

Client Software

Brief History of the Web Browser

The idea of a hypertext browser is not new. Many word processing packages such as FrameMaker and formats such as PDF generate or incorporate hyperlinks. The idea of basing a hypertext browser on common standards such as ASCII text and Unix sockets was an advance first made by the Gopher client and server from the University of Minnesota. Gopher proved to be extremely light and quick, but the links were presented in a menu separate from the text, and Gopher did not have the ability to automatically load images. The first drawback was solved by the invention of HTML, and the second was solved in the first graphical HTML browser, Mosaic, produced in 1993 at the University of Illinois National Center for Supercomputing Applications (NCSA).

Many of the original students who developed Mosaic were among the founders of Netscape the following year. An effort by the University of Illinois to commercialize Mosaic led to the founding of Spyglass, which licensed its code to Microsoft for the creation of Internet Explorer. Netscape and IE have been at the forefront of browser advances in the last few years, but the core function of the browser, to retrieve and display hypertext and images, has remained the same.

How Browsers Work

The basic function of a browser is extremely simple. Any programmer with a good knowledge of Perl or Java can write a minimal but functional text-only browser in one day. The browser makes a TCP socket connection to a web server, usually on port 80, and requests a document using HTTP syntax. The browser receives an HTML document over the connection and then parses and displays it, indicating in some way which parts of the text are links to other documents or images. When the user selects one of the links, perhaps by clicking on it, the process starts all over again, with the browser requesting another document. In spite of the advances in HTML, HTTP, and Java, the basic functionality is exactly the same for all web browsers.

Let's take a look at the functionality of recent browsers in more detail, noting performance issues. To get the ball rolling, the browser first has to parse the URL you've typed into the "Location:" box or recognize which link you've clicked on. This should be extremely quick. The browser then checks its cache to see if it has that page. The page is looked up through a quick hashed database mapping URLs to cache locations. Dynamic content should not be cached, but if the provider of the content did not specify an immediate timeout in the HTTP header or if the browser is not clever enough to recognize CGI output from URLs, then dynamic content will be cached as well.

If the page requested is in the cache and the user has requested via a preference setting that the browser check for updated versions of pages, then a good browser will try to save time by making only an HTTP HEAD request to the server with an `If-modified-since` line to check whether the cached page is out of date. If the reply is that the cached page is still current, the browser simply displays the page from the cache. If the desired web page is not in the cache, or is in the cache but is stale, then the browser needs to request the current version of the page from the server.

In order to connect to a web server, the client machine needs to know the server's 4-byte IP address (e.g., 198.137.240.92). But the browser usually has only the fully-qualified server name (e.g., *www.whitehouse.gov*) from the user's manual request or the HTML of a previous page. The client machine must figure out which IP address is associated with the DNS name of a web server. It does this via the distributed database of domain name to IP mappings, that is, DNS. The client machine makes a request of its local name server, which either knows the answer or queries a higher-level server for the answer. If an IP answer is found, the client can then make a request directly to the server by using that IP address. If no answer is found, the request cannot proceed and the browser will display "No DNS Entry" or some other cryptic message to the user.

The performance problem here is that DNS lookups are almost always implemented with blocking system calls, meaning that nothing else can happen in the browser until the DNS lookup succeeds or fails. If the local DNS server is overloaded, the browser will simply hang until some rather long operating system timeout expires, perhaps one minute. DNS services, like most other Internet services, tend to get exponentially slower under heavy load. The only guaranteed way to avoid the performance penalty associated with DNS is not to use it. You can simply embed IP addresses in HTML or type them in by hand. This is hard on the user, because DNS names are much easier to remember than IP addresses, and because it is confusing to see an IP address appear in the "Location:" box of the browser. Under good conditions, DNS lookup takes only a few tenths of a second. Under bad conditions, it can be intolerably slow.

The client-side implementation of DNS is known as the *resolver*. The resolver is usually just a set of library calls rather than a distinct program. Under Unix, for example, the resolver is part of the *libc* library that most C programmers use for their applications. Fortunately, most DNS resolvers cache recently requested DNS names, so subsequent lookups are much faster than the first.

Once a browser client has the IP address of the desired server, it generates the HTTP request describing its abilities and what it wants, and hands it off to the OS for transmission. In generating the HTTP request, the browser will check for previously received cookies associated with the desired page or DNS domain and send those along with the request so that the web server can easily identify repeat customers. The whole request is small, a hundred bytes or so. The OS attempts to establish a TCP connection to the server and to give the server the browser's request. The browser then simply waits for the answer or a timeout. If no reply is forthcoming, the browser does not know whether it is because the server is overloaded and cannot accept a new connection, because the server crashed, or because the server's network connection is down.

When the response from the server arrives, the OS gives it to the browser, which then checks the header for a valid HTTP response code and a new cookie. If the response is OK, the browser stores any cookie, parses the HTML content or image, and starts to calculate how to display it. Parsing is very CPU-intensive. You can feel how fast your CPU is when you load a big HTML page, say 100K or more, from cache or over a very fast network connection. Remember that parsing text is a step distinct from laying out and displaying it. Netscape, in particular, will delay the display of parsed text until the size of every embedded image is known. If the image sizes are not included in the HTML <IMG> tag, this means that the browser must request every image and receive a response before the user sees anything on the page.

The order in which an HTML page is laid out is up to the particular browser. In Netscape 4.x, web pages are rendered in the following order, once all the image sizes are known:

1. The text of the page is laid out. Links in the text are checked against a history database, and if found, are shown in a different color to indicate that the user has already clicked on them.

2. The boundary boxes for images are displayed with any ALT text for the image and with the image icon.

3. Images are displayed, perhaps with *progressive rendering*, where the image gains in definition as data arrives rather than simply filling in from top to bottom. It is common for Netscape to load and show an image before showing any text.

4. Subsidiary frames are loaded starting over at step 1.

A browser may open multiple connections to the server. You can clearly see this by running *NetStat -c* to poll network activity on a Linux client, and then using Netscape to request a page with multiple embedded images. You'll probably see about five connections open, indicated by the word ESTABLISHED in the state column. The number of simultaneous connections is a tunable option in some browsers. Clients with fast Internet access will benefit from simultaneous connections. Clients with slow Internet access may see no improvement from simultaneous connections because they are already using all of their bandwidth. It is more efficient to use HTTP 1.1's persistent connections and to pipeline requests than to use multiple TCP connections. *Pipelining* means starting another request before the previous request has returned a complete response. HTTP 1.1 will be used automatically if your browser and the contacted server support it.

You can see the progress of the various downloads in the Netscape footer messages: every flash of a URL is an HTTP connection for an HTML page, an image, or a Java *.class* or *.jar* file. It is usually too confusing to try to figure out which connection being shown in the footer corresponds to an image on the page. The Hot-Java™ browser has a much clearer display of the progress of downloading as several parallel lines getting longer as files load.

If the user hits the browser's Stop button, a TCP reset, also called an abortive release, is sent to the server immediately. See *TCP/IP Illustrated, Volume 1*, by Richard Stevens (Addison Wesley), for the TCP details of a reset. If the server is calculating CGI output when the Stop button is hit, the CGI process will not hear about it until it completes and tries to send the output back to the web server for forwarding to the client. Under Unix, the CGI process will get a SIGPIPE signal because the socket to the web server is no longer valid.

Popular Browsers

There are a lot of browsers, but only a few are widely used. See *http://www.boutell.com/openfaq/browsers/* for a comprehensive list. The following five browsers are distinguished either by their market share or their features.

Netscape

As of this writing, Netscape Navigator, usually called "Netscape," still has the largest browser market share, but it has been losing ground to Internet Explorer. Netscape 4 was a major overhaul of Netscape 3. Netscape 1.0 and later versions all have persistent connection ability, but use it via a `Connection: Keep-Alive` header rather than as part of a full implementation of HTTP 1.1. See Chapter 10, *Network Protocols*, for more about HTTP. Netscape exists as native code for Linux, Solaris, Macintosh, Windows, and many other platforms.

Netscape has made the source code for their browser available on the Web at *http://www.mozilla.org/*. This opens the door to performance improvements by the Internet community as a whole. I'm personally hoping that someone will write a filter which eliminates blinking GIF advertisements.

Internet Explorer

Internet Explorer is bundled with every copy of Windows 3.1, 95, and NT. Because Windows has a monopoly on commercial PC operating systems, Internet Explorer is already installed on nearly every PC desktop. This fact, combined with the similarity of the two browsers, removes the incentive to even take the time to install any other browser. Whether Microsoft may continue to bundle IE with Windows is in the courts as of this writing because the bundling looks very much like an abuse of monopoly power.

That said, Internet Explorer does have a few performance features to recommend it. First, it outputs document requests with the HTTP 1.1 header, implying that it has full HTTP 1.1 support. Beyond keepalives, HTTP 1.1 has support for byte range downloading, the continuation of interrupted transfers, and other features that improve performance under certain conditions. IE also seems always to display the text of a page first, before any images, so that you can start to read immediately and decide whether you want to stop the download.

IE exists for Windows, the Mac, and Solaris, although the non-Windows versions have less functionality. There is also a look-alike version for Linux running *fvwm95*, an X Window manager that looks just like Windows 95, available as shareware from *http://jungfrau.ptf.hro.nl/explorer/*, but of course this version contains no code from Microsoft and runs only on Linux.

Appendix C of *Professional Web Site Optimization,* by Scott Ware et al. (Wrox Press) shows that Netscape 3.0 is about twice as fast at loading and displaying web pages than Internet Explorer 3.0. The difference is attributed to IE's need to support the COM threading model.

Mosaic

The original web browser developed by Marc Andreessen and others at the University of Illinois at Urbana-Champaign is NCSA Mosaic. The feature that continues to distinguish Mosaic is support for *gzip* decompression. On the server side, you can configure Apache to report to Mosaic that a file is *gzip* compressed by adding the following lines to Apache's *srm.conf:*

```
# AddEncoding allows you to have certain browsers (Mosaic/X 2.1+) uncompress
# information on the fly. Note: Not all browsers support this.
AddEncoding x-compress Z
AddEncoding x-gzip gz
```

This is useful for large text files, where *gzip* can decrease the size by half, but is not worth the trouble for very small files, because the download difference will not be noticeable and you will still have the overhead of starting *gunzip*.

Mosaic supports Unix, Windows, and Macintosh. It has the additional advantage that it is available at no cost along with the source code.

Lynx

Lynx is a text-only web browser available from *http://lynx.browser.org/*. It was originally developed at the University of Kansas. It is capable of displaying images via helper applications. Advantages of Lynx are that it's free along with the source code, you can run it over shell accounts as well as directly via PPP, it has a *-source* option that is convenient for scripting the retrieval of data, and it's very fast. We saw a use of the *-source* option in Chapter 3, *Web Performance Measurement.*

HotJava

HotJava is a web browser from Sun Microsystems written entirely in Java. The performance is lower than native-code browsers, but it has the advantage of pure Java portability. Sun also sells HTML-rendering JavaBeans™ that can be used in Java applications where browser functionality is needed.

Non-Browser Web Clients

Given the simplicity of programming basic web functionality, it is entirely practical to write your own HTTP clients for specific uses. Currently, the most popular non-browser web clients are robots that index the Web for search engines and link checkers that find broken links, but there are an infinite number of possible client programs and devices. In fact, connecting telephones, TVs, copiers, and other devices to the Web is the main business strategy of Spyglass (*http://www.spyglass.com/*), the Mosaic code licensee. See *Web Client Programming with Perl*, by Clinton Wong (O'Reilly & Associates).

The appletviewer program that ships with Sun's Java Development Kit™ loads applets much faster than Netscape or other browsers, probably because it has no cache to check for previously loaded classes. The appletviewer works well with Java *.jar* files.

Browser Speed

The web browser is probably not going to be your bottleneck simply because the average performance of a point-to-point TCP connection on the Internet is only about 50KByte per second,* while most browsers are able to parse and display data faster than that. My own seat-of-the-pants benchmark is that Netscape 4 running on a 75MHz Pentium laptop under Linux 2.0 can parse a large HTML file from memory cache or from a 10Mbps LAN connection at a rate of about 80KB per second. On the other hand, Netscape 4 running on a Mac PowerBook 5300cs seems to achieve only about 4KB per second reading from memory cache or a LAN.

One might think that browsers would store cached documents in a parsed format for quicker subsequent display, but an examination of the cache shows that this is not the case. This raises the interesting possibility of pre-parsing HTML on the server and storing it in parsed format. There is no standard format for parsed HTML, so the performance gain would be at the expense of portability and human readability. In any case, it is unusual for the Internet to return enough data in HTTP replies to overwhelm the parsing capability of the browser. What this means for capacity planning is that performance is not currently a factor in choosing web browsers, although this may change as Internet infrastructure is upgraded.

In the outbound direction, web browsers do not need to make sustained HTTP requests any faster than a human can digest the replies. Web browsers are generally capable of about 10 HTTP connections per second. Even a person ready to click away furiously could not click on 10 distinct links in one second, but it is possible for a multithreaded browser to reach this rate when parsing HTML pages with many embedded images or applets. Even a burst of 10 requests in a second from one browser is no particular problem for most servers. A typical average rate for requests from a browser is less than 1 HTTP operation per second.

---

* See *http://www.keynote.com/measures/top10.html* and *http://www.orckit.com/* for Internet performance statistics.

Browser Tuning Tips

General Tips

Upgrade

Try to get the latest non-beta version of your browser. Newer versions usually include new features like HTTP 1.1 persistent connections to improve performance. Still, there are some things to be said for the older versions. First of all, beta versions of new browsers often have bugs and performance problems associated with them, while the older non-beta versions are more stable. Netscape 4.0 beta ran Java especially slowly, but this was fixed in the version that was officially released. You may want to wait until a browser is officially released before trying it. Second, browsers have been getting fatter very fast. Netscape 3 for Linux takes about 5M of memory when you first start it up; Netscape 4 takes about 8M. As you use them, they both grow through the loading of features and through memory leaks. If you're memory-constrained, you will get better performance with the older version, especially if it makes the difference between swapping to disk or not.

Do less

You can change your browser's settings so that the browser does only the minimum necessary to get and show you a page. First, turn off automatic loading of images, since they take up most of your bandwidth, and each requires a separate connection unless both your browser and server understand persistent connections. You'll see placeholders for unloaded images that you can click on individually for loading, or you can load them all at once through a menu option. Similarly, you should probably turn Java off if you are bandwidth- or memory-constrained.

To get the browser to start a little more quickly, set it to load only a blank page on startup. Load as few plug-ins as possible, because they add to your startup time. On a Macintosh, load fewer fonts.

To prevent any network access when you have a page in the cache, set the verify option to "never". This risks your viewing out-of-date pages, but it is a significant performance boost if you do have the page in cache.

You can clear your history cache for another slight performance boost, but you will no longer see visited links in a different color. In Netscape 4.0, you clear the history cache like this: Edit → Preferences → Navigator → Clear History button. If you find this is a significant help, you can set your history of links visited to always expire immediately so that you never spend time recognizing and colorizing visited links. This does not affect your browser's cache.

Not accepting or sending cookies will give another slight gain in performance and a large gain in privacy, but this will break many web sites that depend on cookies for their functionality, such as sites that personalize content for you.

Save frequently accessed pages, such as search engine home pages, to a local file on your hard disk with File → Save As, and bookmark where you saved them. The next time you go to one of these saved pages, you won't have any network traffic, and it won't expire from the browser's cache. You may have to modify the HTML in the saved file so that all links are absolute, that is, so they include the server name, because relative links are now relative to the filesystem on your own machine rather than to the document root of the original web server. The easiest way to do this is to add a <BASE> tag to the HTML head, like this:

```
<html>
<head>
<base href="http://www.search.engine.com/">
</head>
...
```

This is also an opportunity to eliminate the lines of HTML that put in the blinking GIF ads so you won't have to see the ads right away. Once you get a page back from the original server—for example by submitting a search request—the HTML you'll get back will be new, and you'll have ads again.

You can cache whole sites in a similar way by choosing a new cache location with Netscape's preferences, then simply browsing the site you want to cache. The new cache will contain the site, and you can keep it there permanently by setting the cache location back to the cache used for most of your browsing. In Navigator 4, you change the cache location with Edit → Preferences → Advanced → Cache → Cache Folder.

Finally, make good use of the Stop button. Stop page downloading if you know you don't want the rest, and stop animated GIFs if you are CPU constrained. Infinitely looping animated GIFs can easily waste 10% of your CPU capacity and will continue to do so until you stop them. This is an issue if you are running the browser and some other CPU-intensive applications at the same time. Some Java applets may also consume CPU time even when you're not using them, or even after you've left that web page. This happens because the applet programmer did not override the applet's `stop()` method, for whatever reason. Applets cannot be stopped with the Stop button, but you can turn off Java to stop them. In Netscape 4, to turn off Java, select Edit → Preferences → Advanced and deselect "Enable Java".

Use shortcuts

A number of shortcuts can improve the user's performance in handling the browser, rather than improving the browser's performance itself.

First of all, you don't always have to type in complete URLs. Most browsers will fill in the rest of a URL with the default "http://www." and ".com" if you just type in the domain name. So, for example, you can type "sun" instead of "http://www.sun.com/". This may actually slow performance or not work at all in some cases. For example, if you are in an organization named Zort, Inc., that has set up its DNS to assume that incomplete URLs should end in your organization's domain name, "zort.com," then entering simply "sun" in your browser will cause a lookup of *http://sun.zort.com*. If there is no local machine named "sun," your DNS may or may not redirect the browser to *http://www.sun.com/*, depending on how DNS was configured.

If the web server machine name is something other than "www," you can still leave off the "http://" part. So if the server is named "web" at zort.com, you can type in "web.zort.com" instead of "http://web.zort.com".

Second, use keyboard shortcuts when they are available, like the Escape key for Stop. You'll find that you can type the keys for Stop, Back, Forward, Open, etc., much faster than you can move the mouse to select them. You have to know what they are, but once you get used to them, you'll never go back. This is also why Unix command-line users tend to disdain GUIs. It's much faster to type a command than to move the mouse. If you are presented with a GUI menu or set of buttons, note that Tab or Alt-Tab will sometimes change which one is currently selected, but it may be quicker here to use the mouse than to tab around in a GUI.

Third, use the Go menu to select a page from your history of recently viewed pages rather than hitting the back button repeatedly. It's much faster. IE has a nice feature that automatically tries to complete the URL you are typing with recently viewed URLs.

Increase caches

Pump up the memory and disk cache in your browser if you can afford it. Clearing your browser's memory and disk cache may help a little if you are hitting new sites, since the browser will have less to check, but it will hurt a lot if you are hitting sites you've seen before, since all the data must be downloaded again. As a rule, you want to set the cache to be as big as your machine can handle.

Reboot

It is unfortunate but true that Netscape and Internet Explorer both tend to take memory from you and not give it back. This can be due to inadvertent memory leaks or to the accumulation of features loaded into memory as you use the browser. If you notice that your browser runs much faster after you quit and restart it or after you reboot your machine, that's an indication that your browser is hogging memory. There's not much you can do in that case but restart the browser regularly or not load features like Java or the mail reading tool.

Multitask

If a page is taking a long time to load, you can open a new browser window and continue browsing in the new window while the old one churns away. In Netscape, use File → New → Navigator Window, or even better, Alt-N.

Stop it

The Stop button can actually speed things up. Hitting Stop will cause Netscape to stop loading and to display what it's got so far, which may be all you need. If you hit Stop and it turns out nothing was loaded, hit Reload and you may find that the server responds much more quickly the second time around. It is possible that the packet containing your request was lost somewhere on the Internet.

A major flaw with browsers right now is the fact that you cannot stop Java from starting once you've begun to download an applet, and you can't do anything else until Java is fully initialized.

Use Activator

There is an ActiveX control and Netscape plug-in called Activator that will download a current and correct Virtual Machine (VM) from JavaSoft™. Simply refer to the Activator VM in your HTML, and if the new VM is not already installed, the browser will ask you if you'd like to download and automatically install it. Not only does this insure that your clients will consistently have the latest and fully functional VM, but it also solves some performance problems with other implementations of the VM. Netscape has been known to download and instantiate Java classes several times more slowly than IE, but this problem goes away with Activator. See *http://www.javasoft.com/products/activator/*.

Internet Explorer Tips

Don't redraw while scrolling

If your machine doesn't have enough spare CPU cycles to keep the images smooth when you scroll in IE, you can turn off smooth scrolling with View►Internet Options → Advanced → Disable Smooth Scrolling. You will be spared the ugly image of your machine struggling to keep up, and scrolling will feel snappy.

Browse in a new process

If hitting the back Button on IE causes a long delay and always gets the page via modem regardless of whether or not you told it to get pages from cache, try setting View → Internet Options → Advanced → Browse In A New Process. This will start new copies of IE which do not share system resources. The idea behind the option is to isolate IE from your system in case IE crashes, but it may have the side effect of making the Back button work quickly and correctly.

Netscape Tips

Prestart Java

Rather than get stuck watching the Java VM start up the first time you hit an applet, you can ask Communicator to initialize Java with the browser itself by using the command line *netscape.exe -start_java*. This option is not available for the Unix versions of Netscape.

Use fewer colors

If you don't really care about accurate colors in Netscape on a PC, you can use approximate colors for a significant speed gain. On Communicator 3.0, select General Preferences → Images → Substitute Colors. On Communicator 4.0, select Edit → Preferences → Appearance → Colors and check "Always Use My Colors". This doesn't work on the Macintosh or on Unix.

Make smaller buttons

You can save a little bit of valuable screen real estate by showing the buttons as text only. In Netscape, Edit → Preferences → Appearance → Show Toolbars As → Text Only. Or, you can eliminate them altogether if you know all the keystroke shortcuts.

Figuring Out Why the Browser Is Hanging

Is your modem still on and connected to your computer?

If you have an external modem, diagnosing problems is easier. At the least, a power light should be lit to indicate that the modem is on. If the modem is definitely on, try manually sending something to the modem to prove it is connected to your computer. On Linux you can do this:

```
% echo AT > /dev/modem
```

From a DOS shell on a Windows machine you can do this:

```
> echo AT > COM1
```

If your modem is connected, you will see the send and read lights flash. If the lights do not flash, either the modem is not connected, or you have configured it for the wrong COM port, PCMCIA slot, or other attachment point.

Are you still online, transmitting and receiving?

Your modem should also have a light labelled CD (Carrier Detect) to indicate if there is a carrier signal, that is, whether you are online. If it is not lit, it may be that the remote end hung up on you, or you lost your connection through too much noise on the line.

If you have carrier detect and can manually get your modem to respond but your browser cannot, then the browser is not communicating correctly with your operating system, implying a TCP/IP stack problem or a PPP problem.

Open another window and make another request. If you have an external modem, look at the modem lights. The read and send lights should be flashing. The send light will tell you that your modem is trying to send data out to the Internet. The read light will tell you if your modem is getting anything back from the network. If you cannot see these lights flashing, there is no data flowing through the modem.

Can you do anything at all?

Browsers have been known to hang. On the other hand, your browser may just be thinking some deep thoughts at the moment. Give it a minute, especially if you just requested a page. The system call to resolve DNS names often hangs the browser for a minute if the DNS server is slow. If you give it a minute and it's still stuck, kill the browser and try again.

Can you still resolve names?

Maybe your DNS server is down. Try a known IP address in the browser. In case you don't keep the IP addresses of web servers around, here are a few: 198.137.240.91 (*www.whitehouse.gov*); 192.9.9.100 (*www.sun.com*); and 204.71.200.66 (*www.yahoo.com*). Make a request with a URL like this: *http://198.137.240.91/*. If that works but *http://www.whitehouse.gov/* does not, your problem is DNS resolution.

If you're on a Unix system, try *nslookup* or *dig* on any domain name. You'll know immediately whether you can still resolve names.

Is the remote web server still up and available?

Try to *ping* the server you're interested in. If *ping* replies, then the web server is definitely alive. Telnet to it on port 80. From a Unix command line, to check on the White House web server, you would type this: `telnet www.white-house.gov` 80. If telnet connects, the web server is up and accepting connections on port 80. If you can't *ping* or telnet, try a *traceroute* to the server to see how far you can get. The traceroute program comes packaged with most versions of Unix, but there is also a commercial NT version called Net.Medic from VitalSigns software. If *traceroute* stops within your ISP, it could be that your Internet provider is down. Sometimes your whole region may be down because of a NAP or Internet backbone issue.

Did you already get most of the page?

Maybe everything is working fine, but you are stuck waiting for that last GIF. Hit the Stop button and see if the page renders.

Key Recommendations

- Set the browser to check cache only once per session, or never.

- Increase the memory and disk cache as much as feasible.

- Use the latest browser version for HTTP 1.1 and other advantages.

- Set the browser to load a blank page on startup.

7

Client Operating System

Volumes have been written about optimizing desktop systems, so here I'm going to touch on only a few points that directly relate to your web browsing performance.

Macintosh

68K Emulation

Apple's change of CPU from Motorola's 68000 series to the PowerPC increased Mac performance in one way, but hurt it in another. Performance is helped because the PowerPC is a much faster, more modern CPU. Performance is hurt because most of the software available for the Mac was written for the 68K chip and runs on the PowerPC chip only in emulation. Not only the applications but also parts of the Mac OS themselves were left in 68K binary format. There are a few things you can do to minimize the impact of emulation on your performance:

- First, always try to get a native PowerMac version of your browser in preference to a 68K version.

- Second, try replacing the emulator that ships with the OS with Speed Doubler from Connectix, *http://www.connectix.com/.* Connectix also makes a well regarded RAM Doubler product.

- Finally, upgrade to Mac OS8, which has more native PowerPC code and faster and more robust TCP/IP.

Networking

For the best networking performance, make sure you're using a recent native-binary Open Transport TCP/IP stack. See Open Transport Mac tips at *http://ogrady.com/FAQ/powerbook/9.html#29.*

Macintosh PPP programs can usually be configured to automatically dial the modem and start PPP when an application such as a browser needs network connectivity. This makes start-up a little easier on the user.

Use the Mac TCP Monitor to check whether TCP packets are timing out and retransmitting, that is, if they're being reported as lost when they're really just pokey. Retransmits can happen if you are on a slow connection or if there are errors in the data received. If the TCP Monitor shows retransmits, you may want to set the TCP retransmit timeout higher and see if that helps. If the retransmits were happening because of errors instead of a high latency connection, increasing the timeout will actually hurt performance.

Another network parameter you can modify is the Maximum Transmission Unit (MTU), which is the largest IP packet your machine will send. You want to limit this to the size of the largest MTU allowed along the route to any particular web server. If you hit a router with an MTU smaller than yours, then your IP packets may be fragmented from that router on, which will slow them down. Try changing MTU in PPP from 1500 to 576, which is the largest MTU size guaranteed not to fragment. Again, be careful to check performance before and after because this will definitely slow down performance if fragmentation was not your problem.

Memory and Disk

If you've used Netscape on a Mac after using it on Windows or Unix, you may have noticed that the Mac seems to be missing a memory cache in the Netscape configuration options. There is a memory cache for Netscape, but it isn't handled from the Netscape preferences. Rather, it is handled from the Control Panels as general disk cache, in the sense of caching disk data in memory rather than in the sense of explicitly caching web pages on disk. You want to have a disk cache large enough to improve performance by avoiding a significant number of disk accesses, but not so large that you starve applications of memory and hurt their performance. A rule of thumb is to have about 32K of cache for every 1M of RAM in the computer; so, for example, a 24M computer should have 768K of disk cache. To change the disk cache setting, select Control Panel → Memory → Disk Cache.

Macintosh applications, at least under System 7, cannot dynamically take memory as they need it, as they can under other operating systems; you have to specifically allocate more memory to an application if needed. To find out how much memory is allocated to Netscape and to change it, first make sure Netscape is not running, then select the Netscape icon and click on File → Get Info.... You'll see two values: the minimum size (what Netscape minimally needs to run), and the preferred size (the most Netscape is allowed to have). You can't do much about the minimum size, but if you give a larger preferred size, Netscape may run a little faster. 16MB is a reasonable value for Netscape 4.0.

Extensions

Extensions consume system resources, so removing all unnecessary extensions will improve overall performance as well as making boot time shorter. You can turn off all extensions by holding down the Shift key when the Macintosh is booting, but this will also turn off extensions that help performance, like the Symantec JIT.

When you use Netscape to browse a Java-enabled page, Java will start more quickly if you move the Symantec JIT, labelled "Java Accelerator for the Power PC," out of the *Netscape* folder and into the *Extensions* folder. This ensures that it will be loaded on startup. Make sure you move it and don't just copy it.

Microsoft Windows

The most effective way to improve the performance of PC hardware running Windows is to erase Windows and install a version of Unix for Intel, such as Linux, Solaris x86, FreeBSD, BSDI, or SCO Unix. Unfortunately, this is not an option for most people because of the complexity of installing an operating system and the need to run applications that run only on Windows. If you have to live with Windows, there are some things you can do to improve browser performance.

System Clutter

Back up your system files, then remove utilities you don't use from your *win.ini* and *system.ini* files. As with eliminating unused Mac extensions, the utilities that are left will run faster.

Specific Video Drivers

A device driver written specifically for your video card should give you better performance and stability than the default VGA driver. Here are some indications that you need a better video driver:

- Changing Control Panel → Display → Settings causes crashes if you are using particular screen sizes or number of colors but not otherwise.

- Setting Control Panel → System → Performance → Graphics → Maximum Hardware Acceleration causes the machine to crash.

- The browser bombs reliably at certain web sites. This could also be due to a Windows or JavaScript security problem.

You can usually download the correct driver from the web site of your video card manufacturer, or from the web site of the manufacturer of the chip on your video card.

Newest drivers

Newer versions of device drivers usually give better performance than older versions. Also check to see that you have the latest Windows service packs and TCP/IP stacks. BIOS should also be upgraded every other year or so for BIOS improvements, but your PC will probably be obsolete in two years anyway.

Memory and Disk

Windows disk caching schemes can help or hurt you. On one hand, the disk cache will make most writes to disk appear to be much faster, because the data is not being written out to disk synchronously with the write command, but queued up to be written some time later. This is known as "write behind" caching. This was the function of the `smartdrv.exe` line in your *AUTOEXEC.BAT* file under Windows 3.1. Disk cache can also be used to read ahead, anticipating that you will probably want more data from the disk after the current read completes. This is known as *read ahead* caching and can be turned on in Windows 95 like this: Control Panel → System → Performance → Advanced → File System → Read Ahead Optimization → Max.

On the other hand, some older hard disk drivers delay lower-priority interrupts while synchronizing disk with disk cache. This would be okay, except that low-priority COM port interrupts must be handled before the UART buffer overflows. If the disk has the COM port locked out and data is lost, the data must be retransmitted, slowing perceived network performance. The best solution is to get an updated driver for your disk, but you could also turn off the disk cache for a quick fix of network performance at the expense of disk performance. For Windows 3.1, the */X* switch to *smartdrv.exe* will turn off write behind caching. For Windows for Workgroups, the write behind cache is turned off by adding a line to the `[386enh]` section of *system.ini* that says `ForceLazyOff=C` where C is the letter of the disk drive. Turning off write behind cache should be only a temporary measure to help network performance until you can get updated disk drivers.

Being short on disk space will hurt Netscape performance, as it will have to search around for enough open space to write its cache and work files. Defragmenting your disk regularly with the *defrag* or *scandisk* utilities will help disk performance. You can defragment under Windows 95 like this: My Computer → Hard Drive → Properties → Tools → Defragment Now.

You can also help disk performance with 32-bit disk access, which you can turn on in Windows 3.1 like this: Control Panel → 386 Enhanced → VM → Change → 32-Bit Disk Access Enabled. Also, when you're about to shut off the machine, you can safely delete files that end in *.swp* or *.tmp* or that begin with a tilde (~), for additional disk space.

System Monitor

Windows 95 has a useful System Monitor tool that you can use to help pinpoint bottlenecks. To use it: Start → Run → enter **sysmon** → Add all of the options, but especially these:

- Memory Manager: Swapfile in Use
- Memory Manager: Free Memory
- Dial-Up Network Adapter: Buffer Overruns

You don't want to see any network buffer overruns. If there are overruns, you are not retrieving data from the UART as fast as it is filling up. This could be due to COM interrupts being starved for attention, an old UART (not likely on anything better than a 386), or the buffer being too small. You can change the buffer size under Windows 95 like this: Start → Settings → Control Panel → System → Device Manager → Modem → Connection → Port Settings → use slider to increase capacity of Receive Buffer. You do want to see a bit of headroom in Free Memory and not too much swapfile in use.

You can detect whether there is noise on your line by looking for Cyclic Redundancy Check (CRC) errors with *sysmon*: Start → Run → enter **sysmon** → Edit → Add → Dial-Up Networking Adapter → CRC errors. You shouldn't see any errors on a reasonably good line.

If your CPU is shown to be overloaded, the solutions are to upgrade to a faster CPU or reduce the number or kind of applications you are running.

Network Utilities

There are a few Unix network utilities available for Windows. Windows 95 has versions of *ping* and *traceroute*. To run *ping*: Start → Run → type command → at C:\ type **ping www.someserver.com**. *Traceroute* is called *tracert* under Windows; run it just like *ping*. There is also a third-party version of *traceroute* for Windows called QuickRoute, from Starfish's Internet Utilities 97 (*http://www.starfishsoftware.com/*).

MTU

If you are on a LAN, leave your MTU at the default of 1500 bytes. If you're dialing up and dealing with the Internet, try setting the MTU to 576 bytes. You may see some increased performance due to reduced fragmentation, as described previously in the Macintosh section. See *http://www.sysopt.com/maxmtu.html* for additional information on MTUs under Windows.

Active Desktop Problems

Active Desktop on Windows 95 consumes a lot of system resources and doesn't provide much essential benefit. You'll probably see better performance if you disable it: right-click on the desktop → Active Desktop → Customize → uncheck "View my active desktop as a web page".

Unix

Any Unix workstation can run a web client, but it is probably overkill to dedicate workstation hardware to web browsing when Macintosh or PC hardware will do just fine. Linux is the most popular version of Unix* for commodity PC hardware, partly because it is free along with all of the source code. Given identical PC hardware, you can get much better performance from Linux than from Windows, but until recently there has been little commercial software available for Linux because of its origins in the hobby world. Linux does have sufficient software to be a good web client because there is Netscape for Linux and a good Java Virtual Machine as well as all the usual Unix tools that make it relatively easy to figure out exactly what's going on in the system and the network: *top*, *vmstat*, *strace*, *traceroute*, *ping*, etc. Linux is a boon for anyone interested in operating systems. Here are a few of the things you can do to figure out exactly what is going on in your Linux web client:

- Start *top* and use M to sort all processes by memory usage. Leave it running. You'll probably see that Netscape is your single largest process and that it keeps growing as you use more of its features.

- Leave *netstat -c* running and you can see Netscape open connections as you retrieve web pages. Connections are open when *netstat* says they are in the ESTABLISHED state. The connections should all eventually be closed, except perhaps for connections such as the one to your POP mail server that polls for new mail.

- You can run Netscape with the *strace* command to see all system calls as they are made and understand a bit more of what Netscape is doing. Netscape's

---

* Though Linux is not Unix in a legal sense.

performance will probably be unbearably slow while you're tracing it, but it is instructive. You can also get the Netscape source code from *http:// www.mozilla.org/*, if you want to try to modify the code to improve the browser's performance yourself.

- You can use *ping* to see what the latency to any given web server is. Most web servers are configured to respond to *ping*. If you *ping* yourself and the latency is significantly over 1 ms, this indicates that you have a poor implementation of IP. Pinging a web server on the same LAN should have a latency under 10 ms. If not, you may have an overloaded LAN or a very poor implementation of IP. If you're pinging a web server across the Internet, anything under 50 ms is good, but latency up to 200 ms is quite normal. When latency gets close to 1 second, you have a poor connection to that server. The *traceroute* command can tell you at exactly which router things start to slow down. This is useful for detecting the quality of an ISP.

If a server is not responding at all, try using *nslookup* or *dig* on the web server name. It may just be that you can't resolve the name, not that the web server itself is actually down. DNS service, like most Internet services, does not degrade linearly but instead hits a wall at a certain load. You can use *nslookup* with DNS servers outside your own organization, find the correct IP for a site, and then browse by using the IP address in place of the web server's name in the URL. You can even point your machine to the other DNS server permanently if your ISP's DNS server is not satisfactory, but this is rather rude unless you have some explicit agreement with the owner of the other DNS server. Consider running a DNS server on your own machine. A private DNS server will cache your frequent queries and provide much better response time for those queries. See *DNS and BIND*, by Paul Albitz and Cricket Liu (O'Reilly & Associates), for instructions on setting up your own DNS server.

Use the latest Linux kernel for the latest TCP/IP fixes and speed improvements, but don't feel the need to upgrade more than once or twice a year. Compile in only the drivers you need, and no others. For example, you don't need floating point emulation on most modern chips, because a floating point unit is now standard. Compile in the TCP retransmit interval to be one second, if it isn't already. Change the */etc/rc.d/** files to run as few daemons as necessary.

Key Recommendations

- Use your OS's tools to tell you if you're running out of RAM or mistransmitting or misreceiving packets, and if the server is up and responding.
- Increase receive buffer size if possible.
- Use the latest and best implementation of drivers and TCP/IP.

8

In this chapter:
- *PC Hardware*
- *Key Recommendations*

Client Hardware

PC Hardware

The client hardware for the Web is mostly standard PC hardware these days, even though there still are a significant number of Macintoshes and network appliances like the Javastation and WebTV are gaining in popularity. In this chapter, I will concentrate on the components of PC client hardware, because the components differentiate the packages. There is still a great deal of standardization and inter-changeability of components at this level, resulting in healthy competition and many price versus performance options.

CPU

Do you need a fast CPU?

The most important thing to remember about web client CPUs is that they're not terribly important. PC hardware is almost always overendowed with CPU relative to bus. That is, an extremely fast CPU will probably spend most of its time wait-ing for the bus to catch up with it. Nonetheless, the CPU frequency and model is what sells the machine, so manufacturers are forced to supply the latest and fast-est CPU even if the previous generation of CPU would do just fine for most peo-ple. Web access speed is influenced much more by disk and network I/O than by CPU or even bus speed.

That said, there are some reasons to have a good CPU on your web browsing machine. For one thing, HTML and image rendering does take some CPU power. If you use a performance monitor and watch your CPU load while parsing a large HTML page, you'll see that parsing creates a significant CPU load. To prove the load is from parsing and not network access or something else, you can see that the CPU is again heavily loaded when you hit the back button to go back to a large page in memory cache, not touching the network. On the other hand, most web pages are small, so you often don't even notice the time it takes to parse them.

A better reason to buy a client machine with a fast CPU is to be able to run emulated programs as quickly as possible. Your machine has value in proportion to the number of useful programs it can run. In principle, any machine can emulate any other machine, but emulation is costly in terms of CPU cycles because there is rarely a one-to-one mapping of system calls between operating systems, or of machine code instructions between CPUs. If you have a Sparcstation and want to run Office 97, you have to do it in emulation (with SoftPC, for example), and this will slow you down. You can run Mac programs on your Linux machine with Executor. And note that the Power Macintosh runs all old 68K Mac programs in emulation. As CPUs increase in power, emulation becomes a more realistic alternative to being locked in to any one platform by your applications. The most important sort of emulation for a web client is emulation of the Java virtual machine. Java, by its nature, does not produce native code for any existing CPU, so it requires emulation. The need for this kind of emulation in the future is justification for a faster CPU, even if your native code applications are fast enough for you now.

Finally, your graphics performance will be better if you have a faster CPU. VRML, in particular, requires intense calculation in order to run smoothly.

Two clues that you need a faster CPU are silent delays during your work (when you cannot hear disk activity) and a consistently high reading on your CPU monitor program.

What to look for in a web client CPU

Here are some of the things you should look for when buying a faster CPU:

- More on-chip cache, also known as *level 1* (L1) cache, helps because L1 cache is directly in the CPU and so has excellent access time.

- A higher CPU clock is invariably better within the same generation of chip, but not necessarily between different kinds of chips. For example, a 400MHz Pentium II should be faster than a 300MHz Pentium II, but you can't say right off whether it will be faster than a 300MHz version of a chip from another generation or another manufacturer.

- Pipelining, where several instructions are simultaneously in various stages of execution, helps because instruction addresses are sequential most of the time. Sequential flow is faster than branching, which takes a cycle and breaks the pipeline, though some CPUs try to do branch prediction so as not to break the pipeline.

- Floating point units are not particularly important for web clients, but they are included on most CPUs these days anyway.

- Reduced Instruction Set Chip (RISC) CPUs such as the PowerPC or SPARC are generally faster than Complex Instruction Set (CISC) CPUs such as the Intel x86 family, because there are fewer instructions and they are all the same length in bits. This means the RISC CPU design can be streamlined in ways the CISC CPU cannot. The tradeoff is that you need more RISC instructions to do what one CISC instruction can do, so RISC executables are slightly bigger, and you need more memory and disk space.

A 64-bit CPU won't necessarily help if all of your software is written for a 32-bit CPU, as most software currently is. 64 bits can refer to a number of things: the size of CPU registers, the width of busses, and the address space size. For the C programmers out there, the address space size is the size of a pointer. CPUs with 64-bit registers can do arithmetic operations directly on 64-bit operands.

If you have a slowish Pentium, you might be able to increase your power with the OverDrive Processor, depending on the slots on your motherboard. A similar product for the Mac is the MAXpowr card from Newer Technologies.

Low-voltage CPUs, such as those found in laptops, run more slowly than the same CPU models running at a higher voltage. This is because each transistor on a CPU has a certain capacitance determined by the size of the wires on the CPU. At a higher voltage, the wires fill with electricity and flip the state of the transistor more quickly, just as a garden hose fills with water more quickly if you turn the spigot further. You sometimes hear the phrase "submicron technology," which refers to the size of the wires etched on the chip. At the same voltage, a smaller chip with thinner wires runs more quickly, partly because the sheer physical distances on the chip are smaller, but also because of capacitance. Laptops often use the exact same chip as desktop machines, but at a slower clock speed to save power. All of this also holds for other chips, like memory. The point to remember is that performance fights power conservation for a given generation of chip.

The bizarre thing about the semiconductor industry is that a given number of transistors in each new generation of chips are not only denser, but also use less power and are faster because of their increased density. They are also cheaper per transistor, because more transistors can be etched into a single silicon wafer.

RAM

More RAM is almost always better, so that you can support a bigger cache and bigger browser binaries, but more RAM won't necessarily help performance if the problem is elsewhere. Use your system's monitoring tools to tell you if you're using all your RAM. If you browse a very large web page on a machine without much RAM, you may crash the browser. This is particularly easy to do on Windows 3.1 machines with 16M RAM.

RAM in PC hardware usually sits on a fast system bus connected directly to the CPU, not on the EISA or PCI bus. The RAM is arranged in a bank that has as many chips as there are data lines on the bus. During a memory access, one bit is retrieved in parallel from each RAM chip in the bank.

The two principle flavors of RAM are dynamic (DRAM) and static (SRAM), with DRAM being the most common. DRAM must constantly be refreshed, because each bit storage location is, in effect, a tiny capacitor that is always leaking charge. SRAM does not need to be refreshed constantly by some external logic, because each bit storage location is an arrangement of five or so transistors called a *flip-flop*, which is self-refreshing. DRAM is denser and cheaper because of its simplicity. SRAM is more expensive, but much faster. DRAM multiplexes the row and column address onto the same set of wires, so addresses are asserted in two phases: first row, then column. An SRAM address is asserted in one phase, which is one reason it is faster.

DRAM comes in various permutations. Note that DRAM chips can contain quite a bit of logic in addition to the raw storage. The advertised speed of RAM is how fast the bits are provided to the chip's internal controller logic. It can take as long again to set up the address internally and prepare for a new cycle once the current access cycle is over, so the speed the chip claims is not exactly what your memory bus will see. Each bit is referred to by a row address and a column address. Fast Page RAM allows the controller to start setting up a new row address before the current cycle is over. Extended Data Output (EDO) RAM allows the controller to start setting up new row and column addresses before the current cycle is over. You need a specific kind of motherboard for each kind of RAM. See *http://www.dataram.com/bytes/edo.htm.*

Cache

Note that RAM typically runs at about 70 nanoseconds and can provide data at about 30Mhz (33 nanoseconds), while all new CPUs run faster than this. *Level 2* (L2) cache, (which is off the CPU, as opposed to L1 cache, which is on the CPU) is used to bridge the difference, but the utility of L2 cache decreases with multitasking machines like Unix servers, since different areas of memory will be accessed and there will be more cache misses. L2 cache is usually SRAM, which runs much faster (3 to 8 nanoseconds), but is bigger (less dense), hotter, and about ten times more expensive than DRAM.

Bus

PCs originally had memory on the same bus as everything else, but recent hardware all has a distinct memory bus for increasing memory access speed. Workstations and high-end PCs often have additional busses for I/O.

The memory bus, also known as the external CPU bus, would run best in exactly two cycles: assert address, then read/write data. Unfortunately most RAM is slower than the memory bus, so several *wait states*, or unused bus cycles, are inserted to give the RAM time to get at its data. Five wait states is quite common.

The ISA and EISA system bus clock frequency can often be increased with a CMOS, or BIOS, setting to some integer fraction ($\frac{1}{8}$ or $\frac{1}{10}$, for example) of the CPU clock speed. If you increase the system bus clock too much, data on the bus will be corrupted and the system will crash, but a moderate increase helps the performance of all cards connected to the bus, such as the disk controller, video controller, and network interface cards.

PCI is now the standard bus in new PCs. It has very good bandwidth and the added advantage of being a cross-platform standard, so that Apple, SGI, Sun, and DEC all use it, making the resulting card market much bigger. PCI runs at 33MHz and 66MHz and is available in 32-bit and 64-bit versions. PCI motherboards often come with legacy EISA slots that allow you to continue using your old cards. See Chapter 11, *Server Hardware*, for more information.

If you're surfing from a local network, the bus can bottleneck your receiving speed. If you're on the Internet, the Internet is your bottleneck.

Disk

Parameters

The two most important parameters for a client disk are the maximum seek time and the rotation speed. Maximum seek time is the time it takes for the disk arm to move from the edge to the center of the disk surface. This puts an upper bound on how long it will take you to get any piece of data. A maximum seek time of 12 milliseconds is pretty good. Do not confuse maximum seek time with access time, average seek time, or any of the other terms used by disk manufacturers. The other important parameter is rotational speed. Typical IDE PC disk rotational speed is 4500 rpm, but SCSI disks run at 7200 and 10000 rpm.

Maximum seek time is more important for random access patterns, and rotational speed is more important for sequential reads.

IDE

The Integrated Drive Electronics (IDE) interface is a hard disk standard that specifies the connection between the disk and the system bus. It is also known as the AT bus Attachment (ATA) standard. The interface is 16 bits wide and was originally intended for use with the ISA bus. There are now adapter cards that let you use IDE drives on a PCI bus. IDE drives are currently the cheapest and most common option. As of this writing, IDE drives have a transfer rate ranging from 1MB per second to 20MB per second and sizes ranging up to 9GB.

Though IDE has control circuits integrated with the drive itself, a separate IDE controller card is still required. One controller card can handle one or two drives, but if there are two drives, they do not operate independently: only one can be active at any time. If you would like to use multiple IDE drives in parallel for performance, you can do so by installing multiple controller cards, though you would probably be better advised to upgrade to SCSI disks.

There have been many extensions to IDE, such as EIDE and Ultra ATA. Ultra ATA is a standard developed by Quantum and Intel that specifies a faster rotation rate and faster transfers between disk and memory than EIDE.

SCSI

The Small Computer System Interface (SCSI) is a general standard for connecting peripherals to computers. Disks which use the SCSI standard are more expensive and higher performance than IDE disks. IDE disks are inexpensive and have good enough performance to make them a reasonable choice for most client hardware, but you will want SCSI disks for servers. See Chapter 11 for more information on SCSI.

Fragmentation

When the disk gets very full, new files must often be written into whatever open space the disk can find. A file will probably have to be split up, with pieces stored in several places on the disk, making access slow because multiple seeks must be done to read one file. Defragmentation utilities rearrange the files on your disk to be contiguous wherever possible, thus increasing access speed.

Video

Cards

Your display monitor is not as important as your video card for performance. Laptop displays are slower than the standard Cathode Ray Tube (CRT), but both are much faster than the video cards that drive them. You want a card with enough video RAM (VRAM), sometimes called Windows RAM (WRAM), to hold your entire display at its full color depth. Your video speed will increase with additional video RAM only up to this point. 2MB is usually enough, but you can get up to 8MB.

You can get a feel for your graphics performance by noting how quickly and smoothly you can scroll or drag around a window, or flip between different open windows.

Some high-performance video cards currently on the market (for example, the 64-bit Matrox MGA Millennium II and Intergraph's Intense3D) are Accelerated Graphics Port (AGP) cards, which run at the same speed as the processor.

Some motherboards have a video controller built in, which makes the computer a little cheaper, but also more difficult to upgrade.

MMX

Intel's MMX CPU instruction extensions do help graphics and video performance, but the software that can take advantage of them is not portable to other CPUs, with the exception of AMD CPUs. MMX's primary mechanism for speeding performance is an on-chip 16K cache for graphics. A good video card will give you a similar or even larger graphics performance boost.

Colors and resolution

Video card manufacturers like to brag that their cards can display millions of colors, but they're ignoring the fact that the human eye cannot distinguish that many, and that the calculations to display the colors are a drag on performance. Eight-bit color (256 colors) is satisfactory for most web browsing, but doesn't display photographs well. For a high-quality display, you need 16- or 24-bit color. If you run multiple applications simultaneously and have only 8-bit color, you may run out of video card buffer space for your color map. This may force one application or the other to use non-optimal colors, or to give up its color map when it is inactive, causing a flashing effect.

Resolution, the number of pixels on your screen, is more important than colors. Computer screen resolution is nowhere near the level of the human eye, so improvements are very noticeable. You may get better performance with lower resolution, but the speed is usually not worth the loss of image quality. At this point, 800×600 pixels is a minimum standard for web browsing. Manufacturers often quote screen size in diagonal inches rather than pixel density. This is misleading: size is nice, but a larger display of a low-resolution image does not make it any more pleasant to look at.

You can change the number of colors and sometimes the video resolution with your computer's configuration utilities. Sometimes this also requires you to move jumpers on the motherboard. Jumpers are little links between two pins which can be moved around to configure the machine.

Drivers

As with disk drive drivers, the latest video drivers are recommended. Some video cards from S3 and other vendors will gain graphics performance by interrupting your CPU and using spare CPU cycles while you're not busy. However, this can keep your CPU from servicing COM interrupts and can result in overrun buffers, lost packets, and ultimately, worse network performance. Good video drivers such as those from Number Nine will give you the option to turn off cycle-stealing.

3D and video clips

You rarely need a 2D or 3D video accelerator card for surfing the Web. The exceptions are when you're trying to play interactive games via the Web, browsing VRML, or using a video conferencing application. This may change if Internet bandwidth increases enough to make heavy visual content practical. AGP cards provide a faster and wider data path for graphics applications like these.

Video card benchmarks

Some popular video card benchmarks include Cbench, Wintach 1.2, VidSpeed 4.0, SpeedMark, and Xbench for Xfree86. Cbench (short for ChrisBench), is intended to measure the speed of DOS games. See *http://sneezy.dcn.ed.ac.uk/simnews/96AUG/ HARDWARE.HTM* for information about Cbench. Many other PC benchmarks have links from *http://www.cam.org/~agena/bench.html.*

I/O Port

The I/O capacity of PC hardware is small relative to that of dedicated server hardware, but sufficient for web browsing. Let's describe how PC I/O works. When a web browser makes a request, it simply asks the OS to forward the request to the remote server. The communications part of the OS—Winsock or your TCP/IP—stack, makes a connection to your serial (COM) port. The chip that controls your serial port is called a Universal Asynchronous Receiver and Transmitter (UART).

The UART

The UART is a buffer with some logic for talking between the (usually RS-232) modem connection on the one hand and the system bus on the other. To continue forwarding a web server query, the OS signals the UART to listen to the bus, then forwards data. The UART reads the data off the bus and signals the modem that it has data to send. The modem accepts that data and eventually is ready with a reply from the web server, which it begins to write into the UART, which generates an interrupt request (IRQ) asking for the OS to come and get the data.

So far, so good, but a problem arises: some older PCs have UARTs like the 8250 or 16450, which accept only 1 byte before demanding service through an IRQ. The CPU may be busy dealing with a higher-priority interrupt, while the modem continues to accept and pass on data at whatever rate you've set for the serial port. The result of an IRQ service delay is that UART buffer gets overwritten before the CPU has a chance to read it. The network routines in the OS find that the data does not match the associated checksum of the link layer (probably PPP or SLIP) and ask for the data to be retransmitted. This slows down your perceived network access speed. One-byte UARTs can handle up to ISDN speeds if your OS is doing very little else, as in the case of DOS, but a Windows machine with a 1-byte UART will probably find itself limited to 14.4kbps or lower.

One solution to serial port overruns is to slow down the the serial port setting—the rate at which the machine tells the modem it can accept data. This may give you better data integrity and fewer retransmits, but faster network access is our goal here. A better solution is to use a machine with a newer UART, like the 16550A. The 16550A can hold 8 to 16 bytes in its buffer, giving the OS more time to deal with the IRQ. A PC with a 16550A or better should be able to handle even 500kbps if the OS's network code is efficient. It is difficult to upgrade the UART on a motherboard because it is usually soldered in place, but you can use an internal modem for a similar performance boost, because internal modems come with a UART on the modem card itself.

Hardware compression can increase overruns

Remember that modems often use hardware data compression by default unless you tell them otherwise. The modems think they're helping you out, but an old UART may be overwhelmed, because it is reading 2 or 3 bytes of compressible data, like text, for every compressed byte transmitted by the modem. This may be confusing if you think you've set the serial port rate low enough for your UART. Again, the best solutions are to upgrade the UART or to use a newer PC with a better UART.

BIOS

The Basic Input Output System (BIOS) is the lowest level of software on your PC. It is also called the Complementary Metal Oxide Semiconductor (CMOS), after the kind of chip that stores the BIOS settings. The BIOS is the first thing that starts when you turn on the computer. It consists of three main parts: the Power On Self Test (POST), the interrupt handlers, and the system options. The POST is run immediately when you switch on the computer, and it checks that the CPU has access to memory, and that the video card, disk drive, and other components are installed correctly. It also installs some basic interrupt handlers, such as one for the keyboard. If the right key combination is pressed, the BIOS will run a program that allows you to change system options. This key combination is different for different BIOSes, such as Phoenix BIOS and AMI BIOS. On my laptop, I can get into Phoenix BIOS by pressing a special key. With AMI BIOS, you hold down the Del key while booting; with some other machines, you press Ctrl-Alt-Insert. See your computer's documentation and the web site of the BIOS maker.

There are some things you can do with your BIOS to get better performance. Set CPU speed to "fast" if that's an option. Enable the floating point unit (FPU) and all caches. Lower the number of wait states for memory or bus to speed memory access. You probably wonder why these settings are not enabled by default: the answer is stability. If you push your machine harder with all of these settings, it may crash more frequently because you've crossed the hardware's physical limits of performance. Since these settings are in the BIOS, you are assured that you can at least boot far enough to change them back if they are a problem.

If your BIOS doesn't have many options, you can install utilities that will give you more. See *http://www.sysopt.com/bios.html.*

Another useful BIOS option is resume mode, especially on laptops. Resume mode usually dumps the state of RAM to the hard disk and then restores it on power-up, saving a great deal of boot time. Also note that using BIOS to configure the hard disk to spin down after a period of inactivity will give you longer battery life but will insert annoying delays if the disk is off and you try to run or save something that requires the disk. On the Macintosh PowerBook, you can control many of these things through the control panels. For example, Control Panels → Powerbook → Better Performance will cause the disk to wait longer before spinning down.

Key Recommendations

- Don't worry about getting the latest CPU.
- Use PCI bus rather than ISA or EISA.
- Buy enough RAM that you rarely need to swap.
- Buy a SCSI disk rather than IDE.
- Use a PC or modem card with a 16550A UART or better.

9

Network Hardware

Lines and Terminators

In this chapter, I'll cover the various kinds of lines and terminators at each link in the chain between client and server, pointing out when higher-speed connections are worth the investment, and suggesting how you can get connections to work better.

A line is a connection between two points. Every connection segment on the Internet is composed of a physical line made of metal, optical fiber, or simply space, and a pair of terminators, one at each endpoint. The physical properties of the line put theoretical bounds on the performance of the line, but the terminators determine the low-level line protocol and, ultimately, how close you can get to that theoretical maximum performance. The copper telephone line most people use to connect to their Internet Service Provider (ISP) is bounded by two modems, although there is a telco switch in the middle. At the ISP, there are probably two Ethernet cards connecting a modem bank and a router. The router feeds a T1 bounded by two CSU/DSUs. And so on.

Millions of web surfers curse their local lines and modems because of slow access, but their wrath is, in part, misdirected. Even with infinite throughput to their local ISP, web surfing would not be incredibly fast. The bottleneck would simply move to the ISP's access point, and if you could defeat that bottleneck, it would move to the closest Network Access Point (NAP), which is where ISPs exchange packets. The Internet as a whole, on average, gets a point-to-point throughput of only about 50KB per second. And remember that most servers are not connected to a backbone, but dangle off an ISP several layers down the tree of connectivity.

You can see the law of diminishing returns in action if you upgrade web client access from 28.8kbps to ISDN and then to cable modem. The 28.8kbps to 128kbps

ISDN increase is impressive, but the 128K ISDN to 500K cable modem increase is not as noticeable, though much larger in absolute terms.

Forwarding and Latency

Every physical line has at least the latency imposed by the speed of light, but most latency on the Internet is caused by the number of terminators and connection points, such as routers, that the bits must pass through. The fewer the termination and decision points, the lower the latency. In particular, you want few connection points where the medium or speed is different between the two sides of the connection.

The interface between lines of two different speeds or protocol types is a choke point. A packet on a slow line cannot instantly be forwarded bit by bit onto a faster line, because the data is always kept in packets in which all bits are adjacent to one another in time. A packet must be received in its entirety before it can be forwarded onto the higher-speed interface. This adds latency. The same story is true for converting protocol types, such as Ethernet to token ring. The moral is to have as few connection points as possible, and to use as few protocols and as few different speeds as possible. The lowest latency comes from a direct connection between the browser and the server, but this is rarely possible.

Your Modem, the Information Driveway

Analog modems convert a stream of digital data into an audio-band analog format that can be sent over Plain Old Telephone Service (POTS), to another analog modem. (The telephone network is also sometimes referred to as the Public Switched Telephone Network, or PSTN.) The increases in modem performance of the last few years have come as modem makers learn to cope better with the difficulties imposed by sending digital data over a quirky analog system.

POTS was built and optimized for voice traffic. There are filters in the phone system that amplify the portion of the audio spectrum humans hear best, 300Hz to 3300Hz, at the expense of other frequencies. There are also filters for echo cancellation. Many phone lines have poor quality. The analog data is sampled at 64kbps, losing some information, and is sent in digital form to the remote phone switch, where it is reconstructed into analog form (see Figure 9-1). All of these voice-oriented characteristics of the phone system present problems to modem manufacturers, but modem performance has risen to near the theoretical maximum of 64kbps imposed by the switches with the current generation of 56kbps modems. For speeds beyond 64kbps, the data signal must bypass the phone switch analog-digital-analog conversion or bypass the phone system altogether.

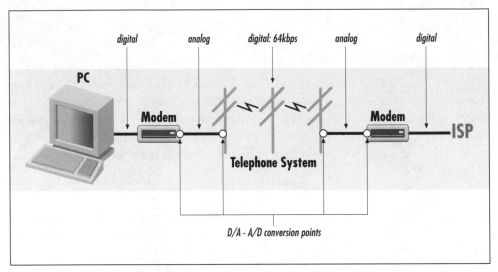

Figure 9-1. Signal conversions with modem use

Modems usually send bits by altering the state of a carrier signal of a given frequency. The carrier's signal state varies by combinations of phase and amplitude.
Note that the actual rate at which distinct states can be transmitted (the baud rate)
has not increased appreciably from earlier modems, but clever encoding schemes
have increased the number of possible states so that more bits can be encoded in
each baud. For example, V.32 modems send one of 64 distinct states with each
state change, so each state encodes 6 bits (2^6 = 64). V.32 modems run at 2400
baud, so 2400 × 6 = 14400 bits/second can be sent. V.34 modems run at 3200
baud, but send 512 distinct states, so each state encodes 9 bits (2^9 = 512). V.34
modems can therefore send 3200 × 9 = 28800 bits/second. There is often confu-
sion between baud and bits per second, because in early modems they were the
same number. That is, early modems, up to 2400 bits per second, transmitted only
one of two possible states at any moment, corresponding to a single bit.

Latency and throughput modem to modem

Modem latency is high relative to the latency of a purely digital Internet connection, even an Internet connection through several routers. I made a simple test to
confirm this. A *ping* between two machines directly connected by modems in the
same city took 160 milliseconds, while a *ping* between two machines connected
via digital links from one coast of the U.S. to the other took 120 milliseconds, even
though it went through eight routers. The latency is distributed between the phone
system, the transport encoding, and the modem itself, but the point is that any use
of a modem imposes a small, but noticeable, latency penalty.

Make sure your modem's throughput is the same or better than your ISP's modems' throughput. Most modems can interoperate with lower-speed modems, so you can buy a modem better than your ISP's modems, use it now, and be ready when your ISP upgrades. There is a catch: 56K modems are not all mutually compatible, so you may buy a 56K modem and not be able to get 56K even after your ISP upgrades. The two standards are the K56flex and US Robotics' x2. The International Telecommunications Union (ITU) was scheduled to choose a standard in mid-1998. Even if the modem is compatible with your ISP's modems, you may still only get about 45kbps because of line quality. However, 33.6kbps modems run at the rated speed more reliably.

Getting synchronous

Modem bandwidth is limited not only by the protocols and line quality, but also because the connection is *asynchronous*, so transmission can begin whenever there is data to send. To give the other side a demarcation of valid data, modems by default send an extra 2 bits per byte to mark the start and stop bits for that byte, so 10 bits are transmitted for every byte of data. A 14.4kbps modem's maximum throughput of data is therefore 1400 bytes per second, rather than 1800 bytes per second. Analogously, a 28.8kbps modem has a throughput of 2800 bytes per second, and so on.

This overhead of 20% can be avoided through the use of Link Access Procedure for Modems (LAP-M) or one of the Microcom Network Protocols (MNP). By using LAP-M or MNP, an entire PPP frame can be sent continuously, with no start or stop bits between the bytes. Of course, the modems at both ends of the phone call must understand and agree on which protocol to use.

Note that LAP-M and MNP happen in the modem, so the serial port will actually see the rated modem speed without any 20% penalty. This means that turning on one of these options will increase the load on the serial port, and could result in UART buffer overruns if the computer was only marginally able to handle the load before.

Hardware compression

Another commonly available modem option is hardware compression. This is compression done by your modem hardware rather than by software in your computer prior to sending the data to the modem. Hardware compression is most useful for large transfers and for text, which is highly compressible. Remember that not all files are compressible, so there is no guarantee you'll see any benefit from turning on hardware compression. Hardware compression is usually part of one of the MNP options.

Error correction

Modems are now clever enough to deal with noise on the telephone line by slowing down the baud rate and/or using simpler state encoding symbols, rather than repeatedly asking for retransmission of damaged data or giving up altogether and ending the call. They are also clever enough to increase the transmission rate when the phone line gets cleaner.

Remember that modems know only that they are sending blocks of raw data to each other. The fact that you are sending an HTTP request wrapped in a TCP segment wrapped in an IP packet wrapped in a PPP frame is unknown to the modem. PPP frames are checked for errors once the data percolates up into the IP socket connection, but this takes a relatively long time to happen, and PPP's only option on error is to ask for the whole frame to be retransmitted. It is much faster to have the modem correct an error, if it can.

V.42 modems have built-in error correction that should be left on. If you turn it off, you'll have more PPP frame check errors. On a good phone line, you may not notice that it's off, but on a noisy line, this may be enough to cause the modem to hang up.

Disable Xon/Xoff flow control, also known as *software handshaking*, because it uses characters in the data stream itself to start and stop transmission. This is the cause of many situations in which transfer stops, for no apparent reason, because a flow control character happens to be in a binary data stream. Enable RTS/CTS flow control, or *hardware handshaking*, if your ISP supports it. This happens faster and does not offer the opportunity to confuse data with flow control instructions.

Line quality

You can sometimes tell that you have a noise problem on your phone line by listening to what ought to be silence during a phone call. If it's clearly not silence, you may have a problem. You might have some luck getting your local telephone company to improve it if you complain; then again, you might not. Local phone companies are, after all, still monopolies for now. (Other performance tuning tips: pay attention to the FCC rules, and write your congressperson asking for more competition.) Of course, the problem could also be the wire in your house, which you have to pay to repair. Hanging up and redialing, that is, rebooting the phone, often helps.

You may see a CONNECT 14400 message when you have a 28.8kbps modem, for example, if you are connecting over a noisy line. The rate can vary as the modem adapts to the line noise. Your modem control program should have an option to tell you exactly what throughput you're really getting and whether there are Cyclic Redundancy Check (CRC) errors. CRC errors imply line noise. A strange number (not one of the standard speeds 14.4, 28.8, etc.) below your modem's rated speed also implies that you are dealing with noise. If you are getting a lower number that is one of the usual modem speeds, then your modem may have dropped to a lower rate to compensate for noise, or you may have simply dialed in to a lower-speed modem.

If you have an external modem, it is connected to your machine via an RS-232 modem cable. Modem cable is not all alike. Capacitance makes some RS-232 cables suitable for high-speed modems, and some less so. If you are using a 14.4kbps modem or better, you need a high-speed cable. If you use a slow cable, you will see many errors and retransmits.

Internal modems are faster

Internal modems have several performance advantages if you are willing to go to the trouble to open up your computer and install one. There is no RS-232 cable involved, so you can't pick the wrong cable. The modem will have its own UART or will emulate one, so you don't have to worry about having an obsolete UART. Finally, internal modems are directly on the bus, so there is less latency in moving bits between the modem and the computer.

There are also parallel port modems that connect to your printer port. You need to install a software driver to use them, but they also have less latency than an external serial port modem.

UART buffer overruns

The UART chip that controls your machine's serial port has a FIFO buffer of probably eight bytes, which must be cleared before the UART can accept any new data. If your machine does not clear the UART data in the time it has told the serial port it would, data will be overwritten and lost, resulting in PPP frame check errors and costly retransmits. The modem's error correction can't help you here—it's already done its job in delivering data to the UART.

The cause of UART overruns is the failure of the computer to get the data from the UART's buffer in time. How long does the computer have? The UART assembles a byte as the bits arrive, then pushes the byte into the FIFO buffer. Say that you have a 28.8kbps modem. It therefore takes 1 second / 28800 bits × 8 bits = .28 milliseconds to receive one byte. This sounds like a very short time, but remember that a 33MHz bus could go through 33 million × .28 × 10^{-3} = 9240 bus cycles in that time, and it should take only one bus cycle to move a byte from the UART to the bus. Starting from an empty buffer, your computer has eight bytes worth of time (2.2 milliseconds) to come and get at least one byte before an eight-byte buffer wraps and begins to overwrite data. So it's not much of a challenge for a lightly loaded PC to retrieve data from the UART.

The ultimate origin of UART overruns is usually an interrupt request (IRQ) from a poorly written disk drive driver or video driver that monopolizes the CPU. The trick is to know when your communication problem is due to an overrun and not to line noise. If it is a driver problem, you probably need a new driver. Fortunately, the UART itself knows when an overrun has occurred, because it can detect when data is unloaded from the buffer. In the case of an overrun, a flag will be set in the UART's status register, which can be read by your Winsock or other networking software. The networking software, in turn, should have a mechanism for notifying you of overruns. If you see a PPP frame check error and no overrun, the problem is likely to be line noise. If you see a PPP frame check error with an overrun, the problem is likely to be a poor device driver or even poor networking code, which can be fixed only by upgrading the drivers or the operating system.

AT commands and dialing time

If you use a Hayes compatible modem, try setting the S11 register lower than the default value of 70 milliseconds. 35 milliseconds often works just fine, and cuts the dialing time in half; that may not be a huge improvement, but it is noticeable. Use the modem AT command ATS11=35. Similarly, you may be able to get away with starting to dial after only 1 second of waiting for a dial tone, rather than the default of 2 seconds; use ATS6=1. Neither of these options is guaranteed to work with any particular modem or local phone line.

Bonding channels

You cannot do much about the latency inherent in using modems, but it is possible to get better than 56K throughput by using multiple analog lines in parallel. This is called *bonding channels* and requires that both ends have multiple modems and the correct bonding software. Diamond Multimedia (*http://www.diamondmm.com/*) sells its Shotgun product, which bonds two 56K analog modems to 112K. Ramp Networks' WebRamp M3t lets you multiplex three modems. Of course, you then need three phone lines, but this may still be cheaper and more reliable than ISDN.

ISDN

Integrated Service Digital Network (ISDN) provides an entirely digital connection between your home and the phone company switch, so there is no loss of data in an analog-to-digital conversion. This allows you to get the full 64kbps that the phone system uses internally for transmitting voice data. An ISDN modem looks and acts quite a bit like an analog modem, but dials and connects very quickly (often in under 1 second) and makes no noise. It is possible to run a web server from ISDN and save connection fees by having your ISP dial your modem and set up a connection to a web server at your home when anyone surfs to a web page at your IP address. This adds a noticeable delay for the surfer, however, and is non-trivial to set up. ISDN is customarily provided as two "B" channels of 64kbps each that can be bonded into one 128kbps channel. There is no loss of start and stop bits because the connection is synchronous, so the actual throughput can be 16000 bytes per second. Some telcos provide only 56kbps B channels because they use one bit out of eight for error correction or synchronization.

A direct ISDN connection from home to your LAN at work does provide enough bandwidth that it feels distinctly better than any analog modem. Video conferencing, for example, is much more reasonable over ISDN than over analog modem. If you can make a local toll-free ISDN call to the same ISP that your employer uses, and your company allows Internet access to the LAN (perhaps with a password), you should also get very good throughput and latency because your packets will remain within your ISP's private network rather than being routed over random points on the Internet. It takes a bit of detective work to find out your company's ISP (use *traceroute*), whether the ISP has a local dial-in number near you (use the ISP's web page), and whether an ISDN call to that number is a local toll-free call (use the front of your phone book).

A significant disadvantage to ISDN is that it is still not available everywhere and is not well supported. In fact, even if your local telco offers ISDN, their service representatives may know nothing about it. This happened to me: I called the information number and asked if ISDN was available. The service representative had never heard of ISDN, and asked me to spell it. Hmmm. I spelled it. Then I was asked what it stood for. I said, "I Still Don't kNow," and the representative seemed satisfied with that, and asked for some time to find someone who had heard of it. I eventually got a call back and was told the service was available.

The setup was very hard because only certain brands of ISDN modems work with the particular kind of switch your telco has in its local office. Furthermore, once you have found out what kind of switch your telco has—for example, a 5ESS— and you've found a modem that is supposed to be compatible with it, you still need to configure many parameters on the modem. Worse, the telco switch also has to be configured for the service, and you need the help of someone at the phone company central office switch to do that. Once it was finally configured correctly, the ISDN performance was good, but I would not recommend ISDN where any other option for high-speed access is available.

Cable Modems

High-speed access over the same coaxial cable that brings you cable TV is a good alternative to ISDN. Installation is usually simple: Your cable company provides you with the cable modem, and will probably install it. It's a very simple box that takes a coaxial connection in one side and provides you with an Ethernet connection on the other side. There are no user-configurable parameters. Most cable modems use the same Rockwell chip set, so if you have to buy one, it may be portable to other cable modem service areas. You need to configure your computer to use the IP address the cable company gives you, but you have to do that with most ISPs, anyway.

The downstream bandwidth is 500kbps, which is excellent, and especially nice if you are getting data from a fast server close to you in router hops. You'll be ahead of the average speed of the Internet; you will still hit bottlenecks, but now the bottlenecks will not be at your connection. Upstream bandwidth is 100kbps, which is sufficient for a small web server. There are no connect-time charges, and there is not even an on/off switch on the modem. It is always on when plugged in.

A disadvantage is that your connection is shared with your local neighborhood. An area with many busy users will give you lower performance. There is also nothing to stop your neighbors from snooping on your IP packets, if they are so inclined, since you are all effectively on the same LAN. Finally, cable modem is available only in a few areas as of this writing, but services such as @Home (*http:// www.home.com/*) are expanding rapidly, after a long period of indecision on the part of the cable companies. Pricing is inconsistent, and you may pay anywhere from $30 per month to $100 per month for the exact same service.

xDSL

The physical characteristics of the copper lines into your home are not what is limiting the speeds you can achieve via analog modem. The limiting factor is the conversion into a 64kbps stream at the telephone company switch. What if you could bypass the telephone switch and hook directly into a digital line at the telco office? ISDN does this, but it connects to a 64kbps digital line, which is not a vast improvement over 56kbps modems. A direct connection to a digital line into the Internet from the other end of the pair of copper wires in your home sets apart Asymmetric Digital Subscriber Line (ADSL) and its cousins, grouped as xDSL.

xDSL speeds vary, but 1.5Mbps downstream and 500kbps upstream are common numbers. This is faster than cable modem, but it may occupy your telephone line, while cable modem does not. xDSL is not yet widely available, and where it is available, you often have to get two accounts to use it: one with your telco, and one with the ISP that has an agreement with your telco to place its xDSL equipment at the telco's local Central Office (CO).

Higher Capacity Lines

Here is a brief overview of the high-speed connectivity options for web servers, each with its own kind of router or switch and termination hardware. These options are all overkill for a simple web surfing client. See *Getting Connected*, by Kevin Dowd (O'Reilly & Associates), for a detailed explanation of these kinds of lines.

56K, T1, and T3

You can get a direct digital connection between your home or organization and your ISP through special services provided by your local telco. These direct digital lines typically come in speeds of 56kbps, T1 (1.544Mbps), and T3 (45Mbps). You can also get a fraction of a T1 or T3 and upgrade it later via a software switch in the CO.

A 56K dedicated digital line might seem useless since there are now 56K analog modems, but remember that the 56K line is more reliable, less subject to noise, and synchronous, so there is less overhead per packet.

T1 and T3 are synchronous serial lines, so no overhead is wasted on start bits. Actual throughput can be very high, better than 90% of the rated capacity, and latency is very low. The downside to these lines is that they are expensive. It is common for a T1 connection from you to an ISP in the same city to cost $1000 per month. Long-distance T1 connections cost much more.

Frame Relay

Frame Relay is a packet switched wide area networking protocol. It provides a virtual point-to-point connection called a permanent virtual circuit (PVC). Frame Relay is a far more cost-effective option than a long-distance T1 line, because with Frame Relay, the long-distance hardware of cable is shared among many customers, though customers see only their own packets. Customers thus have virtual circuits to themselves. Frame Relay is an unreliable protocol, meaning there is no guarantee that packets will arrive on time, or that they will arrive at all. It is up to higher layers of software to ask for retransmits of missing packets. This is transparent to the user in a well-managed ISP.

Frame Relay has built-in prioritization of Committed Information Rate (CIR) packets. Frame Relay generally has good price per performance, especially for the long haul between the U.S. and abroad, but that's often because it's underutilized. When a carrier fills up their capacity, performance drops. Judge Frame Relay service on the packet drop rate, regardless of the CIR, because a high drop rate will make the CIR irrelevant.

ATM

Asynchronous Transfer Mode (ATM) is a packet switched protocol with quality of
service (QOS) guarantees. Actually, ATM does not switch packets per se, but
rather fixed-length (53-byte) *cells.* ATM routing equipment does not have to calculate the length of the cell, and the cells are short; both factors contribute to ATM's
very low latency capability. Voice and video services can be provided over ATM
links without fear that some data will be arbitrarily delayed. ATM is often run over
copper at 16Mbps and is also used over optical fiber. Common fiber speeds are
Optical Carrier 3 (OC3), which runs at 155Mbps, and OC12, which runs at 622
Mbps. These options are expensive.

Satellite

There are various services available via satellite. Asymmetric web client services
require a modem connection to request pages, which are then received via a satellite dish at 1Mbps or so. Symmetrical services are expensive, but may be cheaper
than dealing with government phone monopolies in poor countries. Satellite services always involve considerable latency because of the sheer distances involved,
but low earth orbit (LEO) satellites can have one-tenth the latency of the much
higher orbit geosynchronous satellites. The disadvantage to LEO satellites is that
they regularly move out of range, so there must be provisions for handing off the
signal to another satellite in the group. Geosynchronous satellites remain posi-
tioned over one spot on the earth.

See *http://www.intelsat.int/* for more information on symmetrical satellite services.

Intranets

An Intranet is a TCP/IP network within an organization. Intranet planners have the
luxury of having much more control over the network and client software than is
possible on the Internet. This control makes it possible to guarantee a better quality of service and to use available bandwidth more efficiently, so that time-critical
applications like streaming audio or video run smoothly.

Partitioning

You can't randomly expand an intranet forever without overloading some parts.
You will start to need a hierarchy in your network. The general rule is to keep the
machines that frequently talk to one another close together in the network, prefer-
ably on the same IP subnet, where communications will be fastest. See Chapter 12,
Performance Analysis and Tuning, in *Managing NFS and NIS* by Hal Stern
(O'Reilly & Associates) for more details on partitioning networks.

Where to put the web server?

When deciding where to place a web server on your intranet, consider whether it will be accessed by the outside world as well as from inside your organization, and who has priority. If you have two distinct sets of web content, one internal and one external, you should run at least two web servers, perhaps two virtual servers on the same machine.

Web servers that talk to the Internet should have their best connection be to the Internet, but if internal users are also sharing that connection for email and Usenet traffic, for example, then outside web surfers may be starved for network bandwidth. A full duplex connection to your ISP helps to mitigate this, since your internal users have mostly inbound traffic, while external users have mostly outbound traffic. If you have many internal Internet users, or plan to provide essential services to the Internet community via your web server, you should consider a dedicated Internet connection for the web server, even if it is lower in bandwidth than the connection your organization uses for outbound access. Place the web server outside your firewall and try to minimize traffic (such as database access) across the firewall. Two gateways to the Internet often work better than one gateway with twice the nominal capacity.

If you're forced to share one connection for an important web server with other traffic, or if external access to your web server is swamping an internal LAN, the four Ps for dealing with the problem are: policy, prioritization, proxies, and partitioning:

- Tell users what sort of traffic is acceptable by policy.
- Use one of the traffic management products below to prioritize packets so the most important ones get through.
- Set up a proxy web server where the connection comes into your organization.
- Be sure to place the internal web server on a segment that does not have much broadcast traffic or NFS traffic.

Hardware for partitioning

The hardware boxes that break up your LAN into segments and connect you to the Internet all add latency to traffic, so don't use them gratuitously. Here's a quick summary:

Repeaters

Repeaters are used to extend the effective length of a cable and do not partition at all. They repeat whatever you put on them, with bits sharpened and amplified.

Hubs

> Hubs also repeat, but they repeat out to multiple machines, creating a network structure that looks like the hub and spokes of a wheel.

Bridges

> Bridges contain a table of local MAC-layer addresses such as Ethernet addresses, and they forward packets that don't belong to any local machine to the next network over. This allows easy segmentation of Ethernet traffic, but bridges aren't suitable for large-scale networks because they use broadcasts for all dynamic configuration, which would flood a large network with configuration packets.

Routers

> Routers divide networks by IP network number, the next higher level of protocol. You can put multiple NIC cards in a machine and force it into router duty with the appropriate software, but you'll get better throughput and latency from purpose-built routers.

There is some information on routers later in this chapter, but a detailed analysis of performance issues for all these network devices is beyond the scope of this book. See *Managing IP Networks with Cisco Routers*, by Scott Ballew (O'Reilly & Associates), for more information.

One critical issue with network devices is matching IP Maximum Transmission Units (MTUs) between different protocols. For example, if you are routing from Ethernet to token ring, FDDI, or ATM, you will deliver IP packets more efficiently if they do not need to be fragmented at this boundary, that is, if the MTUs match. FDDI has a larger default MTU than Ethernet (4500 bytes rather than 1500 bytes), so packets originating on FDDI may get fragmented when they hit Ethernet. Any protocol conversion has some overhead, so you should avoid conversions that you don't absolutely need. See the IP section in Chapter 10, *Network Protocols*, for more information about MTUs.

Ethernet

Ethernet is currently the dominant LAN medium. Most installed Ethernet is 10baseT Ethernet, which runs at 10Mbps, but 100Mbps Ethernet is increasing rapidly. The Solaris *ifconfig -a* command will usually show 10Mbps Ethernet as interface le0 and 100Mbps Ethernet cards as hme0 or be0. Note that 10Mbps Ethernet is normally half-duplex, meaning traffic can flow in only one direction at a time, while hme0 cards can autodetect the speed of the card on the other end and do anything from half-duplex 10Mbps to full duplex at 100Mbps.

Ethernet cards are now cheap commodity items, and Ethernet is easy to set up, but it has a significant drawback. Because Ethernet is a shared medium, multiple machines can begin to transmit at the same time, resulting in collisions. The algorithm Ethernet uses for retransmits is to back off for a random amount of time on the first collision, but for an exponentially larger, but still random, amount of time with each subsequent collision that occurs when trying to send the same packet. This works quite well for light loads, but causes throughput to degrade dramatically above 70% utilization, so you should consider Ethernet to have a maximum throughput of 7 Mbps (see Figure 9-2). You can monitor Ethernet collisions under Linux, Solaris, and some other versions of Unix with the *netstat -i* command.

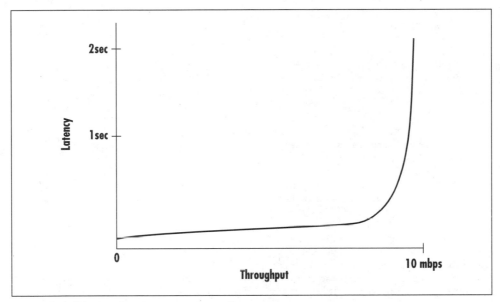

Figure 9-2. Ethernet latency versus throughput

The minimum packet length for Ethernet is 72 bytes, so there is quite a bit of overhead for interactive sessions, where individual characters are sent with 71 bytes of overhead as they are typed. This is not a problem with web transmissions, where data is returned in relatively large chunks that can fill the default packet size of 1500 bytes.

Packet snooping

An Ethernet card will, by default, discard packets that are not addressed to its globally unique MAC address. There is also a "promiscuous" mode, however, which looks at all packets on the LAN, regardless of destination. Solaris comes bundled with the *snoop* tool which is very useful for placing an Ethernet card into promiscuous mode and unwinding the layers of protocols around packets. You must be *root* to run *snoop*. It lets you see that the Ethernet holds an IP packet, and that the IP packet holds a TCP segment, and will even show you the data contents of the packet. Here's an example *snoop* of a browser's HTTP request going to a proxy server:

```
# snoop -v -x 0
ETHER:  ----- Ether Header -----
ETHER:
ETHER:  Packet 4 arrived at 11:33:12.22
ETHER:  Packet size = 337 bytes
ETHER:  Destination = 0:60:5c:f3:71:57,
ETHER:  Source      = 8:0:20:7b:87:4c, Sun
ETHER:  Ethertype = 0800 (IP)
ETHER:
IP:   ----- IP Header -----
IP:
IP:   Version = 4
IP:   Header length = 20 bytes
IP:   Type of service = 0x00
IP:          xxx. .... = 0 (precedence)
IP:          ...0 .... = normal delay
IP:          .... 0... = normal throughput
IP:          .... .0.. = normal reliability
IP:   Total length = 323 bytes
IP:   Identification = 27865
IP:   Flags = 0x4
IP:          .1.. .... = do not fragment
IP:          ..0. .... = last fragment
IP:   Fragment offset = 0 bytes
IP:   Time to live = 255 seconds/hops
IP:   Protocol = 6 (TCP)
IP:   Header checksum = 450d
IP:   Source address = 10.15.6.126, guest
IP:   Destination address = 10.15.19.32, webcache.zort.com
IP:   No options
IP:
TCP:  ----- TCP Header -----
TCP:
TCP:  Source port = 38685
TCP:  Destination port = 8080 (HTTP (proxy))
TCP:  Sequence number = 1844000715
TCP:  Acknowledgement number = 1830043605
TCP:  Data offset = 20 bytes
TCP:  Flags = 0x18
TCP:          ..0. .... = No urgent pointer
TCP:          ...1 .... = Acknowledgement
TCP:          .... 1... = Push
TCP:          .... .0.. = No reset
TCP:          .... ..0. = No Syn
TCP:          .... ...0 = No Fin
TCP:  Window = 8760
TCP:  Checksum = 0xe027
TCP:  Urgent pointer = 0
TCP:  No options
TCP:
HTTP: ----- HyperText Transfer Protocol -----
```

```
HTTP:
HTTP: GET http://patrick.net/ HTTP/1.0
HTTP: Proxy-Connection: Keep-Alive
HTTP: User-Agent: Mozilla/4.02 [en] (X11; U; SunOS 5.6 sun4u)
HTTP: Pragma: no-cache
HTTP: Host: patrick.net
HTTP: Accept: image/gif, image/x-xbitmap, image/jpeg, image/pjpeg, */*
HTTP: Accept-Language: en
HTTP: Accept-Charset: iso-8859-1,*,utf-8
HTTP:
```

```
  0: 0060 5cf3 7157 0800 207b 874c 0800 4500    .`\.qW.. {.L..E.
 16: 0143 6cd9 4000 ff06 450d 8199 067e 8196    .Cl.@...E....~..
 32: bf20 971d 1f90 6de9 37cb 6d14 3fd5 5018    . ....m.7.m.?.P.
 48: 2238 e027 0000 4745 5420 6874 7470 3a2f    "8.'..GET http:/
 64: 2f70 6174 7269 636b 2e6e 6574 2f20 4854    /patrick.net/ HT
 80: 5450 2f31 2e30 0d0a 5072 6f78 792d 436f    TP/1.0..Proxy-Co
 96: 6e6e 6563 7469 6f6e 3a20 4b65 6570 2d41    nnection: Keep-A
112: 6c69 7665 0d0a 5573 6572 2d41 6765 6e74    live..User-Agent
128: 3a20 4d6f 7a69 6c6c 612f 342e 3032 205b    : Mozilla/4.02 [
144: 656e 5d20 2858 3131 3b20 553b 2053 756e    en] (X11; U; Sun
160: 4f53 2035 2e36 2073 756e 3475 290d 0a50    OS 5.6 sun4u)..P
176: 7261 676d 613a 206e 6f2d 6361 6368 650d    ragma: no-cache.
192: 0a48 6f73 743a 2070 6174 7269 636b 2e6e    .Host: patrick.n
208: 6574 0d0a 4163 6365 7074 3a20 696d 6167    et..Accept: imag
224: 652f 6769 662c 2069 6d61 6765 2f78 2d78    e/gif, image/x-x
240: 6269 746d 6170 2c20 696d 6167 652f 6a70    bitmap, image/jp
256: 6567 2c20 696d 6167 652f 706a 7065 672c    eg, image/pjpeg,
272: 202a 2f2a 0d0a 4163 6365 7074 2d4c 616e     */*..Accept-Lan
288: 6775 6167 653a 2065 6e0d 0a41 6363 6570    guage: en..Accep
304: 742d 4368 6172 7365 743a 2069 736f 2d38    t-Charset: iso-8
320: 3835 392d 312c 2a2c 7574 662d 380d 0a0d    859-1,*,utf-8...
336: 0a
```

While this is interesting and may show you some unexpected kinds of load on your LAN, you can also send the output to */dev/audio* (turn down the volume first) for continuous feedback on the activity of your LAN. *snoop -a* will do this, or you can simply redirect *snoop* output to */dev/audio,* using your shell. It's kind of fun to leave it on and hear the patterns of various kinds of activity.

snoop is good for looking at, capturing, or listening to collections of packets, but it can drown you in data. *snoop* does not give statistical output or characterize your traffic patterns, such as excessive retransmits. For this, you need to use network sniffing hardware (Sniffer is a trademark of Network General) or one of the many LAN analyzer software packages such as Sun's *traffic* program. Solaris' *netstat -s* provides summary data: look at the number of bytes retransmitted relative to the total number of bytes sent. SNMP tools also characterize network traffic.

The freely available *tcpdump* program does many of the same things as *snoop*.

NIC buffers

Like serial port cards, Ethernet Network Interface Cards (NICs) have limited buffer sizes. Ethernet cards have far larger buffers, because they are accumulating data at a much faster rate. Eight-bit cards tend to have 8KB buffers, and 16-bit cards tend to have 16KB buffers. Ethernet is serial, so bits enter the buffer one at a time. Whether a card is 8-bit or 16-bit refers to how many bits it can transfer from its buffer to the system bus in one bus cycle. This is much less important than buffer size because the bus can empty the NIC buffer very quickly.

At 10 Mbps, Ethernet can fill an 8KB buffer in (1 sec / 10×10^6 bits) $\times$ 8 $\times$ 1024 $\times$ 8 bits/byte = 6.6 milliseconds. This is a bit more leeway than the 2.2 milliseconds that we calculated it takes to fill an 8-byte buffer from a 28.8kbps modem. Remember that Ethernet packets are 1500 bytes by default, so an 8KB buffer can hold only five complete packets. Your OS may reserve a part of your NIC buffer for outgoing data, leaving you a smaller buffer for receiving data. As with modems, problems arise because the computer may not be able to get the data from the card's buffer before more data arrives, resulting in costly retransmissions. Your alternatives for eliminating this problem are better device drivers, a faster machine, better TCP/IP implementation, or simply a NIC card with bigger buffers.

See *http://www.spade.com/* for more information on NIC buffer sizes.

Fast Ethernet

Fast Ethernet is the same technology as Ethernet, only ten times faster, or 100Mbps. This alone reduces collisions, and improves performance under heavy loads. Gigabit Ethernet, which runs at 1Gbps, 10 times the rate of fast Ethernet, has now appeared (see *http://www.yago.com/*). FDDI is an alternative that is very similar in performance to fast Ethernet.

A web server showing greater than 20% Ethernet collisions should be connected to its router to the Internet via fast Ethernet. But the downside to fast and gigabit Ethernet is cost. You have to upgrade both NICs and hubs.

Switched Ethernet

An Ethernet switch is a lot like a hub, only better (and more expensive). With switched Ethernet, all packets are held in a buffer at the switch until the connection to the destination is open. The time waited is usually very small, and the time saved in avoiding a collision is relatively large. The destination may try to send a packet back out to the switch at the same time the switch is forwarding a packet on to that destination, resulting in a collision, but it is at least guaranteed that there will be no inbound collisions to any destination on the LAN. For this reason, switched Ethernet gives large performance gains over ordinary Ethernet segments connected via a hub. Another reason for improved performance is that multiple machines on the same segment can simultaneously talk to one another, which is not possible on a hub.

Allowing 20% for packet overhead, assuming each transfer is 10KB, and ignoring switch latency, a switched Ethernet connection between a client and web server has a theoretical potential of .8 × 1 HTTP transfer/10240 bytes × 1250000 bytes/second = ~100 HTTP transfers/second.

One problem here is that multiple clients on the switch may be contending for the same web server. If the web server is on the same speed segment as several clients simultaneously trying to get at it, most of the performance advantages of a switch are lost. The solution here is to put the web server on a 100Mbps segment if the clients are all on 10Mbps segments. Many switches can handle having some segments at higher speeds than others.

Ethernet switching is often called layer 2 switching because Ethernet corresponds to layer 2 of the OSI network model. Layer 3 switching is really just fast routing at the IP level, often with special route lookup hardware rather than the traditional software lookup. See *Computer Networks*, by Andrew Tannenbaum (Prentice Hall), for more information on the OSI network layers.

Ethernet cabling

Keep in mind that electrical cables effectively transmit signals only up to a certain cable length because of capacitance, which is essentially the rate at which the cable fills with electricity. If your cable is too long, a high-frequency signal will smear, and you'll lose packets. You can use repeaters to get around cable-length limitations to some degree. For Ethernet, you can use only four repeaters between any two nodes; more will probably increase the transit time beyond the maximum time to live of the packet.

Category 5 (Cat 5) unshielded twisted pair (UTP) works well up to 100BaseT Ethernet. Gigabit Ethernet may not work well over Cat 5 cable, because it uses all four pairs of wires in the cable rather than two pairs, leading to more electrical crosstalk. Because of this problem, the first specification for gigabit Ethernet is for optical fiber. Another hazard is connectors that have a lower rating than your cable and therefore generate a high number of errors. The coaxial "thicknet" variety of Ethernet cable is now obsolete.

Noise

Improper termination of Ethernet lines will cause reflection noise that will hurt throughput. Other causes of reflections are kinks or sharp bends.

It is also easy to destroy LAN performance by running the Ethernet cable in drop ceilings next to fluorescent lights, which generate a lot of radio-frequency noise. If you have a walkman and know of a store with a neon sign, turn on the walkman and get near the neon light. You'll hear a loud hum, because the sign is acting like a radio transmitter. I once met a system administrator who inadvertently clipped Ethernet cable to the antenna line of a dispatch radio system in the office. While anyone was transmitting by radio, Ethernet performance would drop to zero. Avoid large power cables for the same reason; if your computer monitor is showing a distorted image in one part of the office but is OK in another part, you may have a power cable running in the wall or through a pillar.

Noise not only garbles valid messages, but can also cause spurious interrupts that the computer assumes are signal data. When the computer tries to get the message, it hears only nonsense.

IP Traffic Management Products

One problem with IP is that all packets are treated the same regardless of the latency and throughput requirements of higher-level protocols. This can be solved with one of the recent IP traffic management products (also known as "traffic shaping" products), quality of service (QOS) boxes, or bandwidth management products. Some of these products are actually hardware boxes, while others are new software for network hardware.

These products classify and tag IP packets as belonging to different priority levels. When packets are queued up at a router, the traffic shaping product will rearrange the queue depending on priorities. In addition, measurements are taken of network health and of which classes are using what fraction of the bandwidth. Packets from streams that have exceeded a bandwidth allocation may be thrown away. Note that quality of service is relative here: some packets are treated as more important than others, but no guarantee is made about overall latency or throughput. Contrast this with ATM, which does provide hard latency and throughput specifications for different classes of service. ATM can do this because as a connection-ful layer 2 protocol, it has direct control of the physical wire from one end of the connection to the other. IP is a layer 3 protocol and has no direct control over the layer 2 protocol that carries it (ATM, Ethernet, Frame Relay). So you won't find any guarantee that you can make an acceptable voice call over the Internet.

While you can't control the Internet, you can control your own intranet, so you can dictate packet policies and put them into your organization's routers or other network hardware. You may need a single-vendor network to do it, so lock-in is a problem. RSVP, an Internet protocol to accomplish essentially the same thing, has a similar problem because it requires that every router along an RSVP path obey the protocol. A couple of disadvantages to these products are that they add an amount of latency proportional to the number of QOS classes you define, and they don't help at all in cases of extreme congestion, where packets of all classes may be thrown out anyway.

Here are some of the leading IP traffic management products:

CheckPoint Software (http://www.checkpoint.com/)
> CheckPoint was first known for firewall software but now has the FloodGate-1 product to allow data prioritization on LANs.

Cisco's Internet QOS (http://www.cisco.com/)
> Cisco is the 800-pound gorilla of IP networking, with by far the largest market share for routers. It is adding QOS features to its router operating system, IOS 11.1. These features will communicate and synchronize prioritization policy between routers. The product seems designed to keep networks locked in to Cisco.

Packeteer (http://www.packeteer.com/)
> Packeteer has a hardware product that allocates bandwidth and figures out what sort of web response a client can handle by the rate at which the request came in; it can distinguish a 14.4 client from T1 client and generate a reply that the client can handle.

Structured Internetworks (http://www.thestructure.com/)
> Structured Internetworks offers another hardware product that allocates bandwidth and prioritizes packets. The IPath product examines each packet for the identity of the user and prioritizes it, holding lower priority packets in a cache.

Sun Bandwidth Allocator (http://www.sun.com/software/band-allocator/)
> Sun's Bandwidth Allocator software is a streams module that performs policy-based bandwidth allocation, for example, to prevent FTP from using more bandwidth than HTTP, or to control which domains get the best service.

Torrent (http://www.torrentnet.com/)
> Torrent supposedly has a guaranteed minimum bandwidth mechanism for IP, not just a reprioritization mechanism.

Xedia (http://www.xedia.com/)
> Xedia's Access Point hardware and software products handle IP traffic shaping, monitoring, and management. They are mostly appropriate for ISPs.

Network Modeling Tools

You can play out various intranet configuration scenarios with network modeling software to see if your proposed web server location will have a significant impact on your LAN traffic. Three such network modeling products are Cisco's NETSYS (*http://www.netsystech.com*), Mil3's OPNET (*http://www.mil3.com/*), and Optimal Networks' Optimal Application Expert (*http://www.optimal.com/*). Also see *http://www.cisco.com/warp/public/734/toolkit/index.shtml* for useful background.

The Internet

The Internet is intrinsically less predictable than well-characterized private networks because it was built by a heterogeneous group with many different motives, budgets, and technical skills. This is not to say you can't make some good assumptions about the throughput and latency of the Internet based on physics, the behavior of the components, and past experience.

While the latency of the Internet can be arbitrarily high, it has a fixed lower boundary given by the speed of light. The minimum latency for any information to travel 2,000 miles, for example, is (1 second / 186,000 miles) × 2,000 miles = 10.8 milliseconds

So even under the best possible circumstances, say a direct 2,000-mile ATM link over optical fiber, you're going to have at least 10.8 ms of latency. Remember that you'll have to send a request before getting a response, so the latency between the start of the request and the start of the response will be double that, even with infinitely fast processing time at the server. The amazing thing is that a *ping* across the country shows that the Internet is operating fairly close to the theoretical maximum, frequently only 30 ms or so from one coast to the other.

If you want to get a feel for the latency of your connection, run a telnet session over a long distance. Be sure the telnet server puts the telnet session in character mode rather than line mode. In character mode sessions, each keystroke is echoed across the link. In line mode, the client data is sent only when the client hits the Return key. Line mode of course has a much better feel to it, but it limits you to sending and receiving entire lines, so you cannot use applications such as *vi*, which react to individual keystrokes. Line mode is also more efficient: the minimum IP overhead per packet is 42 bytes, so you're going to send 41 times as much overhead as data when sending single characters across a character mode line.

In addition to the latency imposed by the speed of light, each router also injects several milliseconds of latency because it has to receive your data to a buffer before it can decide what to do with it. So the fewer routers you go through, the better. In addition, small cells impose less latency, because they can be received in their entirety and forwarded in a shorter amount of time. This is one reason why all of the national ISPs backbone connections are switched ATM, which uses 53-byte cells, rather than routed IP using variable-length packets. If you know where your customers are, you can reduce the number of routers on the path by choosing a close ISP, as described in the section "ISPs," later in this chapter. One millisecond of router savings is worth about 200 physical miles of distance. Packets pick up the performance characteristics of the worst link in the chain from source to destination; if you have fewer links, you have less chance of producing delinquent packets.

Keynote Systems is in the business of measuring actual Internet performance from many different points and has published very interesting findings on its web site (*http://www.keynote.com/*). They have found that on the average, the Internet delivers web data at about 5000 characters per second, or 40000 bits per second for any single point-to-point TCP connection. You might think this makes it useless to buy a 56kbps modem or better service, but remember that this is only an average, and furthermore, this average is dragged down by the large number of users on slow (that is, modem) connections. You will still see a client side performance improvement from a 500kbps cable modem because web sites close to you, or on high-bandwidth connections to you, will have better throughput than the 40000bps average. Cities served by poor internet infrastructure have slower access, as expected. Keynote reports that some of these cities (as of January, 1998) are Phoenix, Dallas, Houston, Kansas City, and Miami. CompuServe, CWIX, and SAVVIS offer the best backbone performance because they are relatively obscure and uncrowded national providers. Internet performance improves on holidays, when most people are not surfing. Packet loss in the Internet itself (not losses caused by an inadequate TCP retransmit timeout) is about 10%. You can check this with *ping*, which reports packet loss statistics.

There are some attempts to document the overall state of the Internet in graphical form at *http://www.mids.org/weather/* and *http://www.internetweather.com/*. They are Internet "weather" reports documenting latency in a graphical way or over many different ISPs. There are also statistics on routing performance and latency at *http://www.merit.edu/ipma/*.

Bypassing the Internet

The joys and pains of packet switching are displayed on the Internet. On one hand, the Internet is very cheap relative to a circuit switched call, for which you're charged in whole-minute increments but latency and throughput are guaranteed. On the other hand, you have to share the bandwidth, so your packet has to wait its turn. Low cost and shared bandwidth lead inexorably to a wait. What happens when an ice cream shop is giving away samples on the street? A big crowd forms and you have to wait a long time to get it, even if it's free.

The Internet is not the ideal solution to all communication needs. If the uncertainty and delays of the Internet are not acceptable, and you control both ends of the connection, you still have the option of renting a private dedicated line, or simply making a phone call. A 56kbps modem connection back to the office LAN is acceptable for many uses. You can also buy long-distance, dedicated TCP/IP service, but this is expensive.

NAPs

Network Access Points (NAPs) are points where large ISPs exchange traffic with one another. NAP is a poor acronym, because the "network access" part sounds like a place where ISPs get access to something larger, when in reality, it is simply a place where each ISP exchanges traffic with its peers, though some peers are better connected than others. NAPs put the "Inter" in Internet: without exchange of traffic between ISP's private networks, you have, well, private networks.

Note that the backbone lines and routers of the Internet are all owned by individual ISPs. NAPs interconnect the ISPs with one another via high-speed Ethernet and FDDI switches, and help them maintain routing tables. Other Three-Letter Acronyms (TLAs) for NAP are MAE (now Metropolitan Area Exchange, originally Metropolitan Area Ethernet) and FIX (Federal Internet Exchange). The MAEs are all run by Worldcom, which recently merged with UUNet. Here are the major NAPs:

- CIX, the Commercial Internet Exchange.

- FIX West at NASA's Ames Research Center in Mountain View. FIX West is directly connected to MAE West.

- Genuity's NAP in Arizona.

- MAE Chicago.

- MAE Dallas.

- MAE Los Angeles.

- MAE New York.

- MAE East in Washington, D.C. (also handles incoming European connections).

- MAE West in San Jose (also handles incoming Pacific Rim connections).

- PacBell NAP in San Francisco.

- Sprint's NAP in Pennsauken, NJ.

Where do NAPs come from?

In the early 1990's, WorldCom and a few ISPs like Metropolitan Fiber Systems (MFS) arranged to exchange traffic for their mutual benefit. In 1993, the National Science Foundation paid to have its NSFNet connected to this hub in Washington, D.C. This was the beginning of MAE East (see *http://www.mfsdatanet.com/MAE*).

Because NAPs are very crowded and busy, they tend to lose packets and to introduce delays. By some estimates, they lose about a third of all packets at peak times. This is one reason that communication within a single ISP is usually faster than communication that crosses ISPs, even if the two ISPs are in the same city. ISPs have no control over how NAPs are run or what hardware and software they use, and they have to pay a large fee for interconnection privileges.

Most traffic may go through NAPs, but there is no law that says it has to. Any ISP can set up a *peering agreement* and hardware to connect to any other ISP or other private network. This gives both parties independence from the NAPs' and the major ISPs' backbone lines. If almost all of your users are on AOL, for example, get a direct connection into AOL. Some ISPs, such as InterNex, have aggressively pursued redundant connections. InterNex connects to 6 major carriers and 90 other ISPs at the time of this writing.

ISPs

Placement

If you're running a web site, your principal weapon in dealing with network hardware owned by someone else is deciding where to position your servers on the Internet. You want two things from a position: proximity (topological and physical) to your customers and big available bandwidth.

Being topologically close to your customers means that there are relatively few routing hops between you and them. Remember that the Internet is a tree; you want as few branch points as possible between you and the target for minimum latency. If you have customers or telecommuters who are using the Internet for access to your server, you definitely want them to be on your ISP, if possible. If your ISP has no local access points near your users, the next best thing is to find them an ISP that connects to the same upstream ISP or NAP as your ISP. Or, of course, you can move your server to their ISP. You can do a *traceroute* to yourself to find out how many routers separate any two points and what sort of latency they are introducing. If your users are scattered nationally, you will probably do best with a national ISP like Netcom, MCI, or Sprint. See *http://nitrous.digex.net/* for cool lists of who's connected to which NAP. Figure 9-3 shows a map of ISPs and their connections to the Internet backbone.

There is an occasional hazard associated with being on the same ISP as your customers, though. Sometimes your ISP will be overloaded, and the fastest possible route will be to use another ISP for a few hops. This is sort of like taking side streets to get around a traffic jam. Unfortunately, routing packets manually, or *source routing*, is not allowed for security reasons, and the ISP's equipment will not even think of routing your packets elsewhere if it sees that both origin and

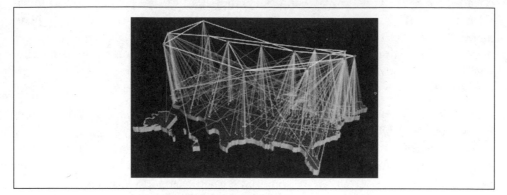

Figure 9-3. ISP connections to Internet backbone

destination are on its network. This means you will get stuck using a slow route sometimes. That's the way things work right now.

ISP performance

The economics of the Internet, where ISPs buy lines and higher-level access at a flat rate and then sell flat-rate access, means that ISPs have an incentive to oversell their services, at least until the point where customers are so unhappy with the performance that they begin to leave. At peak times, in particular, access may be very poor. Before you blame the ISP, consider that ISPs are forced to oversell; otherwise, they could not offer rates competitive with other ISPs that also oversell. Airlines overbook flights for the same reason. Furthermore, an ISP can comfortably oversell by a large margin before customers begin to notice. Your ISP may have a single T1 to its upstream provider and turn around and sell 15 or so T1s to customers, yet still provide them all with satisfactory bandwidth. This is because most users need access only for short and randomly scattered periods of time. The ISP is providing a service by aggregating packets. You will get much better throughput by sharing a T1 to a major backbone than by having a dedicated connection with one-fifteenth of the bandwidth.

If you really want guarantees of performance, you have to pay for them. The ISP can guarantee only the performance of its own network, but this may be good enough if your audience is on the same ISP. If you're very serious about performance and have a lot of money, you can get a direct, unshared connection to a major ISP or even a NAP.

There are no good, comprehensive statistics on ISP performance. There are only scattered statistics such as the page on Montreal ISP performance at *http:// cgat.bch.umontreal.ca:8080/sps2.html*. Even if comprehensive statistics were available, they would have to be constantly updated, because usage patterns shift and

ISPs upgrade hardware and connections. So how should you choose an ISP? There are many things to look for.

First of all, ask the ISP how they're doing. They should be able to provide you with statistics, and asking for the statistics lets them know that you're paying attention. How big is the provider's network backbone? How many users are there, and how many times oversold is the upstream connection? Exactly what is their connectivity to an upstream provider or NAP? Can you get statistics from that provider? How many packets do their routers drop, and what percentage is this? Be sure to cover both incoming and outgoing lines. Also look for outage reporting. See Chapter 3 of *Getting Connected*, by Kevin Dowd, for a numerical method of evaluating your ISP. Also see Appendix B of that book.

You would ideally like a first-tier ISP to have ATM backbones and redundant connections to the NAPs. Be aware that an ISP's claim of FDDI to the local NAP really doesn't mean much to you if the ISP's network backbones are much smaller than that. You'd like a second-tier ISP to have peering agreements with several other ISPs, or multiple connections to first-tier providers. A good proxy cache is also a plus, because it reduces the load on your server. (AOL has a proxy that stores frequently requested pages. You can "seed" the proxy simply by getting an AOL account and spidering your way across your site from the account.)

You can get some feel for the performance of your current ISP by looking in your modem program or TCP/IP tools for timeouts and retransmits. If there are a lot of timeouts, you'll also notice that Netscape itself will time out frequently and give you an error message when you try to connect.

One questionable thing ISPs may do to save money is have many dial-in POPs (Points of Presence) which are really just forwarded lines that get around tolls by keeping each forward distance within a local toll-free limit. The end result is that your call may be bounced through several switches before getting to a computer that's actually connected to the Internet, increasing latency and reducing the quality of the line, and therefore of throughput.

The performance of other ISPs can affect you even if you don't use them at all. If AOL's mail system crashes, so many message for AOL users may back up on your ISP's servers that they crash too, cutting off your access. No ISP is an island.

Co-location and mirroring

Many companies now provide server hosting facilities. The cost can be steep, but the benefits are also large. You can offload all the worry of keeping the server and connection up, and concentrate on content. These co-location companies usually have excellent connectivity to the local NAP, redundant connections, backup power, and they also provide mirroring to other parts of the country or the world.

For example, GlobalCenter (*http://www.globalcenter.net*) has a 100Mbps connection to the NAP in San Jose and mirroring locations on the East Coast and in London. It hosts *Yahoo!*, *Playboy*, and part of the Netscape site on racks of Sun and SGI servers. It has a diesel generator on-site for backup power.

Routers

Every router injects latency into the path a packet takes, because a packet must be received and its destination address examined before it can be routed on its way. Fast routers may add only 1 or 2 milliseconds, but slow routers can add 10 milliseconds or more. Router latency can easily be more significant than the latency imposed by sheer distance.

Old workstations used as routers may have fine bandwidth, but they will have much worse latency than purpose-built routers. Not only should you have real routers, but you should also get the fastest routers you can afford. Real routers don't have to deal with most of the tasks of regular OSs, such as managing multiple users and tasks, so they can be optimized for the one thing they do. Real routers have better buffering, more efficient interrupt handling, and busses specialized for moving data from one interface to another. For most routers, the bottleneck is not CPU power, but the bus traversal when copying data between the different interfaces. Even though dedicated routers are expensive, as hardware goes, they are actually quite cheap per port if you buy a router with many ports.

You can prioritize some kinds of traffic, like telnet traffic, at the router level. This is a kind of traffic shaping like that done by the dedicated boxes described in the "IP Traffic Management Products" section earlier in this chapter. Cisco Systems Internetwork Operating System (IOS) 11.1 for its routers explicitly gives the ability to tag certain IP packets as higher priority than other packets, helping to give some sessions better quality of service and leaving the remaining sessions whatever bandwidth is left over. Some routers also have useful tracing features that help you optimize router use.

IP switching (Layer 3 switching) has recently become popular. The name is a little misleading. IP switching isn't really switching at all in the sense of setting up a temporary dedicated connection. IP switches still produce packets that share the line with other packets. IP switching is basically route table lookups in hardware using special-purpose chips rather than software. IP switches are 2 to 3 times faster than conventional routing. See *http://www.ipsilon.com* for more information.

Link-level compression in routers does not necessarily bring any advantage, because the compression is usually done in software, putting an additional burden on the router's CPU. For heavily loaded routers, this compression load may decrease performance more than the compression increases it. You'll have to experiment to see if it works for you.

Packet size has a very big influence on the CPU power needed for routing. According to Craig Partridge, in his book *Gigabit Networking* (Addison Wesley), a 486 PC can usually route 1Gbps of 1KB packets, but it cannot route the same bandwidth of 128-byte packets. This is because the CPU is primarily occupied in determining where to send the packet, not in the actual sending. Large packets amortize the processing time over more data.

Placing Blame

It is possible to figure out more or less who's to blame for slow external network performance. If network performance varies considerably between day and night, the problem is likely to be the greater congestion of the Internet as a whole during the day. Remember that different parts of the U.S. and the world vary in Internet infrastructure, so you will see different performance depending on where you are. See *http://www.keynote.com/measures/business/business40.html.*

Here's a very cool trick for figuring out whether the problem is with your ISP or with a remote web server's ISP: Say you're getting poor download speed from a remote web server. Try simultaneously loading another remote web site in another copy of the browser. If your modem control program or network tool tells you that you're getting better total throughput when you simultaneously load from a different remote web server, then it's clear that your ISP had some room on the wire to send more packets to you, and the bottleneck is not in your ISP but in the overloaded remote web server or router along the path. If simultaneously loading from another remote web site makes no difference in throughput, then your ISP is at fault and you should complain (or you've reached the maximum throughput of your local connection). Be careful to start the experiment with empty caches.

The Future of the Internet

There are at least two alternative Internets being built right now to try to correct some of the deficiencies in the current system. Merit, at *http://www.merit.edu/*, has a lot of information on the latest happenings.

Internet2

Internet2 is a consortium of educational institutions that are building a network to include definable and measurable qualities of service, including latency and jitter specifications, bandwidth interrogation and reservation capabilities, and packet delivery guarantees. See *http://www.internet2.edu/.*

NGI

The U.S. government's Next Generation Internet (NGI), will also have very specific goals for service quality. The NGI will connect research institutions with high-speed networks that are one hundred to one thousand times faster than today's Internet and use the latest networking technologies. See *http://www.hpcc.gov/*.

PTTs

In some parts of the world, the phone company is a national monopoly called the PTT (Post, Telephone, Telegraph). Don't expect much from a PTT. Dealing with a PTT in some countries, both poor and rich, is like going back in time. There may be only rotary service, or even operators with patch cords. It may take many months, or even years, to get an ordinary phone line, and it is likely to be more expensive than in the U.S. It's ironic, but you can get a high-performance PC almost anywhere on earth, though more than half the world population does not have access to a telephone and has never made a telephone call. The situation is changing, as cellular infrastructure is being installed in many poor countries because it is cheaper and more flexible than installing land lines.

Key Recommendations

- Use the best modem that matches your ISP's modem.

- If on an Ethernet LAN, buy a card with 16K buffers or bigger.

- Use an ISP close in hops to your most-visited sites, like work.

- Use your employer's ISP if you will be accessing the employer's web site frequently, or dial in directly to the office LAN.

- Buy a real router rather than pressing an old workstation into service.

- Dedicate an Internet connection to your server. Don't use the connection for browsing, system management transmissions, or system administration traffic.

- Remember that you must have good data integrity to get good bandwidth.

10

Network Protocols

Power and Protocols

Let's take a minute to consider the politics of protocols, because politics are more likely than performance to determine which protocols are actually used and which remain only theoretical. Protocols have value in proportion to the number of users: a widely used protocol gives you the desirable ability to communicate with a large number of people. So when a protocol has enough users, it tends to attract even more users. Let's call this the snowball effect, because a simple snowball thrown down the side of a mountain can grow to be an avalanche. The snowball effect doesn't particularly care if the communications protocol is high performance. Just being able to communicate at all with huge numbers of people is valuable. This is exactly what happened with HTTP. It's not a particularly efficient protocol, but it has provided great value through its ubiquity.

Open protocols are at the core of the Internet and the Web. TCP/IP, HTTP, HTML, Java, and CORBA are all open protocols. There are many competing definitions of "open" that serve the needs of the parties doing the defining. I say a protocol is open if the complete specification is publicly available for use or implementation at no cost. Open protocols tend to spread faster than closed protocols because they add nothing to the price of software that uses them. Open protocols were essential to the development of the free Internet software that gave rise to the Web. Paying even a small price for software is always a barrier to acceptance, if only because of the overhead involved in making the payment.

Open protocols also tend to benefit the end user more than closed protocols, because multiple compatible implementations of the protocol compete in quality, performance, and cost. For example, because no one owns the HTTP protocol, there are many different web servers and clients, which vary in both price and performance, and the efficiency of these implementations has been increasing. Another critical factor in the success of HTTP is its simplicity. The most common cause of death among open protocols is sheer bloat and complexity. All of the above mentioned protocols, with the exception of CORBA, are relatively simple and have excellent prospects for the future.

If open protocols benefit users, why do we still have closed protocols? One reason is that businesses are motivated not by user benefit, but by money. There is a huge monetary incentive to be the sole implementor of a successful closed protocol, while it is much harder, though not impossible, to make money from an open protocol. Many open protocols come out of government research projects because these projects are not usually profit-oriented. The incentive to remain closed comes from the possibility that the closed protocol may snowball into a world-wide de facto standard. If this happens, the sheer ubiquity of the protocol will force users to purchase the implementation to communicate, increasing the company's market domination still further. Eventually, everyone will have to purchase the implementation, regardless of its quality. This is not good for users, but it is great for business.

Still, closed protocols are not all bad: centralized control assures that the protocol will not fragment into incompatible dialects. If you consider that operating system APIs are actually protocols for communication between applications and operating systems, then you can see that this fragmentation is exactly what happened with Unix. Unix has better performance than Windows, but Unix vendors tried to distinguish themselves with proprietary features which made it impossible for any one application to run on all versions of Unix. That is, it became impossible for Unix applications to communicate with other Unix operating systems, although the situation has improved with the widespread use of the Posix standard. Windows became a monolithic success partly because there was exactly one API; however, that has now changed with the introduction of various flavors of Windows 95 and NT.

Java is an interesting twist on this situation. The Java specification is publicly available at no charge, and others are free to reimplement it from this specification,* yet the specification remains the property of Sun Microsystems. Customers can be assured that the Java specification will not fragment, but they don't have to worry that they will be trapped into using only one implementation. On the other hand, Sun retains quite a bit of power because it can extend Java in ways favorable to itself. This seems to be a good compromise between open and closed protocols.

In the larger sense, the story of communication protocols is really nothing new. The English language is an example of how an open protocol can benefit its originators. The British imposed English as the official language in their colonies

---

* A license to Sun's implementation of Java, however, is not free.

around the world. Now that English is the most widespread business language, it continues to snowball in market share because it is valuable for communication. The British (and Americans) still benefit from this, as they can travel and do business widely without learning another language. What's new with the Internet is the speed with which protocols can propagate.

Factors Affecting Network Protocol Performance

Network protocols have a combination of properties that affect their performance. Most of the properties in this list are discussed in Andrew Tannenbaum's book, *Computer Networks* (Prentice Hall):

Fixed- versus variable-sized packets/cells/frames
> You can build more efficient hardware for fixed-length packets (usually called cells) such as ATM cells because you know, for example, the exact buffer sizes needed for a given performance. You also know that you can use the very efficient cross-bar switch, where each input is directly connected to each output.

Piggybacking
> Some protocols allow you to send an acknowledgment of the previous packet attached to the current packet for greater efficiency. TCP supports piggybacking with *delayed ACK*, where an acknowledgment is delayed for a moment, allowing the acknowledging application to send a data reply along with the ACK. See RFC 1122 for details.

Pipelining versus ACK-ing each packet
> The *window* is the number of packets that you send without getting an acknowledgment. The optimum window size depends on the length of the cable in bits, that is, the maximum number of bits in transit on the cable at any moment. For a longer or more reliable cable, a larger window is more efficient. See Tannenbaum's book for a detailed explanation.

Full/half duplex
> Full-duplex protocols can transmit in both directions simultaneously. Half-duplex protocols transmit in both directions, but not at the same time.

Errors
> The optimum packet size depends on the error rate. If no errors are possible, bigger packets amortize the header overhead and network interrupt handling time better. If there is a high likelihood of errors, small packets make retransmissions less costly.

Number of hops
> If there are a large number of hops between you and a particular destination, you can take advantage of parallelism with smaller packets. You can't move

data from one router to the next until the entire packet is received, so if you have large packets, the bits spend a longer time within one router before beginning to move on to the next. If you have small packets, then many of them can be in transit between the endpoints at the same time. It's like using trucks versus small cars for carrying goods: it's inefficient to carry freight in lots of small cars on a highway, but in a town with many stop lights, the cars will start up faster than the trucks and get the goods through more quickly, even though they have more overhead.

Layers

Remember that networking is built on layers of protocols: HTTP runs on TCP which runs on IP which usually runs on Ethernet. Tuning a high layer will not help if the layers below are the problem. Start with the physical layer and work your way up when looking for network inefficiencies.

The Protocols of the Web

Following are descriptions of the most important network protocols for the Web with performance information on each. Lower layers are presented first.

ARP

The Address Resolution Protocol (ARP) is what translates IP addresses to Ethernet's hardware addresses, also known as Media Access Control (MAC) addresses. A host needing to get an IP packet to a final destination on the same LAN as itself sends out an ARP broadcast asking if anyone knows the MAC address assigned to the desired IP. The machine with the target IP should answer the ARP request.

ARP is cached for a timeout period, and is generally quite efficient. It can be a problem, however, if it is used in place of true routing. Clients should be configured to send packets directly to the local router if no one on the LAN claims them. It may seem clever to have the router send an ARP reply for all addresses (called proxy ARP), rather than just the addresses not on the local subnet, but this puts a big load on the router and network because all packets then have to be examined by the router. See *Managing IP Networks with Cisco Routers*, by Scott Ballew (O'Reilly & Associates).

PPP

PPP is a link-level protocol for carrying any network-level protocol, unlike SLIP, which carries only IP. If you are using a modem to connect to the Internet directly, chances are you're using PPP. PPP frames use checksums to flag errors in transmission; a frame with an invalid checksum is retransmitted, slowing perceived speed. A PPP frame is often 1500 bytes because that size allows it to carry one Ethernet packet, but the size of the frame is negotiated by the copies of PPP at both ends of the link. PPP generally drops the connection of a line with too many checksum errors.

Routing Protocols

Routing protocols such as RIP, OSPF, and BGP are beyond the scope of this book. See the aforementioned *Managing IP Networks with Cisco Routers*, by Scott Ballew, for a good explanation of router configuration. *TCP/IP Illustrated, Volume 1*, by Richard Stevens (Addison Wesley), also has good explanations of routing protocols.

IP

The Internet Protocol (IP) is the network-layer protocol of the Internet. HTTP runs on TCP, which runs on IP. See *TCP/IP Illustrated* for an in-depth explanation of IP. The basic facts you need to know for performance tuning are that DNS names are mapped to 4-byte IP addresses, and that IP packets find their destinations through routers, which make decisions at branch points in the Internet about where the packet should go next. Both of these facts are sources of latency: names have to be resolved and route decisions have to be made for each HTTP request.

In spite of all the hype about the Internet making distance irrelevant, distance—at least distance as measured in terms of router hops—still matters, since each hop adds latency. For this reason, it is important to look at your server logs for customer distribution and try to locate servers near your customers.

Keep in mind that IP was designed to use dynamic routing to bypass down or slow routers, so the route between two hosts on the Internet may change from one moment to the next. It is possible for the sending host to request an exact path through the Internet to another host. This is known as *source routing*, but it works only if all the routers along the way agree to it. They generally don't, for security reasons; a user could use source routing to make a packet appear to come from somewhere it didn't. On an intranet, where you have control over the routers, you can set up static routing tables rather than letting the tables dynamically update depending on conditions. This has a performance hazard: an error in the static routing table can cause a time-consuming ICMP redirect message to be generated for every packet sent to an incorrect gateway, even if the redirect message lets the packets find their correct destination.

The maximum IP packet size is 64 kilobytes with a minimum of 42 bytes of overhead per packet, so most HTTP transfers could fit easily in a single packet, given that the average HTTP transfer is 10 kilobytes. This does not mean that only one packet is sent per request and reply—the TCP setup and teardown is complex and requires multiple packet exchanges. In addition, packets are subject to fragmentation into smaller pieces to fit routers along the path with a Maximum Transmission Unit (MTU) of less than 64K. TCP has a similar parameter called Maximum Segment Size (MSS) that should be 40 bytes less than the MTU, which is an IP parameter. The IP header and TCP header are both 20 bytes, so the maximum TCP data segment can be only the MTU minus 40 bytes without fragmentation. Fragmentation slows down a transfer, because the fragments have to be reassembled into a coherent whole by TCP. A well-tuned intranet will have the same MTU from end to end, but there is not much you can do about small MTUs on the Internet as a whole.

Your MTU setting is the size of the largest IP packet you will accept from the network. It should be set to your ISP's MTU; there is no point in setting it larger, because you will never get a packet larger than the ISP's MTU, and there is no point in setting it smaller, because you don't need to worry about fragmentation once a packet has reached you. If you are using PPP, the MTU will be 1500 by default. This is a reasonable value because it is also the maximum Ethernet packet size and most ISPs use Ethernet internally. To see the MTU of your network interfaces under Unix, use the command *ifconfig -a*.

When a packet size exceeds the MTU of the sender or the MRU of the receiver, it must be broken up and resent as multiple packets. Here's a little script I wrote to *ping* my ISP's router with packets ranging in size from 64 bytes to 4000 bytes and to save the output to a file easily plottable with *gnuplot*:

```perl
#!/usr/local/bin/perl -w

$| = 1;   # Don't buffer so we can interrupt and not lose data.

open(OUT, ">out");
print OUT "# Latency vs ICMP ping packet size.\n";

LOOP:
for ($i=64; $i<4000; $i++) {
    $_ = `ping -c1 -n -s$i 1.2.3.4`;
    m!100% packet loss! && next LOOP;
    m!(\d+) data bytes.*= (.*)/(.*)/(.*) ms!s;
    print OUT "$1 $3\n";
}
```

Figure 10-1 shows the resulting plot. The MTU of my machine was 1500, but perhaps the MRU of the receiving machine was less, accounting for the displacement of discontinuity from multiples of 1500. The overhead for IP is at least 20 bytes, overhead for ICMP is 8 bytes, and there is also a `struct timeval` which should be simply 2 `ints` of 4 bytes each. So the overhead in the packet cannot account for the fact that fragmentation seems to be occurring at about 1250 bytes.

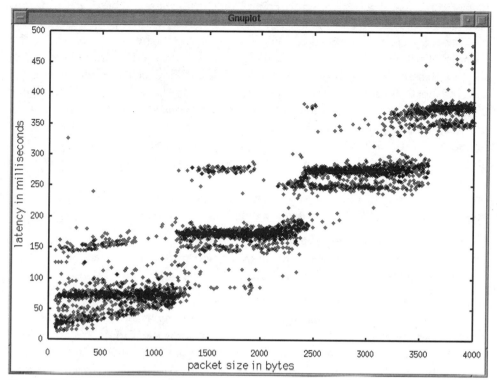

Figure 10-1. Packet fragmentation

You can get the source code for a version of *traceroute* that finds MTUs along the route from the code associated with Stevens, *TCP/IP Illustrated, Volume 1*, which is at *ftp://ftp.uu.net/published/books/stevens/tcpipiv1.tar.Z*. Also note that Solaris 2.*x* includes MTU discovery in the kernel. There is now a standard for MTU discovery, specified in RFC 1191. MTU discovery works by a machine's sending out a large IP packet with the Don't Fragment (DF) option set in the IP header. When the packet hits a router or bridge with a lower MTU, the router will generate an ICMP "Can't Fragment" reply. The sending machine will get the reply and then try a smaller MTU. This continues until an MTU that works along the entire route is discovered.

DNS and Trivial FTP (TFTP) use packets of only 512 bytes maximum because fragmentation is guaranteed not to occur for packets of less than 576 bytes. So you could say that 576 is the minimum maximum transmission unit. On an Ethernet LAN, the MTU is generally set to 1500 bytes; this is the default configuration for many clients, such as Windows 95, but on the Internet it is sometimes a better idea to set the MTU to 576. You can use the modified *traceroute* program mentioned earlier to find out about the MTU between yourself and points you commonly visit.

IP can carry messages intended to control the IP flow itself. These are appropriately called Internet Control Message Protocol (ICMP) packets. Some of the possible messages are that the packet could not be sent, that the packet exceeded the number of router hops allowed, that the packet was directed to an incorrect gateway, or that the remote host is reachable. This last kind of ICMP message is the basis of the Unix *ping* program used to check on the status of remote hosts. *ping* is disabled on many ISPs because it has often been abused; it is simple to use *ping* to send so many ICMP status check messages that the ISP's servers' performance is ruined. This can also be done with TCP SYN packets asking to initiate a connection. These abuses are known as ping flooding and SYN flooding, which are instances of *denial of service* (DOS) attacks. It is possible to track down the origin of *ping* and SYN flooding: there is a free tool from MCI called DOS Tracker that helps you do so at *ftp://ftp.mci.net/outgoing/dostrack742812.tar*.

See Chapter 2, *Capacity Planning*, for information on IP multicasting, which is an effective way to save bandwidth on information sent to many users at a specific time, for example, in real-time audio broadcasts.

Note that TCP/IP implementations vary in efficiency. The latency of a TCP/IP implementation is proportional to how much buffering is done before the user process can receive incoming data, and to how long the CPU takes to process each segment. A big IP packet will monopolize the line until it gets through, potentially blocking a smaller but more time-critical packet, like a packet of real-time voice data.

Van Jacobson compression reduces IP header size by using the fact that the headers in a group of sequential IP packets are mostly the same. It compresses only the headers, not the data being sent, and is most useful for large transfers.

TCP

Transmission Control Protocol (TCP) was designed to create a reliable connection on top of unreliable media by breaking up a transmission into IP packets, assigning them numbers, and retransmitting packets that are not acknowledged as received within a certain time interval. It also takes into account that the packets may not be received in the same order as they were transmitted, and automatically rearranges them. TCP was designed with certain assumptions in mind, for example, that connections would be relatively infrequent, that the amount of data transferred would be relatively large, and that correctness and completeness were much more important than performance. These assumptions fit FTP, but not HTTP, which typically requires many very short-lived connections in rapid sequence, each transferring only a few kilobytes. The importance of absolute correctness and completeness for HTTP transfers is debatable.

To set up or shut down a TCP connection requires several exchanges of packets between client and server, which is considerable overhead on a typical HTTP data transfer of 10KB. Since we need to send or receive three packets to set up the connection, a minimum of two packets to send a request and get a reply, and two packets to tear down a TCP connection, a minimum of seven IP packets must go across the network for even the smallest request.

You cannot change the fact that web servers use HTTP, so what can you do about the performance hit associated with the use of TCP? Since implementations of HTTP and TCP are becoming more aware of each other, one thing you can do is use the most recent implementations of each. TCP is built into the Unix kernel and is upgradable with patches if you don't have the most recent kernel. Solaris 2.6, in particular, is aware of HTTP's needs. As for HTTP, use a web server that understands HTTP 1.1, which has the ability to use one TCP connection for many file transfers, a process known as persistent connections, or less formally, *keepalives*. See Chapter 13, *Server Software*, for information on which servers use HTTP 1.1.

TCP parameters

TCP has many parameters that can be adjusted to affect network performance. A primary concern is avoiding retransmission of packets that are received intact but are delayed because of the latency inherent in the Internet. The default settings may work fine on a low-latency LAN, but then may wind up causing unneeded retransmission on the Internet. Under Solaris, many TCP/IP parameters can be changed in a running kernel with the *ndd* command. The *ndd* timing parameters are in milliseconds. You can see *ndd* parameters, even if you are not *root*, by using the command ndd /dev/tcp \?, but you cannot change anything with *ndd* unless you are *root*.

Listen queue length

TCP keeps connections that it cannot immediately handle in a queue of fixed size, often called the *listen queue* or the *backlog*, and simply drops connections beyond that. To the user, a server that cannot accept new connections is as bad as a server that has died. The bursty nature of HTTP traffic conflicts with the low default setting, resulting in dropped connections that actually could have been handled. Increase the queue length to be at least as large as the listen queue configured for the web server software, but note that a larger queue will take more RAM. The Netscape Commerce server defaults to a 128-entry listen queue, for example, so the queue should be adjusted to 128 or more. Some people recommend going as high as 1024, but most servers won't ever have that many pending connections. Under Solaris, the listen queue parameter has been split into a "completed handshake" queue and a "connections with an incomplete handshake" queue. Limiting the number of connections with incomplete handshakes protects against SYN flooding, a kind of denial of service attack. You can adjust the Solaris completed handshake listen queue size like this:

```
/usr/sbin/ndd -set /dev/tcp tcp_conn_req_max_q 128
```

Under Linux 2.0, change the listen queue by changing SOMAXCONN in the *include/linux/socket.h* file from its default of 128 and recompiling the kernel.

Retransmission delay

If TCP does not receive a segment acknowledgment within a certain interval of time, it considers the segment lost and sends another copy. The default timeout is 200 milliseconds, which is fine on a LAN, but sometimes inadequate for the much larger latencies of the Internet. If you simply use the default, you may end up sending several identical packets, when you could just be sending one—a waste of bandwidth. A reasonable setting for a high latency environment is 1000 milliseconds. The Unix *snoop* utility can give you a feel for how your network is running and whether you are retransmitting unnecessarily. The Mac TCP Monitor tool is a good way to see retransmissions on the client side if your clients are Macs. The retransmission delay parameter is known as *RTOmax* on Windows.

The tradeoff with retransmission delay is that an increase in the timeout will make a lossy connection run more slowly than it would otherwise. It is usually best to leave the settings as they are by default under Solaris 2.6.

A more precise way to monitor the number of retransmissions under Solaris is to use the command:

```
netstat -s
```

In the output from the command, compare tcpOutDataSegs to tcpRetrans-Segs and tcpOutDataBytes to tcpRetransBytes. If you are retransmitting more than 20% of the segments or bytes, try setting the retransmission interval higher and reexamine the *netstat* output.

```
/usr/sbin/ndd -set /dev/tcp tcp_rexmit_interval_initial 1000
```

CLOSE_WAIT interval

This is how long a socket will be unavailable for reuse by another client after it has been closed. If it is set too low, you may reuse the socket and get garbled data if a TCP segment that actually belonged to the last connection arrives late. If it is set too high, you may run out of TCP connections. Ideally, you should set it to wait just long enough that no valid TCP segments for that socket could still be in transit. Sixty seconds is a good starting point, and this is what BSD uses for a default. For an explanation of the tradeoffs, see Chapter 18 of *TCP/IP Illustrated.*

```
/usr/sbin/ndd -set /dev/tcp tcp_close_wait_interval 60000
```

Keepalive interval

TCP has a keepalive option that is not related to the HTTP 1.1 keepalive (persistent connection) option. TCP connections do not carry any traffic at all unless one side needs to send data to the other, so there is no polling or other network overhead on an idle connection. This means that one side of a connection can go down and the other side won't know about it until it tries to contact the other side, if ever. This is not a particular problem for web clients, but it can be a resource-sapping hazard for servers maintaining memory buffers for network connections that no longer exist. Clients frequently disappear without properly shutting down the connection because users shut off the modem or computer; eventually, the server would run out of memory if there were not some way to detect a connection that won't be used again. It may be the proper responsibility of the web server to check these connections, but there is a TCP Keepalive option in most TCP implementations to check the other end at regular intervals. The default interval is typically two to eight hours, but for a busy web server it should be reduced to the maximum amount of time a user might reasonably be idle while loading or using a page, say half an hour.

If *netstat* shows you a large number of connections in the `FIN_WAIT_2` state, that means that clients are not properly shutting down TCP connections. Try reducing the keepalive interval to fix this. If you reduce it too much, clients who are still actually using a connection will find themselves disconnected abruptly. See *http://www.apache.org/* for a discussion of the `FIN_WAIT_2` problem. It seems that clients disconnected for exceeding the `KeepAliveTimeout` for HTTP 1.1 may not be shutting down the connection correctly.

```
/usr/sbin/ndd -set /dev/tcp tcp_keepalive_interval 1800000
```

Receive window

The TCP receive window is also known as the Receive WINdow (RWIN) or Rx Window. It is the amount of data allowed to be outstanding on the Internet without acknowledgment at any one time. This limits the number of TCP segments the sender can push out at any one time. A typical receive window is 32KB, so a server could send at most 32KB without getting an ACK that data was received. This is how a slow TCP receiver such as a web client deals with a fast TCP sender such as a web server; it is a flow control mechanism.

With every acknowledgment, the TCP receiver also sends the amount of data it can still accept at the moment. This amount is known as the *offered window*, and is the receive window less the amount of data the receiver still has to drain from its socket connection. The offered window is necessarily less than or equal to the receive window. See section 20.3 of *TCP/IP Illustrated* for a detailed explanation.

You want a receive window large enough to keep the pipeline as full as the receiver can handle, but too large a window will have negative effects. ISPs often allocate only a fixed number of IP packet buffers on their routers per dial-in port; a typical number of IP packet buffers is 10. This means that a window that is too large will result in buffer overflow and costly retransmits. Another hazard of a too large receive window is that a lost packet will result in the retransmission of all data after the last ACK, even though most of the data may have been successfully received.

It is a good idea to set the receive window size to be an integer multiple of the TCP Maximum Segment Size (MSS) so that a large data stream can efficiently fill the receive window without fragmentation. Try setting your receive window at four or eight times your MSS.

The receive window is limited by your socket buffer size. Applications may ask for larger socket buffers, but there is no guarantee that the OS will give it to them. The OS may have a hard limit on socket buffer size written into it.

If you browse and download primarily from one ISP, use the ISP's MTU, MSS, and receive window settings for maximum efficiency.

An interesting flaw in TCP is that a sufficiently long and fast connection will cause it to break, because the TCP sequence numbers will wrap around past 64K back to 0 before the receiving end can ACK the first segment. This is solved in the next generation of TCP.

On a Solaris client, you can set the receive window like this:

```
/usr/sbin/ndd -set /dev/tcp tcp_recv_hiwat 65536
```

Slow start

Some recommend disabling TCP slow start, which is flow control from the TCP sender's point of view. Using slow start, the sender will put only one TCP segment (and therefore only one IP packet) out onto the network, and wait until it is acknowledged. If the first packet is successfully acknowledged, the sender will send two segments, then four, and so on, up to the congestion window maximum of the sender, which specifies the maximum amount of data that can be in transit at any point. In this way, the amount of data put onto the network is guaranteed to be within the capacity of the receiver to absorb it. See page 285 in *TCP/IP Illustrated* or RFC 2001 for more about slow start.

One problem with slow start on the Web is that new TCP connections are very frequent and very short-lived. Slow start tends to waste time figuring out an optimum transmission rate for a connection that is about to be closed anyway, although it may indeed be useful for large web transmissions over slow links.

A more serious problem with slow start is that Windows clients have a TCP/IP stack that expects a server to send out two packets to begin a slow start, rather than one packet. This is not correct behavior, but most Unix servers have adapted to it. The exception is Solaris, which by default sends out only one packet and then waits for an ACK. Windows clients of such servers receive the first packet and silently wait for the second one. The client times out, then sends the ACK, so there will be a timeout delay when you have the default configuration of a Solaris server and a Windows client. This delay happens for each TCP connection, that is, for each image and other component of a web page, unless HTTP 1.1 persistent connections are being used. The repeated timeouts can double the time it takes for a client to get a page. The solution here is to tell Solaris 2.6 (or Solaris 2.5.1 with TCP patches loaded) to start TCP transmissions with two packets instead of one:

```
/usr/sbin/ndd -set /dev/tcp tcp_slow_start_initial 2
```

Another problem with slow start is that the congestion window is limited to 64KB in most implementations of TCP. It is quite easy to exceed this on a 100Mbps Ethernet LAN. If a 100Mbps LAN has a latency of 10 milliseconds, you could have 1Mbit (= 125KB) in transit. The RFC 1323 TCP Large Window Extensions allows you to expand the congestion window for these cases, and this is implemented in Solaris 2.6.

You can set the maximum congestion window on Solaris like this:

```
/usr/sbin/ndd -set /dev/tcp tcp_cwnd_max 65536
```

A server that uses slow start may cause problems for a client using delayed ACK, described in the section "Piggybacking" earlier in this chapter. If the server is sending more data than can fit in one packet, then the client application may not send a response until it gets all the data. The delayed ACK is wasted here. NT clients have this problem, but Solaris clients do better because they do not use delayed ACK on the first packet of a transmission.

Maximum Segment Size

The Maximum Segment Size (MSS) is the largest TCP segment that a connection will accept. It is announced by the TCP requester when the connection is established. The sender can use any smaller segment size but may not exceed the MSS.

The tradeoff here is to make the MSS small enough to avoid fragmentation, yet large enough so that the overhead of the IP and TCP headers is a relatively small fraction of the entire IP packet. The Solaris default is 536, which is a reasonable value for web services.

Please see Appendix C, *Solaris 2.x—Tuning Your TCP/IP Stack and More*, taken from Jens-S. Voeckler's web page, for a much more detailed treatment of Solaris TCP parameters.

Monitoring TCP

Volumes have been written about network monitoring, so I'm not going to try to duplicate that content here. See *System Performance Tuning*, by Mike Loukides (O'Reilly & Associates).

Regardless of exactly which tools you use to monitor TCP, there are a few patterns to look for. Input errors have many causes: Your cable may be too long, damaged, or just the wrong kind. You may have NIC connector problems. CRC errors may mean network problems or just that the network device driver has buffer overflows. Output errors may imply that the NIC connector is damaged or that the network is simply not responding.

You can figure out if you're retransmitting due to timeouts: Compare output segments to segment retransmissions or output bytes to bytes retransmitted. If you're retransmitting more than 20%, try increasing the TCP retransmit interval. If you're not replying in time for the server, it will retransmit to you, resulting in unacceptable TCP segments or TCP resynchronization pauses. Look for dropped packets, which imply that you have buffer overflows that could be solved with bigger buffers.

Here are several of the better known network monitoring programs:

netstat
> *netstat* is a standard Unix program for monitoring network connections. Type `man netstat` on almost all Unix systems for more information. *netstat* is usually available to all users, not just *root*. *netstat -a* shows you all the current connections on your machine.
>
> *netstat* gives statistics on network performance such as buffer overruns and packet drops. Under Linux, you can simply look at */proc/net/dev* for much of the same information.

snoop
> *snoop* is a Solaris utility that puts the Ethernet card into promiscuous mode, meaning that it can see every packet on the local Ethernet segment. You must be *root* to have permission to use this. It is extremely useful for seeing the contents of network data packets, but it tends to produce a flood of data.

tcpdump
> *tcpdump* is another Unix utility using the promiscuous mode of Ethernet cards. For more information, see *TCP/IP Illustrated* and the associated source code.

UDP

The User Datagram Protocol (UDP) is a transport layer protocol on top of IP, like TCP, but connectionless and unreliable, unlike TCP. UDP, however, has better performance than TCP because it does so little. It is very useful for situations where the application can handle reliability (that is, it can request retransmission of missing packets) and where not every packet is needed but speed is very important, for example, when sending streaming audio over the Internet. DNS, NFS, and the RealAudio protocol all use UDP.

DNS

Domain Name Service (DNS) is a UDP-based service that resolves fully qualified names (FQNs) like *www.umich.edu* to IP addresses like 141.211.144.53. This is critical for the Web, because most sites are referred to by FQN both when typed in by hand and when used as links in a web page. One DNS performance tip is that you don't have to use it. If DNS is very slow for you, use IP addresses rather than domain names in your HTML so that the browser does not have to take time to find the IP address. It is a bit confusing for users to see an IP address appear in their browsers' "Location:" field, but the title of the web page should be able to orient them well enough.

DNS is a hierarchical distributed database. If your local DNS server doesn't have the IP address you're looking for, it knows whom next in the hierarchy to ask. Looking up an uncommon name may take a few seconds because the request may get bumped up the hierarchy several times.

Unix users can also use FQNs entirely without a DNS server by resorting to the primitive original method for mapping FQNs to IP addresses: simply add an entry to your */etc/hosts* file. This makes for very fast lookup, but is not dynamically updated like DNS servers and is considered very bad form in system administration. You can rely on */etc/hosts* only for addresses you control, but there is nothing stopping you from putting in any name-address mapping. Here is an example */etc/hosts* file from a Linux machine:

```
#
# hosts          This file describes a number of hostname-to-address
#        mappings for the TCP/IP subsystem.  It is mostly
#        used at boot time, when no name servers are running.
#        On small systems, this file can be used instead of a
#        "named" name server.  Just add the names, addresses
#        and any aliases to this file...
#

127.0.0.1        localhost
141.211.144.53   www.umich.edu

# End of hosts.
```

Unix users can easily set up a DNS server on their own client machines. The advantage here is that DNS servers cache entries they've looked up, making subsequent access much faster. Netscape Navigator's DNS helper also caches DNS entries automatically for you.

Although DNS servers generally don't see a very large load, try to be sure that your DNS server and web server are not competing for bandwidth on your Internet connection. This may mean placing a DNS server inside your organization rather than relying on your ISP's DNS server. Note that DNS servers, like most Internet servers, tend to degrade in a nonlinear way, with performance dropping off rapidly after a certain load.

See Chapter 2, *Capacity Planning*, for a discussion of round robin DNS.

NFS

The Network File System (NFS) from Sun Microsystems is a method of making a set of files on a remote system appear to be on the disk of local computer. "Remote" can mean across a WAN, but NFS is much more commonly used on LANs because its performance over WANs is usually not good. NFS is a stateless protocol. NFS Version 2 runs over UDP, and Version 3 runs over TCP. A well-tuned NFS server has much better throughput than most web servers, given the same hardware. This means it is feasible to use an NFS server to help scale web services, particularly if you are serving static content. You can set up multiple web servers and provide the content to each server from the same central NFS server to keep the content synchronized across all servers.

There is a caching mechanism for NFS called *cachefs*, which keeps a local copy of files served by NFS and greatly improves read performance for subsequent access. Write performance is much lower than read performance for NFS because writes must be committed to a non-volatile medium such as disk, according to the NFS protocol. Note that each directory requires an NFS lookup, so looking up a path with many directories over NFS results in a big performance loss the first time you do it. See *Managing NFS and NIS*, by Hal Stern (O'Reilly & Associates).

Poor NFS usage can hurt web server performance a lot. For example, you don't want your web server log file NFS mounted, because a block of the log will have to be appended and copied back to the NFS server for each hit. In fact, I had a similar problem when appending mail messages to my *mbox*. The *mbox* file was on the NFS server because it was in my home directory, which was NFS mounted. I noticed that as the *mbox* grew bigger, appending new messages to it got slower. A quick use of *snoop* showed that a large piece of my *mbox* was being copied to my machine, appended, and copied back to the NFS server. The answer for me (there are many) was to simply make the *mbox* in my home directory a link to */opt/mbox,* which was actually on my local disk. The performance problem went away, but the local disk is not backed up by my system administrator, as the NFS server is.

HTTP

HyperText Transfer Protocol (HTTP) is the protocol at the core of the Web. It was created at the CERN research institute in Switzerland by Tim Berners-Lee, originally as a way for scientists to share research papers. It was designed to be simple and extensible, but it was also designed for delivering static content, which is the origin of its inefficiency as a protocol for transaction processing. It certainly is a simple model: the client requests a document, the server returns it, and the connection is closed. That's all there was to it, at first. Although there's a significant amount of overhead involved in setting up the connection and tearing it down right away, this wasn't a problem at first, because most web servers were not getting hit hard enough for the webmaster to worry about performance issues. HTTP worked well.

HTTP was intended to serve the HyperText Markup Language (HTML), but note that there is nothing in the HTTP specification that says that the server must return HTML. HTTP can serve any document type. MIME types were later added to the headers created by web servers to help the client know what to do with the document type received. "Well-known" port 80 was quickly assigned to HTTP, freeing users from typing the port number in a URL and securing HTTP a place in the */etc/ services* file of Unix servers around the world.

Be sure to distinguish between browser page views and HTTP hits. From a user's perspective, he or she simply loads a page and gets text and graphics and maybe an applet or audio clip. The download seems unified. From the server's perspective, there is no page view, only a series of requests for files: first an HTML file, then some images, then an applet and a video. The server does not know or care that the initial HTML file contained references to later files that it serves. In fact, when responding to requests from multiple clients, it is common to see in the server log files that the replies to those clients are actually interleaved in time. The operation of sending a file to a client is referred to as a *hit* on the server, or as an HTTP operation.

Stateless and connectionless

HTTP is stateless, meaning that the protocol does not have any provision for memory about what the server or client has done in the past; multiple states for the server or client do not exist. HTTP is also called connectionless, because there is no persistent connection between server and client. (At least, there wasn't until HTTP 1.1.) Every page the user requests appears to the server as if this were the first time it has dealt with this user. The server simply sets up another connection and returns the requested page. This allows the HTTP protocol to be very simple, which in turn allows it to be rapidly implemented on every kind of machine that speaks TCP/IP.

Connectionless protocols contrast with typical client/server transactions, where the client opens a connection to the database (in two-tier) or application server (in three-tier) and the server keeps the connection open until the client explicitly logs off. The client/server user can be in different states: logged in, authenticated, editing a document, and so forth. Statefulness is essential for many complex functions, such as authentication and transaction processing. Although not provided by HTTP, statefulness and/or persistent connections can be provided by extra software written using CGIs, Java, or CORBA. The actual state mechanism can be cookies passed back and forth between browser and server, information logged on the server and indexed by the requester's IP address or cookie, or direct socket connections, among other mechanisms.

Connectionlessness does have the good side effect that HTTP scales much better than client/server. When a client is disconnected, which from the server's point of view is nearly all the time, the server does not need to maintain any network resources for that client. This means that a single HTTP server can support far more clients than if the connections were continuous.

Ironically, even though HTTP is connectionless, the individual HTTP connections are carried over TCP, which does maintain the state of a connection in order to assure that all packets in a transmission are received and assembled in the correct order. There is considerable overhead in setting up or tearing down a TCP connection, known as a *three-way handshake*. See the "TCP" section earlier in this chapter for a more detailed explanation of TCP and performance. The real TCP performance hit comes from the fact that this handshake must be performed by server and client for every file sent, both for the HTML and for each embedded image, applet, etc. It might have been a better choice to use UDP, which does not require any initialization, and to leave the checking for packet completeness and ordering up to the browser, but that's not the way things happened.

Asymmetric

Note that HTTP data transfer is very asymmetric; requests are quite small, in the tens or perhaps hundreds of bytes, while replies are much bigger. So the output from the server is much more likely to be a bottleneck than the input to the server. Even though the throughput from the server is much larger, the *number* of packets flowing in each direction is similar because the client needs to send TCP ACKs back to the server to acknowledge data packets.

Text-based

HTTP is a text-based protocol, so it is possible to interact with a web server simply by telnetting to the correct port (usually 80) and feeding it HTTP commands via the keyboard:

```
% telnet www.umich.edu 80
Trying 141.211.144.53...
Connected to www.umich.edu.
Escape character is '^]'
GET / HTTP/1.0

HTTP/1.1 200 OK
Date: Sun, 08 Feb 1998 18:35:25 GMT
Server: Apache/1.2.5
Connection: close
Content-Type: text/html

<html>
...
```

Seeing what a browser is up to is a little trickier, since the browser must make the first move. You can't just connect to someone's browser and start giving it commands. You can, however, write a little "server" that will accept a browser request and print out the request verbatim. In this way you can see exactly what the browser sends to the server. Here is the code for such a server written in Java:

```java
import java.io.*;
import java.net.*;

class Server {

    public static void main(String[] args) {
        try {
            String str;

            ServerSocket ss = new ServerSocket(new
Integer(args[0]).intValue());
            Socket s = ss.accept( );
            DataInputStream dis = new DataInputStream(s.getInputStream());
            while ((str = dis.readLine()) != null)
                System.out.println(str);
        }
        catch (Exception e) {}
    }
}
```

Compile and run it:

```
% javac Server.java
% java Server 8888
```

Now make a request from Netscape to retrieve the document at *http://local-host:8888/* and you see the request printed to standard output:

```
GET / HTTP/1.0
Connection: Keep-Alive
User-Agent: Mozilla/4.04 [en] (X11; I; Linux 2.0.0 i586)
Host: localhost:8888
Accept: image/gif, image/x-xbitmap, image/jpeg, image/pjpeg,
image/png, */*
Accept-Language: en
Accept-Charset: iso-8859-1,*,utf-8
```

In this request, you see several name-value pairs being sent by the browser. This is allowed by the HTTP standard. Note the use of the `Connection: Keep-Alive` header, which keeps the TCP connection open for receiving all of the embedded items in the page, such as images. Keeping the connection open is the default behavior of HTTP 1.1, but this requires the `Connection: Keep-Alive` header under HTTP 1.0. For a detailed explanation of browser-host communication, see *Web Client Programming with Perl*, by Clinton Wong (O'Reilly & Associates).

Compression

One of the header name-value pairs of interest from a performance perspective is the kind of compression used. There is currently no standard for compression of web documents, but Apache and some other servers are capable of producing the name-value pair `Content-encoding: x-gzip` to indicate the experimental (the **x-**) use of *gzip* compression of web documents. Remember that not all files can be compressed (or else you could compress every file down to a single bit) so sometimes it's not worth the time involved in applying compression and decompression to a file. As far as I know, only the Mosaic browser understands *gzip* compression directly, but others can be configured to look at the *.gz* suffix and run the file through *gunzip*.

Cache control

Another header name-value pair that can help performance is the `If-Modified-Since` header, which tells the server to return the document only if it has been modified since the last time the server looked at it. You can achieve a similar effect with the HTTP HEAD command, but this may involve two connections to the server: one to get the header of the document, and another to get the document if the cached copy is obsolete. The `If-Modified-Since` header can fulfill the request in the same connection that checks the currency of the document. It is automatically added by the browser for documents in the browser's cache. The server can send back an `Expires` header that forces pages to expire from the cache after a certain amount of time. This has a legitimate use, say, for pages of stock prices, but it has been abused to get a more accurate hit count for advertise-

ments (at the public network's expense), since advertisers are otherwise not able
to tell when an ad has been viewed out of the browser's cache.

The trailing slash

A URL pointing to a directory is technically supposed to end in a slash to indicate
to the server that the URL points to a directory. Nonetheless, most people leave off
the slash, forcing the server to figure out that the user is requesting not a file, but a
directory. Servers figure it out, but they have to go through the step of looking for a
nonexistent file first, which slows things down. They could then give you the index
file for the directory you gave them, but in practice, servers respond with a redirect
to the client, adding to network traffic and delaying the eventual response. It is better for your server if users provide the correct syntax with the trailing slash, so if
you publish a URL or embed links in HTML, use the correct syntax, e.g. *http://
www.someco.com/dir/*.

For example, Apache 1.2.4 responds with an HTTP redirect, sending a `Location:`
URL back to the client, which is the same URL with a slash appended. If we
request a directory named "dir" without the trailing slash from a server at
www.someco.com, this is what we would see on the network:

```
% telnet www.someco.com 80
Trying 127.0.0.1...
Connected to www.someco.com.

Escape character is '^]'.
GET /dir HTTP/1.0

HTTP/1.1 301 Moved Permanently
Date: Thu, 14 May 1998 03:41:58 GMT
Server: Apache/1.2.4
Location: http://www.someco.com/dir/
Connection: close
Content-Type: text/html

<HTML><HEAD>
<TITLE>301 Moved Permanently</TITLE>
</HEAD><BODY>
<H1>Moved Permanently</H1>
The document has moved <A HREF="http://www.someco.com/dir/">here</A>.<P>
</BODY></HTML>
Connection closed by foreign host.
```

HTTP 1.1 improvements

The World Wide Web Consortium (W3C) has considered the shortcomings of
HTTP 1.0 and made a large number of performance improvements, which are part
of the HTTP 1.1 specification. The specification for HTTP 1.1 is available at *http://
www.ics.uci.edu/pub/ieft/http/rfc2068.txt*.

The most significant improvement is the use of one TCP connection to retrieve multiple documents, known as persistent connections. This provides an economy of scale, since the overhead of setting up and tearing down the TCP connection is spread over several documents. By examining the header lines in the request issued by Netscape browser versions 1.0, you can better understand persistent connections even though they do not show "HTTP 1.1" in the server logs. The persistent connection timeout becomes an important web tuning parameter, especially when most clients are on slow connections, because each open connection consumes memory and other resources. When you have a great many HTTP 1.1 clients on slow connections, you accumulate so much simultaneous overhead that you should probably turn down the time of inactivity allowed before the connection is closed. You can see how many connections are open at the moment by running *netstat*, grepping for ESTABLISHED, and then piping that to *wc -l*, like this: `netstat | grep ESTABLISHED | wc -l`. Note that persistent connections work only for static content, not for CGI or server API output.

In addition, HTTP 1.1 allows multiple requests to be pending simultaneously, so you can issue another request before the current one has finished. This is known as pipelining. HTTP 1.0 forced each transfer within a single TCP connection to finish before the next one was allowed to begin. Browsers deal with this HTTP 1.0 restriction by opening several simultaneous TCP connections to the server, but it is no longer necessary for them to do so.

Downloads of a range of bytes in a document are also now allowed; previously, documents had to be downloaded in their entirety. Byte range downloads allow users to download part of a document to see whether they want to load the rest, then continue on to the rest without starting over. This also helps in cases where the transfer has been interrupted by a network failure.

Finally, HTTP 1.1 specifies MD5 digest authentication, meaning that a user password can be validated on the client, which not only is far faster than sending it to the server for validation, but also increases security, because the password is never sent over the network in the clear.

In summary, you should definitely use HTTP 1.1 if you can. It is already part of the Apache server and Netscape Enterprise Server 3.0. Internet Explorer 4.0 reports that it uses HTTP 1.1. Netscape Navigator 4.0 reports that it uses HTTP 1.0 but has some 1.1 features, such as persistent connections.

HTTPS

Secure HTTP (HTTPS), uses the Secure Socket Layer (SSL) protocol on port 443 by default. HTTPS encrypts all traffic, so you can be confident that your content will not be intelligible to anyone snooping Internet packets. HTTPS uses public-key encryption just long enough to exchange keys, and then it switches to private-key encryption for better performance. See *PGP: Pretty Good Privacy*, by Simson Garfinkel (O'Reilly & Associates), for more information on public versus private key encryption. HTTPS has a significant performance penalty associated with it that can be as high as tenfold. The problem is not the exchange of certificates at the beginning of the secure connection, but rather the overhead of encrypting and decrypting every byte sent across the wire. This is not a particular problem for small text transmissions, but it becomes onerous for larger web pages. You should use HTTPS only for the times you really need good security, not for your home page.

HTTP proxy request format

HTTP proxies accept HTTP requests in a slightly different format. Because your browser has connected to the proxy and not directly to the desired web server, the browser must tell the proxy which server to connect to. So rather than saying `GET / HTTP1.0`, the browser says `GET / http://server/index.html` and leaves the protocol up to the proxy.

FTP

The file transfer protocol (FTP) is an older cousin of HTTP. FTP uses many of the same design patterns as HTTP (for instance, status numbers to indicate connection results) and the setting up and tearing down of a TCP connection for every data transfer. FTP is different from HTTP in that it sets up a TCP control channel connection and leaves that connection up as long as the client desires to remain connected. The principal thing you need to know about FTP with respect to the web is that most browsers understand FTP and accept URLs beginning with "ftp://". Downloads using FTP have better performance than HTTP downloads. The browser knows enough to send the anonymous user ID to anonymous FTP sites. FTP fits the model that the TCP protocol was created for: relatively large transfers and infrequent connections.

NNTP

Network News Transport Protocol (NNTP) is usually used only for replicating articles posted to Usenet news groups, but can also be used to replicate web content, in effect distributing a site around the world for quick access. It also makes censorship of a web site much more difficult.

SNMP

The Simple Network Management Protocol (SNMP) is a standardized way to track the machines, applications, and bandwidth of your network. It is a valuable tool for performance tuning. SNMP originated in the Unix community, but it is now available on most platforms. There are many SNMP management tools to choose from, such as HP's OpenView and products from IBM, 3Com, Cabletron, Sun, and Cisco. You can avoid having SNMP traffic add to your production traffic by setting up a separate SNMP management network, although this is not always practical, for financial reasons.

Each monitored device or application is referred to as an *agent* and has a Management Information Base (MIB) that defines the information the agent tracks and what sort of remote control of the agent is allowed.

Remote MONitoring (RMON) is a set of extensions to SNMP that allow monitored devices to be more proactive about signalling errors, unlike the traditional polling mechanism used by SNMP. RMON II can monitor what kind of application traffic is on your network.

WebNFS

WebNFS is a new protocol from Sun Microsystems, the inventor of NFS. WebNFS eliminates the need for FTP by allowing read and write access to NFS servers over the Web. This avoids the tedious process of downloading, editing, and uploading to make simple changes to files. You can edit a file that you refer to with a URL of the form *nfs://server/path/filename*. WebNFS is more efficient than ordinary NFS because it does not require network traffic to look up each directory in a pathname. WebNFS is part of the Solaris 2.6 operating system, but it is not yet used in any browsers.

CORBA

The Common Object Request Broker Architecture (CORBA) is a specification for software object interaction across multiple platforms. CORBA has been under revision for many years, and it finally seems to be gaining widespread acceptance because it works well with the Web and, in particular, with Java. It allows access to legacy applications from anywhere on the Web by wrapping the applications in an object-oriented interface definition language (IDL). A component called an Object Request Broker (ORB), directs requests for services to the appropriate object. Java ORBs can be downloaded from the Web, making CORBA servers available to any web client that understands Java. Netscape now includes Visigenic's ORB. Other Java ORBs are available from Iona, Orbix, and Expersoft. There are also publicly available Java ORBs, such as JacORB.

Because the use of CORBA is so new, there is not much performance information available. It seems that the principal performance issue with CORBA is the number of times data must be copied between buffers in order to fulfill a request. If there is too much middleware involved, performance will suffer. Still, CORBA clearly has a large advantage over CGI in that you can invoke methods and services across the network without starting a process just to handle that call. CORBA also scales well, since objects can run on as many servers as you need, with the ORB dispatching method calls to appropriate objects, or even creating new objects if need be. Disadvantages of CORBA are that it is unnecessarily complex and that it does not gracefully handle remote object instantiation failure.

Remember that it's about a million times slower to instantiate an object over the network than locally, and that there is often no good mechanism to deal with instantiation failures or partial failures, which are much more likely over the network. Distributed objects work well for cases where most of the work is local computation, with occasional communication, but not very well in cases where lots of objects have to move back and forth across the wire.

The Voyager product from Objectspace (*http://www.objectspace.com*) had better performance than CORBA in simple *ping* tests I ran and is more elegant and easier to use. It is a freely available distributed object system for Java, but it does not yet specify integration with legacy systems, as CORBA does. It will eventually include CORBA compatibility.

X

Redirected X displays can easily use up all the bandwidth you throw at them. Every blink of a cursor, the flying stars of the Netscape logo—everything will generate network traffic. A busy screen saver redirected over the network is especially bad. You don't want your web server on a network that is being used for such traffic.

Key Recommendations

- Set a larger timeout for TCP retransmits for the Internet, because the Internet is slower than a LAN.

- Increase the TCP listen queue if you know it is overflowing.

- Don't let unused connections hang around for more than half an hour (not eight hours, as TCP originally specified).

- Use HTTP 1.1 if possible.

11

Server Hardware

Here we revisit computer hardware from the server perspective. Even though each client receives exactly as many bytes as the server sends, the server hardware needs to be more powerful than client hardware because the servers must be capable of handling many clients simultaneously. On the other hand, it is common for small web sites to overestimate just how much server power they really need. If your server is handling only one client every several seconds, then you can probably make do with the same hardware that would make a good web client. For the majority of sites, the network connection is more likely than server hardware to be the limiting factor.

Server tuning is the subject of many entire books, and the subject is much larger than I can present in a single chapter. For in-depth detail, some good books on the subject are: *System Performance Tuning*, by Mike Loukides (O'Reilly & Associates); *Sun Performance and Tuning, 2nd Edition*, by Adrian Cockcroft (Prentice Hall); *Configuration and Capacity Planning for Solaris Servers*, by Brian Wong (Prentice Hall); and *Optimizing Windows NT*, by Russ Blake (Microsoft Press).

How Server Hardware Is Different

Box on a Wire

A web server is essentially remote storage that copies data from its RAM or disk to the network connection upon request. It may not be a simple copy, since dynamic content or database access may be involved, but from the user's point of view, your web server is just one more mass storage device. Now, does a disk drive have a windowing system? No. Similarly, your web server does not need a windowing system, a video card, a monitor, or even a keyboard! In fact, a windowing system occupies a great deal of RAM and CPU time, so it is a drain on server performance. You don't have any choice if you're using a Windows or Mac web server, but on Unix systems you can simply turn off X Windows. NT and Unix have an additional reason not to use a windowing system: the currently active window has a higher execution priority than other processes. On Solaris for example, processes belonging to the currently selected window are bumped up in priority by 10 points (out of 100 or so). If you're not very careful with the windowing system, you can hurt web server performance simply by moving the mouse. It is better to do web server administration remotely over one or more telnet sessions from a different computer.

Web servers without monitors are known as *headless* servers.

Good I/O

The fundamental distinguishing feature of server hardware is high-performance I/O. Commodity PC hardware is limited by its legacy I/O subsystem, while server hardware is designed around I/O and can easily have ten times the I/O performance of the best PCs.

Multiple Busses

Servers usually have separate busses for L2 cache, I/O, RAM, and peripherals. This reduces contention and allows the use of appropriate hardware for each bus. Server busses may be packet switched, in the sense that a request is made over the bus and the bus is released until the response is ready, allowing requests to be interleaved with responses and improving throughput. Bus throughput is critical for servers, because a great deal of what a server does is simply copy data between network devices and storage devices.

Fast Disks

Servers should have separate high-speed SCSI disks for content and logging. IDE disks are not acceptable. Striping data over disk arrays is highly recommended to allow seeks to proceed in parallel.

Lots of Memory

Servers should have large amounts of RAM to reduce disk accesses. A good rule is to allow enough RAM to hold the complete OS and the most frequently accessed parts of your data set. Servers also tend to have large L1 and L2 caches, and may have the cache split between data and instruction caches, because data and instructions have different access patterns. The only memory faster than L1 cache is the set of registers on the CPU. Many megabytes of L2 cache is becoming common.

Unfortunately, the effectiveness of caching for server CPUs is reduced by the context switching that happens with every network interrupt. *httpd* code and network handling code displace each other from the caches.

Scalability

A server should be scalable to smoothly handle an increasing workload. Unix workstations have far more capacity for scaling by adding CPUs and RAM than PCs. Unix workstations scale up to 64 or 128 CPUs, depending on whom you ask, while PC hardware cannot generally handle the contention between more than 4 CPUs, as of this writing. Workstations also have better I/O bandwidth and more RAM expandability.

Network Interface Card

The Network Interface Card (NIC) provides the connection between the network cable and the server's bus. NICs fill a conceptually simple niche, but their variety reflects the many permutations possible between network cable, cable signalling protocol, and host computer bus. NICs take an incoming serial stream of bits and output a parallel stream onto the bus, and vice versa. Until recently, it could be assumed that the network connection would be far slower than the CPU and bus, but LAN network speeds have been increasing faster than CPU and bus speeds, so it is no longer a safe bet that your network card can be handled by your machine. Still, at the interface to the Internet, you can be fairly sure that your server will be more constrained by Internet access than by any other component, save perhaps disk.

NICs have on-board buffers, and a bigger buffer always gives you more flexibility. The buffer has historically been important for holding outgoing data until the network can deal with it all, but as mentioned, that situation is reversing, so the buffers will in the future tend to hold incoming data, waiting for the computer. In either case, a larger buffer makes a buffer overflow and consequent data loss less likely. Lost TCP/IP data is simply retransmitted, adding to overhead. Typically, 8-bit Ethernet cards have 8K buffers, while 16-bit cards have 16K buffers.

When a NIC has a complete unit of data from the network and is ready to forward it on to the computer's bus, it generates a hardware interrupt, which forces the CPU to save its current state and run the network card interrupt handler, which retrieves the data from the NIC's buffer and fills a data structure in memory. Therefore, a critical performance factor is how many interrupts per second the CPU, memory, and bus can handle from the NIC.

Another important measure of a server is how quickly it can get data from RAM or disk out to the network interface. This involves copying data from one place in memory to another, which is typical of server activity. Data is copied from the server's memory to the network interface card memory. Given a 1500-byte outgoing Ethernet packet, the OS must copy it—probably 4 bytes at a time—from RAM or cache out to the NIC buffer, so this copy would require 375 bus cycles to complete. The bcopy or memcpy library calls are often used here, so the efficiency of your server's implementation of these library calls is significant. This is also where the implementation of TCP/IP in your kernel becomes significant. If you have a poor implementation, it probably means the wait between the NIC's interrupt and the retrieval of a packet from the NIC's buffer is large, so additional packets arriving on the NIC may not find sufficient buffer space and may be dropped or overrun data in the buffer. This results in a costly retransmission of the lost packet.

You will get the best performance from the most recent network cards. Many network cards can now be upgraded by loading new code into their flash memory. The latest non-beta release of this code should give you the best performance.

It is possible to sidestep the use of the CPU for retrieving NIC buffer data by using a "busmastering" NIC, which is capable of moving data directly between the NIC buffer and the machine's memory without interrupting the processor. Busmastering cards have a performance advantage over non-busmastering cards but are more expensive, because they need more on-card intelligence. Intel has specified a method for interfacing NICs directly to PC hard disk, called the I2O specification, which will need operating system support. I2O should be available by the time you read this.

Bus

A bus is a set of parallel wires (usually 32, 64, 128, or 256 wires, plus error and protocol handling wires) embedded in a board forming the backbone of the computer. Other components, including CPU, disk, memory, and network cards, are connected to each other by their shared bus.

There may be more than one bus in a computer. PCs may have only one bus connecting everything. Server hardware, however, typically has at least two separate busses: a high-speed bus for connecting memory to the CPU, and a slower bus for connecting I/O to the CPU. System busses lag CPU speed by a large margin, meaning that CPUs spend a great many cycles simply sitting and waiting for the bus to catch up. On the other hand, busses are usually faster than network connections. As already mentioned, this has been changing recently. Fast Ethernet, for example, runs at 100Mbps, which is more than ISA or EISA busses can handle. Gigabit Ethernet runs at 1000Mbps, which is even more of a challenge. At gigabit rates, the server bus and CPU generally become the bottleneck, especially if the CPU is trying to do database access or run CGI applications at the same time.

While a throughput of 1056Mbps from a 32-bit 33MHz PCI bus is technically possible, your true throughput will be far lower because of contention, network packet overhead, OS implementation, and many other issues. 10Mbps is good TCP/IP throughput for a PC. A Sun Ultra 1 should get much better than 40Mbps of TCP/IP throughput. (The advertised rates you see will be the far higher theoretical rates.) The 66MHz PCI bus exceeds memory access speeds, moving the bottleneck to RAM.

Multiple PCI busses, provided on some Compaq PCs, may give you parallel access to peripheral devices. Sun uses the IEEE 1496 standard for its peripheral SBus, but recently started building machines with PCI peripheral busses, so you can use off-the-shelf PCI cards if you install Sun-specific device drivers. Sun implements 64-bit PCI at 66MHz for the throughput needed for 622Mbps ATM, gigabit Ethernet, and Fibrechannel.

Memory

It is difficult to exaggerate the time difference between accessing memory and accessing disk. Although in human terms there is little perceptible difference between a single 100 nanosecond access of RAM and a single 100 millisecond access of hard disk, there is literally a factor of one million between them. The perceptible difference comes in repeated access, when the value of having enough memory quickly becomes clear.

RAM Characteristics

Most physical chip memory these days is Dynamic Random Access Memory (DRAM). Random access refers to the fact that you can access any location on the memory chip with equal speed. Dynamic refers to the fact that the memory is repeatedly being refreshed because the charge on each individual cell is constantly leaking away. DRAM was invented during the 1980s when it was realized that memories could be made much denser by storing a bit on a single transistor rather than on a set of transistors, with the caveat that the entire chip would have to be constantly refreshed because of the charge leakage problem. The older kind of memory is now referred to as Static Random Access Memory (SRAM). SRAM uses *flip flops*, sets of four or five transistors that keep state by refreshing each other. SRAM is more expensive and not as dense as DRAM, but has far faster access time, on the order of 20 nanoseconds rather than 80 nanoseconds for DRAM. SRAM is used for L2 caches. DRAM has dropped a lot in price recently. You should be able to find commodity DRAM for $3-5/MB as of this writing.

Even though RAM is very fast relative to disk, it is not infinitely fast. Most RAM these days has better than 100 nanosecond access time. Let's compare that to a 100MHz CPU, which has a 10 nanosecond clock cycle ($1/10^8$ = 10ns). Most instructions on an Intel CPU take from one to five clock cycles to complete and may require additional memory accesses to retrieve operands. Even at five clocks per instruction, the CPU would still have to wait an additional five idle clocks for the next instruction. This is an overly simplified example that ignores the bus, pipelining of instructions, and superscalar CPUs (which execute more than one instruction at a time), but you can see that, in general, CPUs are faster than the RAM serving them.

RAM itself is often rated in *wait states* for a particular CPU. Each cycle that the CPU has to wait for the RAM is a wait state, so the best RAM for your CPU has zero wait states. Wait states are the reason CPUs have caches, which are a special kind of RAM kept on board the CPU (L1 cache) or very close to the CPU (L2 cache). Cache memory can be accessed at full processor speed. Caches overcome some of the mismatch between bus/RAM speeds and CPU speeds by keeping frequently used data and instructions close to the CPU. Note that some kinds of memory chips have on-chip caches too: that's how EDO, BEDO, and SDRAM differ. The rated speeds for RAM are only theoretical maxima because, in reality, there are latencies internal to RAM between row and column assertion.

Multiple memory controllers allow multiple RAM access setups to proceed in parallel, for greater overall throughput.

CPU

Look at any PC advertisement. the first specification given is usually the CPU speed, because PC buyers like to be able to compare numbers, and this is an easy number to use for comparisons. Ironically, most PC systems are not balanced: a high-power CPU is wasted on an inferior bus and disk. (On the other hand, the CPU isn't really wasted from the PC maker's point of view if that's what gets you to buy the system.) A low-end Intel Pentium CPU running at 100MHz will end up spending most of its time waiting for its EISA bus and IDE disk. What you really want is a fast bus, a low-latency disk, and a lot of RAM. Systems sold as servers are generally better balanced, because they are rated on actual throughput.

Still, sometimes you are really utilizing 100% of your CPU and could benefit from more power. Extensive database searches or calculations, generating graphics on the fly, or running server-side Java may all tax your CPU to its maximum. Use readily available Unix tools to monitor your CPU usage. Run **vmstat 1** for a while and look at the last three columns, which are usually **user**, **system**, and **idle** time. If the idle time is usually very low, say under 5%, then you may need more CPU power. You can measure the same things with *top* or *perfmeter.*

How much CPU power you need also depends on the speed of your client connections, the size of the content being served, and the number of clients. Say you're serving a large (100K) file to hundreds of clients at the same time. If the clients are all on high bandwidth connections, maybe you can serve the entire file in the time you have to run before the OS runs another process. Solaris timeslices are 10 milliseconds by default, but that can be changed. Whether you can efficiently serve the file in the number of timeslices you get will depend on your I/O subsystem. If the clients are all on slow bandwidth connections, then you'll spend most of your time switching between processes, and a good CPU will become more important than the I/O subsystem. A critical point to remember is that when the Internet becomes congested, say at peak times of the day, even fast clients look like slow clients to the server, and the kind of server you need changes from one with the best I/O possible, to one with the best CPU possible and a great deal of RAM to hold all the concurrent connections. (Thanks to Jim Barrick of Keynote for that tip.)

CPU Construction

Let's take a look at CPU construction with an eye on performance. At the most basic level, after a reset, the CPU reads the instruction from a hardwired start address in memory (usually not address zero), executes it, increments its internal program counter to one, reads the next instruction, executes it, and so on. This is a bit of a simplification, but not much of one. The instructions are probably of variable length, so the next one may not be at the next address, and the CPU may need to load operands in order to execute an instruction. It is very likely to jump to an instruction at a non-sequential address, depending on the result of the previous instruction, but the basic pattern holds: read instruction, execute, increment program counter. In fact, if all of memory were filled with "no op" commands, the CPU would just zip right through all memory in sequence. (And it wouldn't take very long: this is pretty much what happens in the memory check when you boot.) When you got to the end, the CPU would just wait for an interrupt in its idle state.

Many optimizations have been done to help the basic "fetch, decode, execute" process along. For example, CPUs now pipeline instructions, meaning that they don't read just one instruction at a time from memory, but several, queuing them up and executing portions of them at the same time. This reduces memory access overhead and speeds execution, but sometimes the next instruction is not at the next memory location, so the pipeline breaks and additional memory accesses must be done. Some CPUs actually look at the upcoming code and use branch prediction algorithms to preemptively read from the most likely part of memory for the next instructions. CPUs also run at different core and bus frequencies. The Pentium, for example, has one bus to the outside world, the "frontside bus," which is 64 bits wide and runs at the PCI clock rate (66MHz), but fetches instructions from its internal cache and runs internally at a higher rate. The frontside bus of Sun Ultra CPUs is 128 bits wide and runs at 83MHz or 100MHz.

When a CPU is referred to as 32-bit or 64-bit, this doesn't mean that it's worth four dollars or eight dollars, but rather that memory addresses are 32 or 64 bits long. On the other hand, a 2-bit CPU actually would be worth about a quarter. The number of bits refers to the size of a pointer, and therefore also determines the address space available. 32-bit machines have a 4GB address space, and 64-bit machines have such a humongous address space that I don't know how to describe it. The Pentium chips are all 32-bit; the UltraSPARC and Alpha are 64-bit. There currently isn't much 64-bit software available, but if you are writing custom software and need a very large address space and extreme performance, a 64-bit CPU may be useful to you. The AltaVista search engine uses custom 64-bit software and needs it, because each of the search engine machines has more than 4GB of RAM.

32-bit software will run on a 64-bit version of the same chip, but you will not necessarily see any performance advantage. It is generally true that software may run on a CPU without being optimized for that CPU. This is true of the SPARC line, for example. Any SPARC executable should be able to run on any SPARC CPU, but it may not have particularly good performance unless it was specifically compiled for that CPU. A good compiler like *gcc* will give you multiple options for each CPU family so that you can take advantage of the latest chip features. Type man gcc for more information. Sun's C compiler has a similar *-xchip* option to tell the compiler which SPARC chip to optimize for.

The next logical step after optimizing compilation for a CPU is simply to apply more of them to a problem. Getting equivalent multiple CPUs to cooperate on a problem within the context of the same address space is known as Symmetric Multiprocessing (SMP). SMP machines usually have CPU modules that you can plug into a bus. Unfortunately, because of the problems of coordinating activity, you don't necessarily get twice the throughput with two processors rather than one; you may even see that performance is worse with multiple CPUs. For software that hasn't been tuned to run on an SMP system, a scalability factor of 1.3 is common. For OSs tuned for SMP, you may see 1.8 to 1.9 scalability. For databases transferring large chunks of data, you may see 1.95 to 1.98 scalability because there's little overhead in figuring out how to allocate the work.

Multi-CPU machines are particularly useful for running multithreaded programs, one thread per CPU. Java threads can also run in parallel on multiple CPUs, but do not do so by default; you must use a native threads package. Unix is far ahead of NT in the SMP arena. The most NT can currently handle is 4 CPUs. Even if an NT machine has slots for more than 4 CPUs, performance is likely to decrease if you go beyond, because the operating system is not efficient at partitioning work among 4 CPUs. Be careful of demonstrations where the vendor sets up several machines side by side and claims good scalability without mentioning that it is extremely difficult to partition most applications among several independent machines. Solaris currently scales up to 64 CPUs with a good scalability factor. This means you can start out with a low-end Solaris machine and add more CPUs as you need more power, without reworking your applications or architecture.

How much bandwidth can a particular CPU handle? According to Brian Wong's book, *Configuration and Capacity Planning for Solaris Servers*, a Sparc 5 can fill a 50Mbit/second line, which is about the same as a T3, but you won't have any CPU cycles left to do anything else. An Ultra or Pentium Pro is capable of saturating a 155Mbit/second ATM connection, while a SPARC Classic or 90MHz Pentium cannot.

CISC instructions are of different sizes, and there are more of them. RISC instructions are generally all the same size, so it is easier to build a RISC CPU for efficiency. There are also fewer RISC instructions (hence the name), so you need to use several of them to get the same effect as with one CISC instruction, and the size of compiled code is larger. You're trading processor speed against storage. Intel CPUs are all CISC and backward compatible to the 8088, but now have a RISC core. Most CPUs now come with a built-in floating point unit (FPU), which is an enormous advantage over software floating point calculations, but few web sites use floating point for anything.

Remember that any digital algorithm implemented in software can also be implemented in hardware, and vice versa. The difference is performance: hardware implementations can be a thousand times faster or more. The Java Virtual Machine (JVM) is in effect a CPU (and some other runtime components) implemented in software. The logical performance enhancement is, therefore, to implement it in hardware. The first Java chips are already coming to market, but don't expect an immediate thousandfold gain in performance. The bytecodes of the JVM are easily translated into hardware; yet more than half of the time, running Java programs are not simply executing bytecodes but are performing more complex actions, such as object creation, that are already in native code in the JVM. Eventually, these actions too will be accelerated by hardware, making Java programs as fast or faster than native code on other platforms.

An HTTP server could also be implemented directly in hardware for speed. Dedicated HTTP chips would also make it easier to embed the HTTP protocol in consumer devices, so that your radio or VCR could be queried and controlled from any web browser. Of course, chips are much more difficult to upgrade than software, but when was the last time you upgraded anything on your VCR?

Disk

Next to your Internet connection, the parameter most likely to affect the perceived performance of your server is the speed of its hard disks. If everything seems reasonable but your performance is still lagging, the problem is probably your disks. Remember how much of a penalty it is to go to disk rather than RAM. The relationship between a 100 nanosecond RAM access and a 10 millisecond disk access is the same proportion as one second to 28 days, a factor of 100,000. And that's assuming a fast disk. So we want to avoid disk access wherever possible.

Disk Architecture and Parameters

Hard disks are literally that: hard platters coated with a magnetic recording material. There are usually multiple platters in a single hard disk unit. The unit is called a *spindle*. Each platter surface has an associated arm that swings in a wide enough angle to be able to position the data-reading and -writing tip of the arm over any point on the radius of the platter. The disks generally start rotating when you boot up your computer and continue until you turn off the power. Laptops and other power-conscious machines may spin down (stop) the disk after a certain period of inactivity, but you should disable this feature on any such machine to be used as a web server, because there is usually a several second wait for the disk to spin up again. Current hard disks typically rotate at 7200 or 10000 rpm. Since the disk has moving parts, for example, the platters and the disk arms, it is the part of your system most likely to fail. One way to gracefully accept the failure of a disk is to have a redundant array of them. One standard for doing this that we'll talk about in a bit is called RAID.

The most important disk parameter is maximum seek time, which is the upper bound on the time it takes for the disk arm to move to any track. Disk arms are subject to forces of inertia when starting and stopping movement, and it is this inertia, as well as the physical distance the arm must travel, that limits overall disk performance. When the disk arm stops over a track, it tends to jiggle a bit, and the disk must wait for the arm to settle down before reading data. Latency for disks is defined as the maximum time needed for any sector on a track to come under the read/write head once the arm is in position. Latency is inversely proportional to disk speed. Seek time is usually much larger than latency, and therefore is the bottleneck. Seek time is also more important than raw throughput because disks spend most of their time seeking, not transferring data.

To reduce average seek time, disks often try to queue up requests and then order them in a manner that reduces the total amount of motion of the disk arm. The exact algorithm used is determined by the disk controller, but disks usually use the "elevator" algorithm, where the disk arm moves in one direction for as long as there are queued reads and writes in that direction before reversing direction.

Disks have memory caches of their own, used primarily to speed up writes to the disk system. The utility of a large disk cache depends on whether you're doing a lot of writes. Web servers read a lot of content and write only small records to log files, so the utility of large disk caches is debatable.

You will get better performance from a disk that is physically on the same machine as your web server software (a local disk) than from one mounted across a network, but a very high speed connection such as Fibre Channel tends to blur this distinction. Furthermore, your web server should probably have at least two disks: one for content and one for web server logging. If you can afford it, consider yet another disk for the operating system itself, which has its own disk needs. Use the faster disk for serving content, because serving is a more intense operation than logging and is directly relevant to perceived performance. Users don't care if you log their access; only you care. You can also increase performance further by using another disk for your swap space. As much as possible, balance the load across all your disks to get the most from each of them.

A separate disk controller card for each disk will reduce contention. If you use a single controller for several disks, make sure that controller has a maximum transfer rate that is equal to or better than the sum of the maximum transfer rates of all the disks connected to it.

Solid state disks are now on the market. These disks use non-volatile memory, either flash RAM or battery backed RAM, but use a SCSI or other disk interface, so they appear to the system to be ordinary disks. There are no moving parts, so they are unlikely ever to break, unlike ordinary disks. Access time is thousands of times faster than that of a rotating physical disk. The main disadvantage to solid state disks is cost, which is comparable per megabyte to that for system memory: around \$5/MB at this writing, compared to 20 cents/MB or so for disk. Another disadvantage is that system RAM is faster than solid state disks, so if you have money to spend, you'll get more performance from spending it on system memory. Still, if you have filled your webserver to its maximum with memory, a solid state disk could be more cost effective than upgrading the web server machine itself.

IDE

The standard sort of disk you get with a PC is known as an Integrated Drive Electronics (IDE) disk. This is a commodity disk, not very expensive, but without high performance, reliability, or scalability. IDE disks should be fine for your web logging needs, but they are not suitable for a high-performance web content disk or database.

EIDE

EIDE is an extended version of IDE. Because it was not designed from scratch but carries some of the legacy problems of IDE, it is also not particularly scalable, but has better performance than IDE.

SCSI

Higher-performance disks use the Small Computer Software Interface (SCSI) standard. SCSI is the interface the disk uses to talk to the computer, not a type of disk per se, but disks that connect via SCSI are referred to as "SCSI disks." These disks are designed to scale from single small systems up to large arrays. SCSI disk controller cards may contain cache memory or have the ability to interleave requests to different disks for higher throughput. If you are interleaving requests, you will get the best performance by balancing the load across equivalent disks. You can also coordinate the use of multiple controllers with SCSI. You should use *iostat* or *sar* under Solaris to monitor the performance of each disk to be sure the load is balanced.

Up to 7 SCSI 1 disks or 15 SCSI 2 disks can be daisy chained, with each disk up to 6GB in size. Plain SCSI transfers data at 5MB/sec to 10MB/sec. Wide UltraSCSI provides 40MB/sec (320Mbit/sec) interfaces, and this is currently the most common variety of SCSI. Wide UltraSCSI disks typically run at 10000 rpm and have very low seek and latency times. Narrow UltraSCSI provides 20MB/sec (160Mbit/sec) interfaces. Both wide and narrow UltraSCSI allow cable lengths up to 3 meters, which sounds like a lot, but this can be constraining for large configurations. Differential SCSI increases the allowed distance to 25 meters but is otherwise the same. SCSI is evolving, with UltraSCSI 2 now available (80MB/sec) at 12 meters.

SCSI is more expensive than EIDE, but it is well worth the extra cost. You should serve all of your content from SCSI disks.

Fibre Channel

You may be able to replace SCSI connections with Fibre Channel connections for better performance. Fibre Channel is a serial connection standard commonly used on Unix servers but still rare on cheaper hardware. Its key advantage is that it is suitable both for connecting peripherals to a server and for connecting servers to each other, up to a distance of 10 kilometers in theory. It competes with SCSI, which is limited to 10 meters, one-thousandth the distance. You can currently get 100MB/s (200MB/s full-duplex) with Fibre Channel.

Fibre Channel was intended for use with optical fiber, but you can use coaxial cable or twisted pair if you want to give up most of the distance advantage for cheaper wire. Fibre Channel lets several servers share the same disk, unlike SCSI, and can be switched or shared, like Ethernet. Because you can talk directly to disk with Fibre Channel, you can remove some of the latency you'd otherwise have with converting from Ethernet protocol to SCSI and back. Fibre Channel is intended for servers and would be wasted on an ordinary PC, which would not be able to fill the wire. Fibre Channel's future is not clear, because Ethernet and SCSI are already in place with clear upgrade paths, and Fibre Channel does not integrate well with them.

RAID

Redundant Arrays of Inexpensive Disks (RAID) are an example of how you can achieve high performance from a collection of relatively low-performance components. The idea behind RAID is to set up a collection of disks in which every bit of information is on at least two disks, so that any one disk can fail with no interruption in service. Because of the number of disks, you can use cheaper disks that have a lower reliability. As a bonus, the performance of RAID systems is very good because the system can run multiple requests in parallel, and because smaller disks may have lower seek times as a result of their physically smaller platters. For example, 4 2G drives will usually have better performance than one 9G drive.

RAID is usually sold as a package that appears to the host machine as a single large disk. Striping is a similar concept, where access to contiguous blocks of data is spread out over multiple disks, increasing the potential for parallelism and reducing seek times because of smaller platters.

See Brian Wong's book, *Configuration and Capacity Planning for Solaris Servers*, for more details on RAID.

Typical Disk Performance

Hard disks now typically run at 7200 rpm and have the ability to do about 100 random I/O operations per second, or up to 500 sequential I/O operations. There are also many 5400 rpm disks, with the ability to handle about 75 random I/O operations per second and 10000 rpm disks, with the ability to handle about 140. One hundred random operations per second implies a seek time of about 10 milliseconds, since a majority of access time is seek time. Disks on PC systems are capable of a sustained 8–16 Mbit/sec throughput, while the same disks on Unix systems can achieve 32–40 Mbit/sec because of Unix optimizations for disk access.

To estimate the number of disks you'd need to support your hit rate from disk (and not from memory), take your average rate of hits per second, multiply by three to get your assumed peak rate, and multiply that by two to get the peak I/O rate you'll need from your disk. Remember that you need to do a read of the directory to get the permissions for a file (the `open()` system call) before you can read the file itself (the `read()` system call). So if you're getting 30 hits/second on average, your peak rate is probably around 90, and you'll need 180 random I/O operations per second from your disk to prevent your users from experiencing noticeable delays. So you would need two RAIDed or striped 7200 rpm disks to handle that. Going backwards, we can derive a rule of thumb that a 100 I/O operations per second disk should be able to handle a system getting 17 hits/second on average. Actually, you might be able to do better than that, because the OS will cache directory names and inodes, saving some lookups.

Fragmentation

As a disk fills up, it becomes progressively harder to find enough contiguous space to write new files, so new files are written in fragments at multiple places on disk. Reads and writes of fragmented files require multiple movements of the disk arm, slowing access. Fragmentation becomes a more significant problem as the disk gets very full, so it is a good idea to leave at least 10% of any given disk free. Disks on heavily used Windows and Mac machines need regular defragmentation, and these systems include defragmentation utilities. Unix disks tend to fragment more slowly because of better disk write algorithms, but eventually they too will need defragmentation. The most effective way to defragment a disk under Unix is to back it up to tape, reinitialize the filesystem with *mkfs*, and then restore the filesystem from tape. This task is a little easier if you combine it with one of your regular backups.

Key Recommendations

- Don't worry about CPU, just concentrate on having a good network connection, fast disk, and enough memory.

- Buy enough RAM to keep the entire HTML document tree in memory if you can afford it.

- Use SCSI rather than IDE disks.

- Use separate disks for log writing and content reading.

- *http://www.sun.com/sunworldonline/* is a good resource for Sun-specific tuning questions.

12

Server Operating System

The operating system sits between the hardware and the web server software, translating the web server's request for services into hardware actions and delivering data from the hardware back up to the web server. The server hardware has a maximum performance that is fixed by its physical specifications. You can approach this maximum performance by appropriate configuration of the operating system. The question for web servers is how to configure the operating system to take requests from the network, find the correct file to return or run the correct program, and push the result back out to the network, all as fast as possible.

Unix and the Origin of the Web

Networking has been central to the development of Unix. Unix was originally developed around 1970 as a research project by AT&T Bell Laboratories, building on multiuser and multitasking ideas from the Multics government research project of the 1960s. Since AT&T was barred from selling software because it was the U.S. telephone monopoly, it allowed universities to use the source code for education and research. The University of California at Berkeley, in particular, continued development on the TCP/IP implementation in the Unix kernel. The Berkeley group introduced enough changes that Unix was for about ten years split into two main camps: Berkeley Unix and AT&T Unix. Around 1988, these were merged into

System V Release 4 (SVR4) Unix, but derivatives of the two original camps continue to exist, such as BSDI and SCO.

The HTTP protocol and the first web server were both developed on Unix platforms and are natural outgrowths of previously existing Unix work. HTTP inherited many characteristics of FTP, but extended FTP with automated requests. The first popular web server software, the University of Illinois' *httpd*, was a classical Unix daemon. At that point, all Unix machines had TCP/IP networking ability and FTP by default, so the technological jump from the existing file transfer protocol to the web protocol was much smaller than would be expected from its subsequent impact on the world. As almost all Unix machines were networked, it was a trivial matter to retrieve *httpd* from the University of Illinois and start it running on your local machine. There was no charge for the software, since it came from a tax-sponsored research project. Web usage exploded because the Internet was primed and ready for a new and simpler front end.

Web servers and clients were quickly ported to other platforms, such as Windows, the Macintosh, and even mainframes and the AS/400, but the majority of web servers remained on Unix platforms. Unix proved superior in stability and performance because of its longer development history and open nature. Simply put, more people have been able to contribute to and debug Unix for longer than any other operating system. Development of proprietary platforms has been limited by the number of paid employees of any one company, while Unix benefited from the work of the entire academic and Internet community. An interesting hybrid approach between proprietary and public code is Netscape's desire to capture the creativity of the Internet community by releasing the source code to its browser for inspection and improvement. The Netscape browser source code is available at *http://www.mozilla.org/*.

Unix Flavors

It might be said that the Unix market enjoys competition, but it could also be said that the Unix market suffers from competition. The problem has been that individual vendors have created their own versions of Unix that are incompatible with all other versions. This means that a binary executable for one version is usually incapable of running on any other Unix, even if the hardware is identical.

The problem is gradually being solved by several forces. First, the SVR4 standard has become dominant. An old joke goes that Sun succeeded in uniting the Unix industry, but unfortunately it united in a coalition against Sun. Nonetheless, SVR4 is now the de facto standard. Programs written to the SVR4 standard have source-level portability to other SVR4 systems, meaning that you should be able to recompile the code for each system without changes. Second, the increasing popularity of Sun Microsystems' Solaris implementation of SVR4 means that Solaris is becoming the de facto standard for binary-level portability, while the future of some other versions of Unix is in doubt. Finally, as more applications are written in Java, small differences between operating systems will become irrelevant. Systems will be forced to compete on performance and cost, not compatibility. Here are the major versions of Unix used for web services:

Solaris

Solaris is Sun Microsystems' (*http://www.sun.com/*) version of Unix. When the Berkeley-derived SunOS was made compatible with SVR4, its name was changed to Solaris. There are versions of Solaris for Sun's SPARC hardware as well as for the Intel x86 architecture. Solaris on the SPARC hardware has the largest Unix market share, so you can be reasonably sure that any commercial multiplatform Unix software will be ported to Solaris first, debugged, and probably optimized for Solaris. This is important because software vendors do not have the resources to port and optimize for every version of Unix. Solaris has the largest market share for web servers, partly due to its performance and reliability, but also because Solaris has the largest share of the computer science education market. Students who learn to program and administer on Solaris systems tend to keep using it once they go out into the business world. One of Solaris's strengths is its efficiency in memory allocation, which happens so frequently that it has a large impact on overall system performance. Memory allocation is accelerated by hardware called with special opcodes available only to the OS, not to applications.

Solaris 2.6, the latest version as of this writing, comes with default parameters more appropriate to web services than previous versions, so a web server run out of the box on Solaris 2.6 will not need much tuning. Solaris 2.6 also includes many fundamental improvements that increase web server performance, such as a more efficient TCP/IP stack with more networking code in the kernel rather than user space, and better use of multiple CPUs. Sun claims a 350% increase in web server performance on Solaris 2.6 over Solaris 2.5 on multiprocessor systems.

Digital Unix

Digital Unix is known for extremely good I/O performance because of efficient disk driver and TCP/IP implementations, which make it very suitable for web serving. Digital Unix is already 64-bit, so it is ahead of most other Unixes there. It is scalable up to very large SMP systems, like the showpiece AltaVista search engine.

Linux

Linux is a free Unix kernel originally written for the Intel architecture, but since ported to the Alpha, PowerPC, and even Sun's SPARC. The project was started by Linus Torvalds of Finland. Remember that Linux is just a kernel and not the utilities that allow user interaction with the kernel. Linux comes in distributions from various organizations, usually including GNU tools such as the *gcc* compiler and *bash* shell, as well as a version of the X Window System called XFree86.

The scalability of Linux is not as mature as that of Solaris. Until recently, you were limited to 256 simultaneous processes and there was no multiprocessor support. Still, Linux is as robust and high-performance as many commercial versions of Unix. There is an information page on Linux at *http://www.li.org* (and a competing page at *http://www.linux.org*). Excellent free support is available via the many Linux Usenet newsgroups, and paid support is supplied by companies such as Cygnus. Now that Oracle has been ported to Linux, Linux is being accepted by the business community as a serious platform. There are several high-volume web sites that run the free Apache server on Linux.

Irix

Irix is the version of Unix developed by Silicon Graphics for the company's high-performance graphics workstations. It runs only on Silicon Graphics hardware. Silicon Graphics hardware has been optimized for graphics manipulation, but many of the graphics features, such as very quick memory and disk access, are also useful for high-performance web serving. Unfortunately, Irix is not as well supported as Solaris by software vendors like Netscape, so there is often a delay before the Irix version is available. See *http://www.sgi.com/* for extensive information on tuning Irix for web services.

BSD

The Berkeley Standard Distribution of Unix (BSD) is similar to Linux in that it tends to be favored at smaller web sites and runs on Intel x86 hardware. Unlike Linux, BSD development includes not just the kernel but all of the utilities and documentation as well. BSDI (*http://www.bsdi.com/*) and FreeBSD (*http://www.freebsd.com/*) are derivatives of BSD, and have continued the development of Berkeley Unix.

Mach OS

The list of Unix versions used for web services would not be complete without Mach OS. Mach was developed at Carnegie-Mellon and provided the foundation for the NextStep operating system, on which the original implementation of HTTP was built by Tim Berners-Lee at CERN in Switzerland.

Let's take a look at how Unix works, keeping in mind the performance perspective.

Processes and the Kernel

Unix work is divided up into processes, which you can think of as tasks to be done. Each process has a unique process ID, which is simply an integer, and an owner, along with priority and many other attributes that you can see with the *ps* command. Unix is multiuser and multitasking, so many processes belonging to many users can be running concurrently. (NT, on the other hand, is multitasking, but not multiuser.) Of course, Unix processes are not all running at *exactly* the same time; it looks that way because the operating system is letting each process run for a bit of time, then interrupting it and letting the next one run, more or less in round robin fashion. The process that does the scheduling runs in the kernel and is known as the scheduler. Processes are scheduled in terms of "clock ticks," which are hundredths of a second, so every process is allocated at least one one-hundredth of a second when it starts its turn.

The kernel is some address space and tasks that do scheduling and other fundamental functions, such as directly interfacing to the hardware to display something on-screen or to write something to disk. Only the kernel has direct access to the hardware, and the kernel is accessible to user programs only through the system calls that define its interface. This has a couple of benefits: the kernel can prevent user processes from doing naughty things with hardware, such as reading someone else's files from disk. Also, the system calls can be the same regardless of the underlying hardware, making the program's source code portable. SVR4 is mostly a specification of system calls, so software written to use just those calls should compile and run on any SVR4 system.

Scheduling

To be more precise, the scheduler does not use round robin exactly, but assigns each process a priority and uses a system-dependent algorithm to decide which process to run next based on that priority, how long a process has waited, hardware interrupts, and other factors. The more processes you have running, the poorer performance you'll get from each one. Changing from one user-level process to another is called a *context switch*, and is rather expensive because it may require clearing out certain caches, such as the address translation cache in the memory management unit (MMU). Switching into kernel mode (a system call) is much faster than switching between user processes, but this also takes some time.

Look at your load average with the *perfmeter* if you have it. If you have a single-CPU machine and see a load average above two, meaning more than two processes are waiting to run on average, and if the CPU utilization is also high, you probably have too many processes running and should think about removing some nonessential processes, moving some load to another machine, or upgrading your hardware. On the other hand, if you see a high load average but low CPU utilization, your system may be misconfigured, the running application may be misbehaving, or you may have a bursty load.

Kernel Context

Limiting hardware access to the kernel has some associated performance penalties. First of all, you must switch to kernel mode to get access to the hardware. Then there is a delay because data has to be copied first from a buffer on the device to the kernel, and then from a kernel buffer to the user process (or in the other direction).

All of this means that there is an indeterminate amount of time involved in Unix hardware access. However small that time interval happens to be, you cannot be sure it will be the same every time you access the hardware, so you cannot yet use Unix for real-time applications, such as flying a fighter plane. For that, you need a real-time operating system, or RTOS. There are real-time priorities of 90 or greater under Solaris, which have precedence over even system-level tasks, but real-time programming under Unix still involves some uncertainties.

There's a tradeoff here in Unix in that kernel routines are much faster in accessing hardware such as the network and disk (most of what a web server does) but good development and maintenance dictate partitioning into user and kernel level rather than having one massive kernel. As of the migration from SunOS to Solaris, the kernel is multithreaded and each process is assigned a kernel-level thread for increased context-switch performance.

Unix and httpd

For web serving, what you want to know about your operating system and hardware is how fast you can get an interrupt from the network interface card, go into kernel mode to get the data, and go back to user mode. You want to copy the request and the output only once within the OS: from/to the device driver's buffer in the kernel to/from the user process. Good implementations of TCP/IP do only one copy, and some experimental systems do no copies at all but simply reallocate the ownership of a buffer between the user and the kernel.

When a web server machine receives an HTTP request, it must schedule some CPU time for the *httpd* daemon to handle the request (see Figure 12-1). Note that *httpd* runs as a user process, so it has lower priority than kernel processes. It must wait for them and share what time is left over with other user processes, so the fewer other processes running, the better. If you can afford it, you should dedicate your web server and not run interactive terminal sessions, database applications, NFS or DNS services, etc. This advice conflicts with the use of Java applets for client-server type applications, because the default security model for Java applets is to allow access only back to the web server from which the applet originated, meaning that the web server machine must not only serve the applet, but also deal with requests from that applet for services such as database access. There

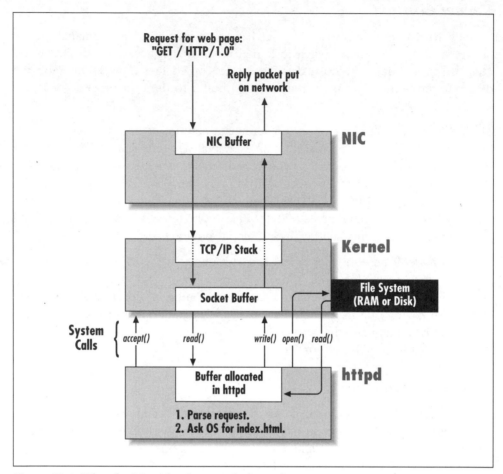

Figure 12-1. What the OS and web server do for each request

are many solutions to this dilemma, such as signing the applet so that it can access other machines, using appletviewer or turning off the browser's network security (only in an intranet), writing a small redirector daemon that copies data from a receiving socket on the web server to another socket on another machine, or mapping the IP address of the web server to a set of machines with one of the load balancing products mentioned in Chapter 2, *Capacity Planning*.

Reducing the Load on the OS

If your web server is going to access a large database, consider using FastCGI or opening a socket to a separate machine running the database and leaving it open. Some "middleware" products will manage a single open connection to a database for you. Interactive sessions, though seemingly innocuous, generate lots of interrupts (for example, one with each keystroke and many with each mouse movement). Another strategy is to increase the priority of your web server process, which you can do as *root* by making the appropriate system call. This could be dangerous on a heavily loaded web server because other essential functions may get starved for attention, possibly crashing your server. Another trick that may improve performance is to configure the scheduler to use longer timeslices, also known as *quanta*, for each process. This will sometimes help a CPU-bound system by reducing the time spent in the scheduler. See *Essential System Administration*, by Æleen Frisch (O'Reilly & Associates), for details on how to configure the scheduler under AIX and Solaris.

I haven't heard of anyone doing this, but there is nothing to stop someone, in principle, from putting their web server directly into the kernel to avoid the overhead of changing into and out of user mode. You would then have a fatter kernel and less flexibility, but you already know that performance fights flexibility. You would need the source code, so Linux and Apache are likely candidates for this merger. Perhaps Apache could be made into a Linux module. It's not clear just how much this would help performance, because most of a web server's CPU time is spent in kernel TCP/IP code.

Process Creation

The creation of new processes under Unix is through the `fork` system call, which copies a process and assigns the copy a new process ID, usually followed by an `exec` system call, which reads a new executable from disk (if not already loaded) and starts it in the current address space. The disk access takes about 50 milliseconds, and the process creation itself maybe 10 milliseconds. The created process consumes something like 50K in the kernel for record keeping as well as its own memory in user space as reported by the *ps* command.

The `fork` and `exec` method is not a particularly efficient way to do things, but it is simple for the programmer. It was expected that new process creation would not occur very frequently, so there was no incentive to make it very efficient. It is exactly this inefficiency that limits the scalability of CGI, which creates and destroys a new process for each hit. The reason `fork` and `exec` are two separate system calls is that `fork` was intended for use in a client-server environment where the ability to generate a new copy of a server process for each client is desirable.

To get around the expense of new process creation, the concept of threading was introduced. Threads are separate strands of execution within the same process. It takes far less time and resources to create a new thread than to create a new process—as much as 100 times less. In addition, switching between threads is very quick. Your entire process still has to wait for the scheduler to run it before any of the threads in that process can run, but the advantages of quick thread creation and switching are still very great. If you have a Symmetric Multiprocessing (SMP) machine, i.e., one with multiple equivalent CPUs, you can often assign one thread to each CPU and take advantage of parallel execution. This is now possible with Java threading, for example. Another advantage of threads is that an entire process can avoid being blocked on I/O by assigning the I/O operation to a single thread and letting only that thread block.

Address Space

When a Unix process requires more RAM than is physically available, it is still possible for the process to run, using part of the disk as its memory space. The memory on disk is known as *virtual memory* because it is not real RAM and the part of disk used for it is called the *swap space*. Memory is segmented into *pages*, so the term for storing some of a process's address space on disk is referred to as paging. If an entire process is suspended and moved out to disk, we say the process is swapped out. A basic rule of thumb is that paging is acceptable, but not desirable, while swapping is an indication of a serious memory problem that will hurt your performance.

You will necessarily see paging in when you start a program, because it must be read from disk, and you will see paging out when programs have been idle for a long time. Neither is an indication of any problem. In the long term, you should monitor your paging and swapping activity with *sar* or *vmstat*, but *perfmeter* gives a good visual indication of how things are going at the moment. If you see continuous paging or any swapping activity, it would improve performance to figure out why it's happening and fix it, probably by buying more RAM or reducing the load on the machine. Tuning memory parameters is a large subject. For more information on Solaris memory parameters, see *Sun Performance and Tuning*, by Adrian Cockcroft and Richard Pettit (Prentice Hall).

Every process in Unix gets its own independent address space and is unaware that its memory space is actually mapped to the far smaller physical RAM installed on the machine. Most machines are currently 32-bit and therefore have a 4GB address space. There is a unified dynamic memory pool, meaning that processes and the filesystem share RAM, with the filesystem's buffer cache occupying whatever memory is not needed by other processes. This buffer reduces disk reads and writes, improving performance, but it may give you the false impression that you're running out of memory when, in fact, processes still have plenty of room to grow by displacing the buffer cache. On Solaris, the scan rate of the pager (*sr* in *vmstat*) and the number of pages moved in or out per second are much better indications of whether you're short of memory than the amount of memory reported as free by *vmstat* or other tools. Also be aware that various tools like *sar*, *vmstat*, and *top* may all have different definitions of what it means for memory to be free. Some deduct memory that a process would like to reserve from the amount calculated to be free even though that memory is not actually in use.

The Filesystem

While everything in Unix is considered to be a file, including data, executables, directories, and devices, the most common type of file is the *regular* file, which is simply a stream of data bytes. There is no distinction in Unix between text files and binary files. Our principal concern in serving web content is how to access regular files as quickly as possible. In order to understand the issues involved in access speed, we have to know a bit about the Unix filesystem.

There are many kinds of filesystems in use in Unix systems, but the most common kind is the Unified File System (UFS), derived from the Berkeley Fast Filesystem. UFS filesystems consist basically of inodes, directories, and data blocks. Inodes are 128-byte records on disk that describe files. Each inode contains a list of pointers to the data blocks on the disk that make up a file. Given the number of pointers in an inode and the size of the data blocks, we can see that each inode can point to only a fixed amount of data storage. The size of the data blocks is often 512 bytes or maybe 2 kilobytes by default, which is fine if you have a lot of small files, but it is suboptimal if you are going to be serving only a few large files. For larger files, at least one of your inode pointers must point to a sort of second level inode called an *indirect block* that contains pointers to other data blocks. And this can continue on to doubly indirect blocks, but there is a performance penalty in accessing parts of large files through an extra level or two of indirection.

If you are going to have mostly very large files, you will get better performance by increasing the size of the data block rather than using the default indirection, at the expense of more wasted disk space for small files. With UFS, you have a choice of block sizes ranging up to 64 kilobytes. Changing the block size is platform-specific and is done when you create the filesystem. The point is that you can tune your filesystem to serve a certain size file at the best speed. Remember that web content often has a bimodal distribution, with many smallish (10KB to 20KB) files for text and images and a few large (greater than 1MB) files for downloaded software, audio, high-resolution images, etc. One solution is to have HTTP links point to a server with a filesystem tuned for serving large files for the big downloads, but the gain in filesystem performance would be swamped by long download times over slow network connections. In the case of streaming video, it would help to have a dedicated server with a specially tuned filesystem.

Another kind of filesystem on Solaris is the temporary filesystem, `tempfs`. If you look in */etc/vfstab* on a Solaris system, you will see that */tmp* is usually mounted as a `tempfs` filesystem. The unique thing about `tempfs` is that it attempts to keep everything in RAM rather than on disk. This means that writing to or reading from */tmp* under Solaris is far faster than reading or writing anywhere else. The drawback to using `tempfs` is that it goes away on reboot and everything in that filesystem is lost. Also note that `tempfs` doesn't guarantee that your files will be in RAM; it just makes an attempt to keep them there. That said, you can use `tempfs` in various ways to help server performance. If your web server is constantly retrieving data to be served out to clients, say stock quotes, you'll probably want to write the data to */tmp*. This kind of data is volatile anyway, and fast access is very important. On Solaris, you can `man tempfs` for more information.

Directories

Note that a directory is a special kind of file that contains a list of filenames mapped to inode numbers, as well as information for each file, such as permissions and the time the file was last accessed. The directory structure of Unix is a linked list. When you refer to a file via a pathname, such as */dir1/foo*, the kernel looks inside the root directory for the name *dir1*. It searches linearly through the names in the root directory until it finds the name *dir1* and gets the associated inode number. It then uses that inode to find the datablock called *dir1* and looks linearly through that data for the file name *foo*. When it finds the name *foo*, it has the associated inode and finally knows exactly where on the disk to find the data in the file *foo*. This is a rather involved process, as you can see, so you will in general see better access performance from a path with fewer components and even a slight advantage from short file names and directory names.

If you must have long names, try to differentiate them at the beginning of the name instead of at the end so that whatever string compare function the OS uses to look up the name will have an easier time. So, for example, instead of naming web content files as *regional.daily.report.12.3.1998*, *regional.daily.report.12.4.1998*, etc., name them *3.12.1998.regional.daily.report*, *4.12.1998.regional.daily.report*, etc. (Netscape Navigator's disk cache tends to violate this principle, but there's not much you can do about it unless you're ambitious enough to modify the browser source code.)

This doesn't mean, however, that you should put all of your files in the root directory or create any other huge directories. Directories are searched linearly for a name matching the one requested, so huge directories will give you very poor performance. The recommendations for keeping file paths short and for keeping directory sizes small conflict if you have a great deal of content. Which one wins? Consider that each element of a path is an indirection that requires disk movement, while searching through a linked list of directory names is a much faster indirection in memory. To balance the time spent in each, several hundred elements per directory is probably optimum. On the other hand, once file system structures are looked up, they are cached, so subsequent accesses favor having longer paths rather than larger directories. You would have to run some benchmarks with your content organized in different ways to find the optimal numbers, but 100 files per directory is reasonable. Some systems have Directory Name Lookup Caches (DNLCs), which reduce the disk access for directory lookups.

The Veritas VxFS filesystem uses hashed directories for very fast lookups but is an extra-cost commercial product. See *http://www.veritas.com/*.

The kernel contains an inode table that serves as a cache for recently opened files. Its size is determined by a constant compiled into the kernel, often MAXUSERS, or INODE or NINODE for SVR4. Linked lists such as directories do not cache particularly well because they don't consist of contiguous memory, but increasing the size of the inode table should help access time somewhat.

Filesystem Caching

When you read a file on Unix, the filesystem stores it in a cache, known as the filesystem buffer cache, so that you can avoid a disk access if you use the file again soon. In SVR4, the cache is whatever memory is free at the moment, so the cache size grows and shrinks dynamically. On other Unix systems, the cache is usually a dedicated part of the process's address space. When SVR4 reclaims memory from the cache, it chooses memory that has not been recently used; this method is known as the Least Recently Used (LRU) basis.

When you write to the buffer cache, the changes are not written to disk immediately, but queued up for later, more efficient writing. This is different from the Mac and Windows, which synchronously commit writes to disk at the time the application considers the data written. This makes Unix systems more vulnerable to data loss in the event of power outage, but higher-performance otherwise. It's one more tradeoff.

You can easily see the buffer cache in action by editing a file you have not recently used, closing it, and opening it again. The second time will be much faster, because both your editor and the file are in the buffer cache the second time around and so do not have to be retrieved from disk. This sort of caching helps HTTP servers quite a lot because the same files tend to get requested over and over.

Fragmentation

The layout of a filesystem on disk tends toward disorder after many reads and writes, with the result that a new file will typically be stored in fragments fit into the available holes in the disk. This hurts performance, because writing and accessing fragmented files forces many motions of the disk arm. If your filesystem has been well used for writing many files, you should use a disk defragmentation utility or simply dump the filesystem to tape, reformat the disk, and write the files back onto disk. Do not make an image of the disk on the tape with *dd*, *dcopy*, or other disk copy utilities, because that image will itself be fragmented. Write the files out as files.

When you put the files back to disk, you can play another trick: write related content together. For example, write an HTML file, then write the images referred to by the file. When you go to access the HTML file and need the images that go with it, the disk arm stands a good chance of being in exactly the right place to get the image files, thus improving performance. Your frequently accessed files are likely to be in the buffer cache already, so this technique will help them only on the first read; it is more suited to large collections of infrequently accessed files.

If your disk is too full, it will rapidly fragment because it will be difficult to find contiguous space to write files, and performance will suffer. Try to keep your disk under 90% full, especially if you're writing to it and not simply serving static content. If your disk is nearly 100% full and performance is intolerable, you may want to try to take advantage of any available space on the disk, such as space the disk itself reserves for temporary storage. How this is done varies with the disk and operating system, but it may be as simple and dangerous as using a tool like *fdisk* or *tunefs* or the Linux *fips* utility to increase the size of a disk partition. I don't know the details, and you didn't learn about this from me if something bad happens to your disk. You did back everything up, right?

Remember what happens when a file is accessed? Among other things, the permissions of the file as stored in the directory are checked against the user ID. This takes time and is not necessary for a dedicated web server isolated from your internal network. If you're a kernel hacker, you can change the kernel to skip the ID check. This would mean that all users would have access to all files on the machine, but it's not as dangerous as it sounds if there is nothing on your web server except content that you'd like to be public anyway, and if login over the network is disabled. The hazard to your web server is greater on the Internet than on your intranet, because hackers are known to commandeer web sites for distribution of "warez," illegal copies of software, and you'd be making it a bit easier to do so. Note that running the web server as *root* is not the same thing as disabling permissions, even though *root* has access to all files. The permission check is done even for *root*.

Another thing that happens when a file is accessed, but which is pointless for web servers, is the updating of the file access time in the directory. It is pointless because the file will be accessed repeatedly, and the access times will be recorded in the web server log in any case. This is particularly important if your HTML files are being read from NFS, where the access time write requires additional network traffic. See Chapter 10, *Network Protocols*, for information on NFS. You'd need to make serious modifications to your filesystem to stop update times from being written, or you can mount a filesystem as read-only.

Avoid symbolic links in your content tree because they are not only a level of indirection but also mean an additional two disk accesses: one to read the link's permissions (remember that a link, like everything else in Unix, is a file) and another to read the contents of the link, which tell you where the target file is located. A symbolic link is a text file containing the path to the target file, marked so that the operating system uses it as a link and not a text file. Hard links, however, can be used with no additional time penalty because they map the link name directly to the inode of the target file, just like the proper filename. But hard links cannot be used to cross filesystems, while symbolic links can.

Keep your PATH and LD_LIBRARY_PATH short and pointing first to the libraries your web server will actually use. If you don't, you'll waste a lot of system calls when executing CGIs or other new processes. Here we should have */lib* first in our LD_LIBRARY_PATH, but it is last instead, causing a lot of wasted open calls:

```
% echo $LD_LIBRARY_PATH
/usr/openwin/lib:/usr/ucblib:/usr/dt/lib:/usr/lib:/usr/local/lib:/lib
```

Here's what happens when we run a CGI (you can see by tracing system calls with *truss* on Solaris or *strace* on Linux). The entire library path is searched before the library is found and opened at the end of the path. We should have had */lib* first in the LD_LIBRARY_PATH:

```
open("/usr/openwin/lib/libc.so.5", O_RDONLY) = -1 ENOENT (No such file or directory)
open("/usr/ucblib/libc.so.5", O_RDONLY) = -1 ENOENT (No such file or directory)
open("/usr/dt/lib/libc.so.5", O_RDONLY) = -1 ENOENT (No such file or directory)
open("/usr/lib/libc.so.5", O_RDONLY)    = -1 ENOENT (No such file or directory)
open("/usr/local/lib/libc.so.5", O_RDONLY) = -1 ENOENT (No such file or directory)
open("/lib/libc.so.5.2.18", O_RDONLY)   = 3
```

There is some hazard in changing your LD_LIBRARY_PATH because you may suddenly find that certain programs depended on certain versions of the libraries and are now using a different version.

It is entirely possible to serve content off a CD-ROM. Since CD-ROMs run at far slower rates than disk drives, this is not recommended for performance reasons.

Another trick to save memory and speed up file access is to use Unix memory mapping of files, via the mmap() system call. This allows you to deliberately put a data file in RAM so that multiple CGI or other processes using that file will all be referring to part of memory rather than disk. Reading a file will bring it into the buffer cache anyway, but it is more efficient to bring it in via `mmap()` because `mmap()` will map the file directly into the user's address space, while `read()` and `write()` will copy the data into the kernel first, and from there into user space. Once the file is in memory, you can use pointers to access data in the file, which is far quicker than the standard I/O routines. Memory mapping files requires programming in C rather than, say, Perl or Java. `man mmap` for more information. BSD and Solaris can map files to memory, but Linux 2.0 cannot.

Finally, note that most Unix shells and web servers understand constructs like *~user* to be a shorthand for the user's home directory. So when you see URLs of the form *http://server/~user/file.html*, the web server has to resolve that tilde to a user's home directory. This can be done in several ways, such as by an NIS lookup or reading the */etc/passwd* file, but it takes significant time in any case. The classic way is to open the */etc/passwd* file and scan down for the user, then move over to get his or her home directory, which is time-consuming even if */etc/passwd* is cached in RAM and lookups are hashed. It is still expensive to look up *~user* many times per second, especially if you don't have *cachefs*. In general, it is a bad idea to use ~ in path names on heavily loaded web servers.

The Windowing System

There is no need for a windowing system on a web server. Users will not benefit from it, because they can't see the server's screen. On the contrary, users will suffer from a windowing system because it uses CPU and a great deal of RAM. Eliminating use of the windowing system avoids problems caused by process priority shifting depending on where the mouse is at any given time. On most windowing systems, it is now standard to increase the priority of processes running in or started from the currently selected window. A web server is likely to suffer when an interactive user is sitting at the keyboard, running jobs with higher priority.

You can see this for yourself with a simple experiment. Say you start a single *httpd* process from an *xterm* under Solaris. Here's a little *sh* script that will show you the priority of that *httpd* once per second. The priority is the number in the seventh column from the left:

```
while true
do
ps -cle | grep httpd
sleep 1
done
```

As you move your mouse out of the xterm and click into some other window, you'll see the priority of *httpd* drop by 10. When you move your mouse back into the *xterm* where you started *httpd*, you'll see its priority increase by 10. This is probably not what you want for a dedicated web server.

It is quite straightforward to avoid starting X on Unix systems, and to do maintenance in terminal mode or through telnet sessions. Windows and the Mac do not give you that option; you are forced to expend resources on their windowing systems even if your machine is a dedicated web server.

Versions and Patches

You should use the latest non-beta version of your operating system with all patches, because performance improvements are always being found and security holes blocked. You can see what version of the OS you are using when you boot up or by using the *uname -a* command on most versions of Unix. You should be aware that patches often introduce their own bugs, so check performance immediately after installing a patch. The Solaris Internet Server Supplement (SISS) patch for Solaris 2.5.1 gives about a 20% performance boost to Internet services under Solaris 2.5.1, both on Sparc and Intel CPUs. The SISS also gives you WebNFS (a file system for the Web) and the Java virtual machine for multi-CPU machines. SISS 1.0 is incorporated into Solaris 2.6. Under Solaris, *showrev -p* shows you the patches installed.

Configurable OS Parameters

Here, we go over optimum parameters for web services. Note that Unix systems are shipped with a generic kernel, optimized not for any particular use, but for acceptable performance for general use. See Chapter 10 for information on configuring TCP. You can see the current settings in a Solaris system by viewing */etc/system* or grepping for "ndd" from *inetinit*. In general, Solaris 2.6 is already tuned for web services, so you shouldn't have to modify anything to get the best performance. Here are a few of the most basic parameters you may want to tune on Linux or another OS. Remember to back up your kernel and configuration files before changing anything:

Number of file descriptors

File descriptors are positive integers by which the kernel keeps track of open files and network connections per process. If your web server software has a very large number of open files and connections in a process, it is possible to run out of file descriptors, meaning that you will not be able to accept new connections until old connections terminate and give up their descriptors. In programmer's terms, the `accept()` system call will fail. What happens after that depends on your version of Unix; it may log an error to the system log or print a message on the console, among other things. Old versions of Unix had

a file descriptor limit of 20 (as `OPEN_MAX` in *limits.h* for SVR4), but every system has increased it far beyond that. It is not unreasonable to want several
thousand file descriptors. The `limit` or `ulimit` shell commands and C functions can both be used in some versions of Unix to change the maximum
number of file descriptors on a "soft" basis, up to a "hard" limit imposed by a
number compiled into the kernel. The limit is 256 in Linux 2.0, and 1024 in
Linux 2.1. To change the hard limit, you may have to change the source code
and recompile the kernel. Under Solaris 2.5.1, set `rlim_fd_max=4096` in *etc/
system* and reboot.

Number of processes

The maximum number of processes allowed to any one user can also be set
with `ulimit` up to the hard limit defined in the kernel. Linux has a hard limit
of 4000 simultaneous processes. Solaris allows a very large number of processes, so you'll run out of other resources first.

Network buffers

Note that the web server's response is written to a network buffer, also called
a socket buffer, not directly to the client. This allows the OS to take care of
forwarding data back to slow clients, freeing up a thread in the web server. If
the network buffer is too small, the web server has to write the response in
buffer-sized chunks, waiting for each chunk to drain before it can write the
next one. The OS should have the right number and size of network buffers to
handle your connections without either wasting memory or forcing the server
to block while waiting for an available buffer. Network buffers belonging to
clients who have ungracefully disconnected for whatever reason are a major
source of wasted memory on web servers; this is one reason to turn down the
TCP keepalive interval.

The size of socket buffers can be set with the options `SO_SNDBUF` and `SO_`
`RCVBUF` to the C-level call `setsockopt()`, at least up to a limit compiled into
the kernel. High-volume servers with lots of RAM will benefit from larger buffers. A small receive buffer size is a way of limiting the backlog of incoming
data. `man setsockopt` for more details.

Apache has a `SendBufferSize` directive to allow a webmaster to control the
size of socket buffers without recompiling the source code. A larger socket
buffer will result in a larger TCP window being advertised. Here is a comment
from Apache's *httpd_main.c* source file:

```
/*
 * To send data over high bandwidth-delay connections at full
 * speed we must force the TCP window to open wide enough to keep the
 * pipe full.  The default window size on many systems
 * is only 4kB.  Cross-country WAN connections of 100ms
 * at 1Mb/s are not impossible for well connected sites.
```

```
* If we assume 100ms cross-country latency,
* a 4kB buffer limits throughput to 40kB/s.
*
* To avoid this problem I've added the SendBufferSize directive
* to allow the web master to configure send buffer size.
*
* The trade-off of larger buffers is that more kernel memory
* is consumed.  YMMV, know your customers and your network!
*
* -John Heidemann <johnh@isi.edu> 25-Oct-96
*
* If no size is specified, use the kernel default.
*/
```

Memory limits

You may also specify the maximum amount of memory that a process may use via the `ulimit` system call or `ulimit` user-level program. This can put a cap on the amount of damage done by a runaway CGI. Unfortunately, some systems do not implement this correctly, allowing processes arbitrary amounts of memory.

Flushing frequency

Writes are not necessarily synchronous in Unix. When you write to a file, the change happens immediately in memory but it is not committed to disk until the operating system gets around to it. In this way, you get better write performance, since writes appear instantaneous to the user but can be queued up in the most efficient order by the disk controller. The downside is that when the write to disk does happen, it runs to completion, meaning that other tasks must be put off during the write, so the user may notice a delay. One way around this is to use a Direct Memory Access (DMA) disk controller card, which controls the transfer of data between memory and disk without use of the CPU. Once the transfer is initiated, the CPU can return its attention to the user so that disk writes do not affect responsiveness.

If you don't have a DMA disk controller, you can trade off memory usage against the frequency of writes by writing to disk at longer intervals. Note that the writes may take longer, since more data has accumulated and that loss of power before a write puts more data at risk. 60 seconds is a good amount of time to wait, rather than the default of 30 in Linux. In Linux, change */etc/rc.d/ rc.S* to have this line: `/sbin/update 60` &. Under Solaris, the synchronization load is spread across 5-second intervals by the *fsflush* process.

Unix OS Monitoring Tools

Most versions of Unix collect performance metrics once per second from the kernel, so most Unix performance monitoring facilities do not allow a sample rate of greater than once per second. You wouldn't want to do much more monitoring of general statistics anyway, because the measurement itself would significantly add to the load. Read the manpage on each of these for more detailed information. Here are the major monitoring tools and some example output on a heavily loaded web server.

ps

The most basic tool to let you know what's going on is *ps*, which displays all your processes along with information on CPU and memory usage. The options to *ps* vary a great deal with OS, so you need to read the *ps* manpage on your system for more details. An important point to remember is that Berkeley-style priorities are opposite from SVR4 priorities. In SVR4, higher numbers mean higher priority. You can display SVR4 priority with the *-c* option. Here's a listing sorted by priority and edited a bit for clarity:

```
% ps -cle | sort -k 7,7 | tail -25
 F S   UID   PID  PPID CLS PRI     ADDR    SZ   WCHAN TTY      TIME CMD
 8 S 10002 24097 24060  TS  58 61518010   346 6101627e ?       0:01 xterm
 8 S 10002 27452 24102  TS  58 61216cd8  1297 6101663e pts/15  0:14 xemacs
 8 S 10003 10417     1  TS  58 60602668   370 60aebd36 ?       0:00 xterm
 8 S 65533 21162 21161  TS  58 613d6670   346 610162a6 ?       0:00 xterm
 8 S 65533 21305 21174  TS  58 612ff9a0   257 6194b156 pts/30  0:00 tcsh
 8 S 65533 29569 27210  TS  58 612f0cd8   231 61017f16 ?       0:00 httpd
 8 S     0   135     1  TS  59 605f0cc8   203 604d3c96 ?       0:00 in.named
 8 S     0   312     1  TS  59 607ce020   214 607ce1f0 ?       0:02 nntp
 8 S     0 19112 19104  TS  59 60efb998   109 60efbb68 ?       0:00 tail
 8 S 10001 12530     1  TS  59 60c0a008   725 60c0a1d8 ?       0:02 java
 8 S 10001 20646     1  TS  59 61260010   726 612601e0 ?       0:02 java
 8 S 10001 22450     1  TS  59 60b26660   726 60b26830 ?       0:01 java
 8 S 10001 29165     1  TS  59 6183ecc0   723 6183ee90 ?       0:01 java
 8 S 65533 11391 11386  TS  59 60029338  1209 60029508 ?       0:40 java
 8 S 65533 27224 27210  TS  59 61a1acd8   231 60d13e10 ?       0:00 httpd
 8 S 65533 29602 27210  TS  59 618e0000   231 60d13290 ?       0:00 httpd
 8 S  6443 11302 11301  TS  60 60028cd8   240 6152e0a6 pts/18  0:00 tcsh
 8 S 65533  4437 27210  TS  60 61a2e020   231 60d13350 ?       0:00 httpd
 8 S 65533 19921 27210  TS  60 60065338   231 60d13310 ?       0:00 httpd
 8 S 65533 29603 27210  TS  60 6120a668   231 60d13190 ?       0:00 httpd
 8 S 65533 29604 27210  TS  60 618eece0   231 60d13210 ?       0:00 httpd
 8 S 65533 29605 27210  TS  60 61988008   231 60d13250 ?       0:00 httpd
 8 S 65533 29606 27210  TS  60 61a0e020   231 60d132d0 ?       0:00 httpd
19 S     0     3     0 SYS  60 60122678     0 1043e194 ?      64:08 fsflush
19 T     0     0     0 SYS  96 10416c88     0          ?       0:00 sched
19 S     0     2     0 SYS  98 60122cd8     0 10439f10 ?       0:00 pageout
```

perfmeter

perfmeter is a very simple graphical tool for viewing the performance of the disk, network, CPU, and so forth. It comes bundled with Solaris. Set it up to view everything to get the best feel for which components affect others. You'll have an easy way to see if your CPU is overloaded, for example, or when there is network traffic when you didn't expect it. *xload* is a similar tool for Linux.

Figure 12-2 shows what *perfmeter* looks like on a Sun Ultra 1 with 64MB RAM, running Solaris 2.5.1. I hit this machine with a load generation tool that asked for a 55K binary file 250 times in 35 seconds. So the server was being hit about 7 times per second, and the throughput was about 3Mbit per second.

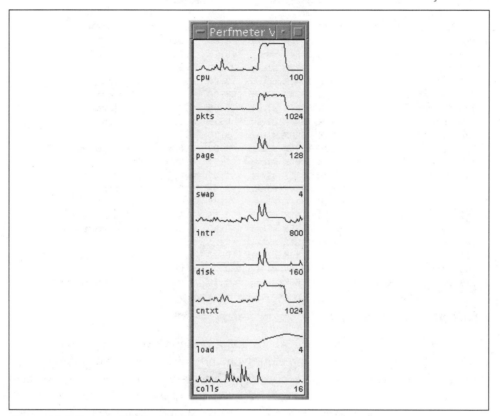

Figure 12-2. Image of perfmeter

rup

rup is useful for seeing which machines running *rstatd* are on your local LAN and what their load averages are, as a first glance at the network.

top

top is a wonderful tool for continuously seeing what processes are at the top of resource consumption at the moment. It is rather like a self-refreshing *ps* that lets you sort the output in several ways. Here is *top* on a large web server:

```
last pid:  1867;  load averages:  1.29,  1.38,  1.40                13:57:59
196 processes: 173 sleeping, 1 running, 21 zombie, 1 on cpu
CPU states: 61.2% idle, 11.7% user, 24.5% kernel,  2.7% iowait,  0.0% swap
Memory: 371M real, 106M free, 260M swap, 181M free swap

  PID USERNAME PRI NICE  SIZE   RES STATE   TIME   WCPU    CPU COMMAND
29390 giacomo    8    0   10M   10M sleep   0:02  1.51%  2.94% buildindex
27210 fred     -25    0 1848K 1384K run   348:16  2.31%  2.36% httpd
 2807 root      33    0  133M  117M sleep  22.8H  2.67%  1.46% dataserver
 1074 patrick   33    0 1880K 1648K cpu     0:00  0.35%  0.27% top
27643 jeffrey   33    0   12M 4824K sleep  67:00  0.15%  0.08% java
 2302 jeffrey   33    0 5648K 5224K sleep   0:05  0.02%  0.05% java
 8450 root      33    0 2136K 1592K sleep   0:38  0.01%  0.03% sshd
   99 root      -3    0  904K  680K sleep   9:30  0.02%  0.01% defrouter
  117 root      33    0 2120K 1176K sleep   3:02  0.00%  0.00% rpcbind
  315 root      33    0 2000K 1000K sleep   1:37  0.00%  0.00% lpd
12828 root      33    0 1672K  816K sleep   1:09  0.00%  0.00% sshd
  445 root      33    0 8248K  904K sleep   0:43  0.00%  0.00% backupserver
11391 aloysiu   34    0 9672K 5368K sleep   0:39  0.00%  0.00% java
    1 root      33    0  440K  192K sleep   0:36  0.00%  0.00% init
  330 root      33    0 2904K 1888K sleep   0:30  0.00%  0.00% defcon
  140 root      23    0 1760K 1184K sleep   0:21  0.00%  0.00% inetd
  217 root      33    0 1504K 1144K sleep   0:20  0.00%  0.00% syslogd
  346 root      33    0 1480K  736K sleep   0:20  0.00%  0.00% at
  213 root      33    0 2752K 1568K sleep   0:10  0.00%  0.00% automountd
```

System Call Tracers

Do you ever wish you could see what's going on inside your computer while it's mulling over some seemingly simple question and driving you crazy in the process? Well, you can, sort of. You can see exactly which system calls are being executed and what the parameters to those calls are with one of the system call tracing utilities, such as *truss* on Solaris or *strace* on Linux. Shared library calls can be seen using *sotruss* under Solaris 2.6. See Chapter 13, *Server Software*, for a trace of what happens when a request is made of a web server.

Network Snooping Tools

Do you ever wish you could see what's going across your Ethernet connection? The *snoop* utility that comes bundled with Solaris will show you exactly what's being transmitted across your segment of the network. You have to be *root* to run it because it allows you to see absolutely everything, down to the content of the packets. *tcpdump* is a similar utility from the Stevens TCP/IP book with source code available from *ftp://ftp.uu.net/*.

There is a snoop of a web request in Chapter 10.

netstat

netstat shows the status of network connections. This is very valuable for determining what connections are up and whether you are wasting a lot of memory holding connection buffers for unused connections. *netstat -c* will start displaying an updated network status every second, which is very instructive if you make a few requests from your browser while running it. Here's some sample output from *netstat*:

```
% netstat -at
Active Internet connections (including servers)
Proto Recv-Q Send-Q Local Address       Foreign Address  (State)    User
tcp      0      0 *:700                *:*              LISTEN     root
tcp      0      0 *:netbios-ssn        *:*              LISTEN     root
tcp      0      0 *:nntp               *:*              LISTEN     root
tcp      0      0 *:auth               *:*              LISTEN     root
tcp      0      0 *:6000               *:*              LISTEN     patrick
tcp      0      0 *:sunrpc             *:*              LISTEN     root
tcp      0      0 *:pop3               *:*              LISTEN     root
tcp      0      0 *:www                *:*              LISTEN     root
tcp      0      0 *:finger             *:*              LISTEN     root
tcp      1      0 cm208144186.cab:1584 nike.veritas.com:www CLOSE_WAIT patrick
tcp      1      0 cm208144186.cab:1580 nike.veritas.com:www CLOSE_WAIT patrick
tcp      1      0 cm208144186.cab:1579 nike.veritas.com:www CLOSE_WAIT patrick
tcp      1      0 cm208144186.cab:1578 nike.veritas.com:www CLOSE_WAIT patrick
tcp      1      0 cm208144186.cab:1577 nike.veritas.com:www CLOSE_WAIT patrick
tcp      1      0 cm208144186.cab:1576 nike.veritas.com:www CLOSE_WAIT patrick
tcp      1      0 cm208144186.cab:1575 nike.veritas.com:www CLOSE_WAIT patrick
tcp      0      0 *:time               *:*              LISTEN     root
tcp      0      0 *:uucp               *:*              LISTEN     root
tcp      0      0 *:ftp                *:*              LISTEN     root
tcp      0      0 *:chargen            *:*              LISTEN     root
tcp      0      0 *:netstat            *:*              LISTEN     root
tcp      0      0 *:daytime            *:*              LISTEN     root
tcp      0      0 *:systat             *:*              LISTEN     root
tcp      0      0 *:discard            *:*              LISTEN     root
tcp      0      0 *:echo               *:*              LISTEN     root
tcp      0      0 *:printer            *:*              LISTEN     root
tcp      0      0 *:shell              *:*              LISTEN     root
tcp      0      0 *:login              *:*              LISTEN     root
tcp      0      0 *:2049               *:*              LISTEN     root
```

vmstat

Use *vmstat* to give you a snapshot of your memory situation in an ASCII format that varies between Unix versions. Your scan rate and page out rate under Solaris are an indication of whether you have enough memory. You want to keep both of them low. Here's some sample output from *vmstat*:

```
% vmstat 1
```

procs			memory		page						disk				faults			cpu		
r	b	w	swap	free	re	mf	pi	po	fr	de	sr	s2	s3	s4	s1	in	sy	cs	us	sy	id
0	0	0	352	888	0	534	18	3	7	0	0	0	1	0	1	271	1	418	3	6	91
6	0	0	192960	111528	0	2139	0	0	0	0	0	0	0	0	0	488	2780	1106	4	23	73
1	0	0	196128	112136	0	4412	0	0	0	0	0	0	0	0	0	1086	3193	2511	7	33	60
0	0	0	194016	111416	0	3419	0	0	0	0	0	0	0	0	0	689	1977	1722	2	22	76
0	0	0	193664	111296	0	4319	0	0	0	0	0	0	0	0	0	890	2597	2231	2	28	69
1	0	0	195608	111992	0	4100	0	0	0	0	0	0	0	0	0	887	2341	2210	4	23	72
0	0	0	196480	112256	0	1234	0	0	0	0	0	0	0	0	0	390	924	785	2	7	92
0	0	0	194720	111720	0	1616	0	0	0	0	0	0	0	0	0	360	1095	738	2	8	91
0	0	0	189440	110016	0	2900	0	0	0	0	0	0	0	0	0	701	1767	1732	2	20	78
1	0	0	195040	111768	0	5486	0	0	0	0	0	0	2	0	1	1046	3969	2729	10	32	58
0	0	0	194280	110808	0	4147	0	0	0	0	0	0	0	0	0	787	2368	1984	2	27	70
2	0	0	191816	110152	0	5556	0	0	0	0	0	0	31	0	0	1122	3268	2840	4	38	58
0	0	0	194368	111528	0	3784	0	0	0	0	0	0	0	0	0	750	2157	1914	4	18	78
2	0	0	194776	112064	0	4684	0	0	0	0	0	0	0	0	0	893	2607	2316	4	28	67
0	0	0	195424	111888	0	2366	0	0	0	0	0	0	1	0	0	526	1433	1240	4	16	81
0	0	0	195424	111888	0	3650	0	0	0	0	0	0	0	0	0	758	2381	1896	2	24	73
0	0	0	194368	111592	0	4166	0	0	0	0	0	0	0	0	0	830	2405	2108	3	24	73
0	0	0	194368	111528	0	3430	0	0	0	0	0	0	0	0	0	676	2116	1724	2	22	76
0	0	0	194360	112000	0	3988	0	0	0	0	0	0	0	0	0	772	2266	1896	2	26	71

sar

sar provides much the same information as *vmstat*, but can save data in a compact binary format suitable for long-term statistics gathering. *sar* itself provides display options for the data collected. It is much more complete and flexible than *vmstat*. Here's sample output from *sar*:

```
% sar -c 5 5

SunOS pokey.patrick.net 5.5.1 Generic_103640-12 sun4u     02/17/98
```

15:03:46	scall/s	sread/s	swrit/s	fork/s	exec/s	rchar/s	wchar/s
15:03:51	2418	5	84	79.64	0.60	1126	537
15:03:56	1703	3	58	57.80	0.00	478	505
15:04:01	1676	10	57	51.70	0.00	640	523
15:04:06	2553	14	93	84.83	0.00	739	559
15:04:11	1807	4	60	56.80	0.60	965	556

Unix Versus NT as the Web Server OS

All of this is not to say there is no competition for Unix as a web server platform. It is simple to set up a web server on any Windows or Macintosh machine and get reasonable performance, as long as the load is light. But for heavy loads, the only competitor to Unix for a web server platform is Windows NT. The creators of NT applied many of Unix's features, such as the concepts of a kernel, user processes, and preemptive multitasking, to the design of NT. Let's take a look at what each OS has to offer.

NT Pros and Cons

NT has the traditional Microsoft advantages of close integration with other Microsoft products, a consistent look and feel, and GUI rather than command line administration for those who don't like to type commands and don't want or need a fine level of control. NT has the ability to run some legacy Windows applications. NT can run on cheap commodity PC hardware, but so can many versions of Unix.

NT does not have especially good performance or scalability for web serving. See the article "The Best OS for Web Serving: Unix or NT?" by Barry Nance (*Byte Magazine*, March 1998) for one experiment confirming this. More important, NT is very unstable compared to Unix, frequently crashing or requiring reboots, which is a serious drawback to using it for important sites. NT comes with no remote administration and no multiuser mode.

Running a high-performance web site on PC hardware is also difficult. Scalability is limited by the PC's legacy I/O architecture, which was never intended for large loads. By some estimates, you cannot handle more than about 250 concurrent transaction processing users on even the best PC hardware. PC hardware is also generally less reliable than true workstation hardware, because it is built for the mass market, where cost rather than reliability is the driving factor.

Microsoft also has some credibility problems. Their "Wolfpack" scalability demonstration used the easily fudged debit-credit benchmark, rather than the more reliable TPC-C and TPC-D transaction processing benchmarks. And Microsoft has been accused of misrepresenting the capability of NT workstation relative to its NT server edition. The cheaper NT workstation was limited to 10 open connections, allegedly because it couldn't handle more than that; users were supposed to pay much more for a supposedly higher-performance version. A binary *diff* showed that the executables were identical, except for a few bytes that were presumably a switch allowing more connections.

Unix Pros and Cons

Unix operating systems are very robust, usually capable of running for many months and sometimes several years without rebooting. Equally important is that Unix has much better scalability than NT, allowing a small site to grow by adding hardware such as CPUs and I/O controllers to existing machines rather than requiring multiple new machines to handle increasing load. Finally, Unix has better performance, partly because it is usually run on better hardware rather than commodity PCs.

A large majority of high-performance web sites run on some version of Unix, so the issues are well worked out.

A professional Unix system will typically have a higher entry-level cost than NT, even if the price/performance ratio at that level is better. If cost is a big consideration, there are many versions of Unix that will run on the same commodity PC hardware as NT and provide the same or better performance, such as Solaris x86, Linux, and BSDI. Pricing for Solaris is similar to that for NT.

Unix also requires more highly trained system administrators, although GUI tools for the Unix-averse are starting to appear, such as Sun's Netra product line.

Key Recommendations

- Don't write back the file access time. Either mount a filesystem as read-only or change the filesystem source and recompile.
- Use short paths.
- Don't use symbolic links.
- Don't run a window system on the server; use terminal mode.

13

Server Software

Inside Web Server Software

At the most basic level, web servers accept requests and return replies. The reply can be a static page, custom dynamic content, or an error. While there is a lot of variation in performance depending on load, an individual request for a static page typically takes only one- or two-tenths of a second from the time the request arrives on the network until the response is pushed back out. Modem latency, Internet latency, and even browser parsing time are all likely to be larger than that, so a lightly loaded web server will not be a bottleneck.

A heavily loaded web server is another story. Web servers tend to go nonlinear when loaded beyond a certain point, degrading rapidly in performance. This chapter is about why that happens and what your options are for getting the most out of your web server software.

The Evolution of Server Software

Servers spawned from inetd

The first generation of web servers were just another Unix service launched on demand from *inetd*, which reads */etc/services* on startup and listens to the ports specified. When a request comes in on one of *inetd*'s ports, it launches the program specified in */etc/services* to deal with requests on that port. This requires calling the `fork()` and `exec()` system calls: `fork()` to clone *inetd* to get a process, and `exec()` to write over that process with another process that can service the request. This mechanism is intended to conserve system resources by starting up daemons only when they're needed, providing better performance for everything else. As an example, consider *ftpd*. Watch the list of processes running on your system, say with *top*. When a request comes in on port 21, *inetd* launches *ftpd*, and you will see *ftpd* appear in the list of processes. When the FTP session is over, the FTP process goes away.

Originally, *httpd* was launched the same way, but from port 80. Trouble started when servers were loaded above one or two hits per second and couldn't keep up. Remember that a single HTML page can have many embedded images, so one page can generate enough HTTP operations to reach the maximum load of an *inetd*-spawned server. The *inetd* mechanism trades off more startup time for reduced overall system load, but this tradeoff works only under very light web serving loads. For anything more, system load is actually increased by the many startups of *httpd,* and performance for both the local machine user and the web client is reduced. Avoid launching *httpd* from *inetd*; run a standalone server instead.

Configure Apache's *httpd.conf* like this:

```
# ServerType is either inetd, or standalone.
ServerType standalone
```

Forking servers

A step up from using *inetd* to `fork()` and `exec()` is to use an instance of *httpd* to simply `fork()` another copy of itself to handle the request, with no need for an `exec()`. This was the original intent behind the `fork()` system call, and it works reasonably well for the client-server world, but because HTTP requests arrive so frequently and are of such short duration, the time spent in creating a new process is larger than the time spent actually servicing the request. The early CERN and NCSA servers were forking servers.

Another improvement came with the Apache server. Apache servers are preforking. For example, when Apache 1.2.4 *httpd* starts up, it immediately starts five additional servers by default to handle multiple simultaneous requests from one browser or from several concurrent clients. Apache will increase the number of server processes in response to a heavier load; this works well even for very large sites, but it is memory- and CPU-intensive.

Threaded servers

To match the lightweight and transient nature of an HTTP connection, server programmers have been turning to threads. Threads are independent streams of execution within a single process. Thread creation and context switching is on the order of ten times faster than for processes. Still, once you have a process created and ready to handle a connection, the bottleneck is in servicing the request rather than the overhead of managing server processes or threads, so you don't see a full tenfold increase in performance with the threaded server. Netscape Enterprise 2.0

and up are threaded servers and can currently serve several thousand connections per second.

Keepalive servers

An additional improvement in performance is available by keeping TCP connections open for serving multiple files in one request. This technique is known as persistent connections, or "keepalive," and is part of the HTTP 1.1 standard. Most browsers and servers now understand keepalive connections even if they don't fully implement HTTP 1.1. Browsers will indicate that they understand keepalive connections by sending a `Connection: keepalive` header with their request. Both preforking and threaded servers use keepalives.

A performance hazard to keepalives is that clients may disconnect without notifying the server, which then has an open connection consuming resources indefinitely. To prevent too many such connections from accumulating, most implementations of keepalive come with a timeout parameter so that unused connections will be closed.

Behind the Scenes

Here's a system call trace (to trace all requests made of the operating system) on Linux 2.0 of what Apache 1.2.4 does in response to a request from a browser. Since this is a preforking server, you need the -*f* option to *strace* to follow child *httpd* processes. You usually can't tell why an application decided to make a particular system call, but this is still a very valuable technique for figuring out where a server is spending its time:

```
# strace -f /opt/apache_1.2.4/src/httpd -f /opt/apache_1.2.4/conf/httpd.conf

accept(15, {sin_family=AF_INET, sin_port=htons(1049),
    sin_addr=inet_addr("127.0.0.1")}, [16]) = 3
fcntl(18, F_SETLKW, {type=F_UNLCK, whence=SEEK_SET, start=0, len=0}) = 0
sigaction(SIGUSR1, {SIG_IGN},  <unfinished ...>
<... sigaction resumed> {0x80040a0, [USR1], SA_INTERRUPT}) = 0
getsockname(3, {sin_family=AF_INET, sin_port=htons(8085),
    sin_addr=inet_addr("127.0.0.1")}, [16]) = 0
setsockopt(3, IPPROTO_TCP1, [1], 4) = 0
getpid()                        = 382
brk(0x804f000)                  = 0x804f000
brk(0x8050000)                  = 0x8050000
brk(0x8053000)                  = 0x8053000
sigaction(SIGALRM, {0x8003440, [], SA_INTERRUPT}, {SIG_DFL}) = 0
alarm(300)                      = 0
select(4, [3], NULL, NULL, {0, 0}) = 0 (Timeout)
read(3, "GET / HTTP/1.0\r\n", 4096) = 16
sigaction(SIGUSR1, {SIG_IGN}, {SIG_IGN}) = 0
time(NULL)                      = 883860478
sigaction(SIGALRM, {0x8003440, [], SA_INTERRUPT}, {0x8003440, [ALRM],
```

```
    SA_INTERRUPT}) = 0
alarm(300)                  = 289
read(3, "\r\n", 4096)       = 2
alarm(0)                    = 300
sigaction(SIGUSR1, {SIG_IGN}, {SIG_IGN}) = 0
getpid()                    = 382
stat("/home/patrick/public_html", {st_mode=S_IFDIR|0775, st_size=1024, ...}) = 0
open("/.htaccess", O_RDONLY) = -1 ENOENT (No such file or directory)
open("/home/.htaccess", O_RDONLY) = -1 ENOENT (No such file or directory)
open("/home/patrick/.htaccess", O_RDONLY) = -1 ENOENT
    (No such file or directory)
open("/home/patrick/public_html/.htaccess", O_RDONLY) = -1 ENOENT
    (No such file or directory)
brk(0x8056000)              = 0x8056000
stat("/home/patrick/public_html/index.html", {st_mode=S_IFREG|0664,
    st_size=2306, ...}) = 0
stat("/home/patrick/public_html/index.html", {st_mode=S_IFREG|0664,
    st_size=2306, ...}) = 0
open("/home/patrick/public_html/index.html", O_RDONLY) = 4
time(NULL)                  = 883860478
open("/usr/lib/zoneinfo/GMT", O_RDONLY) = 5
read(5, "\0\0\0\0\0\0\0\0\0\0\0\0\0\0\0\0"..., 6460) = 55
close(5)                    = 0
sigaction(SIGALRM, {0x8003440, [], SA_INTERRUPT}, {0x8003440, [ALRM],
    SA_INTERRUPT}) = 0
alarm(300)                  = 0
alarm(0)                    = 300
sigaction(SIGALRM, {0x8003440, [], SA_INTERRUPT}, {0x8003440, [ALRM],
    SA_INTERRUPT}) = 0
alarm(300)                  = 0
fstat(4, {st_mode=S_IFREG|0664, st_size=2306, ...}) = 0
brk(0x8057000)              = 0x8057000
read(4, "<html>\n<title>Patrick Killelea<"..., 4096) = 2306
read(4, "", 4096)           = 0
alarm(300)                  = 300
read(4, "", 4096)           = 0
alarm(0)                    = 300
close(4)                    = 0
time(NULL)                  = 883860479
write(16, "127.0.0.1 - - [03/Jan/1998:14:47"..., 69) = 69
sigaction(SIGALRM, {0x8003780, [], SA_INTERRUPT}, {0x8003440, [ALRM],
    SA_INTERRUPT}) = 0
alarm(30)                   = 0
write(3, "HTTP/1.1 200 OK\r\nDate: Sat, 03"..., 2546) = 2546
shutdown(3, 1 /* send */)   = 0
select(4, [3], NULL, [3], {2, 0}) = 1 (in [3], left {1, 780000})
read(3, "", 2048)           = 0
close(3)                    = 0
alarm(0)                    = 30
sigaction(SIGUSR1, {0x8004090, [], SA_INTERRUPT}, {SIG_IGN}) = 0
alarm(0)                    = 0
sigaction(SIGPIPE, {0x8003440, [], SA_INTERRUPT}, {0x8003440, [PIPE],
    SA_INTERRUPT}) = 0
close(3)                         = -1 EBADF (Bad file number)
```

First you see the `accept()` system call, because the server recognizes a request for services from IP address 127.0.0.1, which is the local machine. Some manipulation of the socket is done, along with a few requests for more memory, and then the server begins to read the request from the socket: `GET / HTTP/1.0` and a following blank line, shown by another carriage return and line feed: `\r\n`. The blank line signifies the end of the request, so the server looks at its server root directory */home/patrick/public_html* to make sure that it exists and the server has permission to read it. Then the server does something a little odd: it checks each directory from the system root (/) on down for web permissions.

In this kind of full-path authentication on Apache and some other servers, the current directory and each parent directory (up to the system root, not just up to the document root) are searched by default for a *.htaccess* authentication file, which must be read and parsed, if found. You can speed up Apache by turning off authentication for directories that don't need it, like the system root, by putting the following in the *access.conf* file:

```
<Directory />
AllowOverride None
</Directory>

<Directory /usr/local/mydocroot>
AllowOverride All (or any of the other AllowOverride options)
</Directory>
```

See *Apache: The Definitive Guide*, by Ben Laurie and Peter Laurie (O'Reilly & Associates), for more information on the `AllowOverride` directive.

Once the web server is satisfied that there are no restrictions on the server root directory or that the user has permission, it opens *index.html* in that directory and reads it. Then it gets the time; updates the log file with the time and file served, among other parameters; and finally writes the file out to the socket. Then it closes the socket (in this case twice, for some unknown reason, failing the second time).

This was a simple case with no CGI, but if there were CGI script output, it would be buffered by the web server so that large chunks could be sent in the same IP packet, improving network performance by amortization. If you want to send a smooth stream of output back to the client (say for audio or video streams) you would need to use non-parsed headers. See Chapter 15, *CGI Programs*, for more details.

How Servers Fail

A preforking server with a fixed maximum number of processes (for example, the `MaxClients` parameter in Apache's *httpd.conf*) handles that many clients at one time, and no more. Additional requests are refused by the server, and the user is met with an annoying "connection refused" message in the browser. The refused connections have no impact on the server's ability to handle the requests that it does accept. Similarly, threaded servers hit the maximum number of threads (for example, the `MaxThreads` parameter in Netscape Enterprise's *magnus.conf*) and refuse any more connections.

But let's say that we configure an infinite number of processes or threads, set the TCP listen queue to "infinite," and then we overload the servers by increasing the number of client requests. What happens?

Not only are there too many client connections competing for CPU time, but the overhead of scheduling those processes or threads consumes an ever larger percentage of CPU time. Eventually, the CPU spends almost all of its time scheduling and no real work is done. If you were to graph throughput against number of simultaneous connections, throughput would peak at a certain number of connections, and then fall off as you moved beyond that number.

Performance degrades faster for non-threaded servers because of the larger overhead of scheduling and switching between processes rather than threads. CPU load rises as the number of processes to be scheduled increases. Memory is also depleted faster in the forking server, because processes incur greater overhead than threads. Still, degradation is fairly linear, because the impact is distributed across many fairly small processes.

Threaded servers hold up better at first because of lower overhead in context switching between threads, slowly dropping in performance as more threads are scheduled and switched, until memory is low enough that the machine begins to swap. The downside to threaded servers is that swapping out the huge process with all the threads is a sudden large hit to performance. This is why Netscape advises you to run four processes with 32 threads each rather than one process with 128 threads.

Slow clients have more impact on memory than fast clients because each slow client ties up buffers concurrently with other slow processes. This means that a threaded server fails sooner when most of the clients are on slow connections. Keep in mind that when the Internet is heavily loaded, say in the afternoon, it looks to the web server like everyone is on a slow connection. Fast clients benefit more than slow clients from server I/O improvements.

Some web servers slowly leak memory, that is, they allocate memory and lose all references to it, meaning that memory cannot be used or reclaimed. This eventually makes the server process so large that it has to be restarted. If restarting the web server significantly helps performance, you may have a leak. If you can't get a bug fix, the next best thing is to schedule regular restarts of the web server software or, in the worst case, reboots. You can monitor the size of your *httpd* processes with *ps* or *top*. Server vendors can and do run leak-finding tools like Purify

(*http://www.pureatria.com/*) on their products, but their aggressive release sched-
ules mean that they don't have time for extensive usage tests with Purify.

Common Server Parameters

Server vendors try to tune their servers as best they can for general use before
they send them out to you. They certainly want you to get high performance. The
reason you might change things is that you know more about your particular
needs than they do.

Number of Processes

You'll get better performance by running only the number of server processes
your RAM can hold. If you run too many, you'll start swapping and performance
for each will drop. If you can run only 32 server processes in RAM, then don't try
to run any more than that, even if you often have more than 32 concurrent users.
You can configure the number of *httpd* processes in Apache with the **Max-
Clients** directive. You don't want to run too few *httpd* processes either, because
you need enough processes so that fast clients never have to wait for a slow client to finish and free up a process.

Number of Server Threads

Configure the server only for the maximum number of threads the RAM will support. See Chapter 2, *Capacity Planning*, for some threads-to-memory recommendations.

Persistent Connections

Turn on persistent connections, or keepalives (**KeepAlive On** in Apache's
httpd.conf), and set the number of allowed requests per connection high (**Max-
KeepAliveRequests 200**) to save the overhead of setting up new connections,
but set the timeout fairly low, say 15 seconds (**KeepAliveTimeout 15**) to reduce
the impact of dead or very slow clients.

Access Control

The general web performance tip of keeping search paths short takes on added
importance if your web server uses directory-specific access control. Each directory traversal takes time not only because it follows the file system's linked list and
checks Unix permissions, but also because of the web server's access control,
which is usually even less efficient. See the tip about *access.conf* in the "Behind
the Scenes" section earlier in this chapter.

Logging

Turn off runtime DNS reverse lookup. This reverse lookup is what lets the server, which is given only the IP address of the calling browser, use the fully qualified name in CGIs and in the server's log file. You don't really need reverse DNS because log file analysis programs such as the *logresolve* program that comes with Apache can look up names offline, and CGIs can do a reverse lookup themselves if they really need to.

The hazard to DNS is that it uses blocking system calls, which hang the entire server process until the call completes. DNS calls can take a noticeable amount of time for a single user, so a server servicing many users sees a large drag on performance from DNS lookups. As of Netscape Enterprise 3.5, DNS lookups are off by default.

In Apache's *httpd.conf*, do this to turn off DNS lookups:

```
HostnameLookups off
```

In Netscape's *magnus.conf* file, do this:

```
DNS off
```

And in the **AddLog** directive, do this:

```
iponly=1
```

The less you do in the logging step, the faster it will go. Shorter pathnames for content are written faster, use less disk space, and provide faster lookup. During log file analysis, remember that most servers do not include the headers in the number of bytes transferred, so calculations of how much network throughput you're using will be low unless you take this into account.

You could turn off logging altogether, but that's not recommended. First of all, you'll save only about 15% of request service time, or even less if you are using separate disks for content and logging. The information in your logs is so valuable for performance analysis that you'll do much better to leave logging on.

Servers

Here is a list of the major web servers with a little background on each and some details on the configuration of the Netscape servers. There is a chart comparing features of 125 web servers at *http://webcompare.internet.com/chart.html*, and there are some benchmark comparisons of web servers at *http://www.spec.org*. Site rankings are from *http://www.netcraft.com/survey/* or *http://www.webcrawler.com/WebCrawler/Facts/Servers.html*, as of spring 1998. Remember that you can always figure out what server someone is using by telnetting to port 80 of the web server machine and typing in a GET / HTTP/1.0 request.

Apache (http://www.apache.org/)

Apache, easily the most successful web server, is used in about half of the two million known web sites. Apache was derived from the NSCA server via many patches, therefore the name: "a patchy" web server. One of the best features of Apache is its price: it is freely available along with source code. Apache is a pre-forking server, but performance is very good. A threaded version is in the works for NT. Support, via Usenet newsgroups, is probably better than support for any commercial server.

Apache supports Java servlets and has real-time performance monitoring tools and an optional log format that tells you how long each transfer took. (See *mod_log_config.html* in the server documentation.) Try to ensure that the server has been compiled with the latest C compiler and libraries for your server platform, or compile the server yourself.

One problem I had with Apache is the fancy indexing. If `FancyIndexing` in *srm.conf* is set to "on," then whenever you access a directory lacking an *index.html*, an HTML listing of the directory contents is generated on the fly and returned to the user. The problem with the fancy version of this directory listing is that it assumes that you have installed the icons that ship with the server in the */icons* directory. If you fail to install these icons, users will see broken links for those icon images and, what's worse, every time you go back to that page a bunch of useless network traffic is generated by looking for those icons, holding up the rendering of the page. This occurs every time you view the directory page, even if you set your browser to always use cached content and never check the network, because the missing images are not in the cache. I suppose you could install the icons, but I just set FancyIndexing to "off."

Please see Appendix B, *Apache Performance Notes*, for Dean Gaudet's notes on Apache servers from *http://www.apache.org/docs/misc/perf-tuning.html*.

Boa (http://www.boa.org/)

Boa is a very small and basic web server: single-threaded, single-process, but very fast. It has very little configurability, and is intended for small simple sites. It is available for free.

IIS (http://www.microsoft.com/products/prodref/427_ov.htm)

Microsoft's Internet Information Server is used at about half a million sites. It runs only on Windows NT and, as of Version 4.0, is part of NT Server rather than a distinct product. IIS has an integrated search engine and built-in streaming audio and video, but it works only with Windows clients. IIS can automatically authenticate

Windows clients. It comes with a utility that asks your expected load range and does some tuning based on the answers. It is a commercial product.

There is an interesting clause in the End User License Agreement for NT:

> No Performance or Benchmark Testing. You may not disclose the results of any benchmark test of either the Server Software or Client Software for Internet Information Server to any third party without Microsoft's prior written approval.

Why Microsoft prohibits independent benchmarking of IIS is left as an exercise for the reader.

Java Web Server (http://www.javasoft.com/products/java-server/webserver/)

Java™ Web Server™ is a 100% Java product from Sun's JavaSoft division. Its most remarkable feature is its performance, which is similar to Netscape Enterprise and faster than Apache if run on Solaris 2.6 with native threads: 609 HTTP operations per second SPEC benchmark. It has a simple applet interface for administration, fully supports HTTP 1.1, servlets, CGI, SSL, session tracking, and on-the-fly configuration. There is also a performance logging facility. It is not free, but there is a freely available demo version.

One nice performance feature is a memory buffer for the log, which reduces the number of log disk writes.

There is a web page on tuning your Java Web Server: *http://jserv.javasoft.com/products/java-server/documentation/webserver1.0.2/administration/performance.html.*

Jigsaw (http://www.w3.org/Jigsaw/)

Jigsaw is a 100% Java server, like Java Web Server. It outperforms the CERN server and is comparable to the NCSA server but not as fast as Apache. Jigsaw supports servlets and HTTP 1.1, and it has web-based administration through CGI forms. It is available for free.

NCSA (http://hoohoo.ncsa.uiuc.edu/)

The National Center for Supercomputing Applications *httpd* runs at 68000 sites. NCSA was one of the first web servers after CERN's. It is the ancestor of Apache and Netscape, and through Spyglass, of IIS. Many features found on other servers, like access control and CGI, originated here. It is still only HTTP 1.0 compliant and may never be upgraded. Serious development effort that originated with NCSA has moved to the Apache project, but NCSA is still available for free.

Netscape (http://home.netscape.com/)

The various versions of Netscape have been installed at over 200,000 sites. They are all commercial products. See *http://developer.netscape.com/* for details on configuration. Some come with the Adminserver tool for real-time performance monitoring. The following list describes the different Netscape versions:

Commerce

Netscape Commerce Server 1.12 for Solaris is not multithreaded, but rather preforking, so there is a separate instance of *httpd* for each connection. Commerce Server 1.2 will listen for a maximum of 128 TCP connections before it begins dropping them, but this is configurable to a lower value in the *magnus.conf* configuration file. If you use 128 connections, it makes sense to set the operating system's TCP listen queue to 128 also. For Solaris, you can set the listen queue like this:

```
ndd -set /dev/tcp tcp_conn_req_max 128
```

Enterprise 2.01

Netscape Enterprise Server 2.01 is multithreaded for Solaris as well as NT. You can run it as separate preforked processes if your plug-ins are not thread-safe, but you'll lose some performance. You may want to run only one process with 128 maximum threads for easiest programming, but under heavy loads you'll get better performance from four processes with 32 threads each, for the reason mentioned above.

Enterprise 2.01 includes the HTTP 1.1 keepalives, an early version of the Java servlet API, a performance measurement log option, and real-time performance measurement tools. The server caches frequently used pages, reducing response time at the expense of using more RAM.

Enterprise 3.x

Enterprise 3.0 includes some new features, such as the ability to choose integration with Informix or Oracle and a *perfdump* tool. The "Netscape Enterprise Server 3.0 Performance Tuning Guide," available from *http://help.netscape.com/kb/server/971211-7.html* is reproduced in Appendix A of this book for your convenience, with permission from Netscape.

Fast Track

Fast Track is the entry-level server. It has fewer features than the other servers, but is rumored to be faster than the Enterprise servers. Fast Track knows HTTP 1.1.

Configuration and internals for Netscape servers

The primary configuration files for Netscape Enterprise servers are *magnus.conf* and *obj.conf*, both of which are found in the *suitespot/https-<server name>/config* directory. The *magnus.conf* file is the server's main configuration file, read upon booting. Here are some suggested parameter settings, but your needs may vary depending on your load.

MaxProcs should be one less than the number of CPUs on SMP machines. This reserves one CPU for the operating system. Allocate at least one process for each 32 threads, in any case:

```
MinThreads 4
MaxThreads 32
DNS off
ListenQ 128
KeepAliveTimeout 15
```

The *obj.conf* file controls content-related issues, such as access to directories. It is consulted for every request except for the Init directive. Here are some more suggested settings:

```
Init fn=cache-init cache-size=512 mmap-max=10240 max-file=1048576
```

Netscape servers have an internal cache of URLs. cache-size is the total number of URLs cached and should be set high for best performance, at the expense of using more memory. The effective limit is the number of file descriptors available per process, which can be discovered or set with ulimit. On Solaris systems, you can set the number of file descriptors per process at boot time in */etc/system* with rlim_fd_max. On the other hand, if all your content is generated dynamically, it may be better to set this low to conserve memory.

The mmap-max parameter specifies the maximum amount of memory set aside for memory mapped files; units are in kilobytes. This should be about the same as the total amount of static data you are serving. If you have about 10MB of static data, you should set this to 10240. Never set this above the amount of RAM you can actually spare for caching, or you will have to go to the disk for the content and lose the benefit of caching.

max-file is the largest file to keep in cache. You would rather not have the occasional use of very large files push everything else out of the cache, so set this limit at, say, 1MB.

The following will load */etc/passwd* into memory for faster access to files referred to by paths that contain ~:

```
Unix init-uhome pwfile=/etc/passwd  .
```

This will limit CGIs to 60 seconds in case they run away:

```
init-cgi timeout=60
```

As of 2.0, there is also a `directive_is_cacheable` option in the Request structure. Your API Server Application Functions (SAFs) can use this option to tell the server that identical URL requests can use a cached response, so the API does not need to be run again. Use this option when the response does not depend on the user's IP or browser, but only on the URL.

Netscape servers work through the following seven SAFs for each request, as configured by the *obj.conf* file. Steps may be skipped as appropriate. You can write your own SAFs by programming to the Netscape API and referring to the resulting *.so* file in *obj.conf.* Each SAF returns a response code to the server, telling whether it succeeded, whether to continue, and for the service step, what headers should be returned to the client. Do not use `gethostbyname` or `gethostbyaddr` blocking system calls in your plug-ins, because you may block the whole server process:

1. Authorization Translation, where user-supplied information is translated into a user ID and group ID

2. Name Translation, for doing something out of the ordinary, like redirecting requests

3. Path check, for existence and permissions

4. Object Typing, where objects are mapped to MIME types so the appropriate HTTP header can be supplied

5. Service Selection, for returning the static file, running the CGI, and so on

6. Update log

7. Error handling and informing the client of the error

Zeus (http://www.zeus.co.uk/)

Zeus claims to be the fastest web server available, and some benchmarks at *http://www.spec.org/* give the claim credibility, such as 1837 HTTP operations per second recorded on the SPECWeb96 benchmark. The Zeus web server runs as a single process and uses only non-blocking network I/O. Zeus runs best if started as `zeus -q`, which disables some infrequently used access control features and if run with a very large cache. Zeus is a commercial product.

Proxy Servers

Proxy servers are usually set up at the interface between a large organization and the rest of the Internet, both for security and performance reasons. The main idea behind using a proxy for security is that there will be no direct connections between the Internet and the internal network; when an HTTP request goes out, the proxy intercepts it and makes the request on behalf of the internal user. or if the proxy already has the page in its cache, the cache will simply return the page to the internal user without ever touching the Internet.

If the page requested is not in the proxy's cache, then the request will be significantly slower because of the extra step of intercepting the request and copying it back from the proxy to the client. On the other hand, for all subsequent accesses, access will be far faster because the page is close at hand.

Proxy caches don't work for dynamic content, or at least they're not supposed to. If your proxy is caching dynamic content, the whole purpose of creating custom content on the fly is defeated. There are a few other twists with dynamic content. The images and other embedded static content on a dynamic page will be cached for an increase in performance, but HTTP 1.1 keepalives may actually hinder this use of cached images and lower performance. It depends on the sophistication of your proxy server. If the proxy checks only the first URL of the connection, it will not realize that it has usable images in the cache. Or, if the proxy gets every embedded image before forwarding anything to the client, the client will see long delays.

Proxies are especially useful in cases where the entire organization is likely to view a few pages at a certain time, say, when a news release comes out, or every morning when users look at *www.news.com* or *www.cnn.com*. There is also a very large benefit to caching pages from slow sites.

Another great thing about proxy servers is that you can use them to track and filter out obviously non-work-related web requests, such as those to *www.playboy.com*. This spares your Internet intranet bandwidth and helps in general, once users know these sites won't work. There will then be more bandwidth and better performance for truly work-related hits. But don't get carried away with the Big Brother attitude. You want workers to be very web-literate, so you want them to browse a lot. Just cut out the obvious abuses.

If browsing performance is very important to your organization, it is doubly important for your proxy server because the proxy has to do both client and server duty.

Intel (*http://www.intel.com/*) has a product called Quick Web that seems to do proxy caching of popular pages and lossy image compression, which means dropping information from GIFs and JPEGs, apparently using their native compression. This makes the images take up fewer bits, but it does not make them any smaller on the screen, so the images are fuzzier.

Sun has a proxy hardware/software package called the Netra Proxy Cache Server (*http://www.sun.com/products-n-solutions/hw/networking/netraproxy/*). It features distributed and transparent caching, load balancing, ICP support, and auto-failover across multiple proxy servers. Apache and Netscape also provide proxy caching software. Remember that your users' browsers must be set up to point to the proxy server. Netscape allows you to specify a URL for automatic proxy configuration, as well as domains for which the proxy should not be used.

Hierarchical Caches

Recent research on distributed caching schemes has led to two implementations of hierarchical caching: Harvest (commercial) and Squid (freeware). They both use the same Inter-Cache Protocol (ICP). Hierarchical caching provides increased perception of performance for the entire Internet, but it requires a large infrastructure to be successful. Squid is being used in an elaborate national caching scheme described at *http://ircache.nlanr.net/*. See also *http://squid.nlanr.net/Squid/*.

Firewalls

Firewalls may insulate your intranet from the Internet, but they do so at a cost. Each packet needs to be examined and then routed out to another interface, but the examination is several protocols deep, unlike a normal router that simply looks at the IP headers. So you have all the problems of routers, and then some. Firewalls that encrypt all traffic can increase latency dramatically, easily taking twice as long to make a transfer. Some configurations put the proxy and web server between two firewalls in a "DMZ"; this will slow access from inside the organization still further. A couple of rules for reducing the impact of firewalls are to use dedicated firewall hardware doing nothing but firewall duty, and to put the most used rules at the top of your rules list so they are read first. Multiple firewall machines may be able to work in parallel.

See *Building Internet Firewalls*, by Brent Chapman and Elizabeth Zwicky (O'Reilly & Associates).

Key Recommendations

- Turn off runtime DNS reverse lookup.
- Use a server that understands HTTP 1.1 or at least keepalives.
- Reboot at regular intervals if there is memory leakage.
- Server should not close log between writes.
- Use recent server software since implementations have been getting better.
- Take advantage of the web server's caching features.
- Optimize for type of content and speed of client connection.

14

Content

In this chapter:
• Size Matters
• HTML
• Graphics
• Audio
• Video
• Key
  Recommendations

Size Matters

The network doesn't know or care what type of content you are serving. Bits are bits. Size is all that really matters for network transfer time. The basic performance principle is therefore to send fewer bits and make fewer requests. Try to think of size in terms of download *time* rather than absolute bits, because how long a human being has to wait is the ultimate measure of success. If most of your users are on 28.8 modems, make a rule that no image can be "larger" than 10 seconds. 10 seconds is about 35K if the 28.8 modem is running perfectly.

Compare Yahoo! (*http://www.yahoo.com/*), which has a very light home page, to CNN (*http://www.cnn.com/*), which tends to bloat. The difference in download time is significant. It's easy to get carried away, so lay down some ground rules and try to get your content developers to care about bandwidth issues.

HTML

About HTML and Compression

A slight amount of waste is intrinsic to HTML, because HTML is written in ASCII text. ASCII is defined as using only seven bits of each byte, so one bit in eight, or 12.5%, is wasted. A larger amount of waste is due to the fact that text is highly compressible, but no compression is used for most HTTP transfers. It is normal for a text compression program to reduce the size of a text file by half, meaning that file can then be downloaded in half the time. Right now, transmission bandwidth is the bottleneck and CPU power for decompression is cheap, so compressing web pages would seem to make sense, even if it would make debugging problems harder.

Lack of compression is not an issue for small pages, but large text pages can be sent significantly more quickly in compressed format to a browser that understands *gzip* compression, for example. (I believe Mosaic is the only popular browser that understands *gzip.*) Another option is to compress your content and configure your web server to use a certain MIME type for that compressed content, but you then have to ask your users to configure their browser to launch the decompression utility when a file with a certain content type is received. This requires a bit of work on both the client and server side.

Performance Tips for HTML Authors

Make it easy on the server

When composing HTML, try to keep pathnames short, both in number of directories in the path and in the length of each directory name.

You can scale static content easily by partitioning the content across multiple servers and using HTML links to the different servers. To start out partitioning, consider using one server for images, another for HTML, another for applets, etc. Also keep in mind that your HTML can easily refer to other web sites for embedded content, which entirely removes the load from your servers but creates a dependency on the other servers and makes for thorny copyright issues. The Gamelan (*www.gamelan.com*) applet directory does not have applets itself, but simply links to the sites that do, with the authors' knowledge. There has recently been some legal action against a site that was embedding news from other web sites in frames and selling its own advertising in a top frame.

Conversely, if you need to have a link on your page to a site known to be very slow, consider asking the site's administrator for permission to copy the site to your web server.

Make your links explicitly refer to *index.html* files or end directory references with "/". As discussed in Chapter 10, *Network Protocols*, the trailing "/" in a URL saves the server (and network) the additional overhead of a redirection. Also, explicitly referring to *index.html* saves the server from having to think about whether it needs to do directory indexing. However be ware that *index.html* is just a convention. Some web servers like Jigsaw do not use *index.html* for the directory index.

If your content is a huge number of files with a fairly even distribution of access, say in a large archive, then your OS's buffer cache and the web server's cache will not be effective. You'll have to hit the disk for most accesses, so don't waste too much money on RAM, but get the fastest disks or disk arrays you can afford, concentrating on seek time. Disk striping should help considerably.

Make it easy on the network

The most important thing to do with content, from the network's point of view, is to keep the size down.

If you have a large document, users may appreciate getting the whole thing and not having to click and wait to get more; on the other hand, it may be wise to give them a summary and the first part to see if they really want the whole document. HTTP 1.1's byte-range downloads are capable of downloading part of a document at first, and downloading the rest when the user requests it. This requires a browser and server that understand HTTP 1.1.

Typical HTML size is 4K, which is about two pages of text in a browser. You might want to make the text fit into the MTU, if you know it, so that you'll get it all in one packet. If your MTU is 1500 bytes, which is common on Ethernet LANs, then you'll see better performance from 1500-byte HTML pages than from 1501-byte pages.

Make it easy on the browser

Parsing is compute-intensive, so we want to make it easy on the browser. You can do this by eliminating redundant or useless tags, using few fancy features like nested tables or frames, and giving the browser information it would otherwise have to calculate itself. Also, word processing programs that generate HTML tend to do rather a bad job, often with extra tags that format blank lines. It is simple but time-consuming to clean this up by hand, so it is worthwhile to write a few simple Perl scripts to do some substitutions or eliminations for you. Here's an example of a one-line Perl script that removes <BR> tags that are alone on a line. These tags are often an artifact of using a graphical page composition tool:

```
perl -pi -e 's/^<br>$//i' *.html
```

Don't put much in the <HEAD> of the page, because that section must be completely parsed and acted on before the rest of the page can be displayed. In particular, don't put extensive JavaScript scripts in the <HEAD>. Put the majority of the script near where it is used, for example, within a form that is being validated with JavaScript.

Background images are displayed before the text of the page, so keep them simple or eliminate them. A large single background image, as opposed to background images composed of repeating small elements, can make scrolling painfully slow.

Use the SIZE option to the <IMG> tag to tell the browser the size of the image; this saves the browser some processing time and allows it to lay out the HTML before receiving all of the images. The syntax looks like this:

```
<img src=/images/demo.gif" size height=150 width=100>
```

The Unix *file* command gives the size of images, and can be used in a Perl script to examine images in HTML source and insert their sizes. There are some publicly available utilities to do this, such as *wwwis* (*http://bunge.jump.com/~ark/wwwis/*), or you can write your own.

You can scale an image by including a size that is different from the image's true size in pixels, but it is wasteful to use a size smaller than the pixel size. Scaling an image upward works, but it takes a bit of the browser's time and the image gets coarser.

Frames take some time to retrieve and render. This can be significant for multiple nested frames. There is an interesting recursive abuse of frames at *http://www.vanderburg.org/~glv/*. Be warned that the ziggurat link off this page will try to use up all the browser's memory, and will either crash it or make it so slow as to be useless.

Use IP addresses rather than domain names in your links to avoid DNS lookups. For HTML page links, this puts the IP rather than the server's domain name in the browser's Location box, which might be confusing to the user. For links to images, the user will notice only that the image loads slightly faster.

Make it easy on the user

Why name your web server "www?" It's easy to type, but impossible to say. Please use one syllable rather than nine—name your web server "web." Instead of "www.company.com," use "web.company.com." The radio announcers of the world will thank you.

The first thing the user will see is the text within the <TITLE></TITLE> tags, so try to make it descriptive enough that the user can decide whether to wait for the entire page to load. Many people don't notice the title, so give them a nice clear label for the page in <H1></H1> tags, too.

Make every site's home page load lightning-fast, because it sets the tone for the entire site. Users will wait longer for detail pages further in the site, but if they can't get in the front door right away, they may assume the site is down or go away because they're annoyed. You might want to dedicate a server to the initial home page.

Be sure to give text links that mirror image links in case the user has images turned off for faster loading. Many sites are useless without images because no planning was done for text-only browsing. An alternative to putting a text link under each graphic is to offer a link from the home page to a parallel tree for light graphics or text-only browsing. You can use cookies to track whether the user wants a light-graphics version of the site, but cookie-recognition puts a burden on the server, while parallel content adds more content. Always use the ALT text of image tags so people know if an image is worth getting if images are off.

Making all of your site available via text is also nice for blind people surfing the web with text-to-audio convertors.

Similarly, use alternative functionality between <APPLET></APPLET> tags so that users can turn off Java if they need to for bandwidth reasons. The default action of HTML is to ignore tags it doesn't understand, and if Java is turned off, then the <APPLET> tag is no longer understood. The net result is that you can put any valid HTML between <APPLET> tags, and it will be parsed and displayed only if Java is off. I used this in one project to provide an alternative CGI form for a shampoo selector web site. The form did the same thing as the applet that was the alternative. The applet was more interactive and fun but took longer to download.

Don't tell the user about an FTP site or an email address without providing an *ftp://* or *mailto:* link. It's just common web courtesy to make addresses clickable.

Change your web server's `404 - file not found` page to contain a map of your site so that users don't have to hit the Back button to figure out what the alternatives are on your site. This is a performance issue, because it saves users time. If the link as defined by the HTTP_REFERER variable shows that another link on your site referred the user to a 404 page, set up the server to mail the webmaster about the errors. There's no excuse for having invalid links from within your own site. Users can ask for whatever they want, and should be given a polite answer in every case.

For more information on HTML

Read *comp.infosystems.www.authoring.html* on Usenet.

Graphics

The typical web graphic is 10KB to 20KB, which is larger than the typical 4KB of HTML in a page. The challenge with graphics is mostly how to make them smaller.

Weight watching

Make images small by reducing size in number of pixels and number of colors (8-bit is usually enough) and using a format with compression appropriate to the image. The new PNG format has excellent compression.

Java is often criticized for its long startup time and relatively large memory footprint, but large graphics composed of simple shapes consume less network bandwidth as simple Java *.class* files than as bitmap images. I used Java's `drawPolygon()` method in an applet to encode a map of all the rail tracks in the eastern

U.S. as sets of points connected by lines. This was not only smaller than a bitmap, but had the added flexibility of easy zooming and scrolling, which would not have been possible with a static image.

Consolidation

Avoid the overhead of sending multiple images by consolidating them into one, saving download time as well as display time. If each image is a link, you can make the composite into an imagemap and retain the functionality. Use a client-side imagemap, where the URL is chosen by the client, rather than a server-side imagemap, where the URL is deduced from the click coordinates by a process on the server side.

Use a cached imagemap in place of a frame for navigation to save the download of a master frame and navigation subframe.

Reuse

Reuse graphics wherever possible. The browser's cache is smart enough to find them if you reference them in exactly the same way.

Psychology

A common trick is to put your graphics at the bottom of the page so users don't notice that they're loading, since they're still reading the top of the page. Be sure to include the image size in the <IMG> tag or you will delay display of the entire page until Netscape gets the image and figures out its size.

640×480 is still a very common screen size, but if you're designing on a much higher resolution monitor, it's easy to forget that and create something that users will have to scroll horizontally to see. This makes it more work for users to view your site.

Formats

JPEG

JPEG has better compression than GIF for photos but is lossy, meaning that an image compressed into JPEG format cannot be fully recovered. The compression is good enough that most users will not know any information is missing.

GIF

GIF has better compression than JPEG for line-oriented images because it compresses line by line of pixels. GIF is not lossy.

PNG

The new Portable Network Graphics format (PNG) is in Netscape 4.0 and Internet Explorer 4.0. PNG has yet better compression than JPEG or GIF.

Animation

Animations using either "client pull" or "server push" are now obsolete, and have been replaced by animated GIFs, which not only download quickly but run without any network interaction. Animated GIFs are also quicker to download and start than Java applets, though their functionality is limited to displaying a series of images. The downside to animated GIFs is that they use up a great deal of the client's CPU, even if the user switches from the browser to another application.

VRML

Support for the Virtual Reality Modeling Language (VRML) is now provided in many versions of Netscape with SGI's Cosmo Player plug-in. VRML downloads quickly relative to the level of detail you get but requires a very high performance machine on the client side to be useful.

Audio

Most audio formats encode point-by-point air pressure over time using 8-bit samples, giving 256 possible amplitudes. This technique is known Pulse Code Modulation (PCM). Some formats distribute audio linearly, while others take advantage of the fact that humans hear in a nonlinear way. That is, humans have a harder time distinguishing two loud sounds than two soft sounds, so encodings are assigned more densely at small amplitudes.

All of the following formats use PCM in one way or another:

- Sun's *.au*
- Microsoft's *.wav*
- Apple's AIFF
- mu-law (U.S. telephony)
- A-law (European telephony)

You can also code sound in the frequency domain; that is, the code says something like "play this frequency at this amplitude for this amount of time." MIDI works like this.

The number of samples per second determines the frequency range you can encode: if you have n samples per second, you can encode frequencies up to $n/2$ Hz. (This is the Nyquist theorem.) The sample size and number of samples per second also determine the size of an audio sample, and therefore its download time as well.

In the telephone system, voice is encoded as 8-bit samples at 8KHz, giving an audio bandwidth of 4KHz and reasonable quality. Eight bits at 8KHz comes out to 64 kilobits per second, which is the bandwidth used in telephony between switches for a single voice channel. This is a fundamental limit on the rate of information that a modem can send on a single call over the voice network.

Police and fire department radio systems use a lower resolution and sampling rate or compression to conserve radio bandwidth; this is what gives them that police-radio sound quality. Audio compression for radio has been the subject of many years of research, and very low bit rate speech, down to 1200 bits per second or lower, is now possible, although the quality of the signal is artificial.

At the high end, CD quality sound is 44KHz 16-bit samples in stereo, so you'd need $44000 \times 16 \times 2 = 1.4$ million bits per second.

You can see that it is possible to transmit intelligible speech to most clients on the Internet, but that real-time transmission of CD-quality audio is still not possible. Streaming audio products for the Internet have to cope with the intrinsic unpredictability of IP latency, so they use UDP, which is higher-performance than TCP but makes no attempt to retransmit missing packets. This makes sense, because an audio packet that is even one second late is already useless. In these products, the audio transmission begins with a significant amount of empty time to give the packets a head start. The data coding for any point in time is spread across several packets so that if one of them is lost, the signal will not drop out for a moment, but will degrade in quality for a moment. The whole thing works reasonably well, but sounds more or less like a scratchy AM radio most of the time. You can get a measure of the health of the Internet by listening to Internet "radio stations" from around the country. Streaming audio works quite well on an uncongested intranet, but then again, a conference call works better.

Video

Streaming video gets a better compression ratio than streaming audio, typically 20:1 rather than 5:1 before you really notice the difference in quality, but since video starts out with far more data, it is even harder to do over the Internet than audio. Video compression depends strongly on the content involved. Videos of talking heads giving the news are easily compressed because each frame is so much like the previous one. Action films don't compress well.

Streaming video is not yet ready for wide use on the Internet but may be useful in intranets. Precept Software (*www.precept.com*) has streaming video for intranets, but it's a Windows-only product. Real Networks (*www.real.com*) does streaming video, too, and has cross-platform (PC, Mac, Unix) clients and PC and Unix servers.

Key Recommendations

- Send only as many bytes as needed, whatever the content type. Use the ALT part of the <IMG> tag for those who've turned off images.

- Don't assume the user has better than 640×480 video resolution.

- Use <SIZE HEIGHT=*nnn* WIDTH=*nnn*> for graphics.

- Reuse graphics; the browser's cache is smart enough to find them.

15

CGI Programs

While plain HTML documents stored on your web server can contain whatever text you like, that text is static. Everyone who requests that document through a web browser will get exactly the same document. Quite often, however, you'd like to customize the response for a particular user. For example, a retail chain might want to query a database for the user and return the address of the branch store nearest the user. One way to do this is to have the web server run a program that will query the database and format the result in HTML. The first widely available method for incorporating dynamic content like this into web pages was the Common Gateway Interface (CGI) standard. CGI was introduced as part of the web server developed at the National Center for Supercomputing Applications (NCSA).

CGI provides a standard interface between web servers and programs that can generate HTML or other web content. CGI got its start as a literal gateway between web servers and older Unix programs that send their output to the terminal, but it quickly became clear that the real value of CGI was that it could provide a web interface to almost any software. Programs started by the web server using the CGI interface are referred to as *CGI programs*, or just *CGIs*, though CGI is technically the interface and not the programs that use the interface.

The definitive description of CGI 1.1, the current version, is on the Web at *http://hoohoo.ncsa.uiuc.edu/cgi/*. From here on, I will assume that the reader understands how to write at least a simple CGI program. If you'd like an excellent tutorial on CGI, read *CGI Programming on the World Wide Web*, by Shishir Gundavaram (O'Reilly & Associates). If you already know CGI programming and would like to keep up with the latest developments, read the Usenet newsgroup *comp.infosystems.www.authoring.cgi*.

Server APIs, such as the Apache API, NSAPI, and ISAPI, are a huge performance win over CGI at the expense of portability. Once you've written a program for a server's API, there is a cost to porting it to another server (unlike CGIs or Java servlets), but on the other hand, the APIs have no parameter parsing and no separate CGI process. Programs written using the API run as part of the web server process. Note that some databases are also web servers, which eliminates even the overhead of the separate *httpd* process.

CGI Internals and Performance Problems

Though the CGI mechanism for generating dynamic web content is very versatile, the basic structure of CGI limits its performance. The main performance penalty is that a new instance of the program is executed for each user's request. This process exits immediately after sending its output back to the web server. If the CGI program opens a database connection, the database connection must be reopened for the next instance of the CGI. This load on the operating system severely limits the number of CGI requests that can be serviced per second. CGI execution time is likely to be the bottleneck under any but the lightest loads. CGIs typically take far more CPU and other resources than serving HTML pages. Another inefficiency is that CGIs that are hit more than once throughout the day, say for stock quotes or weather, return mostly unchanged HTML and graphics with only a little bit of new content. This is very wasteful of network bandwidth.

Let's take a closer look at the sequence of events in starting a CGI program and where the performance problems are. When a CGI request comes in, the web server must parse the input URL and the request headers, recognize that the user desires to execute a CGI program, and begin the CGI with the `fork()` and `exec()` system calls. Parsing and `fork()` and `exec()` account for much of the cost of CGI. The server sets up the environment variables and the standard I/O for the child process, then it begins to write the URL-encoded data to the CGI's standard in. The CGI reads the data, stopping when it has read the number of bytes specified in the CONTENT-LENGTH environment variable. The CGI may also read URL-encoded command-line arguments, which are given by placing them after the script name in the URL like this: *http://www.nowhere.com/script.cgi?cmd_line_arg*.

It is then up to the CGI to decode the data and decide what to return to the browser. This is the meat of the CGI and varies widely in complexity. When the CGI is done, it outputs its results to the web server, which adds HTTP headers and forwards everything to the browser.[*] The CGI then exits. There is a rather dated

---

[*] Alternately, many web servers allow the CGI itself to provide all the headers and communicate directly with the client's browser.

but still accurate illustration of CGI events at *http://www.ansa.co.uk/ANSA/ISF/ 1506/1506prt4.html.*

CGI is also problematic because communication between browser and server is limited to parameters that the browser sends and the result the server returns. Ongoing communication within the same connection is difficult to implement.

Given that CGI performance is poor and that all it can do is reply to a request and close the connection, why does anyone use CGI? In fact, a migration to Java and CORBA is already underway, allowing code on the browser to directly call methods on remote Java objects. This will simplify true transaction processing on the Web. Still, there are a number of good reasons that CGI is popular and will probably be around for at least a few more years:

- CGI is conceptually simple.

- CGI is an open standard supported by most web servers, regardless of hardware or operating system. So, your CGI scripts are portable.

- CGIs are easy to write and can be written in almost any programming language.

- CGI scripts won't crash a web server (though they will slow down the server) because they run as separate processes.

- Many CGI scripts are freely available.

General CGI Tips

No matter how optimized your hardware and operating system are, it is easy to get truly awful performance with a badly written CGI. There is no constraint on how long a CGI is allowed to run, so if your CGI is ill-mannered or overloaded, the user will suffer. We should distinguish here between merely inefficient CGIs, infinite loops, and runaways. Coding for efficiency is a huge topic and is highly language-dependent. We will cover efficiency in the section "CGI Language—Specific Optimization Tips," later in this chapter.

Infinite Loops

If your CGI somehow gets into an infinite loop, the web server may well wait forever for the CGI to return results. This, in turn, means that the user will probably be left staring at a blank or partially filled browser for quite some time. Or worse, they'll just hit the Back button and then try again, putting another infinitely long CGI in motion on your server, and thus using up CPU time that produces nothing.

CGI programs don't know if and when the user hits the Stop button on the browser. The program often finds out only when it tries to output HTML and receives a SIGPIPE signal because the socket is no longer valid, but this may depend on the configuration of the operating system and web server.

How to find and kill infinitely looping CGIs

To kill an infinitely looping CGI, you must first find its process ID (PID). The classic way to do this is with the Unix *ps* command. Under Solaris, for example, you can list all of your processes like this:

```
ps -ef
```

Look for unusually large values in the **TIME** column and note the PID for that process. Note that you can't trust the name given by *ps*, because it can be set on some systems by setting **argv[0]** in the executing program. Once you have the PID of the looping CGI, you can kill it with the *kill* command, like this:

```
kill 2353
```

However, this is not guaranteed to stop processes that choose to ignore the TERM signal. If the process is still present after a few seconds, try the *-9* option, as in **kill -9 2353**. This should not be your first option because processes killed with the *-9* option do not get a chance to clean up temp files or finish writing buffered output to a file. The kill command may leave a zombie process on the system, which cannot be killed but occupies only minimal system resources. Zombie processes are marked with **Z** or **defunct** in *ps* output. If a process is not a zombie but cannot be killed, then it is probably waiting on an NFS call or a stuck device.

There are a number of more user-friendly tools for hunting down rogue processes, such as *top*, *skill*, and *killall*.

Runaways

A special case of the infinitely looping process is a process that is not only stuck in a loop, but is also spawning new processes on each iteration of the loop. While an ordinary infinite loop can go on forever, a runaway process uses up its owner's process table in a few minutes at most. One clue that you have a runaway CGI is seeing a large number of processes with the same name and a common parent process ID (PPID) or sequential PPIDs. You should try to kill the common PPID, or, in the case of sequential process numbers, the lowest PPID. It sometimes helps to sort the output of the *ps* command by PPID so you can see patterns more clearly. For example, on Solaris you can do this:

```
ps -el | sort -k 3,3
```

A user who manages to use up the process table or memory will see an error message like **No more processes** or **Out of virtual memory**, and will be unable to start any new process, even the *kill* program, until at least one process exits.

The user may also find that the keyboard has locked up. Just for fun, if you have a Unix system to yourself and have saved all your work and quit your applications, you can easily use up all your processes by creating a shell script with a single command: the name of the script itself. For example, create a file called *x*, insert the single command *x* and make the file executable. When you run *x*, you'll quickly use up all your processes or run out of memory by repeatedly forking shells. Run *ps* a few times, if you can, and you'll see the number of processes created. When you hit the process or memory limit, you'll be unable to fork a new shell, and all of the parent shells will exit.

Web servers, however, typically run as "nobody" and have no controlling terminal, so you will not see error messages, except perhaps in the web server log. The first clue that a CGI has run away will be that the server becomes very slow. If the server keyboard is locked up, it is still usually possible to log in to the machine with the runaway process over a LAN and kill the parent process.

Guarding Against Infinitely Looping CGIs

The best way to guard against infinitely looping CGIs is through careful CGI programming. Be especially sure when using recursion that the recursion will be terminated. When using the `fork()` or `system()` functions, make sure that the created process can not immediately `fork()` itself or call `system()` in the same way. Check to see that the condition of all `while` loops must eventually be false, ending the loop.

Try to crash your CGIs yourself, before your customers do. Put in bizarre input, including quotation marks, newlines, and other unusual characters.

One trick CGI programmers can use is setting an alarm at the beginning of the script and setting up a `SIGALRM` handler, so that if the script does get into an infinite loop for some reason, it will kill itself when the alarm goes off. For example:

```perl
#!/usr/local/bin/perl

$SIG{'ALRM'} = sub {
    syswrite(STDERR, "Caught SIGALRM in script.pl\n", 28);
    exit(-1);
};

alarm(5);    # Alarm will go off in 5 seconds...
while (1) {} # We would be stuck here forever if not for the alarm.
```

There is a `setrlimit` Unix system call to set limits on the consumption of system resources by a process and its child processes. These resources include CPU time, file size, stack size, number of processes, and number of open files. You can achieve the same effect at the shell level with the `limit` or `ulimit` command, depending on which shell you use. Unfortunately, these limits are sometimes not implemented by the operating system even when they seem to be available.

At the web server level, Apache has directives that limit the resource consumption of CGI Scripts. O'Reilly's WebSite also has a Runaway CGI sanity timer that is set at 10 minutes for server-push CGIs. In general, server-push is a bad idea for ordinary animations. You'll put a much lighter load on the server by using animated GIFs or Java. On the other hand, a Scottish company called Graham Technologies (*http://www.graham.com/*) makes a very nice server-push tool for distributing live video over the Internet.

Don't Keep the Customer Waiting

It's a frustrating experience for users to see that their browser has contacted your site but be forced to wait while you create content for them. If you must do some intensive calculation in your CGI, first turn off I/O buffering ($| = 1 in Perl) and get the content type and some text out to the browser before you take time to create the bulk of your content. If you don't at least get the content type to the browser, it will give up on you after a relatively short timeout and close the connection. You'll end up doing all your calculations in vain. After sending out the header, turn I/O buffering back on ($| = 0 in Perl) for the performance benefit of buffered I/O.

One area where CGIs typically get stuck is waiting for I/O with another part of the computer or the Internet. DNS lookups fall into this category. If possible, avoid DNS by using static IP addresses in your CGI scripts.

If your processing has output that makes sense to view as you are creating it, you should give the user feedback on your progress by using a non-parsed header (NPH) CGI script, which bypasses the web server and outputs results directly back to the browser. The great advantage of NPH scripts is that they can keep the connection to the browser open and can output results over a relatively long time. An ordinary CGI, in contrast, has to output all of its results to the web server and close the connection before the web server begins to send the data on to the browser. Another smaller advantage is that the NPH CGI returns its first data to the browser slightly faster than an ordinary CGI, since the data does not have to go through the server first. An example of where you might use this technique is a CGI that needs to report back a constantly changing status, as of a stock price.

Under Apache and NCSA servers, all you have to do to transform an ordinary CGI into an NPH CGI is prefix the script name with *nph-* (for example, *nph-script.cgi*). Note, however, that you are responsible for outputting complete and correct HTTP headers with NPH scripts, which would otherwise be the responsibility of the web server. If you get the headers wrong, the browser will not be able to interpret your output. Also, note that the server cannot log the size of data returned via an NPH CGI.

Push State or Processing into the Browser

One good way to speed up CGIs is to reduce the amount of work they do by pushing some of the work onto the browser, which usually spends most of its time idle, waiting for the server to return data or for the user to read the displayed page. An excellent example of this is the use of JavaScript to validate user input on the client side. Sending extra JavaScript validation code to the browser is a small price to pay for the reduced load on the network and server, not to mention the elimination of wasted CGI calls because of invalid input. The CGI itself can be smaller, because it doesn't need to do validation, though removing all validation is dangerous.

Here is a crude example that checks an input date for correct format before contacting the web server:

```
<HTML>
<HEAD>
<SCRIPT LANGUAGE="JavaScript">

<!-- Hide the script from browsers that don't like JavaScript.

    function validdate(lf) {
        if ((lf.date.value.charAt(0) < '0') ||
            (lf.date.value.charAt(0) > '1') ||
            (lf.date.value.charAt(1) < '0') ||
            (lf.date.value.charAt(1) > '9') ||
            (lf.date.value.charAt(2) != '/') ||
            (lf.date.value.charAt(3) < '0') ||
            (lf.date.value.charAt(3) > '3') ||
            (lf.date.value.charAt(4) < '0') ||
            (lf.date.value.charAt(4) > '9') ||
            (lf.date.value.charAt(5) != '/') ||
            (lf.date.value.charAt(6) < '0') ||
            (lf.date.value.charAt(6) > '9') ||
            (lf.date.value.charAt(7) < '0') ||
            (lf.date.value.charAt(7) > '9')) {

            alert("Invalid date. Please use format MM/DD/YY.");
            return false
        }
        else return true
    }
// End of hiding JavaScript -->
</SCRIPT>

</HEAD>

<TITLE>stuff</TITLE>
...
<FORM name="dateform" action="/myscript/" method="post">
mm/dd/yy <INPUT name="date" size=8 maxlength=8 value="">
```

```
<INPUT name="submit_button" TYPE="submit" VALUE="log on"
    onclick="return validdate(dateform)")>

</FORM>
```

JavaScript is also excellent for constructing simple calculators on the client. Not only is the load taken off the server, but the response time is shorter because all of the calculation is done in the browser.

The downside to using JavaScript for form input validation is that you have to download a little more data, and JavaScript has Netscape versus Internet Explorer incompatibilities and other quirks that make it inelegant and hard to use. Another major downside has been that JavaScript just *stops functioning* when you run out of memory, so a naive server may think its input has been validated when it hasn't. This means JavaScript cannot entirely remove the burden of validation from the server, but it can reduce that burden by limiting server-side validation to detecting some key that shows that JavaScript is still running in the client and refusing input if JavaScript is not running.

Cookies

Another browser feature useful in reducing server load is cookies. Cookies can eliminate revalidation of users or their state, or store information about users so that the CGI does not have to look it up each time the page is accessed. Cookies however, are limited to 4K of data.

HTTP 1.0 browsers will not cache pages that contain cookies.

Java

You can use Java in Java-enabled browsers to eliminate CGIs altogether. Java is a general-purpose language and can make connections back to the machine that served it for access to databases and other facilities on the server machine. While it does take a few moments to start up the Java virtual machine, the benefits can be enormous. For example, I wrote a shipment-tracking applet for a freight company that included a set of data points defining the highways, railtracks, and borders of the U.S. Because all map data was downloaded with the applet, it was possible to zoom and scroll far more quickly than is possible with maps drawn with CGI programs, where substantial network traffic is required for each new view.

You can also use the Java capabilities of browsers to sidestep CGI by making direct method calls to objects on the server. Two standardized ways of doing this are through Java's Remote Method Invocation (RMI) and through CORBA. RMI is easier to program, but it runs more slowly and requires Java on the server as well as the client. CORBA takes a little more time to program, but it runs more quickly and is much more flexible. See Chapter 16, *Java*, for more information on RMI, and Chapter 10, *Network Protocols*, for more information on CORBA. A third alternative is the Voyager product from Object Space (*www.objectspace.com*), which is simple to program and high-performance but is not yet widely used.

Preprocess Queries and Cache the Results

Do you ever wonder how network news programs can have a detailed obituary story ready within hours of the death of a celebrity? What looks like superhuman performance is actually preprocessing. Television networks keep on file prepared obituaries of major celebrities, especially those who are seriously ill. Obviously, the networks don't know when a given celebrity will die, but since there are a limited number of people whose death would be newsworthy, the networks prepare stories on all of these people. The principle here is that the more you limit the input parameters, the fewer possible results there are. A smaller result set means you can do more effective caching of responses.

The point of a CGI is to output different HTML depending on user input and state information; however, if the number of possible input and state combinations is small, it makes sense to run the CGI for all possible input offline and cache each result in a plain HTML file. For example, if a CGI can inform you of tomorrow's weather forecast in 100 cities around the U.S., you will certainly get better performance and scalability by regenerating 100 static HTML pages every night than by running a CGI in response to every query.

Even with a huge number of possible inputs, if there are a few frequently requested pages, it makes sense to dynamically cache those pages. Keep a server-side cache of frequently requested CGI output and have a stub CGI merely return an HTTP `Location:` response pointing to a static HTML page if the page is in the cache. A good way to prune a full cache is to delete the least recently used pages. This is known as an *LRU cache*.

AltaVista users can input a query containing any string at all, currently up to 800 characters. Because the data set (all web pages in the AltaVista database) and the uncertainty of what the user will ask for are huge, the effort required to deal with this uncertainty is also huge. But that doesn't mean that AltaVista has to do a linear search though its entire data set for each query. Like most large databases, the AltaVista database is indexed, so the server can simply use the input keywords as an index to the data set and return any results.

An index is not always faster than a linear search: a linear search has the advantage that the disk heads move only from one track to the next, while an indexed retrieval may require the heads to jump around a great deal. The size of your index and data set determines which method is better. The AltaVista web server also caches the results of the most frequent queries.

As an example of effective indexing, consider a CGI that needs to search through the server's filesystem for a particular file, named *desiree*. While it is easy to have the CGI run the Unix *find* command, it is far more efficient to search a prebuilt index of the file system. To build an index of your entire filesystem, you can simply do this:

```
% find / -print > index
```

Now the two approaches to finding the file are these:

```
% find . -name desiree -print
```

and:

```
% grep desiree index
```

You can time how long these commands take by prefixing them with the Unix *time* command. For example:

```
% time find . -name desiree -print
```

Look at the real (elapsed) time in the output of the time command. See the manpage for *time* for more information about your system's output format. You should see that the grep of the index is 10 to 100 times faster. This is the benefit of indexing.

You should also notice that if you run either *find* command again soon, it will run more quickly than it did at first. Why is this? It's because your program has been loaded into RAM and probably has not been swapped out, and because the part of the filesystem that you were accessing is also now cached in RAM. This is how Unix operates, and it will automatically work to your advantage.

Another feature of Unix related to caching: the text segment that is the executable code part of programs is shared between concurrent instances. Code shared between concurrent instances of a program is referred to as *re-entrant* code. For a quick example of the kind of speedup you get by using re-entrant code, start a copy of Netscape and note how long it takes. Then go to Netscape's menu bar and choose File → New Web Browser. It will start in a flash.

The key is that the code or text segment is already loaded and ready to run. When you get many hits on the same CGI over a short period, the second and subsequent hits use the same text segment as the first hit, meaning that the RAM needed to run the second and subsequent copies is smaller than the RAM needed for the first copy. This also reduces the risk of paging or swapping. For these reasons, the second and subsequent copies usually run faster than the first, subject to the limits of your system. Eventually, the 10th or 100th or 1000th instance will not have enough resources to run and must be queued or simply dropped.

Almost all browsers have RAM and disk caches so that you can retrieve a previously requested page from cache instead of wasting time loading the same page again. There are some cases, however, where you want to override the browser cache. You generally do not want the browser to cache the output of CGI scripts, so CGI scripts typically specify the `Cache-Control` header in HTTP 1.1 or `Pragma:No-cache` header in HTTP 1.0. The hazard to performance is that the CGI writer will use these headers too often, putting an unnecessary load on the web server.

Small Is Beautiful

Smaller programs are easier to understand and to maintain, and they load and run more quickly than larger programs, while reducing the risk of paging or swapping. Though there is always a temptation, known as "creeping featurism," to add features to a program, this should be resisted as much as possible. It runs counter to the well-known KISS principle in engineering. KISS stands for "Keep It Simple, Stupid." Keeping your programs small and quick is also Unix tenet number one of *The Unix Philosophy*, an excellent book by Mike Gancarz (Digital Press).

One way to make CGIs smaller is to move some error checking code to the client via Java or JavaScript, as mentioned earlier. It is much more dangerous to use JavaScript because forms still work when JavaScript is turned off. With a Java form, the input field won't even exist if Java isn't running, so it is harder to submit bad input.

A very simple form of error checking is to use HTML to limit the length of text fields so that users know when they have tried to enter too many characters. For example:

```
<input name="date" size=8 maxlength=8 value="">
```

Scaling Issues

CGI does not scale well. Performance degrades quickly with increased load because of the large load imposed by each CGI process and its child processes.

If you have multiple different CGIs using independent data, then the simplest and best way to scale is to run different CGIs on different web servers. The servers don't even have to be in the same country. If the CGIs do have to share data, another excellent way to scale is to put just the CGIs on additional machines, leaving the web server to decide which machine should run the CGI and the web server as the conduit for returning results back to the client. This is the essence of the FastCGI standard discussed in the "Daemonize It" section later in this chapter. The round-robin DNS scheme described in Chapter 10 does not work with CGIs that maintain state (typically using cookies) because the state information on a particular server must be synchronized with that of a particular client.

Break Up Long Forms into Several Small Forms

Breaking up a long CGI form into several pages does hinder the use of multiple servers for scaling, but it gives you better performance per page. Breaking up long forms also gives you the flexibility to turn a single page into a tree of pages, eliminating the need to send inappropriate questions to the user.

Server DNS Lookup

Be sure to turn off DNS lookup in the web server. Some CGIs expect to use REMOTE_HOST (corresponding to REMOTE_ADDR, which is the IP). This reverse lookup takes time. How you turn off DNS in the web server depends on what server you use. See the "Logging" section of Chapter 13, *Server Software*, for more information. For Sun's Web Server, for example, you set:

```
cgi_dns_enable "no"
```

Debug and Optimize

A final general tip is to test your script offline, where you can time and debug it more easily than from a web server. You can easily write a test script that will set up the environment variables and run `time prog.cgi`. Ignore the difference between the first and second run; look at the difference between the second and third for the reasons mentioned previously in this chapter.

CGI Language-Specific Optimization Tips

While any programming language that includes the concept of standard in and standard out can be used to write a CGI, some languages are intrinsically more suited to the task than others. In this section, I will review the most common CGI languages (*sh*, Perl, and C), point out their strengths and weaknesses for CGI use, and give some language-specific optimization tips. But first, here are a few performance tips general to all languages:

- Keep loops small.
- Use table lookups rather than calculation, where practical.
- Use integer rather than floating point math.
- Avoid dynamic memory allocation.
- Profile your code and optimize the most-used parts.

Shell Scripts

Unix Bourne shell scripts have the advantages of portability across Unix systems, easy file manipulation, and filtering. However, shell scripts are very slow to execute because they are interpreted and because they rely on other Unix programs for advanced functionality, with the result that *sh* scripts tend to `fork` a lot of new processes. This consumes time and resources. For example, if you wanted your *sh* CGI to search in all the files in the current directory for the word "foo" and output a sorted list of the results, eliminating duplicate lines, the programming is remarkably easy. Here is an entire CGI program that does exactly that:

```
#!/bin/sh
echo "Content-type: text/plain"
echo
grep -h foo * | sort | uniq
```

Although the time it took to write this program is negligible, we pay a large price at runtime. This script starts six processes in response to a single CGI request: *sh*, two copies of *echo*, and one each of *grep*, *sort*, and *uniq*. This is very bad for performance.

If you feel you must write a CGI program in a shell script language, use a more modern shell like *csh* or *bash*. With these shells, you can frequently use shell built-in commands to avoid the overhead of a `fork` and `exec`. For example, *csh* has a `time` command that is much faster to use than the */bin/time* program because the built-in `time` executes as part of the shell. You do lose some portability if you rely on built-ins that are unique to the shell you're writing in, but the performance gain is worth it.

If you have to run multiple programs from within a shell script, don't run them all in the background because they will compete for resources. It is better to run them sequentially, so that each program has more resources available to it and will finish faster.

Another tip to use when writing in shell languages is to keep your environment as small as possible. Each `fork` of the shell (which happens when you execute any external command) must initialize itself. If you keep the number of user-defined environment variables and shell functions small, the `fork` will be slightly quicker.

Perl

Perl is the most popular CGI language, due to its portability (though the portability is easily broken by using the `system()` function), excellent text handling and regular expressions, and extensive library of built-in functions. It is more complex than *sh*, but it has an astounding array of features. A coworker of mine likes to insist that Perl "includes every hack known to mankind." While Perl is an interpreted language like *sh*, its performance is substantially better, though usually not as good as the performance of compiled C code. It is far easier on the programmer to write text handling routines in Perl than in C.

Since Perl is so widely used, a lot of effort has been put into Perl optimization. A good place to start reading about Perl optimization is the "Efficiency" section in Chapter 8 of *Programming Perl*, by Larry Wall, Tom Christiansen, and Randal Schwartz (O'Reilly & Associates). Another good source is a newsgroup archive like *www.dejanews.com*.

Here are a few basic tips:

* Avoid calling Unix programs if there is an equivalent Perl function, such as sort. This saves the overhead of starting a new process.

* Hashed lookups are faster than linear searches.

* Use everything you know about the pattern you are looking for to reduce runtime load. For example, if you are looking for a pattern that you know occurs only at the end of a line, use the $ anchor to tell Perl it does not have to search the whole line for the pattern.

There is a Perl compiler that generates C code out of Perl scripts. While Perl is already optimized enough that this may not make a huge difference in the actual runtime of the program, compiled C programs do not have the overhead of starting up the Perl interpreter, so for frequently accessed CGIs, this could improve performance considerably. The compiler is currently available from *ftp.ox.ac.uk* in */pub/perl/Compiler-a1.tar.gz*, and it is distributed with the Perl core as of release 5.005. Also see *http://www.perl.com/*.

Perl performance can be improved with a Perl module for the Apache web server, known as mod_perl. There is an introduction to the Perl module at *http://www.osf.org/~dougm/apache/*. Because the Perl interpreter becomes part of the Apache web server when you use mod_perl, the overhead of starting a new process, let alone the rather large Perl interpreter, is entirely avoided. Users have claimed execution speedups of 400% to 2000% by using mod_perl. You may well get better performance out of Perl scripts using mod_perl than out of compiled C code run as an ordinary CGI. You do, however, need to make a few changes to your Perl scripts and web server configuration to use mod_perl.

C

The first CGI programs were written in C, and C is still an excellent choice for cases where speed of execution is important. Remember that CGI programs written in C are still separate processes, so even if a C CGI program were to execute infinitely fast, it would still have to contend with process-creation time. C is very portable at the source code level, although it must be recompiled for each platform. There are regular expression libraries for C, but text handling requires more attention to detail than Perl does.

C optimization is a large enough topic to merit its own book, but here are some tips to get you started:

- Use your compiler's highest optimization level. For the GNU C compiler, *gcc*, this option is *-O3*. Note that optimizers are not infinitely wise and have been known to slow down, rather than speed up, code execution time. Be sure to time your program at different optimization levels to make sure you've actually improved performance. Higher optimization may expose subtle bugs in your code; use *lint* to find these problems. The latest compiler is likely to optimize best. Read your compiler's manpages to find out which other options may be of use to you.

- Increase speed by using fewer functions to avoid the overhead of pushing and popping some stack frames. Replacing a function call with the actual code of the function is called *inlining* code. The speed savings add up if you inline a function that would otherwise be called many times in a loop. Similarly, you can *unroll* loops for a speed increase: instead of incrementing a counter and making a comparison on each iteration, code all the iterations in a row yourself. Manual inlining and unrolling are considered poor programming practice because they make the code more difficult to read and maintain, so use your compiler's options to do these. The *gcc* compiler has options for both inlining and unrolling. Another disadvantage to these techniques is that both increase the size of the code, meaning that it takes longer to load and is more likely to be paged out.

- Use library calls rather than system calls. System calls are notoriously expensive in terms of time and resources. Even though library calls may end up calling the same system call, the library call is often more efficient in its use of system calls.

- Always use buffered I/O. It is far more efficient to read as much as you can at a time than to read single bytes off the network or from a file. You don't want to keep the user waiting while you read, either, so put reading in a separate thread of execution if you can.

- Statically link in libraries, rather than dynamically loading shared libraries at runtime. The code will be faster because the dynamic libraries do not have to be found and loaded. As with inlining function calls, this will make your executable bigger and slower to load. Do this only if you have plenty of RAM. This is the *-dn* option on SPARC compilers. Link with the *-lfast* library if you use *malloc* a lot.

- Use powers of two (1, 2, 4, 8, 16, . . .) in preference to other numbers where you have a choice. Most CPU architectures do power-of-two math extremely quickly, while other numbers require more CPU cycles. This is a result of the nature of the binary arithmetic all CPUs use. You can insure optimum division and multiplication by powers of two by shifting rather than multiplying (e.g., use x << 2 rather than x *= 2), but if you have a clever compiler, it will note the opportunity to use shifting and do it for you when translating the C source down to binary. I wrote a map applet in Java that zooms in or out by powers of two. It has to do lots of number crunching to display the map, but does it much faster than it could by multiplying everything by a random integer. See Chapter 16 for Java-specific tips.

- Floating point math is far slower than integer math and should be avoided unless truly useful. It may help to shift factional numbers up into integer range, truncate them, do integer math, and then shift them back down into fractional range when they need to be displayed.

- Use a code profiler and optimize most-executed sections, rewriting in assembly language if necessary. Use *gprof* to tell you how much time you're spending in each routine and *tcov* to tell you how many times you execute particular source lines. A good commercial tool is Quantify from Pure Software. A rule of thumb is that your code will spend 90% of its execution time in 10% of the code. Assembly coding is a technique of last resort, given the tediousness of assembly coding, loss of portability, and increased potential for errors.

- Use statically compiled arrays rather than a pointer to `malloc`'d memory.

See Chapter 16 for a discussion of server-side Java as a replacement for CGI.

Daemonize It

The best way to get CGI-like behavior, with far greater performance and scalability, is a common Unix technique I call *daemonization,* after the Unix daemons lurking in the background of every Unix machine waiting for events to handle. The basic idea is this: instead of having a CGI start in response to a query and then die, start up a persistent CGI-like process (a *daemon*) along with the web server. The daemon can even be on a different machine than the web server. When the web server gets a request pointing at the daemon, it simply connects to the daemon, hands over the request, and waits for the results (while still able to handle other requests).

Daemonization is a feature of servlets in Java. You can start servlets running and connect to them as often as you like, avoiding the overhead of startup, exactly as described previously. The fact that Java is interpreted is less significant than the performance gain derived from leaving the servlet running. Servlets are multithreaded, isolating clients from each other. See Chapter 15 of *Java Network Programming*, by Elliotte Rusty Harold (O'Reilly & Associates).

A standard method of daemonizing CGIs has been defined by Open Market, called FastCGI (see *www.fastcgi.com*). FastCGI programs are persistent, and they are also extremely scalable, because they can be run on machines other than the originating web server. FastCGI uses a single TCP socket to connect the web server and FastCGI application, unlike the standard CGI method of using pipes and environment variables. This connection provides the environment information, standard in, out, and error, all multiplexed together. Because of this, and the need to run in a loop, source code changes are required to transform an ordinary CGI into a FastCGI.

One downside of FastCGI is that it does not work natively with most common web servers requiring an ordinary CGI stub (Apache is the exception), which reduces the performance advantage. There is a collection of FastCGI performance tuning tips at *http://www.fastcgi.com/kit/doc/fastcgi-whitepaper/fastcgi.htm*. BMC "Patrol CGI Server" works like FastCGI: see *http://www.bmc.com/cgiserver/*.

Recent versions of NT's active server pages are similar in that a loaded CGI service does not exit, but remains resident, waiting for the next request. Apache's `mod_perl` works the same way.

Daemonized CGIs have a memory leakage hazard because you leave them running all the time. If the daemon leaks any memory at all, you will eventually lose so much RAM to it that you'll have to restart the daemon. You can try to use `ulimit` to limit the amount of RAM the daemon can use, but this isn't always reliable and you still have to come up with something to do when you hit that limit. A better approach is to make sure your code is clean to begin with. Tools like Purify, CodeCenter, Bounds Checker, or PURE can tell you if you have a leakage problem and often exactly where the problem is. Typically, leakage is the result of failing to clean the heap (free memory) of intermediate stack frames when returning from a subroutine.

Note that you can easily bypass CGI yourself and still run server-side programs on machines other than your web server. It is straightforward to set up a program that will accept connections on port 80 and process them, outputting HTML back to the browser. CGI has the advantage that browsers know how to use it to package forms data.

Another replacement for CGI is simply to use a named pipe, also known as a FIFO, in place of an HTML file. Note that named pipes do not take arguments like CGIs.

Finally, you could also write a CGI stub to use shared memory or a memory mapped file to communicate with a resident process if you do not like CGI or FastCGI.

CGI Database Access Performance

The principal performance concern with CGI database access is in eliminating the overhead of opening the database connection for each instance of the CGI. Opening a database connection can be very time-consuming and may require the loading of large libraries. It is worthwhile to buy or write a connection manager that opens the connection only once and brokers CGI requests to it, rather like FastCGI, but for database connections. RDBMS makers have realized this need for a fast or persistent connection and are now releasing products to fill the gap.

Another performance trick is to use one complex SQL query rather than multiple smaller queries, the results of which must be integrated by the CGI process before presentation to the user. Not only is the time spent in the SQL engine shorter overall, but the CGI does less work. Make the database do the work. See Chapter 17, *Databases*, for more tips.

Key Recommendations

* Set sanity timers in CGIs.
* Get some output from the CGI to the user right away.
* Don't write CGIs in a shell scripting language.
* Daemonize CGIs.
* FastCGI scales much better than CGI.
* Use `mod_perl` if your CGIs are in Perl and your server is Apache.

16

Java

What Java Does for You

Java provides an elegant solution to many long-standing programming problems and even solves a few new problems that became apparent only with the rise of the Web.

Since Java bytecode runs in a virtual machine, the same program will run on very different computers without porting or recompilation as long as there is an up-to-date Java virtual machine (JVM) on the target computer. There are JVMs already for all major architectures, from handhelds to mainframes, and the same bytecode can run on all of them. This frees software developers from the onerous task of porting while giving them the largest possible market for their software.

Since applets are distributed just before use, there is never a revision control prob lem or any cost to distribution of new code. Java's flexibility also gives end users the freedom to choose whatever hardware and operating system fit their needs best.

There is no advantage to the programmer or consumer in limiting the platforms software will run on; the benefit is solely to the platform vendor. There is also no benefit to the consumer in limiting the choice of operating systems, yet as of this writing, it is impossible to buy an assembled PC without paying for Microsoft Windows, whether you want it or not. Java levels the playing field, producing more competition and more choice for consumers in the hardware and OS arena while making it possible to scale business applications across the entire range of available hardware. This fact alone saves billions of dollars of legacy mainframe hardware from the scrap heap.

While Java is not the first programming language to make use of a virtual machine (Smalltalk has been around for years), it rose to prominence because it solved a fundamental problem limiting the commercial potential of the Web: HTTP was designed to distribute text, not to process transactions. Business computing, however, is fundamentally about transaction processing. When Java is included in a web browser, it becomes easy to give users transactional ability on demand.

CGI was an early attempt to overcome the limitations of HTTP and does have the advantages of ubiquity and simplicity, but it is difficult to scale and to integrate with legacy systems. Java and CORBA were designed with scaling and integration in mind. Because Java allows arbitrary functionality to be pushed to the browser, it reduces the load on both the server and the network. Once Java objects are loaded in the client, they need a standard method of communicating with the server. CORBA, as a standard for interobject communication, fills this role nicely, as well as providing a uniform interface to legacy software.

Another very significant advantage of Java is that the programmer does not have to worry about traditional memory leaks, which can eventually force a reboot. This is not to say that you can leave your Java applets running forever inside your browser, because both Netscape and Internet Explorer, which are written in C, have memory leakage problems themselves. Even on the server side, it's quite possible to find that your virtual machine (VM) has a leak or simply fails to reclaim classes. Threading, in particular, is prone to leaking; every time you create a thread you may lose some memory and not be able to get it back. This may be OK on the client side, where rebooting is normal, but it is definitely a hazard on the server side. You are dependent on the quality of your VM, but then, you have always been dependent on the quality of your operating system. Note that the programmer still has the ability to leak memory at a high level by allocating objects and never releasing all references to them.

Java Compared to Native Code

Java is a typical example of the conflict between portability and performance. Java's portability solves many problems, but there is a performance cost to these solutions. Java is compiled into bytecodes, which are then interpreted. Because the bytecodes are not the instructions of any existing CPU (any actual machine, so to speak), they must be interpreted by a virtual machine, i.e., translated into instructions that can be directly executed by the CPU. This is the primary reason that the simple interpretation of Java bytecodes is 30 to 100 times slower than optimized C, although just-in-time compilers (JITs) can bring this down to 5 to 10 times slower.

Code written in C is compiled into instructions that are native to a particular CPU, so interpretation is not needed, but these instructions have no binary-level portability. Furthermore, C code is not as efficient as hand-coded assembly, but it is much easier to write and good enough for most uses. Source-level C portability is also generally problematic because C programs often take advantage of platform-specific features, and because the C standard itself includes platform dependencies, such as the number of bits in an int. In C, integers can be different sizes on different platforms, so int i means one thing on one platform and another thing on another platform, leading to different results at runtime even if the code compiles smoothly. Java is completely portable at the source level, but that's irrelevant because it's portable at the binary level.

In addition to the instruction set, some other features of the Java VM do not map especially well to the architecture of existing CPUs. For example, C compilers can use CPU registers for quick access to frequently used variables. Java stores parameters and local variables on a stack and has no notion of CPU registers, although a clever VM might. The stack is of indeterminate size, so it is easiest to implement a VM by putting all of the stack in RAM. This in turn means that each frequently used local variable will require a RAM access, which is much slower than a CPU register access. Also note that Java and C++, being object-oriented, have a lot more indirection than C programs.

Another large performance hit comes from referencing classes. The VM has to follow several levels of indirection simply to find the class, then has to check for synchronization locking, whether the class access allows you to see it, and so on. There are other locks that might also affect the performance of your application, such as locks for garbage collection, class linking, loading, verification, and thread creation or destruction. The VM can implement these locks as it wishes, leading to variations in the performance of different VMs.

There are a number of other tradeoffs between features and performance in the Java language and runtime environments. Browsers tend not to start the Java VM until you have downloaded some Java, resulting in a delay while the browser initializes its VM before the first time you run Java in a session. Then, as you download classes, each superclass of any loaded class must be located in the client-side libraries or downloaded. The downloaded classes must all be run through the bytecode verifier as a security measure, which takes significant time. At runtime, array bounds are checked, which is a welcome relief to many programmers used to C/C++, but this can also be a penalty that is especially noticeable in tight loops. All method calls in Java are resolved at runtime—unlike C, where the location of functions is compiled into the code. This dynamic method binding gives the ability to swap methods at runtime, but incurs a significant overhead.

Another cost to using Java rather than C++ is that all objects are on the heap rather than the stack. This is done to eliminate a source of memory leakage and to improve security, but it requires time to manage the memory of objects on the heap.

Unfortunately, there is nothing in Java like the Unix `select()` system call, which can be used to tell when a socket has data ready for reading by the program. All reads in Java are blocking reads, which means that they must be in a separate thread if the entire program is not to hang, waiting for input. This is rather wasteful, since the reading thread will be awakened and put back to sleep repeatedly. It would be more useful to have a function that could generate an event when a socket has data ready.

Note that Java applets are intended to be small, but nothing requires them to be. You can write truly fat, slow applets in Java if you want. Such applets will take forever to download and even longer to run. You have enough rope to hang yourself. Don't do it.

Why It's Getting Better

In early 1997, Java's performance lagged C/C++ by a factor of 10 to 20, depending on the application. Now, at least some runtime environments are running Java as fast as they run C. InfoWorld has verified a report by Cats Software in Palo Alto that Java was only 4% to 10% slower than Microsoft's Visual C++ in a differential equation package.

Before we go into the reasons for the improvements, note that the current performance is quite acceptable for many applications. Java first became popular on the client side, in a web browser, manipulating GUI components. Java does this just fine: it may take 100 milliseconds rather than 10 milliseconds to change the GUI in response to a click or keystroke, but since both are faster than ordinary human perception, the time difference doesn't matter. Furthermore, as CPUs continue to increase exponentially in power, not only GUI operations, but all common computing operations will have performance rates that are indistinguishable, in human terms, from that of native code. Also, certain fundamental operations like arithmetic and string manipulation are implemented directly in the VM rather than in the Java class libraries that ship with the VM. Since the VM is usually written in C and optimized for a specific platform, these operations are already in native C.

Here are some reasons that Java execution speed will approach that of native code. First of all, Java compilers are continuously improving with respect to the bytecode they generate. One source code file can be implemented many different ways in bytecode. As time goes on, compiler writers will find ways to generate ever more efficient bytecode. Then, at the level of bytecode interpretation by the VM, we already have just-in-time compilers that compile stretches of bytecode (from a single instruction up to an entire method) into efficient native code as the bytecode is being executed. The next time the same stretch of bytecode is to be run, the compiled native code is run instead. For example, loops will run far faster under a JIT compiler because the bytecode does not have to be interpreted on every cycle of the loop. On the first cycle, native code for the loop is generated, and on the second and subsequent cycles, this native code is called.

JITs themselves are also improving. As of this writing, the SunSoft™ JIT approximately quadrupled performance (but this still lagged some native code by a factor of about five). Note that a JIT will not necessarily help you, and may even hurt in the case of code with very little redundancy of execution. A JIT must take some time to compile code and must keep track of what it has compiled. JITs are most useful for repetitive code where the compiled fragments are executed repeatedly. Code run with a JIT generally performs better in the CaffeineMark benchmark test, but this is because the test is very repetitive. Your code may be very different. See Chapter 3, *Web Performance Measurement*, for some information on the Caffeine-Mark Java benchmark. Also see the Volano Java benchmark, which is based on a chat application, at *http://www.volano.com/*.

VMs themselves, including the runtime support mechanisms, are improving rapidly. Microsoft's VM was considerably faster than Sun's initial implementation because Microsoft removed one layer of indirection. Where Sun had a handle to a pointer to both the data and instructions of a class, Microsoft had only a pointer to a single block containing both the data and instructions, at the expense of slower garbage collection. Garbage collection algorithms are also improving. Also, clever VM writers will be able to take advantage of CPU registers rather than using RAM for the entire Java stack.

Ultimately, what will bring Java performance up to or beyond that of native code on current CPUs is the implementation of the VM in hardware. At that point, the term "virtual" will no longer be accurate. The JVM was designed to be implemented in hardware eventually, and the Java chip should be quite a bit faster for the bytecodes that can be easily implemented in hardware. Unfortunately, there are bytecodes that require extensive processing to execute (like declaring a new object) and are not easily implemented in hardware. In some software, only 15% of the processing is bytecode interpretation by the VM.

Performance Tips: What You Can Do

OK, so Java performance will improve in future generations of compilers and JVMs, but you need better performance *now*. What can you do? There are dozens of techniques for improving Java performance. Let's go through the major ones, starting at the source code level.

Get the Best VM for Your Runtime Platform

If you know your code will be running on a particular platform, say because it is server-side code, be sure you have the latest VM for that platform. You probably also want a VM written by the operating system vendor because the vendor presumably knows the most about optimizing Java for that OS. So use the MRJ on the Mac, Digital's VM on Digital Unix, and so on. Microsoft also makes the fastest VMs for Windows, but be careful when using Microsoft Java products lest you end up writing code that won't run anywhere except on Windows.

Along with using the best VM for your platform, you should take advantage of all available performance boosters, such as native thread packages and JITs.

Profile Your Code

First, look at your Java code as you would look at C/C++ code, and do all of the optimizations you would do there. Look in Chapter 15, *CGI Programs*, under the section on optimizing C, for the standard ideas.

To do code profiling in Java, you compile with the *-prof* option, like this:

```
javac -prof MyClass.java
```

This does profiling based on actual execution times, but doesn't count the number of times any set of bytecode is used. The result is a profile file. You can interpret this file with a number of free tools available on the Web to find out where your code is spending most of its time, and therefore, where you should concentrate your source code optimization efforts. A number of tools both instrument your code for profiling and display the results: Visual Quantify for Java from Rational, Java™ Workshop™ 2.0 from Sun, and JavaSpec™ from the JavaTest part of Sun.

CPU and memory profilers for Java are also available from OptimizeIt, at *http://www.optimizeit.com/*, and from The KL Group, at *http://www.klgroup.com/*. It is also very instructive to start the Java console in Netscape and press 9 in the console window for detailed statistics as the applet runs. Press ? to see all the options the console gives you. These options are very useful at times.

Use Threads

Threads are far easier to use in Java than in C or C++. This is a very good thing, because threading allows multiple streams of execution within a single program, which is critical to writing high-performance applications in Java. One reason threads are so important to Java performance is that all Java I/O operations block the thread they are in (the thread waits until the read or write operation is complete). So you must use multiple threads if you do not want your entire program to hang whenever the network is slow, for example. If you put an I/O read or write into its own thread, the rest of the program can continue in other threads while the I/O thread blocks. The thread with the I/O can then notify another thread (using the well-named `notify()` method) when its operation is complete. Of course you should also be sure to use buffered I/O rather than single-byte I/O wherever possible, just as you would in C.

All applications and applets start out with one parent thread. If you create and run child threads, you may have to force the parent thread to explicitly give up control with the `suspend()` or `sleep()` methods for the child threads to run with acceptable performance.

Note that Java's threading model depends on the underlying operating system. For example, under Unix, the "green threads" model uses preemptive multitasking, while Windows threads must explicitly give up control. This can lead to differences in behavior across platforms unless the control of threaded operations is carefully thought out. Threading performance also depends on the underlying platform. While the earliest versions of Java did not take advantage of symmetric multiprocessing (SMP) machines, Java 1.2 (at least the Unix version) will allocate one thread per processor on SMP machines, resulting in performance that scales well with the number of processors. For example, you can get almost twice the performance from an application that splits the work into two equivalent threads, since each thread will have its own CPU. There is some overhead in managing the allocation of work.

Be aware that you can assign different priorities to different threads, so you can assign a high priority to tasks that are critical for overall performance, while assigning a lower priority to other tasks.

The JVM does not guarantee that your threads will be free of deadlock. Deadlock, where each of two or more threads is waiting for actions that can only be performed by the other, is fatal to performance. It is your responsibility to use the synchronized `keyword` and `Monitor` classes to insure this does not happen. Synchronized methods run more slowly than non-synchronized methods, but synchronization is critical to thread safety.

Browsers call your applet's `stop()` method when the user goes to another page, and `start()` when the user returns. Be sure to stop all your threads from doing anything when the `stop()` method gets called. It's rude to use up CPU cycles when the user is not actively using your program (unless this is part of the applet's functionality, and the user knows that).

The downside to threads is that they have associated locks that restrict access to portions of the code to particular threads. It is possible to overuse threads, forcing some threads to wait for others to give up locks, thus hurting overall performance. Don't use separate threads unless you have a clear reason to do so.

Be Clever with Loops

Keep synchronized methods out of loops if you possibly can. I/O classes tend to have a lot of synchronization, so you're often better off doing I/O all at once rather than in a loop, because each loop will waste time on locking and unlocking. You should read an entire stream (for example, with the `readFully()` method) and do any type conversions later on the entire data set, rather than looping through a read of a certain type and doing the conversion on the spot. Because each array access requires a bounds check, if you are going to use elements from an array in a loop and the elements do not depend on the index of the array, you'll get better performance assigning the array elements to a local variable and using that in the loop. For example:

```
local = array[4];
for (int i = 0; i < somenumber; i++)
    if (i = local) doSomething();
```

Use Final Methods

Since non-final method names are bound at runtime, if you know you will not override a method in a subclass, you should declare that method as final. (Or if you can, declare the whole class as final.) If you can avoid a method call entirely by including the code for one method in another (*inlining*), you will avoid the overhead of setting up the stack and tearing it down again. This is particularly important in loops.

On the other hand, the HotSpot designers claim that there is no additional advantage to declaring methods final when running with HotSpot.

Load and Use Fewer Classes

Similarly, if you use fewer but larger classes, you'll probably get a slight performance boost because the VM will not have to load as many classes, although this does not necessarily lead to good programming style. Not only should you reduce the number of classes, you should also reduce the number of objects (that is, reuse a class when you're done with it, if possible, rather than reinstantiating it). Even for a small class, you'll get better performance by reusing it than by instantiating it twice. Once again, the HotSpot designers claim this doesn't help for code run with HotSpot.

You can trade off initial download time against smaller runtime penalties by dynamically loading classes as needed with `Class.forname()` or other techniques. This has an added advantage over a single large initial load: code that isn't needed won't be downloaded. On the other hand, you'll probably set up a TCP connection for each of these classes at runtime.

Avoiding extensive subclass chains gives a performance boost because loading any class requires that all of its ancestor classes be loaded. While good object-oriented design would have you abstract out common features of related classes into a parent class, good performance can often be achieved by combining the two classes rather than creating a superclass. Again, this is not necessarily good style. Also, most browsers still require one TCP connection per class downloaded so fewer classes will help there, too. If you have more than two or three classes, however, you'll certainly want to put all of them into a *.zip* or *.jar* file, which will be downloaded in a single TCP connection. Increasing modularity by putting classes with interdependencies or closely related functionality in the same *.class* file, package, or *.zip* file can take advantage of locality of reference. That is, you often need code that is closely related to the code you're running at any moment, so keeping that code together will reduce time spent searching for it.

It's usually faster to use the functions provided than to try to reimplement them. For example, `drawPolygon()` is faster than using `drawLine()` repeatedly.

Be careful when using packages off the Web. Naive implementations of regular expressions, for instance, can be painfully slow. Use the information you have to reduce the work that the regular expression has to do. I once was looking for a pattern at the end of a long string, and found I got 70 times better performance by anchoring the match to the end of the string (using $) than when I left out that single character.

Use String Buffers or Arrays

If you are going to do a lot of string manipulation, be sure to use StringBuffers rather than Strings, since extending a String necessarily involves copying the whole thing, while extending a StringBuffer often means filling in space that has already been allocated. Bare byte arrays may be faster than StringBuffers for certain operations, especially if you use `System.arraycopy()`. Adding on to a StringBuffer is also quite a bit faster than the + operator, which creates a new StringBuffer itself, appends both of the arguments, and converts the result back to a String.

Don't Manage by Exception

Exceptions are expensive to construct and propagate, which is OK if they happen only rarely, but a problem if they are relied on for normal flow of execution. They are, after all, supposed to be exceptional.

Keep the Paint Method Small

Keep your `paint()` method as simple as possible, since it will be called many times. If you have too many calculations in your `paint()` method, the user will suffer greatly while waiting for your applet or application to redraw itself. This is all the more important since calls to `paint()` are queued up by the VM if they cannot be executed immediately. If you have a large `paint()` method and a user needs to scroll or otherwise redraw a lot, the user will probably give up in disgust while the queued up `repaint()` calls are slowly executed, making the screen flash and preventing the user from doing anything else. This problem is especially noticeable under Windows. If you must do a lot of computation in `paint()`, you can use clipping (redrawing just the part of the screen that has changed) to give your machine a fighting chance. Of course, the computation required to redraw a square on your screen goes up with the area of that square.

Double buffer (basically, draw into an off-screen buffer where it happens more quickly, then swap to the screen) where possible for smoother graphics. Likewise, try to fetch the next URL, or whatever data you're going to display next, while the user is busy looking at the current data. This can be a bit wasteful when dealing with URLs, because you may end up making someone's server do a lot of work, then throwing away the data because your user never clicked on the next link.

Use Sockets Rather Than URLs

Making an HTTP connection to get a URL is quite easy in Java, but if you need to transfer non-HTML data, you'll get slightly better performance by making a direct buffered socket connection back to the server the applet came from and downloading your data through that. This is especially helpful if you need to get multiple files, since you can use the same TCP connection for all of the files. Also be aware that you can get a further performance boost from using UDP sockets with Java, although UDP is unreliable, meaning you'll have to check the data integrity.

For some reason, it is far faster to display the Times font at runtime than some other fonts. This may be due to fonts built into the VM versus indirection of a loaded font.

Use Native Methods

If absolutely necessary for performance, you can write code in a compiled language like C and link it to Java code using the native method interface. At first glance, this would seem to destroy Java's portability, but it is not difficult to include pure Java fallback methods that will be used in case your code is run on a platform that does not support your native methods. See *http://www.java-world.com/javaworld/javatips/jw-javatip13.html* for examples.

Compile With -O

You can do a few things when compiling to improve the performance of your Java code. Once you have your code debugged and have used the profiling data to optimize it, you should optimize compilation by using the *-O* option, like this:

```
javac -O MyClass.java
```

This will automatically inline your final, private, and static methods, meaning that the call to those methods will be replaced with the actual code, removing the run-time overhead of pushing the current state on the stack at the expense of making your code larger. Note that optimization may bring out hidden bugs in your code. This is usually because the optimizer takes a stricter view of syntax, but it could also be due to bugs in the optimizer. You should thoroughly test your code after optimization. Suntest™ makes a suite of applet testing tools which can be used for regression tests.

Threads also have the advantages of very fast interthread communication via shared variables, parallel execution on multiprocessor machines, a relatively small memory footprint, and very fast context switching.

Platform-Dependent Compilation

Java's bytecode-level portability is a wonderful thing, but portability assumes that code will be moved from one platform to another. Certainly, applets need to move from a server to an arbitrary client machine, and in the long run, all platforms become obsolete, taking their native code with them. In the medium run, however, many applications are used on one machine for months or even several years. In this case, it may make sense to compile Java into C and from there into highly optimized native code, keeping the original bytecode around for future portability.* Compiling Java down to native code before runtime is known as *static compilation.*

Here are links to a few compilers that take Java source code down to C source code:

- Harissa (*http://www.irisa.fr/compose/harissa/harissa.html*)
- j2c (*http://www.webcity.co.jp/info/andoh/java/j2c.html*)
- JCC (*http://www.geocities.com/CapeCanaveral/Hangar/4040/jcc.html*)
- Toba (*http://www.cs.arizona.edu/sumatra/toba/*; applications only)
- TowerJ (*http://www.towerj.com/*)

---

* There are now also tools that translate COBOL and Visual Basic into Java bytecode.

If you use one of these, bear in mind that what you produce will not have binary portability, and it will be required to link to a library that performs runtime services, such as garbage collection, usually done by the VM. In addition, you will probably lose the ability to dynamically load regular Java classes (those you have not compiled down to C).

If you would prefer to go directly to Wintel *.exe* files, Microsoft's Java compiler allows you to do this, as does Symantec's Cafe Pro 2.0.

Silicon Graphics' VM also does static compilation behind the scenes.

In the next section, I give some runtime tips for performance. As I mentioned earlier, you should use *.jar* or *.zip* files if you have more than one class, because each class requires a separate TCP connection to load (unless you are using HTTP 1.1). Also, it may soon be possible to turn off the bytecode verifier in browsers (it is off for applications by default). This exposes you to some risk in return for performance.

JITs

Just-in-time compilers usually help performance substantially, but be aware that JITs help the most for repetitive code and not much for GUI code. In fact, it's possible that your code will run more slowly with a JIT. One problem is that you really don't want to JIT-compile code that will be used only once. It takes longer to compile the code and run it than to simply interpret the bytecodes. JavaSoft's HotSpot compiler solves this problem by collecting runtime execution data and using that data to compile only the portions of the code that are repeatedly executed, that is, the hot spots.

Here are the JITs available as of this writing, their URLs, the platforms they run on, and whether they're free or not:

Apple (http://www.applejava.apple.com)
    The Apple MacOS Runtime for Java MRJ2.0 includes a JIT for Java 1.1.3. It is free for download and bundled with MacOS 8.1.

DEC (http://www.digital.com/java)
    JDK 1.1.5 on Digital Unix V4.0x only. It is the only 64-bit implementation of Java. Free.

HP (http://www.hp.com/esy/go/java.html)
    JDK 1.1 for HPUX only. Free.

Kaffe (http://www.kaffe.org)
    For Alpha, 68K, PowerPC, MIPS, Sparc, x86. Free.

Microsoft (http://www.microsoft.com/visualj)
   Internet Explorer for Windows and the Mac. Free.

Netscape (http://www.netscape.com)
   Windows 3.1/95/NT, Mac, Solaris. Commercial.

SGI (http://cosmo.sgi.com/code/index.html)
   Irix. Commercial.

Sun (http://www.sun.com/workshop/java/jit)
   Windows 3.1/95/NT and Solaris. Free.

Symantec (http://www.symantec.com/javacentral/index.html)
   Windows 95/NT and Mac. Commercial.

VMs themselves vary in performance. Some poor implementations may not garbage collect classes and methods, meaning you will eventually run out of memory and the VM will stop. VMs generally improve in performance as time goes on and succeeding revisions of the VM specification come out, so you should use the latest version for your platform.

Java's 1.1 event handling is much faster than in 1.02. As an example of an improved VM, here are some of the changes from Sun's 1.1 to 1.2 Java runtime environments:

- Each thread keeps its own heap and monitor caches, reducing the overhead of locking and synchronization.

- Loaded classes are able to take advantage of memory compression and to share `String` objects among classes.

- Object allocation speed is greatly improved, as is garbage collection.

- The 1.2 JDK does not use handles, which are pointers to pointers, but only a single level of indirection to objects. This speeds up object references and allows the elimination of memory fragmentation.

Likewise, always use the latest version of any Java compiler, because compilers tend to generate better code in succeeding generations.

A 64-bit CPU probably won't help improve your performance because the Java virtual machine was defined to have a 32-bit address space and 8-bit bytecode instructions. Dedicated Java chips are more likely to help.

One way to avoid the download time for applets is to cache them locally, which is now possible with Netscape 4.0, Communicator. Marimba's Castanet product also allows caching of applets (and excels at differential updating, which saves bandwidth), but once you write an application to their API, you've lost portability: it requires their runtime to run.

On another level, Gemstone makes an application server that does a good job of storing Java objects in a database so that they don't have to be reinstantiated every time you use them, but again, this ties your software to their product. This ability to serialize and store all of your objects will soon be part of Java. See *http://www.sunlabs.com/research/forest/opj.mail.html.*

A blunt instrument for avoiding Java download time is simply to put your class files in with Netscape's on the client side. Then there will be no download time at all (but you have to go around to all of your clients and install it). See *http://www.javaworld.com/javaworld/jw-06-1997/jw-06-plugins.html.*

If all you're looking for is content replication, Unix has *rdist*, and there are other products such as ClusterCATS from Bright Tiger (*www.brighttiger.com*).

Server-Side Java

Although Java is best known for allowing you to download and execute Java programs in a web browser, there is a place for Java on the server side as well. There is a server API for Java, but not all servers obey it (JavaSoft's Java Web Server and Apache are the primary ones, and Sun distributes a patch for IIS). The Java server API specifies how the server should load and execute class files, or *servlets*. There is even an option to let the user upload servlets from the browser to the server, a reversal of browser/server roles. Performance of servlets is better than traditional CGI but slower than C-level server API programs. You can use Java applications as traditional CGIs, but then you get hit with the CGI penalty, the penalty of starting a VM, and the penalty of Java being interpreted, so it's not a particularly good idea. It is possible to write a server-side classloader without much trouble, saving the overhead of starting a new VM for each CGI, but you will still have the CGI forking overhead. For more information on servlets, see *http://java.sun.com/products/java-server/servlets/.*

One big advantage of Java over CGIs is the ability to distribute functionality between the client and server as needed. Instead of putting all functionality in a CGI program or making the user wait to download an entire applet, you can download some of the applet, letting the rest remain on the server side. This gives you the flexibility to trade off download time against network and server usage. You can even do this in a dynamic way, detecting network performance and deciding at runtime about how you need to distribute functionality. An important performance point to remember is not to poll between the browser and server for events, as this is wasteful of network resources. Use Java's event listeners rather than RMI or CORBA. See Chapter 10, *Network Protocols*, for more tips.

Distributed Object Performance

The browser/server relationship is being transformed by Java and CORBA into a relationship among distributed objects. RMI, the distributed object capability native to Java, is slower than CORBA in most implementations (the OrbixWeb Java ORB is about 20 times faster than RMI), but RMI is much simpler to use. RMI will eventually be merged into CORBA by JavaSoft. Both CORBA and RMI have associated overhead (such as object serialization) that can be avoided by using minimal custom protocols over sockets or HTTP/CGI.

Java ORBs themselves vary in performance, depending to a large degree on which version of Java they support. IONA's OrbixWeb 2.0.1 has a performance advantage because it supports Java 1.1.3's JIT and native threads, unlike, for example, the free JacORB. OrbixWeb is not free. Java ORBs are about as fast as their C++ counterparts. See *Client Server Programming with Java and CORBA*, by Robert Orfali and Dan Harkey (John Wiley & Sons), for benchmark numbers.

The Voyager product from Objectspace (*www.objectspace.com*) is another pure Java distributed object model. It is simpler than both RMI and CORBA and has the performance advantage of CORBA, but it is not yet widespread, perhaps because it is a proprietary offering (though free) from a small company. Voyager will also be integrated with CORBA in the future.

In summary, here are a number of standard tricks for improving distributed object performance:

- Objects should be reused rather than reinstantiated where possible, even across machine reboots. This implies that your objects should also be made persistent. They can then be "rehydrated" and ready for use more quickly than is possible by programmatic reconstruction.

- If you have a cache containing many objects, take the time to index the cache to avoid serial searches.

- If you send serialized objects across the network, be very careful of how many dependent objects, such as member objects and parent objects, are also sent. The number can add up quickly.

- Consider using multiple VMs on the same machine to take advantage of parallelism.

- And, of course, the whole point of distributed Java objects is to make use of multiple VMs scattered across the network. As of Java 1.1, a signed applet can refer to machines other than the server it came from, increasing scalability through the use of multiple servers.

Key Recommendations

- Java benefits from a fast CPU.
- Use a recent compiler and VM, preferably one optimized for your platform.
- Profile your code and optimize the most-used parts.
- Use threads.
- Use buffered I/O.
- Ask the client to cache the applet.
- Java is overkill for small animations or calculators. Use JavaScript or animated GIFs.

In this chapter:
• *Do You Really Need a Relational Database?*
• *Performance Tips*
• *Key Recommendations*

17

Databases

The explosion of interest in the Web is largely due to the promise of relatively cheap and easy global Internet access to legacy databases, Most of this information is on mainframes or in relational database management systems (RDBMSs). Some web site designers begin with the idea of providing web access to a certain data set and design a database with this goal in mind.

There are three standard classes of database access, each with different requirements:

• The individual query of a read-only database, such as AltaVista.

• The very complex query looking for patterns in huge amounts of data, usually for marketing purposes. This is called *data mining*. In a famous example of a data mining, grocery stores correlated sales of all items and found that beer and diapers were often sold together. No one had previously suspected this, but it made sense because both are items that you run out of and may make a special trip to buy. As a result of this discovery, grocery stores now tend to keep beer and diapers close together. Data mining is read-only, and the queries are usually so complex and take so long to run that web access is not advisable.

• Transaction processing, such as online credit card verification and sales, or bank account access. Transaction processing is rapidly becoming a key area of value for the Web.

These three classes of database access vary in their scalability needs and abilities. The read-only simple access class is easily scaled by replicating the database. Data mining databases generally do not need to be scaled, because so few users will be making queries. Transaction processing databases are the most difficult to scale, because it comes down to writing data to exactly one master copy at any moment, which imposes a significant bottleneck.

Database planning and tuning is a huge field, far larger than all of the work done on tuning web services so far. See *Oracle Performance Tuning*, by Mark Gurry and Peter Corrigan (O'Reilly & Associates).

Do You Really Need a Relational Database?

It is common for web developers to jump to the conclusion that they need an SQL-compliant RDBMS like Oracle, when in fact they have a rather small data set that could be organized as one table. Commercial RDBMSs are expensive as well as nontrivial to install and administer.

When You Need a Professional Database

Here are some indications that you need a professional database:

- You have more than a megabyte of data.
- You have multiple tables and want to do complex queries.
- You need extremely high reliability and performance.
- You need transaction processing abilities.

If this sounds like your situation, then you'll benefit from the performance features of commercial RDBMSs, such as the ability to work from raw disk rather than the OS's filesystem, custom threading models, and query optimizations.

Alternatives

Alternatives to the traditional SQL database include the following. Some of these are low-performance, but make for such easy programming that a low-volume web site should consider them.

The most obvious strategy for a small data set that needs to be searched in simple ways is to download all of the data to the client in an HTML page and let the user use the browser's find function to get to the relevant line. For more complex searching of small data sets, consider writing a Java applet to download along with the data, which presents a search interface to the user and simplifies the query.

For data sets that are too big for your client's access speed, a step up is to do the search on the server side with an ordinary CGI, a server API module, or a Java servlet. The Unix *grep* command is reasonably efficient and very easily used in a

CGI. Sometimes grepping a flat ASCII data file has a far better return on invest-ment than any formal database, because the programming is so easy. Perl has easy-to-use hashtables, and Unix *ndbm* files do a similar sort of hashing, for those inclined to write CGIs in C. C programmers can also read a binary file that is mapped into memory and treated as memory structures directly. This approach has extremely good performance if the overhead of CGI startup can be lessened by daemonizing the CGI or writing a server API module.

Finally, if you feel you need SQL for some complex queries but have a fairly small data set, consider MiniSQL, also called mSQL, from *http://www.Hughes.com.au/*. It is available with source code for a small fee, has good performance, and supports a large subset of ANSI SQL. There is also a JDBC™ interface available from *http://www.imaginary.com/~borg/Java/java.html*.

Performance Tips

Planning

A web site that exists for database access should be planned around the database. First, decide what sort of load the database will have to handle, and then choose web server software and hardware based on that load. The database will probably have to do much more work than the web server, so the database will be the bot-tleneck.

If you can afford to cache the whole database in RAM, a technique known as *supercaching*, do it. Also, if you know something about the kinds of SQL state-ments that will be executed, you can be ready for them with the correct amount of memory. Complicated joins take a lot of RAM and may even use all of your virtual memory if you're not careful.

Database vendors have a natural advantage in providing the fastest drivers and connectivity for their databases, but the Java DataBase Connectivity standard (JDBC™) does give you portability options. The best JDBC drivers talk directly to the database in the database's native protocol. The Open DataBase Connectivity standard (ODBC) slows things down a bit.

Multiple Tiers

The browser/web server/database setup happens to be a three-tier system, but doesn't have all the advantages of three-tier unless you plan for them. A two-tier system, where the web server is also the database, will give you better perfor-mance for small numbers of users but will not scale well. For large numbers of users, three-tier systems can reuse business objects on the web server or applica-tion server for both reading and writing without immediately hitting the database again, producing a large increase in performance. A middle tier also lets you join multiple databases to act as one so you can distribute the database. Mid-tier transaction processing monitors can also boost performance by managing access to a database connection, so that the connection does not need to be opened and closed for each query.

Queries

A good schema will reduce the amount of work a database must do to satisfy a query. Here are some guidelines:

- Cache the results of the most frequent queries.

- Do the more restrictive part of the query/update first. The second part will have less data to deal with and therefore will run faster.

- Precompile queries.

- You can push a lot of work onto the database with advanced SQL or stored procedures. The SQL is mostly portable, but the stored procedures will tie you to some particular database.

- Limit locking to the bits of data that you really need to lock.

- A single bad SQL query will create a crushing load on the database. Don't give the general public unrestricted access, not even on your intranet.

Indexes

Build indexes that correlate with what you're likely to be searching for. Otherwise, you've wasted your time building and updating the index, and your disk space in storing it.

Combined Web Server/Databases

Some databases themselves are now HTTP servers, eliminating a layer between the client and the database. These can construct HTML on the fly, like CGI, and can maintain state for transactions. They can be configured to use the same database connection for all requests, improving performance tremendously over opening a connection for each request. The downside is that they are proprietary solutions and do not scale well. The applications you write for one of these hybrid servers will not run on the others. The database may allow access across the network to other databases, but then you no longer have the performance advantage of dealing with only one process. The following are a few web server/databases:

- IBM's Merchant Server uses DB2.

- Informix Web Datablade uses Informix.

- NS LiveWire Pro uses Informix, and now Oracle as well.
- Oracle WebServer uses Oracle.
- Sybase's web.SQL uses Sybase.

Key Recommendations

- Keep the connection to the database open across CGI calls.
- If you don't have a large amount of data, consider non-RDBMS options.
- Build indexes.
- For complex queries, do the most restrictive part first.

III

Appendixes

A

Netscape Enterprise Server 3.0 Tuning

Introduction

This section describes supported tuning parameters and an unsupported utility (*perfdump*) which are built into the Netscape Enterprise Server 3.0. This document also addresses specific performance tuning problems and situations. This information is provided in the hope that it will be useful. However, the interfaces described in this document may, and probably will, change in future versions of the product.

Audience

This guide is intended for advanced administrators only. This is provided in good faith to expose as much information as possible to help administrators make a site that runs well. However, not all of these parameters are supported.

Do not tune the various values listed here without fully understanding exactly what you are doing. We cannot overstate the seriousness of changing these values without understanding them. We've seen many cases where someone heard of the internal tuning parameters we used in 2.0 and then called us with a critical escalation asking us to solve why their server suddenly stopped performing at all. So please, if your webserver is running fine out of the box as it should, please don't change these values.

We believe the default tuning parameters are good for most all sites—with possible exception to the very large sites. The only parameter which we think large sites will regularly need to change is the RqThrottle parameter, and it is tunable from the Administration Server. The rest of these parameters deal with the fine details to help administrators understand how the webserver is working and to design content that will run well on the server.

What Is perfdump?

perfdump is a "service" function which is built-in to the Netscape Enterprise Server. It can collect various pieces of performance data from the web server internal statistics, and it displays it in ASCII format when a request is issued for it.

The components of the web server which can be monitored with *perfdump* are:

- Listen socket status and thread count
- Keepalive data
- Server cache data
- Server DNS cache data
- Asynchronous DNS cache data (Unix only)

Installing perfdump

To install *perfdump*, you'll need to modify two files, *mime.types* and *obj.conf*. These files are found in the *suitespot/https-[servername]/config* directory.

Add the following line to your *mime.types* file (you can add this anywhere in the file):

```
type=perf exts=perf
```

Add the following line to your *obj.conf* (add this as the first **Service** function in the file):

```
Service fn=service-dump type=perf
```

Restart your server software, and you should now be able to access the URL *http:// yourhost/.perf*. This will display the *perfdump* statistics. Similarly, if you request the URL *http://yourhost/.perf?refresh=5*, this will display the *perfdump* statistics and inform the navigator to automatically refresh the statistics every 5 seconds.

Using perfdump Statistics

This section describes the various pieces of information available via *perfdump*, defining what each field represents, and shows how to tune each field, if possible.

First, here is a sample of the *perfdump* output from our site:

```
ListenSocket #0:
------------------
Address               https://INADDR_ANY:80
ActiveThreads         487
WaitingThreads        47
BusyThreads           440
IdleThreads           14

Thread limits         48/512


KeepAliveInfo:
------------------
KeepAliveCount        196/200
KeepAliveHits         2030795
KeepAliveFlushes      840657


CacheInfo:
------------------
enabled               yes
CacheEntries          4096/4096
CacheSize(bytes)      10394342/10485760

Hit Ratio             6806487/8457088 ( 80.48)

pollInterval          5
maxFileSize           537600


Server DNS cache disabled
```

If you are running a 3.0 server, you might notice that there are a few fields which are not described here. These fields are obsolete and will go away in the next release. They do not provide any useful information for tuning the web server. The names of the obsolete fields are listed at the end of each section.

ListenSocket Information

The first subtopic in the *perfdump* screen is the ListenSocket information. For each hardware virtual server you have enabled in your web server, you will find one ListenSocket structure. For most sites, this means only one listen socket will be listed.

Address

This field contains the base address which this listen socket is listening to. For most sites which are not using hardware virtual servers, the URL will be *http://INADDR_ANY:80*. "INADDR_ANY" is a constant value known internally to the server which specifies that this listen socket is listening on all IP addresses for this machine.

Tuning. Create hardware virtual servers from the administration server to create additional sockets and specify their IP addresses.

Threads

The next few fields specify the current thread use counts and limits for this listen socket. Keep in mind that the idea of a "thread" does not necessarily reflect the use of a thread known to the operating system. "Thread" in these fields really means an HTTP session. If you check the operating system to see how many threads are running in the process, it is not going to be the same as the numbers reported in these fields, and that is perfectly normal.

ActiveThreads

The total number of "threads" (HTTP sessions) which are in any state for this listen socket. This will be equal to `WaitingThreads` + `BusyThreads` + `KeepAliveCount`. This equation may vary a little if your site uses multiple listen sockets. This is because the `KeepAliveCount` is shared across all listen sockets.

Note. With 3.01 and later releases, this number will be equal to the `WaitingThreads` + `BusyThreads` rather than `WaitingThreads` + `BusyThreads` + `KeepAliveCount`.

Tuning. Not tunable.

WaitingThreads

The number of "threads" waiting for a new TCP connection for this listen socket.

Tuning. This is not directly tunable, but it is loosely equivalent to the `RqThrottleMinPerSocket`. See "Thread limits," later in this list.

BusyThreads

The number of "threads" actively processing requests which arrived on this listen socket.

Tuning. Not tunable.

Thread limits

The minimum thread limit is a goal for how many threads the server attempts to keep in the WaitingThreads state. This number is just a goal; the number of actual threads in this state may go slightly above or below this value.

The maximum threads represents a hard limit for the number of ActiveThreads that are allowed to be running simultaneously. The server will not allow more than this many threads to run concurrently, and this can be a bottleneck for performance. This limit is tunable from the Enterprise Server Manager and is known as "Maximum Simultaneous Requests."

In the 3.0 server the defaults are 48/128. With 3.01, the limits are increased to 48/512. This is because we found that 128 can be a gating factor for performance even on sites doing as little as 750,000 hits per day. If your site is experiencing slowness and the ActiveThread count remains close to limit, you should consider increasing the Maximum Simultaneous Requests.

Tuning. `RqThrottleMinPerSocket` in *magnus.conf* is the minimum value (the first number). `RqThrottle` in *magnus.conf* is the maximum value.

KeepAlive Information

This structure reports statistics about the server's HTTP-level KeepAlive system. (N.B.: The name "KeepAlive" should not be confused with TCP "KeepAlives".) Also, the name "KeepAlive" was changed to "Persistent Connections" in HTTP/1.1. For the purposes of this document, I will always refer to them as "KeepAlives."

Both HTTP/1.0 and HTTP/1.1 support the ability to send multiple requests across a single HTTP session. Most current web browsers (including the Netscape Navigator) support this feature.

A web server can receive hundreds of new HTTP requests per second. If every request were allowed to keep the connection open indefinitely, the server could become overloaded with connections. On Unix systems, this could lead to a file table overflow very easily.

To deal with this problem, the webserver maintains a "Maximum number of 'waiting' keepalive connections" counter. A waiting keepalive connection is a connection that has fully completed processing of the previous request over the connection and is now waiting for a new request to arrive on the same connection. If the server has more than the maximum waiting connections open when a new connection starts to wait for a keepalive request, the server closes the oldest connection. This algorithm maintains an upper bound on the number of open, waiting keepalive connections that the server will maintain.

KeepAliveCount (KeepAliveCount/KeepAliveMaxCount)

Displays the number of sessions currently waiting for a KeepAlive connection and the maximum number of sessions that the server will allow to wait at one time.

Tuning. `MaxKeepAliveConnections` in *magnus.conf* is the maximum number of KeepAlives.

KeepAliveHits

The number of times a request was successfully received from a connection which had been kept alive.

Tuning. Not tunable.

KeepAliveFlushes

The number of times the server had to close a connection because the `Keep-AliveCount` exceeded the `KeepAliveMaxCount`.

Tuning. Not tunable.

Cache Information

The "Cache" is a URI cache. It caches that a specific URI maps to a specific static file on disk.

enabled

If the cache is disabled, the rest of this section will not be displayed.

Tuning. Inserting the following line to *obj.conf* will disable the server cache:

```
Init fn=cache-init disable=true
```

CacheEntries (CurrentCacheEntries/MaxCacheEntries)

The number of current cache entries and the maximum number of cache entries. A single cache entry represents a single URI.

Tuning. The `cache-init` function in *obj.conf* tunes the cache. Add the following to set the maximum size of the cache:

```
Init fn=cache-init MaxNumberOfCachedFiles=xxxxx
```

CacheSize (CurrentCacheSize / MaxCacheSize)

These parameters represent the current size of the cache in bytes and the maximum size of the cache in bytes. The default size is 10MB, and the cache will not insert new entries once that size has been reached.

Tuning. The `cache-init` function in *obj.conf* tunes the cache. Add the following to set the maximum size of the cache:

```
Init fn=cache-init MaxTotalCachedFileSize=xxxxx
```

The units are in kilobytes.

Hit Ratio (CacheHits / CacheLookups (Ratio))

The hit ratio is one of the most important pieces of data available. It tells you how well your cache is getting used. Hopefully, the hit ratio is above 90%. For many sites, that is true. If the number is 0, you know you have some work to do to optimize your site. See the "Common Performance Problems to Check For" section for more information.

Tuning. Not tunable.

pollInterval

When a file is in the cache, we need to constantly go back to the disk to make sure that it hasn't changed since we last cached it. The `pollInterval` represents a maximum amount of time that can pass before we check the disk again. The default value is 5 seconds. If you'd like to check the file with every access, you can set this value to 0.

Tuning. The `cache-init` function in *obj.conf* tunes the cache. Add the following to set the maximum size of the cache:

```
Init fn=cache-init PollInterval==xxxxx
```

The units are in seconds.

maxFileSize

The `maxFileSize` is the maximum size of a file that we will cache. The default size is 537600 bytes. This means that a file which is 600 KB will not be cached. It is recommended that you avoid caching large files unless you have lots of RAM available.

Tuning. The `cache-init` function in *obj.conf* tunes the cache. Add the following to set the maximum size of the cache:

```
Init fn=cache-init MaxCachedFileSize=xxxxx
```

The units are in bytes.

Obsolete fields

- `OpenCacheEntries`
- `numCacheInsertsOk`
- `numCacheInsertsFail`
- `numCacheDeletes`

DNS Cache Information

The DNS cache caches IP addresses and DNS names.

enabled

If the cache is disabled, the rest of this section will not be displayed.

Tuning. By default, the DNS cache is off. Adding the following line to *obj.conf* will enable the cache:

```
Init fn=dns-cache-init
```

CacheEntries (CurrentCacheEntries / MaxCacheEntries)

The number of current cache entries and the maximum number of cache entries. A single cache entry represents a single IP address/DNS name lookup.

Tuning. The **dns-cache-init** function in *obj.conf* tunes the cache. Add the following to set the maximum size of the cache:

```
Init fn=cache-init cache-size=xxxxx
```

HitRatio (CacheHits / CacheLookups (Ratio))

The hit ratio is the number of cache hits per the number of cache lookups. Typically, the cache hit ratio for the DNS cache should be around 60–70%.

Tuning. Not tunable.

Obsolete fields

- numCacheInsertsOk
- numCacheInsertsFail
- numCacheDeletes

Asynchronous DNS Lookup Information (Unix Only)

enabled

If asynchronous DNS is disabled, the rest of this section will not be displayed.

Tuning. Add **AsyncDNS** on to *magnus.conf*.

NameLookups

The number of name lookups (DNS name to IP address) that have been done since the server was started.

Tuning. Not tunable.

AddrLookups

The number of address loops (IP address to DNS name) that have been done since the server was started.

Tuning. Not tunable.

LookupsInProgress

The current number of lookups in progress.

Tuning. Not tunable.

Common Performance Problems to Check For

This section discusses a few common problems to check for on your web site.

The server is under-throttled

As mentioned earlier, the server will not allow the number of `ActiveThreads` to exceed the "Maximum number of simultaneous connections" value specified via the admin server. If the server reaches that limit, it will stop servicing new connections until it has finished with the old connections. This can lead to increased response time.

The server's default throttle is 128, which means that once the server has 128 busy connections, the server will stop accepting new connections. So, if your server is "at throttle" and you don't want it to be, you should raise the value for this parameter.

The symptom of an under-throttled server is a server which has a long response time. Making a request from a browser will establish a connection fairly quickly to the server, but it will be a long time before the response comes back to the client.

How to check for under-throttling?

The best way to tell if your server is being throttled is to look at the `WaitingThreads` count. If this number is getting close to 0 or is 0, then the server is not accepting new connections right now. At the same time, this probably means that the number of `BusyThreads` is very close to the limit. Also check to see if the number of `ActiveThreads` is close to the limit. If so, the server is probably limiting itself.

How to fix "under-throttling"?

The RqThrottle parameter is tunable from the Enterprise Server Manager, where it is referred to as the "Maximum number of simultaneous requests". Increase this value to something suitable and restart your server. A suitable value can range from 200–2000, depending on the load. If you want your server to use all resources available to it on the system (i.e., you don't run other server software on the same machine), then increasing RqThrottle to a larger value than necessary shouldn't have any negative effects.

The cache is not utilized

If the cache is not utilized, your server is not performing optimally. Since most sites have lots of GIF or JPG files (which should always be cachable), you should be getting some advantage from the cache.

Some sites, however, do almost everything through CGIs, shtml or other dynamic sources. Dynamic content is generally not cachable and will inherently yield a low cache hit rate. Don't be too alarmed if your site has a low cache hit rate. The most important thing is that your response time is low, and it's quite possible to have a 0% cache hit rate and still have very good response time. As long as your response time is good, you may not care that the cache hit rate is low.

How to check for a low cache hit rate?

Under the "CacheInfo" section, check the hit ratio. This is the percentage of times the cache was used with all hits to your server. A good cache hit rate is anything above 50%. Some sites may even achieve 98% or higher.

How to fix a low cache hit rate?

Fixing a low cache hit rate may be difficult or it may be easy. The first thing to do is to find out why your cache hit rate is low. If you are doing a lot of CGI or NSAPI, you may have a low cache hit rate. If you are writing your own NSAPI, be sure to see the programmer's guide for information on making your NSAPI code cachable as well.

KeepAlives are getting flushed

Using HTTP KeepAlives is a good thing. A web site that might be able to service 75 requests per second without KeepAlives may be able be able to do 200–300 requests per second when KeepAlives are enabled. Therefore, as a client requests the various items from a single page, it is important that they be able to take advantage of KeepAlives.

How to check for KeepAlives getting flushed?

Under the "KeepAlive Information" section of *perfdump*, check the Keep-AliveFlushes and KeepAliveHits ratio. On a site where KeepAlives are running well, the ratio of KeepAliveFlushes to KeepAliveHits will be very low. If the ratio is high (greater than 1:1), your site is probably not utilizing the HTTP KeepAlives as well as it could.

How to fix KeepAlive flushes?

To reduce KeepAlive flushes, increase the value `MaxKeepAliveConnections` in *magnus.conf.* The default value is 200. By raising the value, you keep more waiting KeepAlive connections open and thus reduce KeepAlive flushes.

 On Unix systems, if you increase the `MaxKeepAliveConnections` value too high, the server can run out of open file descriptors. Typically 1024 is the limit for open files on Unix, so increasing this value above 500 is not recommended.

Platform-Specific Issues

Unix

The various Unix platforms all have limits on the number of files that can be open in a single process at one time. For busy sites, you'll need to increase that number to 1024:

Solaris

In */etc/system,* set `rlim_fd_max` and reboot.

SGI

Run `systune -i` and set `rlimit_nofile_max` and `rlimit_nofile_cur`, then reboot.

AIX

Run `smit` and check the kernel tuning parameters.

HP-UX

Run `sam` and check the kernel tuning parameters.

Benchmarking the Netscape Enterprise Server

For optimal performance in benchmark situations, make sure that Content Management, Search, and Agents are disabled. These functions are controlled through the admin server. Bring up the admin server and go to `Web Publishing | Server State`. Change the state to `off`, and apply the change. Next, go to `Agents& Search | Search State`. Change this state to `off`, and apply the change. Note that both states may already be set to `off`.

SPECweb96 Tuning

SPECweb96 uses a very large data fileset. This fileset far exceeds the Netscape Enterprise Server's expected fileset size. For instance, on the Netscape web site, we are able to obtain more than an 80% cache hit rate with a 10MB cache. With SPECweb96, a 10MB cache can yield cache hit rates as low as 20% (this number varies depending on the SPECweb96 load requested; larger loads use larger filesets).

To optimize performance in a SPECweb96 test, you should use a machine which has enough RAM to cache the entire fileset. You should also increase the web server's cache size (see the previous section, "Cache Information," for more information).

1. Calculate the number of files used in the SPECweb96 fileset. The SPECweb96 fileset size is based on the number of SPECweb96 OPS requested in the test run. The following formula calculates the number of files:

   ```
   files= ( ( (int) ( (sqrt(OPS/5) * 10.0) + 0.5) ) * 36 )
   ```

   ```
   fileset size = files * 142207.5
   ```

   Example:

Max Requested OPS	Number of files	Fileset size (bytes)
500	3636	517,066,470
1000	5112	726,964,740
2000	7236	1,029,013,470

2. Increase the number of files that the web server's cache will hold to the number of files calculated in step 1.

   In the *obj.conf* configuration file, use the line:

   ```
   Init fn=cache-init
   ```

   Append these values to the **cache-init** line:

   ```
   MaxNumberOfCachedFiles = < Number of files from step 1 >
   MaxNumberOfOpenCachedFiles= < Number of files from step 1 >
   ```

3. Increase the web server's total cache size to be large enough to hold the entire SPECweb96 fileset:

   ```
   MaxTotalCachedFileSize = < Fileset size from step 1 >
   ```

4. Increase the web server's largest cached file size to be large enough to hold all SPECweb files:

   ```
   MaxCachedFileSize = 1024000
   ```

   (The largest single SPECweb96 file is 900kB.)

5. Increase the cache poll interval.

The `cache-init PollInterval` directive may be used to change the cache refresh interval (default is 5 seconds). Using a value of 30000 (8 hours) should keep cache checks from happening within a SPECweb96 run.

6. Miscellaneous.

Some additional directives in *magnus.conf* will further improve performance:

— `DaemonStats` is probably the most important for HTTP GET benchmarks. It disables some of the daemon statistics gathering in the web server.

`RqThrottle` specifies the maximum number of simultaneous transactions the webserver will handle. Changes to this value can be used to throttle the server, minimizing latencies for the transactions that are performed. Default value is 128. `RqThrottle` acts across multiple virtual servers, but does not attempt to load-balance.

— You can set the number of maximum simultaneous requests, which is the number of active requests allowed for the server at one time. However, for general-purpose Internet or intranet use, you probably will not need to change the default value (128 requests).

To compute the number of simultaneous requests, the server counts the number of active requests, adding one to the number when a new request arrives, subtracting one when it finishes the request. When a new request arrives, the server checks to see if it is already processing the maximum number of requests. If it has reached the limit, it defers processing new requests until the number of active requests drops below the maximum amount.

In theory, you could set the maximum simultaneous requests to 1 and still have a functional server. Setting this value to 1 would mean that the server could only handle 1 request at a time, but since HTTP requests generally have a very short duration (response time can be as low as 5 milliseconds), processing one request at a time would still allow you to process up to 200 requests per second.

However, in actuality, Internet clients frequently connect to the server and then do not complete their requests. In these cases, the server waits 30 seconds or more for the data before timing out. Also, some sites do heavyweight transactions that take minutes to complete. Both of these factors add to the maximum simultaneous requests that are required. If your site is processing many requests that take many seconds, you may need to increase the number of maximum simultaneous requests.

— `DaemonStats` are on by default. A `DaemonStats` `off` directive in *magnus.conf* will disable collection of server statistics.

— `ACLFile` is a *magnus.conf* directive to load ACLs. Disable all `ACLFile` directives for maximum performance.

WebStone Tuning

For webstone performance benchmarking, there is no additional web server tuning required as long as the fileset size is relatively small. If the webstone fileset size is large, you should increase the web server's cache size. (See the SpecWeb tuning guide for information on tuning the cache.)

B

Apache Performance Notes

This appendix was written by Dean Gaudet and is used with his permission. The latest version of this page is on the Web at http://www.apache.org/docs/misc/perf-tuning.html.

Introduction

Apache is a general web server that is designed to be correct first and fast second. Even so, its performance is quite satisfactory. Most sites have less than 10Mbits of outgoing bandwidth, which Apache can fill using only a low-end Pentium-based web server. In practice, sites with more bandwidth require more than one machine to fill the bandwidth due to other constraints (such as CGI or database transaction overhead). For these reasons, the development focus has been mostly on correctness and configurability.

Unfortunately, many folks overlook these facts and cite raw performance numbers as if they are some indication of the quality of a web server product. There is a bare minimum performance that is acceptable; beyond that, extra speed only caters to a much smaller segment of the market. But in order to avoid this hurdle to the acceptance of Apache in some markets, effort was put into Apache 1.3 to bring performance up to a point where the difference with other high-end web servers is minimal.

Finally, there are the folks who just plain want to see how fast something can go. The author falls into this category. The rest of this document is dedicated to these folks who want to squeeze every last bit of performance out of Apache's current model and want to understand why it does some things that slow it down.

Note that this is tailored towards Apache 1.3 on Unix. Some of it applies to Apache on NT. Apache on NT has not been tuned for performance yet; in fact, it probably performs very poorly, because NT performance requires a different pro-gramming model.

Hardware and Operating System Issues

The single biggest hardware issue affecting web server performance is RAM. A web server should never ever have to swap: swapping increases the latency of each request beyond a point that users consider fast enough. This causes users to hit Stop and reload, further increasing the load. You can, and should, control the `MaxClients` setting so that your server does not spawn so many children it starts swapping.

Beyond that, the rest is mundane: get a fast enough CPU, a fast enough network card, and fast enough disks, where "fast enough" is something that needs to be determined by experimentation.

Operating system choice is largely a matter of local concerns. But a general guide-line is to always apply the latest vendor TCP/IP patches. HTTP serving completely breaks many of the assumptions built into Unix kernels up through 1994, and even 1995. Good choices include recent FreeBSD and Linux.

Runtime Configuration Issues

HostnameLookups

Prior to Apache 1.3, `HostnameLookups` defaulted to `On`. This adds latency to every request, because it requires a DNS lookup to complete before the request is fin-ished. In Apache 1.3, this setting defaults to `Off`. However (1.3 or later), if you use any `allow from domain` or `deny from domain` directives, then you will pay for a double reverse DNS lookup (a reverse, followed by a forward to make sure that the reverse is not being spoofed). So for the highest performance, avoid using these directives (it's fine to use IP addresses rather than domain names).

Note that it's possible to scope the directives, such as within a `<Location / server-status>` section. In this case, the DNS lookups are only performed on requests matching the criteria. Here's an example which disables lookups except for *.html* and *.cgi* files:

```
HostnameLookups off
<Files ~ "\.(html|cgi)$>
    HostnameLookups on
</Files>
```

Still, if you just need DNS names in some CGIs, you could consider doing the `gethostbyname` call in the specific CGIs that need it.

FollowSymLinks and SymLinksIfOwnerMatch

Wherever in your URL-space you do not have an `Options FollowSymLinks`, or
you do have an `Options SymLinksIfOwnerMatch`, Apache will have to issue
extra system calls to check up on symlinks—one extra call per filename component. For example, if you had:

```
DocumentRoot /www/htdocs
<Directory />
    Options SymLinksIfOwnerMatch
</Directory>
```

and a request is made for the URI */index.html*, then Apache will perform
`lstat(2)` on */www*, */www/htdocs*, and */www/htdocs/index.html*. The results of
these `lstats` are never cached, so they will occur on every single request. If you
really desire the symlinks security checking, you can do something like this:

```
DocumentRoot /www/htdocs
<Directory />
    Options FollowSymLinks
</Directory>
<Directory /www/htdocs>
    Options -FollowSymLinks +SymLinksIfOwnerMatch
</Directory>
```

This, at least, avoids the extra checks for the `DocumentRoot` path. Note that you'll
need to add similar sections if you have any `Alias` or `RewriteRule` paths outside of your document root. For highest performance and no symlink protection,
set `FollowSymLinks` everywhere, and never set `SymLinksIfOwnerMatch`.

AllowOverride

Wherever in your URL-space you allow overrides (typically *.htaccess* files), Apache
will attempt to open *.htaccess* for each filename component. For example:

```
DocumentRoot /www/htdocs
<Directory />
    AllowOverride all
</Directory>
```

A request is made for the URI */index.html*. Then Apache will attempt to open
/.htaccess, */www/.htaccess*, and */www/htdocs/.htaccess*. The solutions are similar to
the previous case of `Options FollowSymLinks`. For highest performance use
`AllowOverride None` everywhere in your filesystem.

Negotiation

If at all possible, avoid content negotiation if you're really interested in every last
ounce of performance. In practice, the benefits of negotiation outweigh the perfor-

mance penalties. There's one case where you can speed up the server. Instead of using a wildcard such as:

```
DirectoryIndex index
```

use a complete list of options:

```
DirectoryIndex index.cgi index.pl index.shtml index.html
```

where you list the most common choice first.

Process Creation

Prior to Apache 1.3 the `MinSpareServers`, `MaxSpareServers`, and `Start-Servers` settings all had drastic effects on benchmark results. In particular, Apache required a "ramp-up" period in order to reach a number of children sufficient to serve the load being applied. After the initial spawning of `StartServers` children, only 1 child per second would be created to satisfy the `MinSpareServers` setting. So a server being accessed by 100 simultaneous clients, using the default `StartServers` of 5, would take on the order of 95 seconds to spawn enough children to handle the load. This works fine in practice on real-life servers, because they aren't restarted frequently. But it does really poorly on benchmarks that might only run for ten minutes.

The one-per-second rule was implemented in an effort to avoid swamping the machine with the startup of new children. If the machine is busy spawning children, it can't service requests. But it has such a drastic effect on the perceived performance of Apache that it had to be replaced. As of Apache 1.3, the code will relax the one-per-second rule. It will spawn one, wait a second, then spawn two, wait a second, then spawn four, and it will continue exponentially until it is spawning 32 children per second. It will stop whenever it satisfies the `MinSpare-Servers` setting.

This appears to be responsive enough that it's almost unnecessary to twiddle the `MinSpareServers`, `MaxSpareServers`, and `StartServers` knobs. When more than 4 children are spawned per second, a message will be emitted to the Error-Log. If you see a lot of these errors, then consider tuning these settings. Use the `mod_status` output as a guide.

Related to process creation is process death induced by the `MaxRequestsPer-Child` setting. By default this is 30, which is probably far too low unless your server is using a module such as `mod_perl` that causes children to have bloated memory images. If your server is serving mostly static pages then consider raising this value to something like 10000. The code is robust enough that this shouldn't be a problem.

When keepalives are in use, children will be kept busy doing nothing waiting for more requests on the already open connection. The default `KeepAliveTimeout` of 15 seconds attempts to minimize this effect. The tradeoff here is between network bandwidth and server resources. In no event should you raise this above about 60 seconds, as most of the benefits are lost.

Compile-Time Configuration Issues

mod_status and Rule STATUS=yes

If you include `mod_status` and you also set `Rule STATUS=yes` when building Apache, then on every request Apache will perform two calls to `gettimeofday(2)` (or `times(2)`, depending on your operating system), and (pre-1.3) several extra calls to `time(2)`. This is all done so that the status report contains timing indications. For highest performance, set `Rule STATUS=no`:

Accept Serialization—Multiple Sockets

This section discusses a shortcoming in the Unix socket API. Suppose your web server uses multiple `Listen` statements to listen on either multiple ports or multiple addresses. In order to test each socket to see if a connection is ready, Apache uses `select(2)`. `select(2)` indicates that a socket has either no connections or at least one connection waiting on it. Apache's model includes multiple children, and all the idle ones test for new connections at the same time. A naïve implementation looks something like this (these examples do not match the code, they're contrived for pedagogical purposes):

```
for (;;) {
    for (;;) {
        fd_set accept_fds;
        FD_ZERO (&accept_fds);
        for (i = first_socket; i <= last_socket; ++i) {
            FD_SET (i, &accept_fds);
        }
        rc = select (last_socket+1, &accept_fds, NULL, NULL, NULL);
        if (rc < 1) continue;
        new_connection = -1;
        for (i = first_socket; i <= last_socket; ++i) {
            if (FD_ISSET (i, &accept_fds)) {
                new_connection = accept (i, NULL, NULL);
                if (new_connection != -1) break;
            }
        }
        if (new_connection != -1) break;
    }
    process the new_connection;
}
```

But this naive implementation has a serious starvation problem. Recall that multiple children execute this loop at the same time, and so multiple children will block at select when they are in between requests. All those blocked children will awaken and return from select when a single request appears on any socket (the number of children which awaken varies depending on the operating system and timing issues). They will all then fall down into the loop and try to accept the connection. But only one will succeed (assuming there's still only one connection ready); the rest will be blocked in accept. This effectively locks those children into serving requests from that one socket and no other sockets, and they'll be stuck there until enough new requests appear on that socket to wake them all up. This starvation problem was first documented in PR#467. There are at least two solutions.

One solution is to make the sockets non-blocking. In this case the accept won't block the children, and they will be allowed to continue immediately. But this wastes CPU time. Suppose you have ten idle children in select, and one connection arrives. Then nine of those children will wake up, try to accept the connection, fail, and loop back into select, accomplishing nothing. Meanwhile none of those children is servicing requests that occurred on other sockets until they get back up to the select again. Overall, this solution does not seem very fruitful unless you have as many idle CPUs (in a multiprocessor box) as you have idle children, not a very likely situation.

Another solution, the one used by Apache, is to serialize entry into the inner loop. The loop looks like this (differences are highlighted):

```
for (;;) {
    accept_mutex_on ();
    for (;;) {
        fd_set accept_fds;
        FD_ZERO (&accept_fds);
        for (i = first_socket; i <= last_socket; ++i) {
            FD_SET (i, &accept_fds);
        }
        rc = select (last_socket+1, &accept_fds, NULL, NULL, NULL);
        if (rc < 1) continue;
        new_connection = -1;
        for (i = first_socket; i <= last_socket; ++i) {
            if (FD_ISSET (i, &accept_fds)) {
                new_connection = accept (i, NULL, NULL);
                if (new_connection != -1) break;
            }
        }
        if (new_connection != -1) break;
    }
    accept_mutex_off ();
    process the new_connection;
}
```

The functions `accept_mutex_on` and `accept_mutex_off` implement a mutual exclusion semaphore. Only one child can have the mutex at any time. There are several choices for implementing these mutexes. The choice is defined in *src/conf.h* (pre-1.3) or *src/main/conf.h* (1.3 or later). Some architectures do not have any locking choice made; on these architectures, it is unsafe to use multiple `Listen` directives:

USE_FLOCK_SERIALIZED_ACCEPT

This method uses the `flock(2)` system call to lock a lock file (located by the `LockFile` directive).

USE_FCNTL_SERIALIZED_ACCEPT

This method uses the `fcntl(2)` system call to lock a lock file (located by the `LockFile` directive).

USE_SYSVSEM_SERIALIZED_ACCEPT

(1.3 or later) This method uses SysV-style semaphores to implement the mutex. Unfortunately, SysV-style semaphores have some bad side-effects. One is that it's possible Apache will die without cleaning up the semaphore (see the `ipcs(8)` manpage). The other is that the semaphore API allows for a denial of service attack by any CGIs running under the same UID as the webserver (i.e., all CGIs, unless you use something like `suexec` or `cgiwrapper`). For these reasons this method is not used on any architecture except IRIX (where the previous two are prohibitively expensive on most IRIX boxes).

USE_USLOCK_SERIALIZED_ACCEPT

(1.3 or later) This method is only available on IRIX, and uses `usconfig(2)` to create a mutex. While this method avoids the hassles of SysV-style semaphores, it is not the default for IRIX. This is because on single-processor IRIX boxes (5.3 or 6.2) the uslock code is two orders of magnitude slower than the SysV-semaphore code. On multiprocessor IRIX boxes, the uslock code is an order of magnitude faster than the SysV-semaphore code—kind of a messed-up situation. So if you're using a multiprocessor IRIX box, you should rebuild your webserver with -D`USE_USLOCK_SERIALIZED_ACCEPT` on the `EXTRA_CFLAGS`.

USE_PTHREAD_SERIALIZED_ACCEPT

(1.3 or later) This method uses POSIX mutexes and should work on any architecture implementing the full POSIX threads specification; however, it appears to only work on Solaris (2.5 or later), and even then only in certain configurations. If you experiment with this, you should watch out for your server hanging and not responding. Static-content-only servers may work just fine.

If your system has another method of serialization that isn't in the above list, then it may be worthwhile adding code for it (and submitting a patch back to Apache).

Another solution that has been considered, but never implemented, is to partially serialize the loop—that is, let in a certain number of processes. This would only be of interest on multiprocessor boxes where it's possible multiple children could run simultaneously, and the serialization actually doesn't take advantage of the full bandwidth. This is a possible area of future investigation, but priority remains low because highly parallel web servers are not the norm.

Ideally you should run servers without multiple `Listen` statements if you want the highest performance. But read on.

Accept Serialization—Single Socket

The above is fine and dandy for multiple-socket servers, but what about single-socket servers? In theory, they shouldn't experience any of these same problems because all children can just block in `accept(2)` until a connection arrives, and no starvation results. In practice, this hides almost the same "spinning" behaviour discussed earlier in the non-blocking solution. The way that most TCP stacks are implemented, the kernel actually wakes up all processes blocked in `accept` when a single connection arrives. One of those processes gets the connection and returns to user-space, the rest spin in the kernel and go back to sleep when they discover there's no connection for them. This spinning is hidden from the user-land code, but it's there nonetheless. This can result in the same load-spiking, wasteful behavior that a non-blocking solution to the multiple sockets case can.

For this reason we have found that many architectures behave more "nicely" if we serialize even the single-socket case, so this is actually the default in almost all cases. Crude experiments under Linux (2.0.30 on a dual Pentium Pro 166 with 128Mb of RAM) have shown that the serialization of the single-socket case causes less than a 3% decrease in requests per second over unserialized single-socket. But unserialized single-socket showed an extra 100 milliseconds of latency on each request. This latency is probably a wash on long haul lines, and only an issue on LANs. If you want to override the single-socket serialization, you can define `SINGLE_LISTEN_UNSERIALIZED_ACCEPT` and then single-socket servers will not serialize at all.

Lingering Close

As discussed in *draft-ietf-http-connection-00.txt* section 8, in order for an HTTP server to reliably implement the protocol, it needs to shutdown each direction of the communication independently (recall that a TCP connection is bidirectional: each half is independent of the other). This fact is often overlooked by other servers but is correctly implemented in Apache as of 1.2.

When this feature was added to Apache, it caused a flurry of problems on various versions of Unix because of a shortsightedness. The TCP specification does not state that the FIN_WAIT_2 state has a timeout, but it doesn't prohibit it. On systems without the timeout, Apache 1.2 induces many sockets stuck forever in the FIN_WAIT_2 state. In many cases this can be avoided by simply upgrading to the latest TCP/IP patches supplied by the vendor; in cases where the vendor has never released patches (i.e., SunOS4—although folks with a source license can patch it themselves), we have decided to disable this feature.

There are two ways of accomplishing this. One is the socket option SO_LINGER. But as fate would have it, this has never been implemented properly in most TCP/IP stacks. Even on those stacks with a proper implementation (i.e., Linux 2.0.31), this method proves to be more expensive (in CPU time) than the next solution.

For the most part, Apache implements this in a function called lingering_close (in *http_main.c*). The function looks roughly like this:

```
void lingering_close (int s)
{
    char junk_buffer[2048];
    /* shutdown the sending side */
    shutdown (s, 1);
    signal (SIGALRM, lingering_death);
    alarm (30);
    for (;;) {
        select (s for reading, 2 second timeout);
        if (error) break;
        if (s is ready for reading) {
            read (s, junk_buffer, sizeof (junk_buffer));
            /* just toss away whatever is here */
        }
    }
    close (s);
}
```

This naturally adds some expense at the end of a connection, but it is required for a reliable implementation. As HTTP/1.1 becomes more prevalent and all connections are persistent, this expense will be amortized over more requests. If you want to play with fire and disable this feature, you can define NO_LINGCLOSE, but this is not recommended at all. In particular, as HTTP/1.1 pipelined persistent connections come into use, lingering_close is an absolute necessity (and pipelined connections are faster, so you want to support them).

Scoreboard File

Apache's parent and children communicate with each other through something called the scoreboard. Ideally, this should be implemented in shared memory. For those operating systems that we either have access to or have been given detailed ports for, it typically is implemented using shared memory. The rest default to using an on-disk file. The on-disk file is not only slow, but it is unreliable (and less featured). Peruse the *src/main/conf.h* file for your architecture and look for either USE_MMAP_SCOREBOARD or USE_SHMGET_SCOREBOARD. Defining one of those two (as well as their companions HAVE_MMAP and HAVE_SHMGET, respectively) enables the supplied shared memory code. If your system has another type of shared memory, edit the file *src/main/http_main.c* and add the hooks necessary to use it in Apache. (Send us back a patch too, please.)

Historical note: The Linux port of Apache didn't start to use shared memory until version 1.2 of Apache. This oversight resulted in really poor and unreliable behaviour of earlier versions of Apache on Linux.

DYNAMIC_MODULE_LIMIT

If you have no intention of using dynamically loaded modules (you probably don't if you're reading this and tuning your server for every last ounce of performance), then you should add -DDYNAMIC_MODULE_LIMIT=0 when building your server. This will save RAM that's allocated only for supporting dynamically loaded modules.

Detailed Analysis of a Trace

Here is a system call trace of Apache 1.3 running on Linux. The runtime configuration file is essentially the default plus:

```
<Directory />
    AllowOverride none
    Options FollowSymLinks
</Directory>
```

The file being requested is a static 6K file of no particular content. Traces of non-static requests or requests with content negotiation look wildly different (and quite ugly in some cases). First we'll look at the entire trace, then we'll examine details. (This was generated by the **strace** program, other similar programs include **truss**, **ktrace**, and **par**):

```
accept(15, {sin_family=AF_INET, sin_port=htons(22283),
    sin_addr=inet_addr("127.0.0.1")}, [16]) = 3
flock(18, LOCK_UN) = 0
sigaction(SIGUSR1, {SIG_IGN}, {0x8059954, [], SA_INTERRUPT}) = 0
getsockname(3, {sin_family=AF_INET, sin_port=htons(8080),
    sin_addr=inet_addr("127.0.0.1")}, [16]) = 0
setsockopt(3, IPPROTO_TCP1, [1], 4)     = 0
read(3, "GET /6k HTTP/1.0\r\nUser-Agent: "..., 4096) = 60
sigaction(SIGUSR1, {SIG_IGN}, {SIG_IGN}) = 0
time(NULL)   = 873959960
gettimeofday({873959960, 404935}, NULL) = 0
stat("/home/dgaudet/ap/apachen/htdocs/6k", {st_mode=S_IFREG|0644,
    st_size=6144, ...}) = 0
```

```
open("/home/dgaudet/ap/apachen/htdocs/6k", O_RDONLY) = 4
mmap(0, 6144, PROT_READ, MAP_PRIVATE, 4, 0) = 0x400ee000
writev(3, [{"HTTP/1.1 200 OK\r\nDate: Thu, 11"..., 245},
    {"\0\0\0\0\0\0\0\0\0\0\0\0\0\0\0\0"..., 6144}], 2) = 6389
close(4)    = 0
time(NULL)  = 873959960
write(17, "127.0.0.1 - - [10/Sep/1997:23:39"..., 71) = 71
gettimeofday({873959960, 417742}, NULL) = 0
times({tms_utime=5, tms_stime=0, tms_cutime=0, tms_cstime=0}) = 446747
shutdown(3, 1 /* send */) = 0
oldselect(4, [3], NULL, [3], {2, 0})    = 1 (in [3], left {2, 0})
read(3, "", 2048)   = 0
close(3)    = 0
sigaction(SIGUSR1, {0x8059954, [], SA_INTERRUPT}, {SIG_IGN}) = 0
munmap(0x400ee000, 6144)    = 0
flock(18, LOCK_EX) = 0
```

Notice the accept serialization:

```
flock(18, LOCK_UN) = 0
    ...
flock(18, LOCK_EX)                      = 0
```

These two calls can be removed by defining **SINGLE_LISTEN_UNSERIALIZED_ ACCEPT** as described earlier.

Notice the **SIGUSR1** manipulation:

```
sigaction(SIGUSR1, {SIG_IGN}, {0x8059954, [], SA_INTERRUPT}) = 0
    ...
sigaction(SIGUSR1, {SIG_IGN}, {SIG_IGN}) = 0
    ...
sigaction(SIGUSR1, {0x8059954, [], SA_INTERRUPT}, {SIG_IGN}) = 0
```

This is caused by the implementation of graceful restarts. When the parent receives a SIGUSR1, it sends a SIGUSR1 to all of its children (and it also increments a "generation counter" in shared memory). Any children that are idle (between connections) will immediately die off when they receive the signal. Any children that are in keepalive connections, but are in between requests, will die off immediately. But any children that have a connection and are still waiting for the first request will not die off immediately.

To see why this is necessary, consider how a browser reacts to a closed connection. If the connection was a keepalive connection and the request being serviced was not the first request, then the browser will quietly reissue the request on a new connection. It has to do this because the server is always free to close a keepalive connection in between requests (i.e., due to a timeout or because of a maximum number of requests). But, if the connection is closed before the first response has been received, the typical browser will display a "document contains no data" dialogue (or a broken image icon). This is done on the assumption that the server is broken in some way (or maybe too overloaded to respond at all).

So Apache tries to avoid ever deliberately closing the connection before it has sent a single response. This is the cause of those `SIGUSR1` manipulations.

Note that it is theoretically possible to eliminate all three of these calls. But in rough tests, the gain proved to be almost unnoticeable.

In order to implement virtual hosts, Apache needs to know the local socket address used to accept the connection:

```
getsockname(3, {sin_family=AF_INET, sin_port=htons(8080), sin_addr=inet_
addr("127.0.0.1")}, [16]) = 0
```

It is possible to eliminate this call in many situations (such as when there are no virtual hosts, or when `Listen` directives are used that do not have wildcard addresses). But no effort has yet been made to do these optimizations.

Apache turns off the Nagle algorithm:

```
setsockopt(3, IPPROTO_TCP1, [1], 4)     = 0
```

because of problems described in the paper "Performance Interactions Between P-HTTP and TCP Implementations" (*ACM Computer Communication Review*, April, 1997) by John Heidemann.

Notice the two time calls:

```
time(NULL)                            = 873959960
...
time(NULL)                            = 873959960
```

One of these occurs at the beginning of the request, and the other occurs as a result of writing the log. At least one of these is required to properly implement the HTTP protocol. The second occurs because the Common Log Format dictates that the log record include a timestamp of the end of the request. A custom logging module could eliminate one of the calls.

As described earlier, `Rule STATUS=yes` causes two `gettimeofday` calls and a call to `times`:

```
gettimeofday({873959960, 404935}, NULL) = 0
...
gettimeofday({873959960, 417742}, NULL) = 0
times({tms_utime=5, tms_stime=0, tms_cutime=0, tms_cstime=0}) = 446747
```

These can be removed by either removing `mod_status` or setting `Rule STA-TUS=no`.

It might seem odd to call `stat`:

```
stat("/home/dgaudet/ap/apachen/htdocs/6k", {st_mode=S_IFREG|0644, st_
size=6144, ...}) = 0
```

This is part of the algorithm which calculates the PATH_INFO for use by CGIs. In fact if the request had been for the URL *cgi-bin/printenv/foobar*, then there would be two calls to stat: the first for */home/dgaudet/ap/apachen/cgi-bin/printenv/foobar* which does not exist, and the second for */home/dgaudet/ap/apachen/cgi-bin/printenv*, which does exist. Regardless, at least one stat call is necessary when serving static files because the file size and modification times are used to generate HTTP headers (such as Content-Length and Last-Modified) and implement protocol features (such as If-Modified-Since). A somewhat more clever server could avoid the stat when serving non-static files; however, doing so in Apache is very difficult given the modular structure.

All static files are served using mmap:

```
mmap(0, 6144, PROT_READ, MAP_PRIVATE, 4, 0) = 0x400ee000
...
munmap(0x400ee000, 6144)                     = 0
```

On some architectures, it's slower to mmap small files than it is to simply read them. The define MMAP_THRESHOLD can be set to the minimum size required before using mmap. By default it's set to 0 (except on SunOS4, where experimentation has shown 8192 to be a better value). Using a tool such as *lmbench*, you can determine the optimal setting for your environment.

You may also wish to experiment with MMAP_SEGMENT_SIZE (default 32768) which determines the maximum number of bytes that will be written at a time from mmap()d files. Apache only resets the client's Timeout in between write()s. So setting this large may lock out low bandwidth clients unless you also increase the Timeout.

It may even be the case that mmap isn't used on your architecture; if so, then defining USE_MMAP_FILES and HAVE_MMAP might work (if it works, then report back to us).

Apache does its best to avoid copying bytes around in memory. The first write of any request typically is turned into a writev which combines both the headers and the first hunk of data:

```
writev(3, [{"HTTP/1.1 200 OK\r\nDate: Thu, 11"..., 245}, {"\0\0\0\0\0\0\0\0\
0\0\0\0\0\0\0\0"..., 6144}], 2) = 6389
```

When doing HTTP/1.1 chunked encoding, Apache will generate up to four element writevs. The goal is to push the byte copying into the kernel, where it typically has to happen anyhow (to assemble network packets). On testing, various Unixes (BSDI 2.x, Solaris 2.5, Linux 2.0.31+) properly combine the elements into network packets. Pre-2.0.31 Linux will not combine, and will create a packet for each element, so upgrading is a good idea. Defining NO_WRITEV will disable this combining but will result in very poor chunked encoding performance.

The log write:

```
write(17, "127.0.0.1 - - [10/Sep/1997:23:39"..., 71) = 71
```

can be deferred by defining BUFFERED_LOGS. In this case up to PIPE_BUF bytes (a POSIX defined constant) of log entries are buffered before writing. At no time does it split a log entry across a PIPE_BUF boundary, because those writes may not be atomic (i.e., entries from multiple children could become mixed together). The code does it best to flush this buffer when a child dies.

The lingering close code causes four system calls:

```
shutdown(3, 1 /* send */)              = 0
oldselect(4, [3], NULL, [3], {2, 0})   = 1 (in [3], left {2, 0})
read(3, "", 2048)                      = 0
close(3)                               = 0
```

which were described earlier.

Let's apply some of these optimizations: -DSINGLE_LISTEN_UNSERIALIZED_ ACCEPT, -DBUFFERED_LOGS and Rule STATUS=no. Here's the final trace:

```
accept(15, {sin_family=AF_INET, sin_port=htons(22286),
        sin_addr=inet_addr("127.0.0.1")}, [16]) = 3
    sigaction(SIGUSR1, {SIG_IGN}, {0x8058c98, [], SA_INTERRUPT}) = 0
    getsockname(3, {sin_family=AF_INET, sin_port=htons(8080),
        sin_addr=inet_addr("127.0.0.1")}, [16]) = 0
    setsockopt(3, IPPROTO_TCP1, [1], 4)    = 0
    read(3, "GET /6k HTTP/1.0\r\nUser-Agent: "..., 4096) = 60
    sigaction(SIGUSR1, {SIG_IGN}, {SIG_IGN}) = 0
    time(NULL)                             = 873961916
    stat("/home/dgaudet/ap/apachen/htdocs/6k", {st_mode=S_IFREG|0644,
        st_size=6144, ...}) = 0
    open("/home/dgaudet/ap/apachen/htdocs/6k", O_RDONLY) = 4
    mmap(0, 6144, PROT_READ, MAP_PRIVATE, 4, 0) = 0x400e3000
    writev(3, [{"HTTP/1.1 200 OK\r\nDate: Thu, 11"..., 245},
        {"\0\0\0\0\0\0\0\0\0\0\0\0\0\0\0\0"..., 6144}], 2) = 6389
    close(4)                               = 0
    time(NULL)                             = 873961916
    shutdown(3, 1 /* send */)              = 0
    oldselect(4, [3], NULL, [3], {2, 0})   = 1 (in [3], left {2, 0})
    read(3, "", 2048)                      = 0
    close(3)                               = 0
    sigaction(SIGUSR1, {0x8058c98, [], SA_INTERRUPT}, {SIG_IGN}) = 0
    munmap(0x400e3000, 6144)               = 0
```

That's 19 system calls, of which 4 remain relatively easy to remove but don't seem worth the effort.

The Preforking Model

Apache (on Unix) is a preforking model server. The parent process is responsible only for forking child processes; it does not serve any requests or service any network sockets. The child processes actually process connections; they serve multiple connections (one at a time) before dying. The parent spawns new or kills off old children in response to changes in the load on the server (it does so by monitoring a scoreboard that the children keep up to date).

This model for servers offers a robustness that other models do not. In particular, the parent code is very simple, and with a high degree of confidence the parent will continue to do its job without error. The children are complex, and when you add in third-party code via modules, you risk segmentation faults and other forms of corruption. Even should such a thing happen, it only affects one connection and the server continues serving requests. The parent quickly replaces the dead child.

Preforking is also very portable across dialects of Unix. Historically, this has been an important goal for Apache, and it continues to remain so.

The preforking model comes under criticism for various performance aspects. Of particular concern are the overhead of forking a process, the overhead of context switches between processes, and the memory overhead of having multiple processes. Furthermore, it does not offer as many opportunities for data-caching between requests (such as a pool of mmapped files). Various other models exist and extensive analysis can be found in the papers of the JAWS project. In practice, all of these costs vary drastically, depending on the operating system.

Apache's core code is already multithread-aware, and Apache version 1.3 is multithreaded on NT. There have been at least two other experimental implementations of threaded Apache (one using the 1.3 code base on DCE, and one using a custom user-level threads package and the 1.0 code base; neither are available publicly). Part of our redesign for version 2.0 of Apache will include abstractions of the server model, so that we can continue to support the preforking model, and also support various threaded models.

C

Solaris 2.x—Tuning Your TCP/IP Stack and More

This appendix is written by Jens-S. Vöckler, and is used with his permission. Patrick Killelea edited and abridged it for this publication. The most recent version of this document is on the Web at http://www.rvs.uni-hannover.de/people/voeckler/tune/EN/tune.html. Use at your own risk!

If your system behaves erratically after applying some of these tweaks, please don't blame me. Always make backup copies of the files you are changing, and have those backups handy before starting to tune. I have carefully assembled the information you see here, but there are no guarantees that what worked for me will work for you. Please don't assume my recommendations are infallible: they are starting points, not absolutes. Always read my reasoning, don't use the recommendations blindly.

Before you start, you ought to grab a copy of the *TCP state transition diagram* as specified in RFC 793. The drawback is the missing error correction supplied by later RFCs. There is an easier way to obtain blowup printouts to staple to your office walls. Grab a copy of the PostScript file pocket guide accompanying Stevens' *TCP/IP Illustrated, Volume 1*. Or simply open that book at Figure 18.12.

Please Share Your Knowledge

I try to assemble this page and related material for everybody interested in gaining more from her or his system. If you have an item that I didn't cover, but that you deem worthwhile, please write to me at *voeckler@rvs.uni-hannover.de*. A dozen or so regular readers of this page will thank you for it. I am only human, so if you stumble over an error, misconception, or blatant nonsense, please have me correct it. In the past, there have been quite a few mistakes.

History and Introduction

This page and the related work have been long in the making. I started out peering wide-eyed over the shoulders of two people from a search engine provider when they were installing a German version of their server for a customer of my former employer. My only alternative resource for tuning information was the brilliant book *TCP/IP Illustrated, Volume 1*, by Richard Stevens. I then started collecting as much information about tuning as I was able to get my hands on. You have the result in front of you on these pages.

Solaris allows you to tune, tweak, set, and reset various parameters related to the TCP/IP stack *while the system is running*. Back in the SunOS 4.*x* days, one had to change various C files in the kernel source tree, generate a new kernel, reboot the machine, and try out the changes. The Solaris feature of changing the important parameters on the fly is very convenient.

Many of the parameters I mention in the rest of the document you are reading are time intervals. All intervals are measured in milliseconds. Other parameters are usually bytecounts, but occasionally different units of measurements are used and documented. A few items appear totally unrelated to TCP/IP, but due to the lack of a better framework, they materialized on this page.

Most tuning parameters can be changed using the program ndd. Any user may execute this program to read the current settings, depending on the readability of the respective device files, but only the superuser is allowed to execute ndd -set to change values. This makes sense, considering the sensitive parameters you are tuning. Details on the use of ndd can be obtained from its manpage. A few example uses of ndd:

```
ndd /dev/tcp ?                    # Show all parameter keys
ndd /dev/tcp tcp_mss_def          # Show the value of this key
ndd -set /dev/ip ip_forwarding 0  # Switch off <I>forwarding</I>
```

All keys starting out with ip_ have to be used with the pseudo device /dev/ip. Analogous behavior is true for the keys which start with tcp_, and so on. Andres Kroonmaa kindly supplied a nifty script to check all existing values for a network component (tcp, udp, ip, icmp, etc.). I do the same thing using Perl. Both scripts are available from my web page.

TCP Connection Initiation

This section is dedicated exclusively to the various queues and tunable variable(s) used during connection instantiation. The socket API maintains some control over the queues. But in order to tune anything, you have to understand how listen and `accept` interact with the queues. For details, see the various books by Stevens mentioned in the "Books" section later in this appendix.

When the server calls `listen`, the kernel moves the socket from the TCP state CLOSED into the state LISTEN, thus doing a passive open. All TCP servers work like this. Also, the kernel creates and initializes various data structures, among them the socket buffers and two queues:

Incomplete connection queue

This queue contains an entry for every SYN that has arrived. BSD sources assign so_q0len entries to this queue. The server sends off the ACK of the client's SYN and sends the server-side SYN. The connection gets queued and the kernel now awaits the completion of the TCP three-way handshake to open a connection (see Figure C-1). The socket is in the SYN_RCVD state. On the reception of the client's ACK to the server's SYN, the connection stays one round trip time (RTT) in this queue before the kernel moves the entry into the completed connection queue.

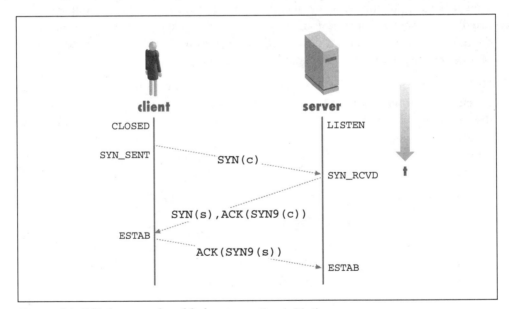

Figure C-1. TCP three-way handshake, connection initiation

Completed connection queue

This queue contains an entry for each connection for which the three-way handshake has completed. The socket is in the ESTABLISHED state. Each call to `accept()` removes the front entry of the queue. If there are no entries in the queue, the call to `accept` usually blocks. BSD source code assigns a length of so_qlen to this queue.

See Figure C-2 for an illustration of the two queues.

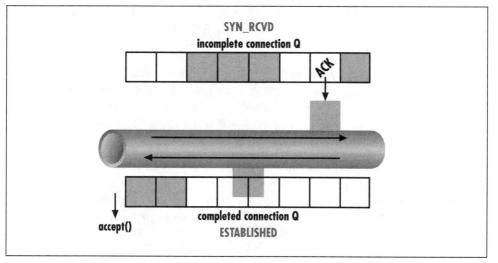

Figure C-2. Queues maintained for listening sockets

Both queues have a limited number of entries. By calling listen(), the server is allowed to specify the size of the second queue for completed connections. If the server is for whatever reason unable to remove entries from the completed connection queue, the kernel is not supposed to queue any more connections.

Historically, the argument to the listen function specified the maximum number of entries for the sum of both queues. Many BSD-derived implementations multiply the argument with a fudge factor of 3/2. Up to and including Version 2.5.1, Solaris systems do not use the fudge factor, but add 1, while Solaris 2.6 does use the fudge factor, though with a slightly different rounding mechanism than the one BSD uses. With a backlog argument of 14, Solaris 2.5.1 servers can queue 15 connections. Solaris 2.6 servers can queue 22 connections.

Stevens shows that for busy servers the incomplete connection queue needs more entries than the completed connection queue. The only reason for specifying a large backlog value is to enable the incomplete connection queue to grow as SYN packets arrive from clients. Stevens shows that a moderately busy web server has an empty completed connection queue 99% of the time, but the incomplete connection queue needs 15 or less entries 98% of the time! A really busy web cache like Squid will need a large incomplete connection queue.

If the queues are full when a SYN arrives, it is dropped, in the hope that the client will resend it and find room in the queues then. Any data for an established connection that arrives before the connection is accept()ed should be stored in the socket buffer.

The system administrator is allowed to tweak and tune the various maxima of the queues with Solaris. There is a change in the available parameters between a (regular) Solaris system up to and including Version 2.5.1, and those systems which either are Solaris Version 2.6 and later, or have applied the TCP patch 103582-12 or above for 2.5.1 systems.

The old semantics contained just one tunable parameter, tcp_conn_req_max, which specified the maximum argument for listen(). The patched versions and Solaris 2.6 replaced this parameter with the two new parameters: tcp_conn_req_max_q0 and tcp_conn_req_max_q. A *SunWorld* (August 1997) article on Solaris 2.6 by Adrian Cockroft tells the following about the new parameters:

> *tcp_conn_req_max* [has been] replaced. This value is well-known as it normally needs to be increased for Web servers in older releases of Solaris 2. It no longer exists in Solaris 2.6, and patch 103582-12 adds this feature to Solaris 2.5.1. The change is part of a fix that prevents denial of service from SYN flood attacks. There are now two separate queues of partially complete connections instead of one.

> *tcp_conn_req_max_q0* is the maximum number of connections with handshake incomplete. A SYN flood attack could only affect this queue, and a special algorithm makes sure that valid connections can still get through.

> *tcp_conn_req_max_q* is the maximum number of completed connections waiting to return from an accept call as soon as the right process gets some CPU time.

In other words, the first specifies the size of the incomplete connection queue, while the second and third parameters assigns the maximum length of the completed connection queue. All three parameters are covered in the following list:

tcp_conn_req_max

Default 8 (max. 32), since 2.5 32 (max. 1024), recommended 128 <= x <= 1024 since 2.6 or 2.5.1 with patches 103630-09 and 103582-12 or above applied: see tcp_conn_req_max_q and tcp_conn_req_max_q0.

The current parameter describes the maximum number of pending connection requests queued for a listening endpoint in the completed connection queue. The queue can only save the specified finite number of requests. If a queue overflows, nothing is sent back. The client will time out and (hopefully) retransmit.

The size of the completed connection queue does not influence the maximum number of simultaneous established connections, nor does it have any influence on the maximum number of clients a server can serve. With Solaris, the maximum number of file descriptors is the limiting factor for simultaneous connections, which just happens to coincide with the maximum backlog queue size.

From the viewpoint of TCP, those connections placed in the completed connection queue are in the TCP state ESTABLISHED, even though the application has not reaped the connection with a call to accept. Solaris offers the option of placing connections into the backlog queue as soon as the first SYN arrives, which is called *eager listening*. The three-way handshake will be completed as soon as the application accept()s the connection. The use of eager listening is not recommended except for experimentation systems.

Solaris systems previous to Version 2.5 have a maximum queue length of 32 pending connections. The length of the completed connection queue can also be used to decrease the load on an overloaded server: If the queue is completely filled, remote clients will be denied further connections. Sometimes this will lead to a "connection timed out" error message.

Naively, I assumed that a huge length might lead to a long service time on a loaded server. Stevens shows that the incomplete connection queue needs much more attention than the completed connection queue. But with tcp_conn_req_max, you have no option to tweak that particular length.

When tuning tcp_conn_req_max, always do it with regard to the values of rlim_fd_max and rlim_fd_cur. This is just a rule of thumb. Setting your listen backlog queue larger than the number of file descriptors available to you won't do you any good. A server shouldn't accept any further connections if it has run out of descriptors. Even though new connections won't be thrown away if you have a large backlog, a server might want to reduce the size to as many connections as can be serviced simultaneously. Again, you have to consider your average service time, too. A short service time implies that file descriptors will be recycled quickly.

There is a trick to overcome the hardcoded limit of 1024 with a patch. SunSolve shows this trick in connection with SYN flood attacks at *http://sunsolve.sun.com/sunsolve/secbulletins/security-alert-136.txt*. A greatly increased listen backlog queue may offer some small increased protection against this vulnerability. On this topic also look at the tcp_ip_abort_cinterval parameter. Better still, use the mentioned TCP patches, and increase the q0 length:

```
echo "tcp_param_arr+14/W 0t10240" | adb -kw /dev/ksyms /dev/mem
```

This patch is only effective on the currently active kernel, disappearing on the next boot. Usually you want to append the line above on the startup script /etd/init.d/inetinit. The shown patch increases the hard limit of the listen backlog queue to 10240. *Only after* applying this patch may you use values above 1024 for the tcp_conn_req_max parameter.

A further warning: changes to the value of the tcp_conn_req_max parameter in a running system will not take effect until each listening application is restarted. The backlog queue length is evaluated whenever an application calls `listen(3N)`, usually once during startup. Sending a HUP signal may or may not work; personally, I prefer to TERM the application and restart it manually or via startup script.

tcp_conn_req_max_q0

Since 2.5.1 with patches 103630-09 and 103582-12 or above applied: default 1024; since 2.6: default 1024, recommended $1024 <= x <= 10240$.

After installing the mentioned TCP patches, or after installing Solaris 2.6, the parameter `tcp_conn_req_max` is no longer available. In its stead the new parameters `tcp_conn_req_max_q` and `tcp_conn_req_max_q0` emerged. `tcp_conn_req_max_q0` is the maximum number of connections with handshake incomplete, basically the length of the incomplete connection queue.

In other words, the connections in this queue are just being instantiated. A SYN was just received from the client; thus the connection is in the TCP SYN_RCVD state. The connection cannot be `accept()`ed until the handshake is complete, even if the eager listening is active.

To protect against SYN flooding, you can increase this parameter. Also refer to the parameter `tcp_conn_req_max_q` above. I believe that changes won't take effect unless the applications are restarted.

tcp_conn_req_max_q

Since 2.5.1 with patches 103630-09 and 103582-12 or above applied: default 128; since 2.6: default 128, recommended $128 <= x <= $ `tcp_conn_req_max_q0`.

After installing the mentioned TCP patches, or after installing Solaris 2.6, the parameter `tcp_conn_req_max` is no longer available. Instead the new parameters `tcp_conn_req_max_q` and `tcp_conn_req_max_q0` emerged. `tcp_conn_req_max_q` is the length of the completed connection queue.

In other words, connections in this queue of length `tcp_conn_req_max_q` have completed the three-way handshake of a TCP **open**. The connection is in the state ESTABLISHED. Connections in this queue have not yet been `accept()`ed by the server process.

On Solaris Version 2.5.1 and later, the `netstat -s` command reports for the counter `tcpListenDrop` the number of dropped connections due to a lack of space in the completed connection queue. If you get many drops, you might need to increase this parameter. Since connections can also be dropped because `listen()` specifies too small an argument, you have to be careful interpreting the counter value. Also refer to the parameter `tcp_conn_req_max_q0`. Remember that changes won't take effect unless the applications are restarted.

tcp_conn_req_min

> Since 2.6: default 1; recommended: don't touch.

This parameter specifies the minimum number of available connections in the completed connection queue for `select()` or `poll()` to return "readable" for a listening (server) socket descriptor.

Programmers should note that Stevens describes a timing problem, if the connection is RST between the `select()` or `poll()` call and the subsequent `accept()` call. If the listening socket is blocking (the default for sockets), it will block in `accept()` until a valid connection is received. While this seems no tragedy with a web server or cache receiving several connection requests per second, the application is not free to do other things in the meantime, which might constitute a problem.

Retransmission-Related Parameters

The *retransmission timeout* (RTO) values used by Solaris are far too aggressive for wide area networks, although they can be considered appropriate for local area networks. Sun thus did not follow the suggestions mentioned in RFC 1122. Newer releases of the Solaris kernel are correcting the values in question:

> The recommended upper and lower bounds on the RTO are known to be inadequate on large internets. The lower bound SHOULD be measured in fractions of a second (to accommodate high speed LANs) and the upper bound should be 2*MSL, i.e., 240 seconds.

Besides the retransmit timeout value two further parameters, R1 and R2, may be of interest. These don't seem to be tunable via any Solaris interface that I know of:

> The value of R1 SHOULD correspond to at least 3 retransmissions, at the current RTO. The value of R2 SHOULD correspond to at least 100 seconds.
>
> [...]
>
> However, the values of R1 and R2 may be different for SYN and data segments. In particular, R2 for a SYN segment MUST be set large enough to provide retransmission of the segment for at least 3 minutes. The application can close the connection (i.e., give up on the open attempt) sooner, of course.

Many internet servers that are running Solaris do retransmit segments unnecessarily often. The current condition of European networks means that a connection to the U.S. may take up to 2 seconds. All parameters mentioned in the first part of this section relate to each other!

As a starter, take this little example: Consider a picture with a size of 1440 bytes, LZW compressed, that is to be transferred over a serial link at 14400 bps and using a MTU of 1500. In the ideal case, only one PDU gets transmitted. The ACK segment can only be sent *after* the complete PDU is received. The transmission takes about 1 second. These values seem low, but they are meant as food for thought. Now consider something going awry:

tcp_rexmit_interval_initial
> Default 500, since 2.5.1 3000, recommended >= 2000 (500 for special purposes).

> This interval elapses before the first data sent is retransmitted due to a missing acknowledgment. Mind that this interval is used only for the *first* retransmission. The more international your server is, the larger you should make this interval.

> Special LAN-only laboratory environments might be better off with 500 milliseconds or even less. If you are doing measurements relying on TCP (which is almost always a bad idea), you should consider lowering this parameter.

tcp_rexmit_interval_min
> Default 200, recommended >= 1000 (200 for special purposes).

> After the initial retransmission, further retransmissions will start after the `tcp_rexmit_interval_min` interval. BSD usually specifies 1500 milliseconds. This interval should be relative to the value of `tcp_rexmit_interval_initial` (e.g., some value between 50% and 200%). The parameter has no effect on retransmissions during an *active open*. (See the document on retransmissions on my web page.)

> The `tcp_rexmit_interval_min` doesn't display any influence on connection establishment with Solaris 2.5.1. It does with 2.6, though. I have yet to research the influence on regular data retransmissions or FIN retransmissions.

tcp_ip_abort_interval
> Default 120000, since 2.5 480000, recommended 600000.

> This interval specifies how long *retransmissions* for a connection in the ESTABLISHED state should be tried before a RESET segment is sent. BSD systems default to 9 minutes.

tcp_ip_abort_cinterval
> Default 240000, since 2.5 180000.

> This interval specifies how long retransmissions for a remote host are repeated until the RESET segment is sent. What's different about the `tcp_ip_abort_interval` parameter is that this connection is about to be established—it has not yet reached the state ESTABLISHED. This value is interesting considering SYN flood attacks on your server. Proxy servers are doubly handicapped because of their Janus-like behavior (they behave like servers toward the downstream cache, like clients toward the upstream server).

According to Stevens, this interval is connected to the active open, e.g., the connect(3N) call. But according to SunSolve, the interval has an effect in both directions. A remote client can refuse to acknowledge an opening connection up to this interval. After the interval, a RESET is sent. The other way around works out, too: If the three-way handshake to open a connection is not finished within this interval, the RESET Segment will be sent. This can only happen if the final ACK went astray, which is a difficult test case to simulate.

To improve your SYN flood resistance, Sun suggests using an interval as small as 10000 milliseconds. This value has only been tested for the "fast" networks at Sun. The more international your connection is, the slower it will be, and the more time you should grant in this interval. Proxy servers should never lower this value (and should let Squid terminate the connection). Web servers are usually not affected, as they seldom actively open connections beyond the LAN.

tcp_rexmit_interval_max

Default 60000, RFC 1122 recommends 240000 (2MSL), recommended 1...2 * tcp_close_wait_interval since 2.6: default 240000.

All previously mentioned retransmission-related intervals use an *exponential backoff* algorithm. The wait interval between two consecutive retransmissions for the same PDU is doubled starting with the minimum.

The tcp_rexmit_interval_max interval specifies the maximum wait interval between two retransmissions. If changing this value, you should also give the abort interval an inspection. The maximum wait interval should only be reached shortly before the abort interval timer expires. Additionally, you should coordinate your interval with the value of tcp_close_wait_interval.

tcp_deferred_ack_interval

Default 50, BSD 200, recommended 200 or 500.

This parameter specifies the timeout before sending a *delayed* ACK. The timeout is to see if the ACKing party has any data that can be sent along with the ACK. See section 19.3 of Stevens, Volume 1. The value should not be increased above 500, as required by RFC 1122. This value is of great interest for interactive services. A small number will increase the responsiveness of a remote service (telnet, X11), while a larger value can decrease the number of segments exchanged.

This parameter might also help HTTP servers that transmit small amounts of data after a very short retrieval time. With a heavy-duty servers or in a laboratory banging environment, you might encounter service times answering a request which are well above 50 milliseconds. An increase to 500 milliseconds might lead to fewer PDUs transferred over the network because TCP is able to merge the ACK with data. Increases beyond 500 milliseconds should not even be considered.

Please note that Solaris recognizes the initial data phase of a connection. An initial ACK (not SYN) is *not* delayed. Therefore, a request for a web service (both server and proxy) which does not fit into a single PDU can be transmitted faster. Web benchmarks will show this as improved performance. Also check the tcp_slow_start_initial parameter.

tcp_deferred_acks_max

Since 2.6: default 8.

This parameter has something to do with the number of delayed acknowledgments or the number of bytes to be collected. My guess is that this parameter specifies the number of outstanding ACKs in interactive transfer mode. In this case, tiny amounts of data are flowing in both directions. In contrast to my prior statement, you need *not* give this parameter a look when tuning bulk transfers, because its impact is on interactive transfers.

Good values for retransmission tuning don't beam into existence from a white source. Rather, you should carefully plan an experiment to get decent values. Intervals from another site do not carry on without change to another Solaris system. But they might give you an idea where to start when choosing your own values.

This next part looks at a few parameters having to do with retransmissions as well:

tcp_slow_start_initial

Since 2.5.1 with patch 103582-15 applied: default 1; since 2.6: default 1, recommended 2 for web services.

This parameter provides the slow-start bug discovered in BSD and Windows TCP/IP implementations for Solaris. More information on the topic can be found on the servers of Sun and in *TCP/IP Illustrated, Volume 3—T/TCP, HTTP, NNTP, Unix Domain Sockets*, by Richard Stevens (Addison-Wesley, 1994).

To summarize the effect, a server starts sending two PDUs at once without waiting for an ACK. This is due to the ACK from connection initiation being counted as data ACK—compare with Figure C-1. The client immediately acknowledges both PDUs, thus undermining network congestion avoidance algorithms. The slow-start algorithm does not allow this behavior; see RFC 2001.

Setting the parameter to 2 allows a Solaris machine to behave as if it had the slow-start bug, too. The IETF is said to want to change the slow-start algorithm, so that this bug will be turned into a feature. Sun also warns:

It's still conceivable, although rare, that on a configuration that supports many clients on very slow links, the change might induce more network congestion. Therefore the change of `tcp_slow_start_initial` should be made with caution. [...] Future Solaris releases are likely to default to 2.

Path MTU Discovery

Whenever a connection is about to be established, the three-way handshake opens negotiation, and the segment size used will be set to the minimum of either the smallest MTU of an outgoing interface or the Maximum Segment Size (MSS) announced by the peer. If the remote peer does not announce a MSS, usually the value 536 will be assumed. If path MTU discovery is active, all outgoing PDUs have the IP *don't fragment* (DF) option set.

If the ICMP error message "fragmentation needed" is received, this means that a router on the way to the destination needed to fragment the PDU, but was not allowed to do so. Therefore, the router discarded the PDU and sent back the ICMP error. Newer router implementations enclose the needed MSS in the error message. If the needed MSS is not included, the correct MSS must be determined by trial and error.

Because the Internet is a packet switching network, the route a PDU travels along a TCP virtual circuit may change with time. For this reason, RFC 1191 recommends rediscovering the path MTU of an active connection after 10 minutes. Improvements in the route can be noticed only by repeated rediscoveries. Unfortunately, Solaris aggressively tries to rediscover the path MTU every 30 seconds. While this is OK for LAN environments, it is grossly impolite behavior in WANs. Since routes may not change that often, aggressive repetitions of path MTU discovery lead to unnecessary consumption of channel capacity and elongated service times.

Path MTU discovery is a far-reaching and controversial topic among ISPs. Remember that MTU discovery is at the foundation of IPv6. The Pittsburgh Supercomputing Center (PSC) tuning page, at *http://www.psc.edu/networking/perf_tune.html*, argues for path MTU discovery, especially if you maintain a high-speed or long-delay (e.g., satellite) link.

My recommendation is not to use the defaults of Solaris versions previous to Version 2.5. Please use path MTU discovery, but tune your system to be RFC-conformant. You may also want to switch off path MTU discovery altogether, although there are few situations where this is necessary.

I was made aware that in certain circumstances, bridges connecting data link layers of differing MTU sizes defeat MTU discovery, and I have to further investigate this matter. If a frame with maximum MTU size is to be transported into network with a smaller MTU size, it is truncated silently. A bridge does not know anything about the upper protocol levels: a bridge neither fragments IP nor sends an ICMP error.

There are workarounds, and `tcp_mss_def` is one of them. Setting all interfaces to the minimum shared MTU might help, at the cost of losing performance on the larger MTU network. Using what RFC 1122 calls an *IP gateway* is a possible, yet expensive, solution:

ip_ire_pathmtu_interval

   Default 30000, since 2.5 600000, recommended 600000.

   This timer determines the interval at which Solaris rediscovers the path MTU. An extremely large value will evaluate the path MTU only once, at connection establishment.

ip_path_mtu_discovery

   Default 1, recommended 1.

   This parameter switches path MTU discovery on or off. If you enter a 0 here, Solaris will never try to set the DF bit in the IP option unless your application explicitly requests it.

tcp_ignore_path_mtu

   Default 0, recommended 0.

   This is a debug switch. When activated, this switch will have the IP or TCP layer ignore all ICMP "fragmentation needed" error messages. By activating this switch, you will achieve the opposite of what you intended.

tcp_mss_def

   Default 536, recommended >= 536.

   This parameter determines the default MSS for non-local destinations. For path MTU discovery to work effectively, this value can be set to the MTU of the most-used outgoing interface decreased by a 20-byte IP header and a 20-byte TCP header—if and only if the value is bigger than 536.

Further Advice, Hints, and Remarks

This section covers a variety of topics, starting with various TCP timers, that do not relate to previously mentioned issues. The second subsection throws a quick glance at some erratic behavior. The final subsection looks at a variety of parameters that deal with the reservation of resources.

Common TCP Timers

This section covers three important TCP timers. First I will have a look at the keep-alive timer. This timer is rather controversial, and some versions of Solaris implement it incorrectly. The next parameter limits the *twice maximum segment lifetime* (2MSL) value, which is connected to the time a socket spends in the TCP state `TIME_WAIT`. The final entry looks at the time spend in the TCP state `FIN_WAIT_2`.

tcp_keepalive_interval
> Default 7200000, recommended $0 <= x <= \infty$

> This is one of the most controversial values in talking with people about appropriate values. The interval specified with this key must expire before a *keepalive probe* can be sent. Keepalive probes are described in the host requirements RFC 1122: if a host chooses to implement keepalive probes, it must enable the application to switch them on or off for a connection, and keepalive probes must be switched off by default.

> Keepalives can terminate a perfectly good connection (as far as TCP/IP is concerned), cost money, and use up transmission capacity (commonly called bandwidth, which is actually something completely different). Determining whether a peer is alive should be a task of the application that should be kept on the application layer. Only if you run into the danger of keeping a server in the `ESTABLISHED` state forever and using up precious server resources should you switch on keepalive probes.

> Figure C-3 shows the typical handshake during a HTTP connection. It is of no importance to the argument whether the server is threaded, preforked or just plain forked. Web servers' work is transaction-oriented, as shown in the following simplified description:

> 1. The client (browser) initiates a connection (*active open*).
>
> 2. The client forwards its query (*request*).
>
> 3. The server (daemon) answers (*response*).
>
> 4. The server terminates the connection (*active close*).

> Common implementations need to exchange 9 or 10 TCP segments per HTTP connection. The keepalive option as an HTTP 1.0 protocol and extensions can be regarded as a *hack*. Persistent connections are a different matter, and are not shown here. Most people still use HTTP 1.0.

> The keepalive timer becomes significant for web servers if in step 1 the client crashes or terminates without the server knowing about it. This condition can sometimes be forced by quickly pressing the Stop button of Netscape or the logo of Mosaic. Thus the keepalive probes do make sense for web servers. HTTP proxies look like servers to the browser, but they look like clients to the

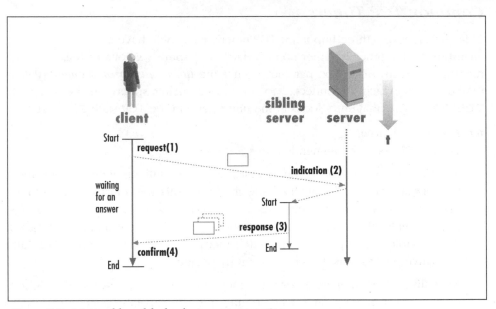

Figure C-3. A typical handshake during a transaction

server they are querying. Due to their server-like interface, the conditions for web servers are true for proxies, as well.

With an implementation of keepalive probes working correctly, a very small value can make sense when trying to improve web servers. In this case, you have to make sure that the probes stop after a finite time if a peer does not answer. Solaris versions up to and including Version 2.5 have a bug and send keepalive probes forever. They seem to want to elicit some response, like a RST or some ICMP error message from an intermediate router, but they never allow for the destination simply being down. Is this fixed with 2.5.1? Is there a patch available against this misbehavior? I don't know, maybe you can help me.

I am sure that this bug is fixed in 2.6 and that it is safe to use a small value like 10 minutes. Squid users should synchronize their cache configuration accordingly. There are some Squid timeouts dealing with an idle connection.

tcp_close_wait_interval

Default 240000 (according to RFC 1122, 2MSL), recommended 60000, possibly lower.

As Stevens repeatedly states in his books, the TIME_WAIT state is your friend. You should not desperately try to avoid it; rather, try to understand it. The *maximum segment lifetime* (MSL) is the maximum interval a TCP segment may live in the Net. Thus, waiting twice this interval ensures that there are no left-over segments coming to haunt you. This is what the 2MSL is about. Afterwards, it is safe to reuse the socket resource.

The parameter specifies the 2MSL according to the four-minute limit specified in RFC 1122. With knowledge about current network topologies and the strategies to reserve ephemeral ports, you should consider a shorter interval. The shorter the interval, the faster precious resources like ephemeral ports are available again.

A top search engine implementor recommends a value of 1000 milliseconds to customers. Personally, I believe this is too low for a regular server. A loaded search engine is a different matter altogether, but now you see why some people start tweaking their systems. I tend to use a multiple of the `tcp_rexmit_interval_initial` interval. The current value of `tcp_rexmit_interval_max` should also be considered in this case—even though retransmissions are unconnected to the 2MSL time. A good starting point might be the double RTT to a very remote system (e.g., Australia for European sites). Alternately, a German commercial provider of my acquaintance uses 30000, the smallest interval recommended by BSD.

tcp_fin_wait_2_flush_interval
BSD 675000, default 675000, recommended 67500 (one zero less).

This value seems to describe the (BSD) timer interval which prohibits a connection from staying in the `FIN_WAIT_2` state forever. `FIN_WAIT_2` is reached if a connection closes actively. The `FIN` is acknowledged, but the `FIN` from the passive side hasn't arrived yet—and maybe never will.

Usually, web servers and proxies actively close connections as long as you don't use persistent connections, and even those are closed eventually. Apart from that, HTTP 1.0-compliant servers and proxies close connections after each transaction. A crashed or misbehaving browser, however, may cause a server to use up a precious resource for a long time.

You should consider decreasing this interval if `netstat -f inet` shows many connections in the state `FIN_WAIT_2`. The timer is used only if the connection is really idle. Keep in mind that after a TCP half-close, simplex data transmission is still available towards the actively closing end. TCP half-closes are not yet supported by Squid, though many web servers do support them (certain HTTP drafts suggest an independent use of TCP connections). Nevertheless, as long as the client sends data after the server actively half-closes an established connection, the timer is not active.

Sometimes, a Squid proxy running on Solaris 2.5.1 confuses the system utterly. A great number of connections, to a varying degree, are in `CLOSE_WAIT`, for reasons that are beyond me. During this phase the proxy is virtually unreachable for HTTP requests, though it still answers ICP requests. Although lowering the value for the `tcp_close_wait_interval` fixes only symptoms, not the cause, it may help to overcome periods of erratic behavior faster than the default. What is needed is some way to influence the `CLOSE_WAIT` interval directly.

Erratic IPX Behavior

I have noticed that Solaris versions previous to Version 2.6 behave erratically under some conditions if the IPX Ethernet MTU of 1500 is used. Maybe there is an error in the frame assembly algorithm. If you limit yourself to the IEEE 802.3 MTU of 1492 bytes, the problem does not seem to appear. A sample startup script available from my web page can be used in `/etc/rc2.d` to change the MTU of Ethernet interfaces after their initialization. Remember to set the MTU for every virtual interface, too!

With a patched Solaris 2.5.1 or Solaris 2.6, erratic IPX behavior does not seem to appear. Limiting your MTU to a non-standard value might introduce problems with truncated PDUs in certain admittedly very special environments. Thus you may want to refrain from using the startup script from my web page (always called *second script* in this document).

Additionally, I strongly suggest the use of a file */etc/init.d/your-tune*, also available from my web page, which changes the tunable parameters. */etc/rcS.d/ S31your-tune* is a hard link to this file. The script will be executed during bootup when the system is in *single-user mode*. A killscript is not necessary. The section about startup scripts below reviews this topic in greater depth.

Windows, Buffers, and Watermarks

This section is about windows, buffers, and watermarks. It should still be considered a work in progress. The explanations available to me were very confusing, though the new Stevens helped to clear up a few things. If you have corrections to this section, please let me know and contribute to an update of the page. Many readers will thank you!

Here is just a short trip through the network layer to explain what happens where. Your application can send any size data to the transport layer, which is either UDP or TCP. The socket buffers are implemented on the transport layer. Depending on your choice of transport protocol, different actions are taken on this level (see Figure C-4).

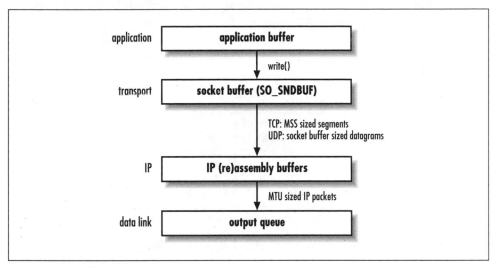

Figure C-4. Buffers and related issues

TCP

All application data is copied into the socket buffer. If there is insufficient room, the application will be put to sleep. From the socket buffer, TCP will create segments. No chunk exceeds the MSS.

Only when the data has been acknowledged from the peer instance can the data be removed from the socket buffer. For slow connections, this implies that some data may occupy the buffer for a very long time.

UDP

The socket buffer size of UDP is simply the maximum size datagram UDP is able to transmit. Larger datagrams ought to elicit the **EMSGSIZE** error response from the socket layer. With UDP implementing an unreliable service, there is no need to keep the datagram in the socket buffer.

Please assume that there is not really a socket buffer for UDP. This really depends on the operating system, but most systems might want to copy the user data to some kernel storage area.

The IP layer needs to fragment chunks which are too large. Among the reasons TCP prechunks its segments is the need to avoid fragmentation. IP searches the routing tables for the appropriate interface in order to determine the fragment size and interface.

If the output queue of the datalink layer interface is full, the datagram will be discarded and an error will be returned to IP and back to the transport layer. If the transport protocol was TCP, TCP will try to resend the segment at a later time. UDP should return the **ENOBUFS** error, but some implementations don't.

To determine the MTU sizes, use the `ifconfig -a` command. We will need the MTUs for some calculations to be done later in this section. With IPv4, you can determine the MSS from the interface MTU by subtracting 20 bytes for the TCP header and 20 bytes for the IP header. This calculation is done repeatedly in the following text:

```
$ ifconfig -a
lo0: flags=849 <UP,LOOPBACK,RUNNING,MULTICAST> mtu 8232
        inet 127.0.0.1 netmask ff000000
el0: flags=863 <UP,BROADCAST,NOTRAILERS,RUNNING,MULTICAST> mtu 1500
        inet 130.75.215.xxx netmask ffffff00 broadcast 130.75.215.255
        ether xx:xx:xx:xx:xx:xx
hme0: flags=863 <UP,BROADCAST,NOTRAILERS,RUNNING,MULTICAST> mtu 1500
        inet 130.75.5.xxx netmask ffffff00 broadcast 130.75.5.255
qaa0: flags=863 <UP,BROADCAST,NOTRAILERS,RUNNING,MULTICAST> mtu 9180
        inet 130.75.214.xxx netmask ffffff00 broadcast 130.75.214.255
        ether xx:xx:xx:xx:xx:xx
fa0: flags=842 <BROADCAST,RUNNING,MULTICAST> mtu 9188
        inet 0.0.0.0 netmask 0
        ether xx:xx:xx:xx:xx:xx
```

I removed the uninteresting things. `hme0` is the regular 100Mbps Ethernet interface. The 10Mbps Ethernet interface is called `le0`. `el0` is the ATM LAN emulation (LANE) interface. `qaa0` is the ATM classical IP (CLIP) interface. `fa0` is the interface that supports Fore's proprietary implementation of ATM. Fore is the vendor of the installed ATM card. As far as I know, you can use this interface to build PVCs or, if you are also using Fore switches, SVCs. You see an unconfigured interface there.

The window sizes for sending and receiving TCP segments and, strange as it may seem, for UDP datagrams, can be tuned with Solaris. With the help of the `netstat` command, you can obtain an output similar to the following one. The data was obtained on a server which runs a Squid with five DNS children. Since the interprocess communication is accomplished via `localhost` sockets, you see both the client side and the server side of each DNS child socket:

```
$ netstat -f inet
```

```
TCP
   Local Address        Remote Address       Swind Send-Q Rwind Recv-Q  State
-------------------- -------------------- ----- ------ ----- ------ -------
blau-clip.ssh        challenger-clip.1023 57344     19 63980      0 ESTABLISHED
localhost.38437      localhost.38436      57344      0 57344      0 ESTABLISHED
localhost.38436      localhost.38437      57344      0 57344      0 ESTABLISHED
localhost.38439      localhost.38438      57344      0 57344      0 ESTABLISHED
localhost.38438      localhost.38439      57344      0 57344      0 ESTABLISHED
localhost.38441      localhost.38440      57344      0 57344      0 ESTABLISHED
localhost.38440      localhost.38441      57344      0 57344      0 ESTABLISHED
localhost.38443      localhost.38442      57344      0 57344      0 ESTABLISHED
localhost.38442      localhost.38443      57344      0 57344      0 ESTABLISHED
```

```
localhost.38445      localhost.38444     57344    0 57344     0 ESTABLISHED
localhost.38444      localhost.38445     57344    0 57344     0 ESTABLISHED
```

The columns titled with `Swind` and `Rwind` contain values for the size of the respective send and receive windows. On the other hand, an application can change the size of the socket layer buffers with calls to `setsockopt`, e.g., with the parameter `SO_SNDBUF` or `SO_RCVBUF`. Windows and buffers are not interchangeable. Rather, the maximum and default socket buffer sizes are tunable with the high watermark of Solaris.

Squid users should note the following behavior seen with Solaris 2.6. The default socket buffer sizes detected during configuration phase are directly connected to the values of `tcp_recv_hiwat`, `udp_recv_hiwat`, `tcp_xmit_hiwat`, and `tcp_xmit_hiwat`. Also note that enabling the *hit object* feature still limits hit object size to 16384 bytes, regardless of what your system is able to achieve.

The following is output from a Squid 1.1.19 configuration script on a Solaris 2.6 host with the previously mentioned parameters all set to 64000. Please note that these parameters might not represent the optimal sizes:

```
checking Default UDP send buffer size... 64000
checking Default UDP receive buffer size... 64000
checking Default TCP send buffer size... 64000
checking Default TCP receive buffer size... 64000
```

Buffers and windows are very important if you link via satellite. Due to the high date rate but the extremely high round-trip delays of a satellite link, you will need *very* large TCP windows and possibly the TCP timestamp option. Only RFC 1323 conformant systems will achieve these ends. In other words, get a Solaris 2.6. For 2.5 systems, RFC 1323 compliance can be purchased as a Sun Consulting Special.

The network research laboratory of the German research network provider did measurements on satellite links. The round-trip time (RTT) was about 500 milliseconds. A regular system was able to transmit 600kbps whereas a RFC 1323 conformant system was able to transmit about 7Mbps. Only bulk data transfer will do that for you.

Squid users beware: as long as Squid does not implement HTTP 1.1 persistent connections, you will not get decent HTTP transmissions via satellite. The average cached object size is about 13 kilobytes, thus you almost never get past the TCP slow start. While this may or may not be a big deal with terrestrial links, you will never be able to fill a satellite pipe to a satisfactory degree. Doing things in parallel might help. Only when reaching TCP congestion avoidance will you see any filling of the pipe.

Window sizes are important for maximum throughput calculations, too. As Stevens shows, you cannot go faster than the window size offered by the received, divided by the RTT. The lower your RTT, the faster you can transmit. The larger your window, the faster you can transmit. If you intend to change your window sizes to the maximum, you might want to give `tcp_deferred_acks_max` another look.

Every socket also has a low watermark, which is important for the `select()` and `poll()` functions. The low watermark for receiving is 1 byte for both TCP and UDP. The low watermark for sending is the amount of space that must exist in the socket send buffer for `select` or `poll` to return the descriptor as writable. The value can be adjusted with Solaris.

tcp_cwnd_max

> Default 32768, since 2.? 65535, recommended 65535 for Solaris <= 2.5.1; since 2.6 262144 (finally!), no recommendations.

> This *congestion window* is opened as large as possible with any Solaris up to 2.5.1. A change to this value is only necessary for older Solaris systems. The Solaris 2.6 default looks reasonable, but you might need to increase this further. Note that the *window scale option* is announced only during connection creation and your maximum window size is 1GByte (1,073,725,440 bytes). Also, the window scale option is employed during the connection only if *both* sides support it.

tcp_recv_hiwat

> Default 8192, recommended 16384 <= x <= 64000;
> Solaris 2.6 *LFN bulk data transfer* 131071 or above.

> This parameter determines the maximum size of the initial TCP reception buffer. The specified value will be rounded up to the next multiple of the MSS. From this the *advertised window size* is determined, the size of the reception window advertised to the remote peer.

> The recommended value depends on the size of the MTU chosen for local interfaces: either 45×1452 or 44×1460. This assumes you are using 10Mbps or 100Mbps Ethernet with either IPX or 802.3 encapsulation. Squid users will be interested in this value with regards to the socket buffer size the Squid auto configuration program finds.

> The previous output shows an `Rwind` value of 63980 = 7 × 9140. 9140 is the MSS of the ATM classical IP interface in host `blau`. The interface itself uses a MTU of 9180. For the standard built-in 10Mbps or 100Mbps IPX Ethernet, you get a MTU of 1500 on the outgoing interface, which yields an MSS of 1460. The value of 57344 in the next `Rwind` line points to the `lo0` (loopback) interface, MTU 8232, MSS 8192 and 57344 = 7 × 8192.

> Starting with Solaris 2.6, values above 65535 should be possible; see the window scale option from RFC 1323. You might need to reboot your workstation in order to have the changes take effect, but then again, you might not.

For HTTP, I don't see the need to increase the buffer above 64k. Imagine a cache servicing 1024 simultaneous connections with HTTP 1.0, e.g., Squid 1.1. If the TCP high watermarks of your system are tuned to 64k, you would need 128M just for your TCP buffers! Squid seems to use the socket option SO_RCVBUF to limit its memory hunger during runtime to 16k.

Only peer hosts implementing RFC 1323 will benefit from buffer sizes above 65535! If one host does not implement the window scale option, the window is still limited to 64k.

tcp_recv_hiwat_minmss
Default 4.

This parameter influences the minimum size of the input buffer. The reception buffer is at least as large as this value multiplied by the MSS. The real value is the maximum of `tcp_recv_hiwat` rounded up to the next MSS and `tcp_recv_hiwat_minmss` multiplied by the MSS.

udp_recv_hiwat
Default 8192, recommended 16384 <= x <= 64000.

This is the highwater mark for the UDP reception buffer size. This value may be of interest for Squid proxies, which use ICP extensively. Please read the explanations for `tcp_recv_hiwat`. Squid users will want at least 16384, especially if you are planning on using the *hit object* feature of Squid.

Remember, if you don't set your socket buffer explicitly with a call to `setsockopt()`, your default reception buffer will have about this size. Arriving datagrams of a larger size might be truncated or completely rejected! Some systems don't even notify your receiving application.

tcp_xmit_hiwat
Default 8192, recommended 16384 <= x <= 64000;
Solaris 2.6 *LFN bulk data transfer* 131071 or above.

This parameter influences a heuristic that determines the size of the initial send window. The actual value will be rounded up to the next multiple of the MSS, e.g., 8760 = 6 × 1460. The recommended value depends on the size of the MTU for local interfaces: either 45×1452 or 44×1460. Also read the section on `tcp_recv_hiwat`.

The `netstat` output displayed earlier in this section shows a `Swind` of 57344 = 7 × 8192. For the standard built-in 10Mbps or 100Mbps IPX Ethernet, you get an MTU of 1500 on the outgoing interface, which yields a MSS of 1460.

Starting with Solaris 2.6 values above 65535 should be possible; see the window scale option from RFC 1323. You might need to reboot your workstation in order to have the changes take effect, but then again, you might not.

For HTTP, I don't see the need to increase the buffer above 64k. Imagine a cache servicing 1024 simultaneous connections with HTTP 1.0, e.g., Squid 1.1. If the TCP high watermarks of your system are tuned to 64k, you would need 128M just for your TCP buffers! Squid does not seem to use the socket option SO_SNDBUF to limit its memory hunger during runtime. This might not be too bad, because the send buffer has to keep a copy of all unacknowledged segments. Thus it should have twice the size of the send buffer.

Only peer hosts implementing RFC 1323 will benefit from buffer sizes above 65535! If one host does not implement the window scale option, the window is still limited to 64k. Host **challenger** supports CLIP on ATM, but it does not support the window scale option. Therefore, I got buffers below 64k even after I increased the related TCP high watermarks to 128k.

udp_xmit_hiwat

Default 8192, recommended 16384 <= x <= 64000.

This refers to the high watermark for send buffers and may be of interest for proxies using ICP extensively. Please refer to the explanations for **tcp_xmit_hiwat**. Squid users will want at least 16384, especially if you are planning on using the *hit object* feature of Squid.

tcp_xmit_lowat

Default 2048, no recommendations.

This parameter refers to the amount of data that must be available in the TCP socket send buffer for **select** or **poll** to return **writable** for the connected file descriptor.

Usually, there is no need to tune this parameter. Applications can use the socket option SO_SNDLOWAT to change this parameter on a process local basis.

udp_xmit_lowat

Default 1024, no recommendations.

This parameter refers to the amount of data that must be available for **select** or **poll** to return **writable** for the connected file descriptor. Since UDP does not need to keep datagrams and thus needs no socket buffer, the socket will always be writable as long as the socket send buffer size value is greater than the low watermark. Thus it does not really make much sense to wait for a datagram socket to become writable unless you constantly adjust the send buffer size.

Usually there is no need to tune this parameter. Applications can use SO_SNDBUF and SO_SNDLOWAT to change the send buffer size and low watermark respectively on a process local basis.

tcp_max_buf
> Default 262144, recommended: see text.
> Since 2.6 1048576, recommended: see text.

udp_max_buf
> Default 262144 (since 2.5), recommended: see text.

> This value refers to the default maximum socket buffer size. The value ought to be adjusted according to the settings of the previous parameters. For many paths, this is not enough, and must be increased. Without RFC 1323 *large windows*, the application is not allowed to buffer more than 64kB in the network, which is inadequate for almost all high-speed paths. Yes, you can use the network as a buffer. You can calculate the capacity of this buffer by multiplying the bandwidth of your path by the RTT. The result is commonly called the *bandwidth-delay-product*.

> When using many connections, like Squid, possibly with an enlarged socket buffer size (see `tcp_xmit_hiwat` and `tcp_recv_hiwat`), you might want to increase the TCP value. On heavily loaded servers, a decrease of this value may decrease the load at the cost of the service time—definitely not recommended.

Tuning Your System

Things to Watch

Did you reserve enough `swap` space? You should have at least as much `swap` as you have main memory. If you have little main memory, then you should have double that amount as `swap`. Do not be fooled by the result of the `vmstat` command—read the manpage and realize that the small value for free memory shown there is (usually) correct.

With Solaris there seems to exist a difference between virtually generated processes and real processes. The latter are extremely dependent on the amount of virtual memory. To test the number of both kinds of processes, try a small program of mine, `testpid.c`, available from my web page. Start it at the console without starting the X Window System, and not as root. The first value is the hard limit of processes, and the second value the number of processes you can really create given your virtual memory configuration. Tweaking your `ulimit` values may or may not help.

General Entries in the File /etc/system

The file */etc/system* contains various very important configurable parameters for your system. You can use these tunings to give a heavily loaded system more resources of a certain kind. Unfortunately, these changes won't take effect until the next reboot.

In *Sun Performance and Tuning*, Adrian Cockroft warns against transporting an */etc/system* from one system onto another, or even worse, onto another hardware platform:

> Clean out your */etc/system* when you upgrade.

The most frequent changes are limited to the number of file descriptors, because the socket API uses file descriptors for handling Internet connectivity. You may want to look at the hard limit of file handles available to you. Proxies like Squid have to count twice for each connection: open request descriptors and either an open file or an open forwarding request descriptor.

You are able to influence the tuning of file descriptors with the reserved word set. Use a whitespace to separate the key from the keyword. Use an equals sign to separate the value from its key. There are a few examples in the comments of the file.

Please, before you start, make a backup copy of your initial */etc/system*. The backup should be located on your *root* filesystem. Thus, if some parameters fail, you can always supply the alternative, original system file on the boot prompt. The following shows two typically entered parameters:

```
* these are the defaults of the system
set rlim_fd_max=1024
set rlim_fd_cur=64
```

Sun does not make any guarantees for the correct working of your system if you use more than 4096 file descriptors.

If you experience SEGV core dumps from your select(3c) system call after increasing your file descriptors above 4096, you have to recompile the affected programs. In particular, the select(3c) call is known to the Squid users for its bad temper concerning the maximum number of file descriptors. Sun remarks on this topic:

> The default value for FD_SETSIZE (currently 1024) is larger than the default limit
> on the number of open files. In order to accommodate programs that may use a

larger number of open files with `select()`, it is possible to increase this size within a program by providing a larger definition of `FD_SETSIZE` before the inclusion of <sys/types.h>.

I tested Sun's suggestion, and a friend of mine tried it with Squid caches. The result was a complete success or disaster both times, depending on your point of view. If you really need to access file descriptors above 1024, don't use `select()`; use `poll()` instead. `poll()` is supposed to be faster with Solaris, anyway. A different source mentions that the redefinition workaround mentioned above works satisfactorily; not for me, nor with Squid.

Some of these tricks are from *http://www.gl.umbc.edu/~vijay/solaris/solartune.html*. I am of the opinion that these pages are not as up-to-date as they could be.

Many parameters of interest can be determined using the `sysdef -i` command. Please keep in mind that many values are in hexadecimal notation without the "0x" prefix. Another program that is very good for looking at your system's configuration is `sysinfo`. Refer to the manpages to learn how to invoke this program.

rlim_fd_cur

Default 64, recommended >= 1024.

This parameter defines the soft limit of open files you can have. The currently active soft limit can be determined from a shell with something like:

```
ulimit -Sn
```

Use at your own risk values above 1024, especially if you are running old binaries. A value of 4096 may look harmless enough, but may still break old binaries.

Another source mentions that using more than 8192 file descriptors is discouraged. It suggests that you ought to use more processes if you need more than 4096 file descriptors. On the other hand, an ISP of my acquaintance is using 16384 descriptors to his satisfaction.

The predicate `rlim_fd_cur <= rlim_fd_max` must be fulfilled.

rlim_fd_max

Default 1024, recommended >=4096.

This parameter defines the hard limit on the number of open files. For a Squid and most other servers, regardless of TCP or UDP, the number of open file descriptors per user process is among the most important parameters. The number of file descriptors limits the number of connections you have in parallel. You can find out the value of your hard limit on a shell with something like:

```
ulimit -Hn
```

You should consider a value of at least 2 × tcp_conn_req_max, and you should provide at least 2 × rlim_fd_cur. The predicate rlim_fd_cur <= rlim_fd_max must be fulfilled.

Use values above 1024 at your own risk. Sun does not make any warranty for the workability of your system if you increase this above 1024. Squid users of busy proxies will have to increase this value, though. A good start seems to be 16384 <= x <= 32768. Remember to change the Makefile for Squid to use poll() instead of select(). Also remember that each call of configure will change the Makefile back, if you didn't change Makefile.in.

maxusers

Default 249 ~= Megs RAM (Ultra-2/2 CPUs/256 MB), min 8, max 2048, no recommendations.

This parameter determines the size of certain kernel data structures that are initialized at startup. There is strong indication that the default is determined from the main memory in megs. It might also be a function of the available memory and/or architecture.

The defaults of the parameters max_nprocs, maxuprc, ufs_ninode, ncsize and ndquot will be determined from this parameter's value. The greater the number you choose for maxusers, the greater the number of the mentioned resources. The relation is strictly proportional: a doubling of maxusers will (more or less) double the other resources.

Adrian Cockroft advises against setting maxusers. The kernel uses a lot of space while keeping track of RAM usage within the system; therefore, it might need to be reduced on systems with gigabytes of main memory.

max_nprocs

Default 3994 (Ultra-2/2 CPUs/256 MB), no recommendations.

This is the system-wide number of processes available. You should leave sufficient space to the parameter maxuprc. The value of this parameter is influenced by the setting of maxusers.

maxuprc

Default −5 (here: 3989), no recommendations.

This parameter describes the number of processes available to a single user. The actual value is determined from max_nprocs, which is itself determined by maxusers. The negative value seems to be a relative distance with regards to max_nprocs, but I haven't been able to test this yet.

ncsize

Default 4323 = 17*maxusers+90 (with maxusers 249), min 226, max 34906, no recommendations.

This parameter specifies the size of the directory name lookup cache. A large directory name lookup cache size significantly helps NFS servers that have a lot of clients. On other systems, the default is adequate.

I don't know about the ties to ufs_ninode, but the formula is the same. The current value is determined by maxusers.

I have heard from a few people who increase ncsize to 30000 when using the Squid webcache. Image, a Squid, uses 16 top-level directories and 256 second-level directories. Thus, you need over 4096 entries just for the directories. It looks as if webcaches and news servers that store data in files generated from a hash need to increase this value for efficient access. Twice the default should be a good starting point. You may want to increase ufs_ninode by the same size.

bufhwm

Default 2% of main memory, no immediate recommendations.

Now, considering the SVR3 buffer cache described by Maurice Bach, this parameter specifies the maximum memory size allowed for the buffer cache. The 0 value reported by sysinfo says to take 2% of the main memory for buffer caches. sysdef -i shows the size in bytes taken for the buffer cache.

I have seen Squid administrators increase this value up to 10%. If you change this value, you have to enter the number of kilobytes you want for the buffer cache.

use_mxcc_prefetch

Default 0 (sun4d) or 1 (sun4m), recommended: see text.

Adrian Cockroft explains this parameter in his article at *http://www.sun.com/ sunworldonline/*, "What Are the Tunable Kernel Parameters for Solaris 2?" The parameter determines the external cache controller prefetches. You have to know your workload: applications with extensive floating point arithmetic will benefit from prefetches, thus the parameter is turned on for personal workstations. On random access databases with little or no need for floating point arithmetic, the prefetch will likely get in the way; therefore, it is turned off on server machines. It looks as if it should be turned off on dedicated Squid servers.

Some services use a multitude of cache files, like Squid or some news servers where names (URLs or articles) are mapped by a hash function to a shallow directory tree, helping the buffer cache and inode caches of the host file system (compared to using unlimited subdirectories like the CERN cache). As is well known in software engineering, the speedup achieved by using the right algorithm usually far exceeds anything you can achieve by fiddling with the hardware or tweaking system parameters. Thus, a new storage scheme for mapped caches should provide food for thought. See *http://www.iaehv.nl/users/devet/squid/new_store/*.

100Mbit Ethernet-Related Entries

Mr. Nebel and Mr. Hüsemann were kind enough to give me a few hints concerning 100Mbit Ethernet interfaces and Solaris. It looks as if these cards default to half-duplex operations. In order to switch to full duplex mode, make sure your router can also run full duplex:

hme:hme_adv_100fdx_cap

> Default 0, recommended 1.
>
> This parameter switches on full duplex mode. Only use this parameter together with the next option.

hme:hme_adv_100hdx_cap

> Default 1, recommended 0.
>
> This parameter switches off half-duplex mode. It must be used together with the previous parameter.

hme:hme_adv_autoneg_cap

> Default 1.
>
> This parameter determines whether the Sun workstation should automatically negotiate the 100Mbit with the router. Usually, Cisco routers also do auto-negotiation, thus it may be necessary to set this switch to 0.

A few mistakes in setting up 100Mbit interfaces result in a downgrade to 10Mbit Ethernet. Check at all available endpoints whether you are really getting the data rate you are expecting.

How to Find Further Entries

There are thousands of further items you can adjust. Every module that has a device in the */dev* directory and a module file somewhere in the kernel tree underneath */kernel* can be configured with the help of ndd. Whether you have to have superuser privileges depends on the access mode of the device file.

For instance, there exists a device /dev/hme and a kernel module /kernel/drv/ hme. This driver is connected, as you might know, to the 100Mbit Ethernet interface. If you want to know what value you can tweak, you can ask ndd:

```
ndd /dev/hme ?
```

Of course, you can change only entries marked for read and write. If you have tweaked enough and want to store some configuration as a default at boot time, you can enter your preferred values into the */etc/system* file. Just prefix the key with the module name and separate both with a colon. You saw this earlier in the subsection on 100Mbit Ethernet and the System V IPC page.

There is another way to get your hands on the names of keys to tweak. For instance, the System V IPC modules don't have a related device file. This implies that you cannot tweak values with the help of ndd. Nevertheless, you can obtain all clear text strings from the module file in the kernel:

```
strings -a /kernel/sys/shmsys # possible
nm /kernel/sys/shmsys # recommended
```

You are seeing a number of strings. Most of the strings are either names of functions within the module or clear text string passages defined within the module. Strings starting with shminfo are the names of user-tunable parameters. Now, how do you separate tunable parameters from the other stuff? I really don't know. If you have some knowledge about Sun DDI, you may be able to help me find a recommendable way, e.g., using _info(9E) and mod_info.

Recommended Patches

It is utterly necessary to patch your Solaris system, if you haven't already done so. Have a look at the DFN CERT patch mirror at *ftp://ftp.cert.dfn.de/pub/vendor/sun/ patches* or the original source from Sun at *http://access1.sun.com/patch.recommended/rec.html*. There may be a mirror closer to you; for example EUNet and FUNET have their own mirrors, if I am informed correctly.

Please remember to press the Shift button on your Netscape Navigator while selecting a link. If the patch is not loadable, a new release has probably appeared in the meantime. To verify this, have a look at the directories of DFN CERT or Sun. The README file on the DNF-CERT server is kept without a version number and thus always up to date:

ip and ifconfig patch
     103630-09 for Solaris 2.5.1 (README)
     103169-12 for Solaris 2.5 (README)

tcp patch (only with ip patches)
     103582-15 for Solaris 2.5.1 (README)
     103447-09 for Solaris 2.5 (README)

Every system administrator should know the contents of Sun's patch page. Besides previously mentioned patches for good TCP/IP performance, you should always consider the security-related patches. Also, Sun recommends a set of further patches to complete the support for large IP addresses. You should really include any DNS-related patch.

Related Books and Software

I started this section after receiving some information from Christian Grimm and Franz Haberhauer on TCP/IP and performance-related literature.

Books

Bach, Maurice, *Design of the Unix Operating System* (Prentice Hall, 1986). ISBN 0-13201799-7. A German translation is available.

Cockroft, Adrian, *Sun Performance and Tuning* (Prentice Hall, 1995). ISBN 0-13-149642-5. Regrettably only up to Solaris 2.4, but most information is still valid for current Solaris systems. The Heise Verlag offers a German translation.

Cockroft, Adrian, *Sun Performance and Tuning, 2nd edition* (Prentice Hall, 1998). ISBN 0-13-095249-4. The improved version on performance and tuning, covers quick tips and Solaris 2.6 as well as Java server technologies.

Stevens, Richard, *Advanced Programming in the UNIX Environment* (Addison Wesley, 1992). ISBN 0-201-56317-7. A German translation is available: *Programmieren in der UNIX-Umgebung*; ISBN 3-9319-814-8, 1995.

Stevens, Richard, *TCP/IP Illustrated, Volume 1—The Protocols* (Addison Wesley, 1994). ISBN 0-201-63346-9. A German translation is available.

Stevens, Richard, *TCP/IP Illustrated, Volume 2—The Implementation* (Addison Wesley, 1995). ISBN 0-201-63354-X. A German translation is available.

Stevens, Richard, *TCP/IP Illustrated, Volume 3—T/TCP, HTTP, NNTP, Unix Domain Sockets* (Addison Wesley, 1994). ISBN 0-201-63495-3. A German translation is available.

Stevens, Richard, *Unix Network Programming, Network APIs: Sockets and XTI*; (Prentice Hall, 1998). ISBN 0-13-490012-X. A German translation is *not* available.

Tanenbaum, Andrew S., *Computer Networks* (I use the second edition; Prentice Hall, 1989). ISBN 0-13162959-X. A German translation of the 2nd edition is available: *Computer Netzwerke* (Wolfram's Fachverlag, 1990). ISBN 3-925328-79-3.

Tanenbaum, Andrew S., *Modern Operating Systems* (Prentice Hall, 1992). ISBN 0-13588187-0.

Wong, Brian, *Configuration and Capacity Planning for Solaris Servers* (Prentice Hall, 1997). ISBN 0-13-349952-9. An up-to-date looking book showing host- and peripheral technologies. Contains hints on tuning. Eases the detection of hardware errors, because it explains about the workings of the hardware (you are then able to determine, if a misbehavior is a bug or a feature).

Internet Resources

- There is an RFC mirror from MERIT near you (*ftp://nic.merit.edu/internet/doc-uments/rfc/*).

- You should also know about other related internet resource documents like IANA assignments (*ftp://ftp.isi.edu/in-notes/iana/assignments/*).

- The Pittsburgh Supercomputing Center maintains a performance related page with some general tuning information for a broad range of systems (*http://www.psc.edu/networking/perf_tune.html*).

Mentioned RFCs and Internet Resources

RFC 793
> Transmission Control Protocol (TCP, STD 7).

RFC 1122
> Requirements for Internet hosts—communication layers (STD 3).

RFC 1123
> Requirements for Internet hosts—application and support (STD 3), updated by RFC 2181.

RFC 1323
> TCP Extensions for High Performance.

RFC 1700
> Assigned numbers (STD 2), outdated, use the IANA assignments instead!

RFC 1918
> Address Allocation for Private Internets.

RFC 2001
> TCP Slow Start, Congestion Avoidance, Fast Retransmit, and Fast Recovery Algorithms.

RFC 2181
> Clarifications to the DNS Specification.

RFC 2324
> HyperText Coffee Pot Control Protocol (HTCPCP/1.0:-)

Unmentioned but Important Internet Resources for Web Services

Compare with Duane Wessel's required reading list for Squid developers, *http://ircache.nlanr.net/Cache/reading.html*, and W3C's history of HTTP change:

RFC 1945

    Hypertext Transfer Protocol (HTTP/1.0).

RFC 2068

    Hypertext Transfer Protocol (HTTP/1.1)

RFC 2069

    An Extension to HTTP: Digest Access Authentication.

RFC 2186

    Internet Cache Protocol (ICP), Version 2.

RFC 2187

    Application of Internet Cache Protocol (ICP), Version 2.

RFC 2227

    Simple Hit-Metering and Usage-Limiting for HTTP.

Please send your suggestions, comments, and ideas for new items to:

    voeckler@rvs.uni-hannover.de

With the hope of supplying useful information,

Jens-S. Vöckler

Index

About the Author

Patrick Killelea currently works for Sun Microsystems Professional Services. Before that, he was a web site developer with a small Internet development company in Chicago. He has worked on many well-known web sites, designing systems and writing software to do useful things such as locating freight trains, selecting the right shampoo for your hair, finding movie reviews, and reporting where your overnight package is. In a previous life, he was an embedded systems programmer, working at Motorola, Intel, and British Telecom. He attended the University of Michigan for much too long and ended up with three undergraduate degrees. For several years, he was a book clerk at the original Borders Book Shop in Ann Arbor, where he first started reading the O'Reilly series. Patrick likes to get email about Web and Java performance tips and tricks, errors in this book, questions on performance issues, and business opportunities. He's available for consulting and teaching engagements in the San Francisco Bay Area. He lives in Palo Alto with his wife and son. Please visit his web site at *http://patrick.net* or email him at *webbook@patrick.net*.

Colophon

Our look is the result of reader comments, our own experimentation, and feedback from distribution channels. Distinctive covers complement our distinctive approach to technical topics, breathing personality and life into potentially dry subjects.

The animal on the cover of *Web Performance Tuning* is a sword-billed hummingbird. There are over 300 species of hummingbird, all found only in the Americas. All of these species are easily identified by their long, tubular bills and iridescent feathers. The iridescence is a refraction effect that can be seen only when light is shining on the feathers at certain angles. Hummingbirds range in size from the bee hummingbird which, measuring 2 inches long and weighing less than an ounce, is the smallest of all birds, to the great hummingbird, which measures about 8.5 inches long.

Hummingbirds are so named because of the humming noise made by their rapidly moving wings. On average, hummingbirds flap their wings 50 times a second; some species can flap as many as 200 times per second. The wings are flexible at the shoulder and, unlike most birds, they are propelled on the upstroke as well as the downstroke. Because of this flexibility, hummingbirds can hover, fly right or left, backwards, and upside down. Most hummingbirds have tiny feet that are used only for perching, never for walking. Hummingbirds will fly to travel even a couple of inches.

Hummingbirds expend a great deal of energy, and need to feed every 10 minutes or so. They feed on nectar, for sugar, and small insects, for protein. Their long, tapered bills enable them to retrieve nectar from even the deepest flower. Pollen accumulates on the head and neck of hummingbirds while they gather nectar. They then transfer this pollen to other flowers and thus play an important role in plant reproduction.

Hummingbirds appear frequently in Native American legends and mythology, often as representatives of the sun. According to some folk beliefs, they can bring love. Since Europeans first spotted these beautiful, colorful little birds, they have often appeared in the art and literature of Europe, as well.

Edie Freedman designed the cover of this book, using a 19th-century engraving from the Dover Pictorial Archive. Kathleen Wilson designed the back cover, and produced the cover layout with QuarkXPress 3.32 using the ITC Garamond font. Whenever possible, our books a durable and flexible lay-flat binding, either RepKover™ or Otabind™. If the page count exceeds the maximum bulk possible for this type of binding, perfect binding is used.

Madeleine Newell was the production editor for this book. Seth Maislin wrote the index. The inside layout was designed by Edie Freedman and modified by Nancy Priest. Text was prepared in FrameMaker by Mike Sierra. The text and heading fonts are ITC Garamond Light and Garamond Book. The illustrations that appear in the book were created in Macromedia Freehand 7.0 by Robert Romano. Quality assurance was provided by John Files, Steve Kleinedler, Nicole Arigo, and Sheryl Avruch. Production assistance was provided by Kimo Carter, Sebastian Banker, Maureen Dempsey, Melanie Wang, and Trisha Manoni. This colophon was written by Clairemarie Fisher O'Leary.

More Titles from O'Reilly

Web Server Administration

Stopping SPAM

By Alan Schwartz & Simson Garfinkel
1st Edition October 1998 (est.)
200 pages (est.), ISBN 1-56592-388-X

This book describes spam—unwanted email messages and inappropriate news articles—and explains what you and your Internet service providers and administrators can do to prevent it, trace it, stop it, and even outlaw it. Contains a wealth of advice, technical tools, and additional technical and community resources.

Writing Apache Modules with Perl and C

By Lincoln Stein & Doug MacEachern
1st Edition January 1999 (est.)
400 pages (est.), ISBN 1-56592-567-X

This guide to Web programming teaches you how to extend the capabilities of the Apache Web server. It explains the design of Apache, mod_perl, and the Apache API, then demonstrates how to use them to rewrite CGI scripts, filter HTML documents on the server-side, enhance server log functionality, convert file formats on the fly, and more.

Web Security & Commerce

By Simson Garfinkel
with Gene Spafford
1st Edition June 1997
506 pages, ISBN 1-56592-269-7

Learn how to minimize the risks of the Web with this comprehensive guide. It covers browser vulnerabilities, privacy concerns, issues with Java, JavaScript, ActiveX, and plug-ins, digital certificates, cryptography, web server security, blocking software, censorship technology, and relevant civil and criminal issues.

Apache: The Definitive Guide

By Ben Laurie & Peter Laurie
1st Edition March 1997
274 pages, includes CD-ROM
ISBN 1-56592-250-6

Despite all the media attention to Netscape, Apache is far and away the most widely used web server platform in the world. This book, written and reviewed by key members of the Apache Group, is the only complete guide on the market today that describes how to obtain, set up, and secure the Apache software. Includes CD-ROM with Apache sources and demo sites discussed in the book.

Building Your Own Web Conferences™

By Susan B. Peck & Beverly Murray Scherf
1st Edition March 1997
270 pages, Includes CD-ROM
ISBN 1-56592-279-4

Building Your Own Web Conferences is a complete guide for Windows® 95 and NT™ users on how to set up and manage dynamic virtual communities that improve workgroup collaboration and keep visitors coming back to your site. The second in O'Reilly's "Build Your Own..." series, this book comes with O'Reilly's state-of-the-art WebBoard™ 2.0 software on CD-ROM.

Building Your Own WebSIte™

By Susan B. Peck & Stephen Arrants
1st Edition July 1996
514 pages, Includes CD-ROM,
ISBN 1-56592-232-8

This is a hands-on reference for Windows® 95 and Windows NT™ users who want to host a site on the Web or on a corporate intranet. This step-by-step guide will have you creating live web pages in minutes. You'll also learn how to connect your web to information in other Windows applications, such as word processing documents and databases. The book is packed with examples and tutorials on every aspect of web management, and it includes the highly acclaimed WebSite™ 1.1 server software on CD-ROM.

O'REILLY™

TO ORDER: **800-998-9938** • *order@oreilly.com* • *http://www.oreilly.com/*
OUR PRODUCTS ARE AVAILABLE AT A BOOKSTORE OR SOFTWARE STORE NEAR YOU.
FOR INFORMATION: **800-998-9938** • **707-829-0515** • *info@oreilly.com*

Web Programming

CGI Programming on the World Wide Web

By Shishir Gundavaram
1st Edition March 1996
450 pages, ISBN 1-56592-168-2

This book offers a comprehensive explanation of CGI and related techniques for people who hold on to the dream of providing their own information servers on the Web. It starts at the beginning, explaining the value of CGI and how it works, then moves swiftly into the subtle details of programming.

Dynamic HTML: The Definitive Reference

By Danny Goodman
1st Edition July 1998
1088 pages, ISBN 1-56592-494-0

Dynamic HTML: The Definitive Reference is an indispensable compendium for Web content developers. It contains complete reference material for all of the HTML tags, CSS style attributes, browser document objects, and JavaScript objects supported by the various standards and the latest versions of Netscape Navigator and Microsoft Internet Explorer.

Frontier: The Definitive Guide

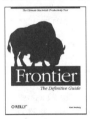

By Matt Neuburg
1st Edition February 1998
618 pages, 1-56592-383-9

This definitive guide is the first book devoted exclusively to teaching and documenting Userland Frontier, a powerful scripting environment for web site management and system level scripting. Packed with examples, advice, tricks, and tips, *Frontier: The Definitive Guide* teaches you Frontier from the ground up. Learn how to automate repetitive processes, control remote computers across a network, beef up your web site by generating hundreds of related web pages automatically, and more. Covers Frontier 4.2.3 for the Macintosh.

JavaScript: The Definitive Guide, 3rd Edition

By David Flanagan & Dan Shafer
3rd Edition June 1998
800 pages, ISBN 1-56592-392-8

This third edition of the definitive reference to JavaScript covers the latest version of the language, JavaScript 1.2, as supported by Netscape Navigator 4.0. JavaScript, which is being standardized under the name ECMAScript, is a scripting language that can be embedded directly in HTML to give web pages programming-language capabilities.

Learning VBScript

By Paul Lomax
1st Edition July 1997
616 pages, includes CD-ROM
ISBN 1-56592-247-6

This definitive guide shows web developers how to take full advantage of client-side scripting with the VBScript language. In addition to basic language features, it covers the Internet Explorer object model and discusses techniques for client-side scripting, like adding ActiveX controls to a web page or validating data before sending to the server. Includes CD-ROM with over 170 code samples.

Web Client Programming with Perl

By Clinton Wong
1st Edition March 1997
228 pages, ISBN 1-56592-214-X

Web Client Programming with Perl shows you how to extend scripting skills to the Web. This book teaches you the basics of how browsers communicate with servers and how to write your own customized web clients to automate common tasks. It is intended for those who are motivated to develop software that offers a more flexible and dynamic response than a standard web browser.

Web Authoring and Design

Photoshop for the Web

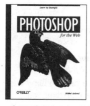

By Mikkel Aaland
1st Edition April 1998
238 pages, ISBN 1-56592-350-2

Photoshop for the Web shows you how to use the world's most popular imaging software to create Web graphics and images that look great and download blazingly fast. The book is crammed full of step-by-step examples and real-world solutions from some of the country's hottest Web producers, including *HotWired*, *c\net*, *Discovery Online*, *Second Story*, *SFGate*, and more than 20 others.

Information Architecture for the World Wide Web

By Louis Rosenfeld & Peter Morville
1st Edition January 1998
226 pages, ISBN 1-56592-282-4

Learn how to merge aesthetics and mechanics to design web sites that "work." This book shows how to apply principles of architecture and library science to design cohesive web sites and intranets that are easy to use, manage, and expand. Covers building complex sites, hierarchy design and organization, and techniques to make your site easier to search. For webmasters, designers, and administrators.

HTML: The Definitive Guide, 3rd Edition

By Chuck Musciano & Bill Kennedy
3rd Edition August 1998
576 pages, ISBN 1-56592-492-4

This complete guide is chock full of examples, sample code, and practical, hands-on advice to help you create truly effective web pages and master advanced features. Learn how to insert images and other multimedia elements, create useful links and searchable documents, use Netscape extensions, design great forms, and lots more. The third edition covers HTML 4.0, Netscape 4.5, and Internet Explorer 4.0, plus all the common extensions.

Web Navigation: Designing the User Experience

By Jennifer Fleming
1st Edition September 1998
288 pages, Includes CD-ROM
ISBN 1-56592-351-0

This book takes the first in-depth look at designing Web site navigation through design strategies to help you uncover solutions that work for your site and audience. It focuses on designing by purpose, with chapters on entertainment, shopping, identity, learning, information, and community sites. Comes with a CD-ROM that containing software demos and a "netography" of related Web resources.

Designing with JavaScript

By Nick Heinle
1st Edition September 1997
256 pages, Includes CD-ROM
ISBN 1-56592-300-6

Written by the author of the "JavaScript Tip of the Week" web site, this new Web Review Studio book focuses on the most useful and applicable scripts for making truly interactive, engaging web sites. You'll not only have quick access to the scripts you need, you'll finally understand why the scripts work, how to alter the scripts to get the effects you want, and, ultimately, how to write your own groundbreaking scripts from scratch.

O'REILLY™

TO ORDER: **800-998-9938** • *order@oreilly.com* • *http://www.oreilly.com/*
OUR PRODUCTS ARE AVAILABLE AT A BOOKSTORE OR SOFTWARE STORE NEAR YOU.
FOR INFORMATION: **800-998-9938** • **707-829-0515** • *info@oreilly.com*

All the Facts. Not the Frills.

UNIX System Administration

Essential System Administration

By Æleen Frisch
2nd Edition September 1995
788 pages, ISBN 1-56592-127-5

Thoroughly revised and updated for all major versions of UNIX, this second edition of *Essential System Administration* provides a compact, manageable introduction to the tasks faced by everyone responsible for a UNIX system. Whether you use a stand-alone UNIX system, routinely provide administrative support for a larger shared system, or just want an understanding of basic administrative functions, this book is for you. Offers expanded sections on networking, electronic mail, security, and kernel configuration.

System Performance Tuning

By Mike Loukides
1st Edition November 1990
336 pages, ISBN 0-937175-60-9

System Performance Tuning answers the fundamental question: How can I get my UNIX-based computer to do more work without buying more hardware? Some performance problems do require you to buy a bigger or faster computer, but many can be solved simply by making better use of the resources you already have.

Using Samba

By Peter Kelly, Perry Donham &
David Collier-Brown
1st Edition January 1999 (est.)
300 pages (est.), ISBN 1-56592-449-5

Samba turns a UNIX or Linux system into a file and print server for Microsoft Windows network clients. This complete guide to Samba administration covers basic 2.0 configuration, security, logging, and troubleshooting. Whether you're playing on one note or a full three-octave range, this book will help you maintain an efficient and secure server.

termcap & terminfo

By John Strang, Linda Mui &
Tim O'Reilly
3rd Edition April 1988
270 pages, ISBN 0-937175-22-6

For UNIX system administrators and programmers. This handbook provides information on writing and debugging terminal descriptions, as well as terminal initialization, for the two UNIX terminal databases.

Managing NFS and NIS

By Hal Stern
1st Edition June 1991
436 pages, ISBN 0-937175-75-7

Managing NFS and NIS is for system administrators who need to set up or manage a network filesystem installation. NFS (Network Filesystem) is probably running at any site that has two or more UNIX systems. NIS (Network Information System) is a distributed database used to manage a network of computers. The only practical book devoted entirely to these subjects, this guide is a "must-have" for anyone interested in UNIX networking.

Volume 8: X Window System Administrator's Guide

By Linda Mui & Eric Pearce
1st Edition October 1992
372 pages, ISBN 0-937175-83-8

This book focuses on issues of system administration for X and X-based networks —not just for UNIX system administrators, but for anyone faced with the job of administering X (including those running X on stand-alone workstations).

How to stay in touch with O'Reilly

1. Visit Our Award-Winning Web Site

http://www.oreilly.com/

★"Top 100 Sites on the Web" —*PC Magazine*
★"Top 5% Web sites" —*Point Communications*
★"3-Star site" —*The McKinley Group*

Our web site contains a library of comprehensive product information (including book excerpts and tables of contents), downloadable software, background articles, interviews with technology leaders, links to relevant sites, book cover art, and more. File us in your Bookmarks or Hotlist!

2. Join Our Email Mailing Lists

New Product Releases
To receive automatic email with brief descriptions of all new O'Reilly products as they are released, send email to:
listproc@online.oreilly.com
Put the following information in the first line of your message (*not* in the Subject field):
subscribe oreilly-news

O'Reilly Events
If you'd also like us to send information about trade show events, special promotions, and other O'Reilly events, send email to:
listproc@online.oreilly.com
Put the following information in the first line of your message (*not* in the Subject field):
subscribe oreilly-events

3. Get Examples from Our Books via FTP

There are two ways to access an archive of example files from our books:

Regular FTP
- ftp to:
  ftp.oreilly.com
  (login: anonymous
  password: your email address)
- Point your web browser to:
  ftp://ftp.oreilly.com/

FTPMAIL
- Send an email message to:
  ftpmail@online.oreilly.com
  (Write "help" in the message body)

4. Contact Us via Email

order@oreilly.com
To place a book or software order online. Good for North American and international customers.

subscriptions@oreilly.com
To place an order for any of our newsletters or periodicals.

books@oreilly.com
General questions about any of our books.

software@oreilly.com
For general questions and product information about our software. Check out O'Reilly Software Online at **http://software.oreilly.com/** for software and technical support information. Registered O'Reilly software users send your questions to: **website-support@oreilly.com**

cs@oreilly.com
For answers to problems regarding your order or our products.

booktech@oreilly.com
For book content technical questions or corrections.

proposals@oreilly.com
To submit new book or software proposals to our editors and product managers.

international@oreilly.com
For information about our international distributors or translation queries. For a list of our distributors outside of North America check out:
http://www.oreilly.com/www/order/country.html

O'Reilly & Associates, Inc.
101 Morris Street, Sebastopol, CA 95472 USA
TEL   707-829-0515 or 800-998-9938
        (6am to 5pm PST)
FAX   707-829-0104

Titles from O'Reilly

International Distributors

UK, EUROPE, MIDDLE EAST AND NORTHERN AFRICA (EXCEPT FRANCE, GERMANY, SWITZERLAND, & AUSTRIA)

INQUIRIES
International Thomson Publishing Europe
Berkshire House
168-173 High Holborn
London WC1V 7AA
United Kingdom
Telephone: 44-171-497-1422
Fax: 44-171-497-1426
Email: itpint@itps.co.uk

ORDERS
International Thomson Publishing Services, Ltd.
Cheriton House, North Way
Andover, Hampshire SP10 5BE
United Kingdom
Telephone: 44-264-342-832 (UK)
Telephone: 44-264-342-806 (outside UK)
Fax: 44-264-364418 (UK)
Fax: 44-264-342761 (outside UK)
UK & Eire orders: itpuk@itps.co.uk
International orders: itpint@itps.co.uk

FRANCE

Editions Eyrolles
61 bd Saint-Germain
75240 Paris Cedex 05
France
Fax: 33-01-44-41-11-44

FRENCH LANGUAGE BOOKS
All countries except Canada
Telephone: 33-01-44-41-46-16
Email: geodif@eyrolles.com
English language books
Telephone: 33-01-44-41-11-87
Email: distribution@eyrolles.com

GERMANY, SWITZERLAND, AND AUSTRIA

INQUIRIES
O'Reilly Verlag
Balthasarstr. 81
D-50670 Köln
Germany
Telephone: 49-221-97-31-60-0
Fax: 49-221-97-31-60-8
Email: anfragen@oreilly.de

ORDERS
International Thomson Publishing
Königswinterer Straße 418
53227 Bonn, Germany
Telephone: 49-228-97024 0
Fax: 49-228-441342
Email: order@oreilly.de

JAPAN

O'Reilly Japan, Inc.
Kiyoshige Building 2F
12-Banchi, Sanei-cho
Shinjuku-ku
Tokyo 160-0008 Japan
Telephone: 81-3-3356-5227
Fax: 81-3-3356-5261
Email: kenji@oreilly.com

INDIA

Computer Bookshop (India) PVT. Ltd.
190 Dr. D.N. Road, Fort
Bombay 400 001 India
Telephone: 91-22-207-0989
Fax: 91-22-262-3551
Email: cbsbom@giasbm01.vsnl.net.in

HONG KONG

City Discount Subscription Service Ltd.
Unit D, 3rd Floor, Yan's Tower
27 Wong Chuk Hang Road
Aberdeen, Hong Kong
Telephone: 852-2580-3539
Fax: 852-2580-6463
Email: citydis@ppn.com.hk

KOREA

Hanbit Media, Inc.
Sonyoung Bldg. 202
Yeksam-dong 736-36
Kangnam-ku
Seoul, Korea
Telephone: 822-554-9610
Fax: 822-556-0363
Email: hant93@chollian.dacom.co.kr

SINGAPORE, MALAYSIA, AND THAILAND

Addison Wesley Longman Singapore PTE Ltd.
25 First Lok Yang Road
Singapore 629734
Telephone: 65-268-2666
Fax: 65-268-7023
Email: daniel@longman.com.sg

PHILIPPINES

Mutual Books, Inc.
429-D Shaw Boulevard
Mandaluyong City, Metro
Manila, Philippines
Telephone: 632-725-7538
Fax: 632-721-3056
Email: mbikikog@mnl.sequel.net

CHINA

Ron's DataCom Co., Ltd.
79 Dongwu Avenue
Dongxihu District
Wuhan 430040
China
Telephone: 86-27-83892568
Fax: 86-27-83222108
Email: hongfeng@public.wh.hb.cn

ALL OTHER ASIAN COUNTRIES

O'Reilly & Associates, Inc.
101 Morris Street
Sebastopol, CA 95472 USA
Telephone: 707-829-0515
Fax: 707-829-0104
Email: order@oreilly.com

AUSTRALIA

WoodsLane Pty. Ltd.
7/5 Vuko Place, Warriewood NSW 2102
P.O. Box 935
Mona Vale NSW 2103
Australia
Telephone: 61-2-9970-5111
Fax: 61-2-9970-5002
Email: info@woodslane.com.au

NEW ZEALAND

Woodslane New Zealand Ltd.
21 Cooks Street (P.O. Box 575)
Waganui, New Zealand
Telephone: 64-6-347-6543
Fax: 64-6-345-4840
Email: info@woodslane.com.au

THE AMERICAS

McGraw-Hill Interamericana Editores,
S.A. de C.V.
Cedro No. 512
Col. Atlampa 06450
Mexico, D.F.
Telephone: 52-5-541-3155
Fax: 52-5-541-4913
Email: mcgraw-hill@infosel.net.mx

SOUTH AFRICA

International Thomson Publishing
South Africa
Building 18, Constantia Park
138 Sixteenth Road
P.O. Box 2459
Halfway House, 1685 South Africa
Telephone: 27-11-805-4819
Fax: 27-11-805-3648